HOW TO SAY IT

HOW TO SAY IT

Third Edition

Choice Words, Phrases,
Sentences, and Paragraphs
for Every Situation

ROSALIE MAGGIO

Prentice Hall Press

PRENTICE HALL PRESS
Published by the Penguin Group
Penguin Group (USA) Inc.
375 Hudson Street, New York, New York 10014, USA
Penguin Group (Canada), 90 Eglinton Avenue East, Suite 700, Toronto, Ontario M4P 2Y3, Canada
(a division of Pearson Penguin Canada Inc.)
Penguin Books Ltd., 80 Strand, London WC2R 0RL, England
Penguin Group Ireland, 25 St. Stephen's Green, Dublin 2, Ireland (a division of Penguin Books Ltd.)
Penguin Group (Australia), 250 Camberwell Road, Camberwell, Victoria 3124, Australia
(a division of Pearson Australia Group Pty. Ltd.)
Penguin Books India Pvt. Ltd., 11 Community Centre, Panchsheel Park, New Delhi—110 017, India
Penguin Group (NZ), 67 Apollo Drive, Rosedale, North Shore 0632, New Zealand
(a division of Pearson New Zealand Ltd.)
Penguin Books (South Africa) (Pty.) Ltd., 24 Sturdee Avenue, Rosebank, Johannesburg 2196, South Africa

Penguin Books Ltd., Registered Offices: 80 Strand, London WC2R 0RL, England

While the author has made every effort to provide accurate telephone numbers and Internet addresses at the time of publication, neither the publisher nor the author assumes any responsibility for errors, or for changes that occur after publication. Further, the publisher does not have any control over and does not assume any responsibility for author or third-party websites or their content.

PRINTING HISTORY
Prentice Hall Press trade paperback first edition / October 1990
Prentice Hall Press trade paperback revised and expanded edition / August 2001
Prentice Hall Press trade paperback third edition / April 2009

Prentice Hall Press third edition ISBN: 978-0-7352-0437-9

The Library of Congress has cataloged the revised and expanded edition as follows:

Maggio, Rosalie.
    How to say it : choice words, phrases, sentences, and paragraphs for every situation / by Rosalie Maggio.—Rev. and expanded.
    p.   cm.
    ISBN 0-7352-0234-6 (pbk.)—0-13-032542-2 (PPC)
    1. Letter writing.   2. English language—Rhetoric.   I. Title.
    PE1483.M26 2001
    806.6—dc21   2001036014

PRINTED IN THE UNITED STATES OF AMERICA

10   9   8   7   6   5   4   3   2   1

Most Prentice Hall Press books are available at special quantity discounts for bulk purchases for sales promotions, premiums, fund-raising, or educational use. Special books, or book excerpts, can also be created to fit specific needs. For details, write: Special Markets, Penguin Group (USA) Inc., 375 Hudson Street, New York, New York 10014.

To DAVID
Liz, Katie, Jason
Matt, Nora, Zoe

ACKNOWLEDGMENTS

Thank you to those who shared their letters and opinions with me: Shelley Sateren; Steve Sikora; Mark Maggio; Dr. Matt Maggio; Patrick Maggio, Esq.; Frank Maggio; Terry Hay Maggio; Mary Maggio; Dr. Paul T. Maggio; Kevin Maggio, Esq.; Irene Nash Maggio; Dr. Paul J. Maggio; Mike Maggio, Esq.; Michael Parker; Bonnie Z. Goldsmith, Patricia Yeager and the Denver Center for Independent Living; Nick Niemeyer; Sheila Hanley and The Dublin Walk; Maggie Parr; Jazzou Jones; Dr. Greg Filice; Katherine King; Debbye Calhoun Spang; Irmiter Contractors and Builders Limited; Jeanne Goerss Novak; and Ben Baughman.

Many of the sentences, paragraphs, and letters are taken from letters I've saved over the years (imagine rummaging through boxes and boxes of them in the attic looking for that great thank-you note). Thanks and love to all my favorite correspondents. You know who you are.

I'm still grateful to Tom Power, the genial and gifted godfather of this book. And many thanks to Maria Gagliano, who gave it new life.

CONTENTS

INTRODUCTION

*All that is requisite to become proficient in any Art, is to know
what to do and how to do it; and the Art of Letter-writing
is no exception to this general rule.*
—F. M. PAYNE,
Payne's Business Letter Writer and Book of Commercial Forms (1884)

How to Say It is a practical, easy-to-use book that tells you what to say and how to say it. Its flexible approach helps you fashion compelling letters in little more time than it takes to handwrite or type them.

Although an impressive amount of business and social interaction takes place today over the telephone and fax, by e-mail, or in person, the well-written letter remains a staple of business success and one of the strongest connecting links between human beings.

Most of us are capable of writing a satisfactory letter, but few of us have the time and mental energy to deal with the countless letters that life today seems to demand of us—especially since all of them should have been written yesterday.

How to Say It features comprehensive, versatile lists of words, phrases, sentences, and paragraphs that allow you to express yourself on any subject in your own voice and style.

Thesaurus-like, these lists provide you with terms relating to your topic. Whether you want to sound formal or casual, traditional or contemporary, businesslike or lighthearted, distant or intimate, you'll find here the words for every letterwriting occasion—from powerful, cogent business letters to warm, sensitive personal letters.

An important message of this book, delivered indirectly in its pages, is that there is rarely "one right way" to write a letter. You may follow, adapt, or ignore the guidelines given here; after all, you know more about your message and your reader than any letterwriting manual. Except for someone like Napoleon, who apparently wrote more than 50,000 letters in his lifetime (and nobody ever said to him, "Get a life!"), almost everyone can use this book to write letters with increased speed, individuality, success—and enjoyment!

HOW TO USE THIS BOOK

Begin by skimming the table of contents to familiarize yourself with the fifty letter topics available to you (for example, sales letters, thank-you notes, references, apologies, acknowledgments, letters dealing with employment).

Next, flip through the appendixes so that you know what kind of help waits for you there: Appendix I deals with the mechanics of letterwriting (what kind of stationery to use, how to address an envelope, the four most common ways of setting up a letter on the page) while Appendix II deals with the content of your letter (writing tips, grammar and usage, frequently misspelled or confused words, redundant words and phrases, correct forms of address).

To find advice about the letter you want to write, either turn to the chapter that deals with that kind of letter or check the index in the back of the book. Its one thousand entries ensure that you will find the help you need.

Each chapter includes a brief introduction, a list of occasions for writing that type of letter, what to include in each letter, what not to say, comments on special situations, and what format to use.

At the heart of each chapter are the lists of words, phrases, sentences, and paragraphs you can use to construct your letter. Sample letters are also given.

The lists "prime the pump"—they start you thinking along the lines of that letter topic. They also provide those who want to compose their own letter with a number of appropriate words, or they allow those using the sample letters as guides to substitute words that fit their needs.

To compose a letter:

- Read through the "How to Say It" section, note the elements your letter should include, and personalize them to reflect your situation.
- Choose from the lists of words, phrases, sentences, and paragraphs those terms that are useful to you.

- Study the sample letters to see if one can serve as a model.
- Combine your checked-off words, phrases, sentences, and paragraphs to produce a letter that says what you need it to say.
- Check your rough draft against the list of what not to say. Have you written something inappropriate? At this point, you may have a question about format or grammar or a social title. Check the index to locate the answer in one of the appendixes.

After writing your first few letters using this book, you may find that it is not, after all, so difficult or time-consuming to write your share of the billions of letters mailed each year.

HOW TO SAY IT

ONE

ACCEPTANCES

*The mind gives us thousands of ways to say no, but there's
only one way to say yes, and that's from the heart.*
—SUZE ORMAN

Once you decide to accept an invitation or grant a request, simply say so; this is one of the easiest letters to write.

A yes that doesn't come from the heart results in an unenthusiastic acceptance and you may even find yourself backing out later. Writing the acceptance is not as difficult as being sure you want to say yes in the first place.

Write Acceptances for

- admissions requests: schools/clubs/organizations
- franchise applications
- invitations: dinner/meeting/party/luncheon/hospitality
- job offers
- membership offers: board/commission/organization
- proposals
- requests: contributions/favors/help
- speaking invitations: conference/workshop/banquet
- wedding invitations (see WEDDINGS)

How to Say It

- Express your pleasure in accepting the invitation/offer/proposal/bid or agreeing to do what was asked.

- Repeat the details of what you are accepting (meeting date and time, amount of the bid or of your contribution, the precise nature of your assistance, the duties you agree to assume).
- Inquire about particular needs: receipt for a tax-deductible contribution, directions to your host's home, wheelchair accessibility, equipment for your speech, list of other organizers.
- Close with an expression of pleasure to come (seeing the person, working for the company, being part of the group) or of future action (what you want to accomplish, actions you intend to take, a reciprocal invitation).

What Not to Say

- Avoid ungracious amplifications: you are busy but you suppose you can manage it; you have two other events on the calendar that evening but you will try to stop by; you probably won't be a good speaker but, sure, you'll try. Let your yes be a simple yes. If you have reservations about your acceptance, it may be better to decline.

Tips on Writing

■ Send acceptances as soon as possible. If you are late, apologize, but do not dwell on it.

■ Acceptances are brief and generally deal only with the acceptance.

■ Noted usage expert Rudolf Flesch says, "If your answer to an inquiry is yes, it's a good idea to make yes the first word of your letter."

■ Be enthusiastic. It is entirely proper to simply state your acceptance and repeat the details of the invitation, but your stock with hosts, employers, or friends will go up if you add a sentence saying something personal, cheerful, or lively.

■ When your invitation is issued in the name of more than one person, mention all of them in your reply. Mail your reply either to the person listed under the RSVP or to the first name given.

■ Always respond promptly to an invitation marked "RSVP" or "Please reply." This is mandatory, obligatory, required, compulsory, imperative, and essential.

Special Situations

■ When offered a position you want, write an acceptance letter that expresses your enthusiasm and pleasure and that confirms the details of your employment.

■ When writing to offer a job to an applicant, include: a congratulatory remark about being chosen and something complimentary about the person's credentials, experience, or interview; information about the job—duties, salary, supervisor's name, starting date; the name and telephone number of someone who can answer questions; an expression of goodwill about the person's employment with the company. Highlight some of the advantages of working for the company to influence the person's decision to accept the offer.

■ In some situations (large weddings, for example), one of a couple may accept an invitation while the other declines. In other cases (large dinner parties), check with your host to see if this is acceptable.

■ White House invitations include the phone number of the Social Office where you telephone your acceptance and can ask questions about protocol, where to park your car, what to wear, how to respond to the invitation. General guidelines are: send your reply within a day of receiving the invitation; write the reply yourself (do not have a secretary do it); handwrite your reply on plain or engraved personal stationery; use the same format and person (first person or third person) to reply but insert "have the honor of accepting"; if the invitation was sent by the President's or First Lady's secretary (in the case of an informal invitation), reply to that person and write "Would you please tell/convey to . . ."

■ Children can write brief acceptances for invitations: "Thank you for inviting me to your Halloween party. Wait till you see my costume!"

Format

■ Model your reply on the format used in the invitation or letter. If it is handwritten, handwrite your reply. If letterhead stationery is used, reply on your letterhead. If the invitation is e-mailed, e-mail your acceptance. When the language of the invitation is informal, your reply is also informal. When replying to a formal invitation, use nearly the same words, layout, and style as the invitation:

Mr. and Mrs. Masterson Finsbury
request the pleasure of
Mr. and Mrs. Edward Bloomfield's company
at a dinner-dance
on Saturday, the seventh of February
at eight o'clock
Gideon Country Club

Mr. and Mrs. Edward Bloomfield
accept with pleasure
the kind invitation of
Mr. and Mrs. Masterson Finsbury
to a dinner-dance
on Saturday, the seventh of February
at eight o'clock
Gideon Country Club

WORDS

accept	gratifying	satisfying	touched
approve	pleased	thoughtful	welcome
certainly	pleasure	thrilled	willing
delighted			

PHRASES

able to say yes	it will be a pleasure to
accept with pleasure	pleased to have been invited
agree to	thank you for asking me to
glad to be able to vote yes	thank you for nominating me for
happy to let you know	we are delighted to accept
I am pleased/happy/honored to accept	we are sincerely happy to join you
	we have accepted your bid of
it is with great pleasure that	we look forward with pleasure
it was so thoughtful of you to	

SENTENCES

After reviewing your application, we are pleased to be able to offer you the funding requested.

I accept with pleasure the position of senior research chemist.

I am happy to be able to do this.

I appreciate very much (and accept) your generous apology.

I'll be happy to meet with you in your office March 11 at 10:30 to plan this year's All-City Science Fair.

In a word, absolutely!

In response to your letter asking for support for the Foscari Children's Home, I'm enclosing a check for $500.

Thank you for inviting me to speak at the Chang-Ch'un Meditation Center next month.

We accept your kind invitation with great pleasure.

We are happy to accept your estimate for refinishing our Queen Anne dining room suite.

We are pleased to grant you the six-week extension you requested to complete your work.

We are pleased to tell you that your application for admission to the Emmet School has been approved.

We look forward to working with you.

PARAGRAPHS

I will be delighted to have dinner with you on Friday, the sixteenth of March, at seven o'clock. Thanks so much for asking me. I can hardly wait to see you and Anders again.

Thanks for telling me how much the children at St. Joseph's Home liked my storytelling the other night. I'm happy to accept your invitation to become a regular volunteer and tell stories every other Thursday evening. Do you have a CD player so that I could use music with some of the stories?

I'm looking forward to your graduation and the reception afterward. Thanks for including me.

Your bid of $6,780 to wallpaper our reception rooms has been accepted. Please read the enclosed contract and call with any questions. We were impressed with the attention to detail in your proposal and bid, and we are looking forward to our new walls.

SAMPLE LETTERS

Dear Selina,

Vickers and I accept with pleasure your kind invitation to a celebration of your parents' fiftieth wedding anniversary on Saturday, July 16, at 7:30 p.m.

Sincerely,

————

Dear Dr. Cheesewright:

Thank you for inviting me to speak at your county dental society's dinner banquet on October 26 at 7:00. I am happy to accept and will, as you suggested, discuss new patient education strategies.

I'm not sure how much time you have allotted me—will you let me know?

With best wishes,

Dear Ms. Thirkell,

I am pleased to accept your offer of the position of assistant director of the Gilbert Tebben Working Family Center.

I enjoyed the discussions with you, and I look forward to being part of this dynamic and important community resource.

The salary, hours, responsibilities, and starting date that we discussed during our last meeting are all agreeable to me. I understand that I will receive the standard benefits package, with the addition of two weeks' vacation during my first year.

Sincerely yours,
Laurence Dean

Dear Dr. Bennett,

I would be most happy to perform twenty minutes of magic tricks at the Five Towns Children's Hospital annual fair to be held on Saturday, November 8. As the date approaches, we can discuss details.

All the best,
Anna Tellwright

Dear Mr. Grandby:

We are pleased to accept for publication your self-help book, tentatively entitled *Don't Give Up*. All of us are excited about its possibilities.

Enclosed are guidelines from the production editor to help you prepare the final manuscript. Also enclosed is a preliminary draft of the book contract. Please look it over, and I will call next week to discuss it.

Sincerely yours,

Dear Ms. Unwin:

Congratulations! Your franchise application has been approved. Welcome to the Sunshine family.

Enclosed is the contract, which we suggest you discuss with your attorney, and a packet of informational materials.

Please call this office to set up an appointment to discuss any questions.

Sincerely,

Dear Violet,

Yes! I will be delighted to stay with the twins while you and Gordon take the horses to the state fair. A week is *not* too long for me. And thanks for the offer of the plane ticket—I accept with pleasure.

Love,

————

Dear Mr. Van Druten,

In response to your letter of February 10, we are pleased to grant you a two-month extension of the loan of the slides showing scenes of our amusement park. We appreciate being able to help you add, as you said, "a bit of amusement" to your corporate meetings.

We offer this extension with our compliments.

Cordially,
Laura Simmons

————

Dear Richard,

I will be happy to write you a letter of reference, and I'm delighted that you thought to ask me. You were one of my favorite students, and I'll enjoy explaining just why to Forey, Harley and Wentworth.

Yours truly,

————

Mr. Clarence Rochester
accepts with pleasure
William Portlaw and Alida Ascott's
kind invitation to dinner
on the sixteenth of June at 7:30 p.m.
but regrets that
Dr. Maggie Campion
will be absent at that time.

————

See also: REFUSALS, RESPONSES

TWO

ACKNOWLEDGMENTS AND CONFIRMATIONS

Life is not so short but that there is always time enough for courtesy.
—RALPH WALDO EMERSON

Letters of acknowledgment and letters of confirmation resemble each other. The letter of acknowledgment says, "I received your letter (telephone call, gift, materials)." The letter of confirmation says, "I received your letter (message, contract) and we agree about the matter"; this letter can serve as an informal contract.

Sometimes a letter of acknowledgment also serves as a thank you. Or it says you received the message or materials but will respond later, or that you passed them on to the appropriate person. Sometimes, too, acknowledgment letters are really sales letters that use the excuse of acknowledging something (an order, a payment) to present an additional sales message.

You always acknowledge expressions of condolence. You generally acknowledge anniversary or birthday greetings, congratulations, apologies, or divorce announcements.

Acknowledge or Confirm

- anniversary/birthday greetings
- apologies
- complaints
- condolences
- congratulations
- divorce announcements
- documents/reports/files/materials received

- gifts (thank-you note to follow)
- information received
- inquiries/requests (will respond as soon as possible)
- letters from constituents
- letters of introduction
- letters received (action underway, will let you know)
- mail in supervisor's absence (assistant writes that message/letter has been received and will be dealt with later)
- manuscripts (under consideration, will give decision later)
- oral agreements, telephone discussions/agreements
- orders (see also ORDERS)
- payments
- proposals
- receipt of orders/merchandise (see also ORDERS)
- receipt of wedding gifts (see WEDDINGS)
- reports
- reservations, speaking dates, invitation times
- sympathy messages

How to Say It

- State precisely what you are acknowledging or confirming (reservation, amount, letter, order).
- Refer to the date and occasion of your last contact (telephone conversation, previous letter, in-person discussion).
- Describe what action, if any, is being taken.
- Tell when the reader will hear further from you or from someone else.
- If indicated, explain why you are not able to respond fully to the letter/request/gift at the moment.
- Express appreciation for the previous contact, for the kindness of the person in writing you, or for the business.
- Close with a courtesy or forward-looking statement.

What Not to Say

- Don't belabor explanations; letters of acknowledgment and confirmation are brief.
- Avoid a negative tone ("thought I'd make sure we're both talking about the same thing"). Repeat matter-of-factly the details of the items you're acknowledging or confirming.

Tips on Writing

■ Write promptly. Acknowledgments are, by their very nature, sent immediately. One exception is acknowledging expressions of sympathy. Because of the hardships involved, responses may be sent up to six weeks later. Or, a close relative of the bereaved may write the acknowledgment: "Mother asked me to tell you how much she appreciated the loving letter of sympathy and the memorial you sent for Dad. She will be in touch with you as soon as she is able to."

Special Situations

■ When a letterwriter asks about an issue better handled by someone else, acknowledge the letter and provide the name, address, and telephone number of the appropriate person. You can also forward the letter to the proper department and so notify your correspondent.

■ Timely and regular business transactions need no acknowledgment: orders are received, merchandise is delivered, payments are sent. You would, however, acknowledge receipt in unusual situations. If the previous order went astray, you will want the sender to know that this one arrived. When you receive payment from someone to whom you've been sending collection letters, let the person know that payment has been received (and, by implication, that there will be no more collection letters). Acknowledge large or important payments, orders, and shipments—or those from first-time customers or suppliers. Acknowledge letters, requests, orders, manuscript submissions, or complaints that cannot be responded to immediately so that the person knows that action is being taken.

■ Acknowledge mail that arrives in a supervisor's or coworker's absence. Mention the absence without offering apologies or explanations. Do not refer to the contents of the letter; an exception is made for the announcement of a death or serious illness. Express sympathy on behalf of the other person and say that a letter will follow as soon as possible.

■ Organizations receiving memorial donations acknowledge receipt of the contribution and also notify the family so it can thank the donor personally.

■ Domestic hotel and motel reservations are often made and confirmed entirely by phone. Occasionally, however, written confirmation is necessary because of special conditions or changes of plans. Include your requirements: date, length of stay, kind of accommodation, price, extras requested (crib in a room, for example), wheelchair accessibility, availability of pool, HBO, entertaining facilities. Request confirmation from foreign hotels or resorts.

Include your e-mail address or fax number or, in some cases, an International Reply Coupon (IRC) for their response.

■ If someone announces a divorce, avoid expressing either congratulations or sympathy (unless you know which is called for); in most cases, simply acknowledge the information.

■ An apology is acknowledged to let the other person know that you have received it (and accepted it, if that is the case).

■ If you cannot respond to a proposal, report, or manuscript right away, acknowledge its receipt to the sender and assure the person that you will communicate further as soon as you have evaluated it. People spend time writing reports, proposals, and manuscripts and are naturally eager for results. They will wait more patiently if their mailing has been acknowledged.

■ When you cannot make an immediate decision among job applicants, acknowledge receipt of their applications or résumés or thank them for their interviews. Tell them you will let them know as soon as a decision has been made. (If you have an idea of when this will be, say so.) Thank them for their interest in your organization.

Format

■ Routine acknowledgments and confirmations (receipt of applications, manuscripts, requests, payments) can be handled by e-mail, preprinted cards, or simple form letters. Note the item received and the date of receipt.

■ For numerous wedding gifts or expressions of sympathy, send printed acknowledgment cards indicating that you'll respond soon. In the case of a public figure whose death inspires many messages of sympathy from people unknown to the family or deceased, printed or engraved cards or foldovers are sent (with no personal follow-up).

■ Use e-mail for routine acknowledgments and confirmations. For business records, keep back-up file copies of all transactions.

■ For complicated business acknowledgments or confirmations, use letterhead stationery or memo paper.

■ Personal acknowledgments and confirmations are handwritten on informal personal stationery; e-mail can be used for casual situations.

WORDS

accept	approve	ensure	reassure
acknowledge	assure	indicate	receipt
affirm	confirm	notice	reply
agreed-upon	corroborate	notify	respond
appreciate	endorse	reaffirm	settle

PHRASES

as I mentioned on the phone

as we agreed yesterday

I enjoyed our conversation of

in response to your letter

I sincerely appreciated

look forward to continuing our discussion

thank you for the package that

this will acknowledge the receipt of

to confirm our recent conversation

want to confirm in writing

we have received

will respond as soon as

SENTENCES

I enjoyed speaking with you this afternoon and look forward to our meeting next Thursday at 2:30 at your office.

Just a note to let you know that the printer ribbons arrived.

Thank you for remembering my ten-year anniversary with Lamb and Company.

Thank you for the wallpaper samples, which arrived this morning.

Thank you for writing me with your views on socialized medicine.

Thank you for your order, which we received yesterday; it will be shipped to you this week.

The family of Annis Gething gratefully acknowledges your kind and comforting expressions of sympathy.

The members of the Board of Directors and I appreciated your presentation yesterday and want you to know that we are taking your concerns under serious advisement.

This is to acknowledge receipt of the rerouted shipment of Doncastle tennis rackets, catalog number AE-78573.

This is to confirm our recent conversation about the identification and removal of several underground storage tanks on my property.

This will acknowledge receipt of your report on current voter attitudes.

This will confirm our revised delivery date of November 6.

We are proceeding with the work as requested by Jerome Searing in his May 3, 2010, telephone call.

We hereby acknowledge that an inspection of the storm drain and street construction installed by the Bagshaw Company in the Rockingham subdivision has been completed.

Your letter of July 16 has been referred for review and appropriate action. We value you as a customer and ask your patience while a response is being prepared.

Thank you for the update on the preparation of the Price-Stables contract. I appreciate knowing what progress you're making.

Thank you for your workshop proposal, which we have just received. Ms. Bramber is out of the office for the next two weeks but will contact you soon after she returns.

Thanks for the samples. As soon as we've had a chance to get them under the microscope and run some tests, we'll let you know what we find.

I've received your kind invitation to join the Friends of the Library committee. I need to review other commitments to be sure that I can devote as much time to the Friends as I'd like. I'll let you know next week. In the meantime, thanks for thinking of me.

The information you sent was exactly what I needed. It will take several weeks to reach a decision, but I'll call as soon as I do. In the meantime, thanks for your promptness.

Thanks for the call this morning, Janet. I'll see you on May 23 at 10:00 a.m. and will bring the spring lists with me.

I wanted you to know that I received your letter this morning, but as I'm leaving for Dallas later today I won't have time to look into the billing problem with the contractor for another week or so. If you need action sooner than that, give Agnes Laiter a call.

I'm glad we were able to reach an agreement on the telephone this morning. I'll have the contracts retyped—inserting the new delivery date of March 16, 2011, and the new metric ton rate of $55—and sent to you by the end of the week.

Thank you for telling me about the divorce. It's been too long since I've seen you. Can we get together sometime? How about breakfast Saturday morning? That used to work for us.

Thank you for your letter of June 9, describing the employee behavior you encountered on three different visits to our store. We are looking into the situation, and will let you know what we find. In the meantime, please accept our apologies for any embarrassment or unpleasantness you experienced.

Thank you for your letter of application and your résumé. We have received numerous responses to our advertisement, which means you may not hear from us immediately. Beginning March 1 we will call qualified applicants to arrange interviews.

We received your request for information on our stop-smoking plan and for a sample of the skin patch. Because of the enthusiastic response to our advertisement, we have temporarily exhausted our supplies of the skin patch. I'm enclosing the literature you requested, and will send the skin patch in approximately two weeks.

SAMPLE LETTERS

Dear Mr. Borkin:

To confirm our telephone conversation, Barry Studio Supplies will be happy to provide you with all your photographic needs. We make deliveries in the metropolitan area within twenty-four hours of receiving an order.

Enclosed is a copy of our current catalog, a pad of order forms, and my card. As your personal representative, I can answer any of your questions and help you with special orders.

Sincerely yours,

————

Dear William Beevor,

We have received the blueprints for the Brass Bottle Hotel. As soon as Mr. Ventimore and the staff have had time to look at them, I'll call you to set up a meeting. Until then, Mr. Ventimore sends his regards.

Yours truly,

————

Dear Mrs. Beddows,

This is to acknowledge your kind expression of sympathy and the lovely floral arrangement you sent on the occasion of Mr. Holtby's death. Mrs. Holtby will be writing you a personal note as soon as she can. In the meantime, she appreciates your friendship and concern.

Sincerely,

————

Dear Mrs. Cammysole,

Thank you for sending the lease for the apartment on Thackeray Street.

We are having our lawyer look at it tomorrow afternoon, and we will be in touch with you as soon as possible after that.

With best wishes,

————

Dear Edna Bunthorne:

This will acknowledge your letter of August 6 addressed to Francis Moulton. Mr. Moulton is on a six-month medical leave of absence, and his interim replacement has not yet been named.

I am enclosing materials that will answer some of your questions, and I will refer the others to the new director as soon as possible.

If the delay is unacceptable to you, you may want to contact Kate Croy at the Lowder Foundation.

Sincerely,

————

Dear Professor Erlin:

Thank you for your paper, "The Rise and the Fall of the Clown Trope," which we received this week. Because of an overwhelming response to our call for symposium papers, our editorial staff will not be able to respond within the usual two to three weeks. It may be five to six weeks before you hear from us. Thanks for understanding.

Yours truly,

————

Dear Member,

Thank you for your order.

Unfortunately, we're temporarily out of stock on the item below. We've reordered it and expect to have a new supply in a few weeks. We'll ship it as soon as it arrives.

Sincerely,

————

Dear Dr. Breeve,

This is to confirm that you have permission to use the Great Organ of St. Luke's Church for an organ recital March 30 at 7:30 p.m. As agreed, you will be responsible for the expense of any organ repairs necessary for the recital.

Please call me to arrange for an extra key when you need to begin practicing.

We're delighted that someone of your talent will be using our wonderful old—but often forgotten—organ.

With best wishes,

————

Dear Geraldine Dabis:

We have received your loan application and will process it as quickly as possible. However, because of the complex nature of the application, it is being reviewed and evaluated by loan officers from two different divisions. This may delay our response somewhat.

If you have questions about the delay or about our process, please call me at 800-555-1216.

Yours truly,

————————

See also: ACCEPTANCES, APPOINTMENTS, FOLLOW-UP, RE-SPONSES, SALES, THANK YOU, TRAVEL, WEDDINGS

THREE

LETTERS OF ADJUSTMENT

A reputation for handling customer claims quickly and fairly
is a powerful public relations tool for any firm.
—L. SUE BAUGH, MARIDELL FRYAR, DAVID THOMAS

Write a letter of adjustment in response to a customer's letter of complaint (also called a claims letter). Business imperfections—incorrect bills, damaged merchandise, late payments—are not as rare as we'd like. In most instances, adjustments are handled routinely. "Keeping an old customer is just as important as gaining a new one." (N. H. and S. K. Mager)

An adjustment letter serves to (1) correct errors and make good on company inadequacies; (2) grant reasonable full or partial adjustments in order to maintain good customer relations; or (3) deny unwarranted claims so tactfully that the customer's goodwill is retained.

In his classic *Handbook of Business Letters,* L. E. Frailey advises treating a complaint with as much respect as an order, letting customers know you are as eager to serve them as to sell them.

"Every unhappy customer will tell ten others about a bad experience, whereas happy customers may tell three." (Lillian Vernon)

The only thing worse than customers who complain are customers who don't complain—and take their business elsewhere. A claims letter gives you the opportunity to win the customer back. You know when you have written a good letter of adjustment because the customer returns.

(To request an adjustment, see COMPLAINTS; this chapter deals only with making them.)

Kinds of Adjustment Letters

- billing/invoice errors
- credit
- damages
- exchanges
- explanations: oversight/error
- newspaper corrections
- refunds/discounts
- refusing to make (see REFUSALS)
- repairing damages
- replacements
- time extensions

How to Say It

- Open with a cordial statement ("Thank you for your letter of June 3"), a thank you for bringing the matter to your attention, or a sentiment such as "We were sorry to hear that . . ."
- Refer to the error, specifying dates, amounts, invoice numbers.
- If the customer was correct, say so.
- State your regret about the confusion, mix-up, or error.
- Explain your company's policy of dealing with customer claims, if appropriate.
- Describe how you will resolve the problem or what you've already done. Sometimes you give customers the choice of a replacement, a refund, or a credit to their account.
- Mention when you expect the problem to be resolved, even if it is only "immediately," "at once," or "as soon as possible."
- Reassure the customer: this error is rare; you do not expect a repeat occurrence of it; the company works hard to satisfy customers.
- Close by acknowledging the customer's patience, asking for continued customer loyalty, offering further cooperation, reaffirming the company's good intentions and the value of its products, or expressing your expectation that the customer will continue to enjoy your services and products for years to come.

What Not to Say

- Don't use the words "claim" or "complaint" even though that's how these incoming letters are commonly identified. To customers, the terms sound accusatory and judgmental, and the majority of them honestly believe they are due an adjustment. Instead of "The damage that you claim was due to improper packing" or "Your complaint has been received," substitute a word like "report" for "claim" and "complaint."

- Don't say how surprised you are ("I can't believe this happened"; "Not once in twenty years have we encountered this problem") unless it truly is an exceptional occurrence. Customers assume that if the error happened to them, it could happen (and probably has) to anyone. You lose credibility.
- Don't repeat all the details of a problem or overemphasize it. A passing reference is sufficient. Focus on the solution rather than on the error. You want the latter to quickly become a vague memory for the customer.
- Avoid long explanations. Customers generally don't care about your difficulties with suppliers, employees, or shippers; they simply want an adjustment. Restrict your explanation, if you wish to include one, to several words ("due to a delayed shipment" or "because of power outages last week").
- Don't be excessively apologetic. A simple "We regret the error" is adequate for most slip-ups.
- Don't blame "computer error." By now people know that human beings run the computers, not vice versa, and this weak and obviously untrue excuse irritates people. And don't imply that these things are bound to happen from time to time. Although this may be true, it makes your company look careless.
- Don't make an adjustment grudgingly, angrily, impatiently, or condescendingly, and don't imply that you're doing the customer a big favor. This cancels the positive public relations effect of righting the error. Make your adjustment graciously or at least matter-of-factly even when the customer is angry or rude. Your attitude must be friendly and understanding; the high road leads to goodwill and customer satisfaction.
- Don't end your letter by mentioning the problem ("Again, we are so sorry that our Great Southwest Hiking Holiday was such an unpleasant experience for you") because it leaves the problem, not your goodwill and adjustment, uppermost in the reader's mind.
- Don't overstate company culpability or indicate in writing that the company was negligent. When negligence is involved, your lawyer can suggest the best approach for your letter.

Tips on Writing

- Respond promptly; this establishes your good intentions.
- Be specific: about the problem, about the steps you are taking, about what

the customer can expect in the future. Vagueness leaves customers expecting more than is offered and unhappy when they don't get it.

■ Assume responsibility when appropriate. Use the active voice ("We sent the wrong monitor") rather than the passive voice ("The wrong monitor was sent to you").

■ When the customer has been inconvenienced, be generous with your sympathy. Sometimes out of fear that the customer will "take advantage" of such openness, businesses fail to give customers their due—and then pay for it in reduced customer satisfaction.

■ In some cases, add a goodwill gesture: a discount coupon or gift certificate, or a reduction on the next order.

■ Adjustment letters are easier to write when your company has a codified strategy for managing customer complaints. You can then follow and appeal to policy and handle similar situations evenhandedly; you will not have to reinvent the wheel for each claims letter.

■ Old but still good advice: "Legalistic quibbles have no place in the answer to a complaint. The customer is rightly or wrongly dissatisfied; business is built only on satisfied customers. Therefore the question is not to prove who is right but to satisfy the customer. This doctrine has its limitations, but it is safer to err in the way of doing too much than in doing too little." (Mary Owens Crowther, *The Book of Letters,* 1923)

■ An excellent resource for those who write letters of adjustment is Cheryl McLean, *Customer Service Letters Ready to Go!* MTC Business Books, 1996.

Special Situations

■ Some problems are partly or wholly the customer's fault (failure to read installation instructions, excessive or inappropriate use). If you decide to grant the adjustment (most companies give customers the benefit of the doubt), don't assign blame to the customer; it undoes the goodwill you are establishing. When neither the company nor the customer is completely at fault, suggest a compromise adjustment or offer several solutions ("Because this item is not manufactured to be fire-resistant, we cannot offer you an exact exchange, but we would be glad to replace the fielder's glove at our wholesale cost, offer you a 30 percent discount on your next purchase, or repair the fire-damaged nylon mesh back"). "A compromise is the art of dividing a cake in such a way that everyone believes that he or she has got the biggest piece." (Ludwig Erhard)

■ When you deny the requested adjustment (a complete refund, for example), explain why: an investigation of the matter did not support it (include documents or itemize findings); standard company policy does not allow it (and violating the policy in this case is not possible); the item is no longer under warranty; the item was used in a specifically prohibited manner. Be gracious but firm. Express your sympathy for the customer's point of view, explain that their letter was considered carefully, appeal to their sense of fair play, and close with a positive statement (expressing your appreciation of past business and cooperation, offering a coupon, saying that this was a difficult letter to write but the only response consistent with your values of fairness and responsibility).

■ Before mailing a product recall notice, consult with your attorney since the wording is important. Most recalls are announced in a form letter that describes the recalled product, tells what the problem is, and explains how the consumer can receive an adjustment, replacement, or refund.

Format

■ Adjustment letters dealing with nonroutine problems are typed on letterhead stationery. For routine adjustment matters, use a half-sheet size memo or form letter with blanks to insert the details.

■ Small companies may return a copy of the customer's letter with a handwritten note: "We apologize for the error. Enclosed is a check for the difference."

■ If you learn of the problem by e-mail or fax, respond that way.

WORDS

accommodate	correct	refund	replace
amend	credit	regulate	return
apologize	rebate	reimburse	satisfaction
arrange	rectify	remedy	settle
compensate	redress	repair	solution

PHRASES

appreciate your pointing out	reduce the price
corrected invoice/statement/bill	sincerely sorry to hear that
greatly regret your dissatisfaction	sorry for the inconvenience/ misunderstanding
I'm sorry to learn that	
make amends for	sorry to learn that
our apologies	until you are completely satisfied
please disregard	will receive immediate credit
prevent a recurrence	you are correct in stating that

I'm sorry about the error in filling your order—the correct posters are being shipped today.

Thank you for bringing to our attention the missing steel pole in the tetherball set you ordered from us.

Thank you for giving us the opportunity to correct the erroneous information published in the last issue of Tallboys' Direct Mail Marketer.

Thank you for your telephone call about the defective laser labels—you will receive replacement labels within two to three business days.

We appreciate the difficulties you have had with your Deemster Steam Iron, but all our appliances carry large-print, bright-colored tags alerting consumers to the safety feature of the polarized plug (one blade is wider than the other and the plug fits into a polarized outlet only one way).

We are pleased to offer you an additional two weeks, interest-free, to complete payment on your formal-wear rental.

We hope to continue to serve your banking needs.

We regret the difficulties you had with your last toner cartridge.

We're sorry you had to write; this should have been taken care of some time ago.

We were sorry to learn that you are dissatisfied with the performance of your Salten personal paper shredder.

Your business and goodwill are important to us.

You're right, the self-repairing zippers on your Carradine Brent Luggage should not have seized up after only two months' use.

You will receive immediate credit for the faulty masonry work, and we will send someone to discuss replacing it.

PARAGRAPHS

Thank you for responding to our recall notices and returning the Small World farm set to us for a refund. Small World has been making quality toys for children since 1976, and we regret the design error that made this set potentially dangerous to young children.

Thank you for calling to our attention the pricing error on our Bluewater automatic pool cleaners. Enclosed is a check for the difference. We look forward to serving you again.

Thank you for your telephone call. You are correct in thinking that you should not have been charged interest this past month. We have credited $2.85 to your account.

After carefully reading your letter of August 4, I consulted our shipping department. It appears that we did comply with the terms of the contract (documents enclosed).

I am sorry that your order was filled incorrectly. Enclosed are the back issues that you ordered. Please keep the others with our apologies.

Thank you for taking the time to let us know of your recent experience with one of our products. We are always interested in hearing from our customers but regret that it was this type of occurrence that prompted your letter.

SAMPLE LETTERS

Dear Mr. Willard:

Thank you for your letter of July 18. We are always happy to hear from our customers and pleased to be of service to them.

We are embarrassed to learn of your unfortunate experience with one of our products. We are always alert to constructive criticism, for we appreciate the enviable reputation our brand names enjoy in the marketplace with consumers the world over.

We would like you to know that as soon as we received your letter we held a special meeting with the resident managers of our Juvenile Puzzle Division, as well as our Quality Control Division. They are now looking into the problem.

In the meantime we are forwarding to you, with our compliments, several of our newest products, which we are certain will bring many hours of pleasant entertainment to your household.

We appreciate your taking the time to write us and hope that you will continue to look for our brand names whenever you purchase "things to do" that are fun for everyone.

Sincerely,

————

Dear Ms. Kenealy,

Enclosed is the Ralph Kello denim dress you ordered six months ago. I can only apologize most sincerely for all the difficulties you have had placing this order.

I am pleased that you are still interested in obtaining the dress. To help compensate you for your troubles I am also enclosing a check for $40—half the amount you sent us six months ago. Thank you for your patience, and I hope we can serve you again soon.

Sincerely,

————

Dear Malcolm Bryant,

We have received your signed copy of the major medical insurance waiver for this school year. The charge of $535 for student health insurance that was included in your fall tuition payment will be credited to your account.

Sincerely,

———

Dear Ms. Jordan,

This will confirm the arrangements made by telephone this morning. We apologize for your conference tables arriving with a center inlay color of Vanilla Illusion rather than the Blackstar Aggregate that you ordered.

The correct order will be delivered on June 7, and the other conference tables will be picked up at that time. As I understand it, only one table of the first shipment was un-boxed. If you can have that one reboxed or protected enough to be returned to us, we will appreciate it.

There will, of course, be no charge and in recognition of the inconvenience to you, we are enclosing a coupon good for $100 off your next order. We have always appreciated your business and look forward to serving you again.

Sincerely,

———

Dear Ms. Carfax,

We are sorry that the flowers you ordered for your holiday office celebration arrived in an unacceptable condition. Thank you for the dated photograph; it was helpful to us in assessing the problem.

It appears that somewhere between our premises and yours, the flowers were exposed to the below-zero temperatures we had that week. This would result in the wilted, browned appearance shown in the photograph. We are following up on this matter with our delivery people.

It is too late to save your holiday celebration, but we would like to make amends by, first, crediting your charge card for the entire amount of the flowers and, second, offer-ing you complimentary flowers of equal value for your next occasion. We appreciate your business and hope to be of service to you again.

Sincerely,

———

Dear Lucy Snowe,

Thank you for your letter requesting a correction of several statements that appeared about you and your company in the most recent issue of *Small Business Today*. The in-formation we were given was not double-checked; we apologize.

The correction appears on page 4 of this month's issue.

Sincerely,

———

Dear Eva Steer:

I am sorry that the Irish linens you purchased from us proved to be flawed.

Please return the order to us, complete with packaging. We will replace it at once and also refund your mailing costs.

I notice that you have been a loyal customer for the past eight years, so you know that our quality control people don't let something like this happen very often. I'm enclosing a discount good for 20 percent off your next order as our way of apologizing for your inconvenience.

Best regards,

Dear Gabriel Bagradian,

Thank you for your letter of July 7, appealing the $50 charge for the non-emergency use of the Werfel Community Hospital emergency room.

A review of the records shows that your son Stephan visited the emergency room on March 19 with a collapsed lung, not for treatment of acne. We regret the error that was made in coding the reason for the visit and have made an adjustment to your account.

We appreciate your spotting the error and letting us know about it so courteously.

Sincerely,
T. Haigasun
Billing Department

Dear Mrs. Painter,

Thank you for telling us about the infestation in our Wheatley cereal. We are sorry you had this experience and want you to know we share your concern.

Consumer satisfaction is most important to us, and we sincerely regret your recent experience with our product. Our company has strict standards of quality control. We carefully examine each lot of raw materials when it arrives. Sanitarians inspect our manufacturing plant continually and, in addition, make periodic checks of our suppliers' facilities. Food samples are collected all through the manufacturing process and are analyzed in our laboratories. We enforce these stringent procedures to ensure the production of high-quality, insect-free products.

The information you gave us about our product is being brought to the attention of the appropriate company officials.

Again, thank you for writing.

Yours truly,

Dear Mr. Steinmetz,

No, the motor on your vacuum should not have "worn out" six months after you purchased it. We can't be sure what the problem is, but this is unusual for our top-of-the-line Costello vacuum.

Please take the vacuum to one of our repair shops (see attached list to find the one closest to you). The personnel there will examine the machine and if they can repair it, they will do so and bill us. If they find that the machine is defective, we will arrange to have a replacement shipped to you.

Please accept our apologies for the inconvenience this has caused you.

———

Dear Mr. Ramsdell:
Re: Claim 02018-1134 WB 753

Enclosed is a check in full settlement of your claim.

Because Shipper's Transit Insurance was not purchased, the carrier's liability is limited to $1.25 per pound times the weight of the load. This conforms with tariff regulations.

To obtain full reimbursement for damages or loss you must file a claim with your corporation traffic department or its insurance carrier. Please check with them about this.

Thank you for your patience and cooperation during the necessary delays in processing your claim.

Sincerely,

———

Dear Mr. Magnus,

We were unhappy to hear that you felt the installation of your fiber-optical cable was "sloppily done" and the electricians "unprofessional."

We now have the report of two inspectors, one from our company and one from an independent oversight bureau, who visited your offices on November 11 and 12. Their evaluations indicate that the installation was meticulously done, that code standards were met or exceeded, that site cleanup was faultless, and that, in fact, there was no findable cause for objection.

Interviews with your staff members who had contact with the electricians turned up no negative information about their behavior.

In the light of these reports, we are unable to offer you the requested deep discount on our services.

———

See also: ACKNOWLEDGMENTS, APOLOGIES, BELATED, COMPLAINTS, CREDIT, REFUSALS, RESPONSES

FOUR

ADVICE

*Advice . . . is a habit-forming drug. You give a dear friend a bit of
advice today, and next week you find yourself advising two or three friends,
and the week after, a dozen, and the week following, crowds!*
—CAROLYN WELLS

Ask for advice only when you are open to it, not when you already know the "advice" you want to receive. That isn't fair to the person who spends time on a response. In addition, you may be unpleasantly surprised.

If you are the advice-giver, respond only to the issues raised by the other person; don't venture further afield.

If you have not been asked for advice, you are on shaky ground to volunteer it. "It is well enough when one is talking to a friend to hedge in an odd word by way of counsel now and then, but there is something mighty irksome, in its staring upon one in a letter where one ought only to see kind words and friendly remembrances." (Mary Lamb)

In general, give advice only when you have been sincerely asked for it.

Kinds of Letters Dealing with Advice

- asking for/requesting
- giving unsolicited
- offering suggestions
- rejecting
- responding to request for
- thanking for

How to Say It

- To ask for advice, briefly outline the issue. Tell what you expect from the other person and perhaps why you chose them in this situation. If you need the advice by a deadline, say so. Reassure them that they are not obliged to respond. Thank them for being available to you.
- To give advice, begin by rephrasing the other person's request ("You asked my advice about your college plans") or by explaining why you are writing (something came across your desk you thought might be of interest, or you had an idea that might be useful). State your opinion, advice, or suggestion. Explain your reasoning, if necessary. Tell what, if any, action you think the person might take. Include a disclaimer: "this is only my opinion," "I know you will use your own good judgment," "just an idea . . ." Finally, assure your reader of your confidence that they will make a good decision, deal with the situation, succeed at any task.
- To thank someone for advice, express your gratitude as you would for any gift, but tell how the advice was useful to you. If you didn't take the advice, thank the person for their time, effort, and concern. When you receive inappropriate or unwanted advice, assume—for politeness' sake—that they meant well and acknowledge their attention.

What Not to Say

- Don't over-explain. Outline your suggestion or course of action in a few sentences. "Whatever advice you give, be short." (Horace) Brevity is difficult in a letter giving advice. We are tempted to offer all the wisdom accumulated over a lifetime. Resist. After writing your letter, delete half of it. The person who wants to know more will ask.
- Avoid "should" as in "I think you should . . ." No one can say what anyone else "should" or "ought to" do. Find a more flexible way of phrasing your suggestion.
- Don't imply that you've found the one, correct answer. Offer instead alternatives, possibilities, fresh approaches.

Tips on Writing

■ When giving advice, use tact, tact, and more tact. Read your letter as though it had been sent to you. How does it make you feel? Have someone read it to make sure it isn't abrasive or patronizing. "Advice is like snow; the softer it falls, the longer it dwells upon, and the deeper it sinks into the mind." (Samuel Taylor Coleridge)

■ Start with a compliment or upbeat remark to frame your advice in a positive context.

■ When possible, attribute the advice to someone else. Especially when your advice is unsolicited, consider getting another person to offer the advice you want to give. Advice that is unwelcome from a parent is often accepted from a third party. Advice from a superior may be better received from a colleague—or vice versa.

■ Be specific. "Get a grip!" or "Shape up!" or "Try harder!" is not advice. Mignon McLaughlin wrote: "'Pull yourself together' is seldom said to anyone who can." When possible, include names and telephone numbers of resources, costs of what you're recommending, clear-cut steps to the goal.

■ When giving unsolicited advice, be respectful and low-key, mildly suggesting that this is something the person might want to think about. In this instance, passive voice or indirect phrasing is useful ("If the loans could be consolidated" instead of "If you would consolidate your loans"). An intermediate step might be to write, "I noticed that . . ." or "Do you need any help?" and, without giving advice then and there, indicate that you are willing to do so.

Special Situations

■ Letters giving professional advice (a lawyer advising a client, a doctor outlining a program of patient health care, a teacher suggesting tests for a child) is written much more carefully than most advice letters. The advice must be professionally defensible and might include references or sources for the advice. Keep copies of the letter (and sometimes send them to third parties). On occasion, another person's opinion may be needed to reinforce the advice and protect yourself. Ours is a litigious society; good Samaritans enjoy no protection under the law for their helpful works and intentions.

■ If you request advice about investing money or about a situation with significant consequences, emphasize that the other person will not be held responsible for the outcome. With a written absolution, the recipient might feel easier about giving advice. You get what you pay for, however, and you might be better off seeing a professional (financial counselor, psychologist, lawyer, realtor).

■ If your first letter of advice is ignored or poorly received, let it be your last letter of advice to that person. "The true secret of giving advice is, after you have honestly given it, to be perfectly indifferent whether it is taken or not, and never persist in trying to set people right." (Hannah Whitall Smith)

■ Don't give advice warning against individuals, companies, or products;

you could create legal problems for yourself. It's generally not a problem to recommend a person or an organization although, if you are a public figure, you might get asked pretty smartly to explain why you didn't mention certain others.

Format

■ Use letterhead stationery to write a business associate outside the firm, memo paper or letterhead to write someone inside the firm, and informal stationery for social relationships.

■ The choice of a handwritten or typewritten letter of advice can set the tone of your letter. A handwritten note to an employee might be perceived as too personal and a bit apologetic, where the typewritten message appears objective and matter-of-fact. On the other hand, writing a personal note in some sensitive business situations indicates that you are writing as a friend as well as a customer, client, or supervisor.

WORDS

advantageous	consult	forethought	precaution	suitable
advisable	counsel	guidance	principle	urge
advocate	debate	guidelines	prudent	useful
appropriate	desirable	insight	rational	valuable
apt	direction	instructions	reasonable	warn
beneficial	encourage	open-minded	recommend	weigh
careful	examine	opinion	resource	wisdom
caution	expedient	persuade	sensible	worthwhile
consider	fitting	practical	study	

PHRASES

alert you to the possibility	I have the impression that
as I understand it	in my estimation/judgment/ opinion/view
backseat driver	
compare notes	I noticed that
consider carefully	I take it that
I am convinced that	it seems to me
I don't like to interfere, but	just wanted to suggest/recommend
I feel/assume/presume/think	keep a lookout for/an eye on
if you don't mind	kick around this idea

look into	think through
might want to	to my way of thinking
piece of advice	to the best of my knowledge
so far as I know	weigh both courses of action
speak for	what you could do
take care of	whether you take my advice or not
take into account	
take it amiss/the wrong way	you've probably already thought of this, but
take to heart	
think about	

SENTENCES

Although I liked what you wrote about switching your major from Physics to Astronomy, I have a suggestion you might want to consider.

Do you have any advice about how I can raise morale in the Accounting Department?

Ever since you asked my opinion about the Middlemarch line, I've been mulling over the situation, weighing the benefits against the rather considerable cost.

I don't usually give unsolicited advice, but this seems to me to be a special case.

I hope this is the sort of advice you wanted.

I'm considering a switch from the technical to the management ladder—do you have any wise, helpful words for me?

I'm writing to you for advice.

I thought I should mention this.

I took your excellent advice and I'm grateful.

I will appreciate any comments or advice you'd care to give.

I would be grateful for your frank opinion about our registering Jermyn for kindergarten this year (he won't be five yet) instead of waiting another year.

I wouldn't ordinarily presume to tell you your business, but I'm concerned.

Thank you for your unerring advice about our hot rolling equipment—we're back on schedule.

There is one thing you might want to consider.

We are unable to take your advice just now, but we're grateful to you for thinking of us.

Would you be willing to tell me quite frankly and confidentially what you think about my interpersonal skills?

You asked for my opinion about switching service providers—here it is.

You must, of course, use your own judgment, but I would suggest this.

Your counsel and advice have meant a great deal to me.

Your idea is excellent and I may regret not going that route, but I'm going to try something else first.

You were kind enough to ask my advice about the Hexam-Riderhood merger—this is what I think.

PARAGRAPHS

You asked what I thought of the new store hours. They are certainly more convenient for customers and will bring us the early evening business that can make a difference in our year-end numbers. However, I wonder if it is profitable to stay open so late on Saturday evenings. Could we keep a record of Saturday evening sales for a month?

We suggest that, instead of external motors and vacuum seals around the driveshafts, you install internal, pancake motors to handle the required tension ranges. Let us know if this takes care of the problem.

You might want to hire an investment banking firm to help with your financial restructuring. Such a firm can assist you in exploring strategic alternatives to rebuild your liquidity and improve value for shareholders.

Have you noticed that the newsletter is not carrying its own weight? I wonder if we ought to continue to subsidize it. I suggest we put it on a subscription basis. This will also oblige it to become more responsive to readers, one of the current complaints being that it isn't. If it can't survive on the income from subscriptions, I question its usefulness.

I would like to suggest that you examine the issue of cooperation versus competition in the school environment. In the three years our children have been students here, I've noticed the school is strongly oriented toward competition, with little value assigned to cooperative learning, cooperative sports, and cooperative activities. I'm enclosing several reports and studies on this issue. May I stop in and speak with you about this next week?

I'm flattered that you want my advice on choosing a college. However, you seem interested in the eastern colleges, and I know little about them. I wonder if you wouldn't want to talk to Ling Ch'ung, who in fact is quite knowledgeable about many of them.

Thanks so much for your advice on the hip roof and preparing for the building inspector. I doubt if she would have given me the building permit the way I was going about things!

I'm grateful to you for the time you took to outline a solution to our current problem. We are interested in your ideas. However, we just started working on another approach last Thursday and I'm going to wait and see how that develops. I'll let you know if we are later able to consider your plan. In the meantime, thanks for your helpful suggestions.

SAMPLE LETTERS

Dear Mr. Brimblecombe:

I was present at the Music Educators' Conference when your elementary school jazz band performed. I was impressed to hear that out of a school population of 640, you have 580 students in your instrumental music program. This is unusual, as I'm sure you know.

Do you have any advice for other elementary music directors trying to increase the number of student musicians? If you do not have the time to respond by letter, perhaps you could indicate on the enclosed postcard a time and date when I could call you long-distance. I'd appreciate any tips you might have.

Gratefully,

Dear Walter,

I hope you will forgive this unasked-for intrusion into your business affairs, but I felt I would be less than a friend if I didn't say something after visiting one of your gift shops last week (the one on Lewis Street).

I was surprised to see the china jumbled together on the shelves, the collector's dolls looking dusty and wrinkled, and some of the figurines chipped and dirty. This hasn't seemed to hurt business—customers were lined up at both counters when I was there—but over the long term it might be unfortunate. I just wondered if you were aware of the situation.

With best wishes,

Dear Tony,

As one of our most aggressive sales representatives, you have an enviable record and I expect you will be up for an award at the end of the year. The flip side of this aggressiveness is, unfortunately, a certain abrasive attitude that has been reported by several customers.

I'd like to suggest two things. One, come in and talk this over with me. I can give you some idea of how people are responding to you and why it's a problem over the long term if not the short term. Two, spend a day or two with Tom Jerningham. He has a manner that is effective without being too insistent.

Let me hear from you.

Sincerely,

————

Dear Shreve,

We are both proud of how well you're doing in college—your grades, your job, your friends. I think we've told you often how much we love you and admire the way you handle things. BUT . . . (did you know there was a "but" coming?) we are extremely concerned about one new thing in your life: cigarettes. Will you please think about what it will mean if you let this habit take hold?

I'm enclosing some literature on the subject.

We won't nag you about this, but we had to speak up strongly at least once and say that, based on our experience, knowledge, and love for you, this is not a good choice.

Love,

————

Dear Marion and Leopold,

Thanks so much for driving all the way into the city just to look over the situation with the house. The decision whether to repaint or put on all new siding was really getting us down. Your advice was excellent, and we feel good about our decision. It was also wonderful to see you again!

Love,

————

Dear Hazel,

I appreciate your concern, and I am sure you have good reasons for feeling that we ought to move as soon as possible. However, after careful consideration of your proposal, I have decided that the situation is fairly stable at present and we should stay put.

Let me know if you have further information that would affect this decision.

Yours truly,

————

Dear Uncle Thorkell,

Thank you for your letter. I appreciated your advice about my earrings. I know it doesn't seem "manly" to you, but my friends and I like earrings. I'm coming home at the end of the month for a visit, and I don't want you to be disappointed when you see that I still have them. Although I am grateful for your concern, I am going to keep wearing earrings. I hope this won't hurt our good relationship.

Love,
_____

See also: EMPLOYMENT, INSTRUCTIONS, REFUSALS, REQUESTS, SENSITIVE, THANK YOU

FIVE

ANNIVERSARIES AND BIRTHDAYS

*I know a lot of people didn't expect our relationship to last—but we've just
celebrated our two months' anniversary.*
—BRITT EKLAND

With the availability of attractive greeting cards today, few people send personal
anniversary or birthday notes and letters. However, anyone who has received a
commercial card with only a signature knows how much pleasure could have been
added with a handwritten line or two. For most people, finding a letter enclosed in
the card is as good as receiving a gift.

Anniversaries once referred primarily to wedding anniversaries. Today, people celebrate business, service, personal, and other anniversaries and they appreciate being remembered on their special day.

Some businesses send birthday and anniversary cards to their customers as a
goodwill gesture.

Send Letters or Cards for

- anniversary of a death
- birthday
- business goodwill (see GOODWILL)
- business or business association anniversary
- customers' birthdays or anniversaries (see SALES)
- invitations to birthday or anniversary celebrations (see INVITATIONS)
- personal achievement or service anniversary
- wedding anniversary (spouse, parents, family members, friends)

How to Say It

- Mention the occasion (if you don't know the number of years, refer to "your service anniversary," "your birthday," or "the anniversary of Beryl's death").
- Include, whenever possible, an anecdote, a shared memory, good-hearted humor, or a sentence telling why the person is important to you.
- End with good wishes for another anniversary period or for the coming years and with assurances of your affection, love, admiration, warmth, interest, delight, pleasure, continued business support, or other appropriate sentiment.

What Not to Say

- Don't detract from your greetings by including other information or news; remain focused on the anniversary or birthday. The exception is the newsy letter to a family member or close friend.
- Don't include "joking" references to advancing age, incapacity, passing years, the difficulties of married life, becoming a fixture at the office. Clever cracks about age and marriage and length of service may evoke reluctant smiles, but they carry little warmth. Avoid negative greeting cards that assume all 21-year-olds can hardly wait to get to a bar, that "the big 4-0" is depressing, and that 50-year-olds are over the hill.

Tips on Writing

■ Birthday or anniversary greetings can be personalized with a quotation: "The great thing about getting older is that you don't lose all the other ages you've been." (Madeleine L'Engle) "The fact was I didn't want to look my age, but I didn't want to act the age I wanted to look either. I also wanted to grow old enough to understand that sentence." (Erma Bombeck) "The marriages we regard as the happiest are those in which each of the partners believes that he or she got the best of it." (Sydney J. Harris)

■ Keep a supply of greeting cards on hand. At the beginning of the year, note dates to remember on the calendar or in a computer file (the gathering of dates is time-consuming only the first time you do it). On the first of each month, choose and address cards to all those celebrating that month. On the upper right-hand corner of the envelope (which will later be covered by a stamp) pencil in the date of the birthday or anniversary—and mail each one a few days before the date.

■ Collect small, flat, useful gifts that can be inserted in a greeting card: handkerchiefs, bookmarks, postage stamps, lottery tickets, art postcards, dollar bills. You can also plump up a birthday or anniversary card with photographs, newspaper clippings, and recipes.

■ A number of Internet sites allow you to choose and personalize greeting cards to be sent by e-mail.

Special Situations

■ Keep track of service anniversaries in your company; sending a note to mark the date creates company loyalty, especially if you add a complimentary remark about the person's work. In the case of colleagues, personalize the note with a recalled shared experience. Goodwill is also built when you remember the anniversary of your relationship with important suppliers or customers.

■ Birthday and anniversary goodwill cards are sometimes sent to individual customers. In businesses where you have access to customers' birthdates or anniversary dates (insurance, for example) sending cards is a way of keeping in touch with people while also reminding them of you and your products or services.

■ In her book *The Bestseller*, Olivia Goldsmith points out, tongue-in-cheek, that it is considered bad form to wish authors on their birthdays "many happy returns" since to a writer "returns" are unsold books returned to the publisher.

■ Congratulations are appreciated on the anniversary of a significant personal achievement—abstaining from smoking or drinking, for example—but only between people who know each other well.

■ Write close friends and relatives who have lost someone on the anniversary of the death. Don't worry about "bringing up sad memories." In one of her columns Ann Landers wrote, "I was among those who had the mistaken notion that it was painful for family members to hear references to a loved one who had died. Many readers called me on it, and I know better now." The person is well aware of the date, and will be grateful that others remember. When someone close to you has lost a spouse after many years of marriage, you might want to send the survivor a special note on the couple's wedding anniversary.

Format

■ For business, sales-oriented, or official letters, send typed or handwritten messages on letterhead or personal-business stationery.

■ Commercial greeting cards are appropriate for nonbusiness uses, as long as you add a handwritten note.

- E-mailed birthday and anniversary wishes are also received happily.
- Many newspapers have columns where family and friends can publish birthday or anniversary congratulations (usually for a fee). Often this is done in conjunction with an open house or reception to celebrate the anniversary.

WORDS

celebration	heartfelt	milestone	remember
congratulations	honored	progress	special
delighted	landmark	prosperity	successful
future	memorable	red-letter day	unique
happy	memories	remarkable	

PHRASES

all good wishes	important day
anticipate another period of success	look forward to the next ten years
celebrate with you	on the occasion of
convey our warmest good wishes	send our love
great pleasure to wish you	

SENTENCES

Congratulations on forty years of outstanding contributions to Heaslop-Moore Plastics.

Congratulations on the tenth anniversary of Stanley Graff Real Estate—it has been a pleasure serving all your stationery needs!

Every good wish to both of you for much health, happiness, prosperity, and many more years of togetherness.

Here's a question for you from Ruth Gordon: "How old would you be if you didn't know how old you were?"

May you enjoy many more anniversaries—each happier than the last.

May you live as long as you want, and never want as long as you live!

May you live long and prosper!

On the occasion of your 25th wedding anniversary, we send you our best wishes for continued love and happiness together.

Today marks the fifth anniversary of Archie's death, and I wanted you to know that we still miss him and that you are in our thoughts today.

Best wishes for a happy anniversary to a couple we have long admired and loved. May your relationship continue to be a blessing to both of you as well as to all those who know you.

This marks the tenth anniversary of our productive and happy business association. In that time, we have come to appreciate Fausto Babel Inc.'s prompt service, reliable products, and knowledgeable staff. I'm sure the next ten years will be equally happy and successful. Congratulations to all of you.

Happy 1st Anniversary! I have such lovely memories of your wedding day. I hope you have been gathering more happy memories of your first year of married life.

Barbara and Dick Siddal celebrate their 50th wedding anniversary on February 14. They have four children, nine grandchildren, and many wonderful friends. Love and congratulations from the whole family.

Sunday is the first anniversary of Vivie's death, and I couldn't let the day go by without writing to see how you are getting along and to tell you that all Vivie's friends here in Cambridge miss her very much.

SAMPLE LETTERS

Dear Muriel Joy,

Happy birthday! I'm sending you 6 quarters, 6 colored bows for your hair, 6 teddy-bear stickers, and 6 tiny horses for your collection.

How old did you say you are today?

Love,
Aunt Dinah

————

Dear Dr. Arnold,

On behalf of the governing board, I would like to congratulate you on ten years of outstanding service as headmaster. Under your leadership the school has established itself among the premier ranks of such institutions.

Be assured of our continued admiration and support.

Very sincerely yours,

————

Dear Winnie and Ed,

Congratulations to you both on the fifteenth anniversary of Leitner's Heating & Plumbing. As you know by now, you're our best (our only!) supplier, and the reason is simple: you're a class act. Quality and competence have paid off for you, and nobody could be happier for you than I. Best wishes with the next fifteen years.

Yours truly,

Dear Auntie Em,

I send you love and hugs on your 80th birthday. If only I were there to celebrate with you!

I read this once: "Years in themselves mean nothing. How we live them means everything." (Elisabeth Marbury) I hope I live my years as well as you've lived yours!

Speaking of which, how is the bridge group? the golf foursome? the church cleaning crew? your birthday luncheon friends? your bowling game? your Monday night dinners with the family? And are you still going to Las Vegas in February?

(Watch the mail for a small package from me!)

Love,
D.

Dear Rabbi Wassermann,

On behalf of the members and officers of the Adath Women's League, I send you best wishes for a joyous birthday and a happy, healthy year!

Karen Engelschall
President
Adath Women's League

Dear Martin,

All of us here at Eden Land Corporation congratulate you at Chuzzlewit Ltd. on your twenty years of solid contributions in the field of architecture.

We know that when we do business with you we can count on superior designs, reasonable costs, and dependable delivery dates.

May the success of these first twenty years lead to an even more successful second twenty.

With best wishes,

Dear Penrod,

Congratulations on your twelfth birthday. I hope you have a wonderful time and get everything you want (although, from what your father tells me, I hope you don't want another slingshot).

Your uncle and I are sorry we can't be there to celebrate with you, but I'm sending you a little something in a separate package. Have a good time and give everyone a hug for us.

Happy birthday!

Dear Grandma Annie,

I know you and Grandpa Oliver would have been married 65 years today, and that you still miss him. I love my photograph of the two of you taken at your 60th wedding anniversary party. I think about him—and about you—a lot.

I hope this day isn't too sad for you. Fortunately you have a lot of happy memories. Maybe they'll be some comfort.

Just thinking about you . . .

> Love from
> Monica

See also: ANNOUNCEMENTS, BELATED, CONGRATULATIONS, FAMILY, GOODWILL, INVITATIONS, THANK YOU

SIX

ANNOUNCEMENTS

It is good news, worthy of all acceptation! and yet not too good to be true.
—Matthew Henry

Announcements, whether formal or informal, make an art of stating essential facts in the fewest possible words. A little like this paragraph.

Announcements Are Made for

- acquisition
- address change
- anniversary: business/wedding (see ANNIVERSARIES)
- baby birth or adoption
- change in benefits (reduced/increased/additional), policies (purchasing/hiring), regulations, procedures (billing dates)
- collection actions on overdue account (see COLLECTION)
- company merger/reorganization
- death
- divorce
- engagement (see WEDDINGS)
- graduation
- layoff (see EMPLOYMENT)
- marital separation
- meeting/workshop/conference
- merger or acquisition
- new company policy/directions/administration/management
- new division/subsidiary

- new home/house/apartment/condo
- new office/business/professional practice/service/career
- new partner/executive/associate/employee
- open house: school/business
- price/rent increase/reduction
- product recall
- promotion
- resignation/retirement (see also EMPLOYMENT)
- wedding (see WEDDINGS)

How to Say It

- Express pleasure in making the announcement (except for death and divorce announcements).
- List key details of the news or event: who, what, when, where, why.
- To announce a meeting, include: the name of the organization, subcommittee, or group; the date, time, place, and purpose of the meeting; a request to notify a contact person if unable to attend. This can be done by preprinted postcard or by in-house memo or e-mail. To announce a directors' meeting, follow the format fixed by corporate bylaws or by state or federal laws; a waiver of notice or a proxy card is often enclosed along with a postage-paid reply envelope.
- To announce the opening of a new business or store, use an invitation format to ask customers to an open house or special sales event.
- To announce changes in company policies, benefits, procedures, or regulations, include: an expression of pleasure in announcing the change; a description of the change; a reference to the former policy, if necessary for clarification; an explanation of what the change will mean for employees or customers; printed instructions or guidelines if appropriate; the reason for the change and why it is an improvement; the deadline for implementing the change; the name and telephone number of a contact person for questions; an expression of your enthusiasm about the change; appreciation for help in effecting the change.
- To announce a birth or adoption, use engraved, printed, hand-lettered, commercial, or designed-by-you notes. Include: the baby's full name and, if not obvious from the name or if still unnamed, whether it's a boy or girl; birthdate (and time, if you wish) or age (if the baby is adopted); parents' full names; siblings' names (optional); some expression of happiness ("pleased to announce"). Baby announcements are made by unmarried parents ("Julia Norman and Basil Fane announce the birth of their son, Alec Norman-

Fane"), by single parents ("Jean Emerson announces the birth of her son, Howard Thede Emerson"), and by married couples where each uses a separate name. Newspaper birth announcements include: the date of birth; sex of child and name, if known; parents' names and hometowns; grandparents' names. Some newspapers allow weight and height information and such sentiments as "welcome with love" or the mention of "many aunts, uncles, and cousins" in listing the baby's relatives. Check with your newspaper about its guidelines.

- To announce a change of address, use forms available from the United States Postal Service, commercial change of address notes, or printed cards: "As of July 1, Sybil Knox (formerly Sybil Coates or Mrs. Adrian Coates) will be living at 15 Morland Drive, Houston, TX 77005, 713-555-1234."
- To announce a graduation, use the printed announcements available through most high schools and colleges. Since space at graduation ceremonies is often limited, announcements are more common than invitations. There is no obligation to send a gift in response to an announcement (a congratulatory card is usually sent), but since many people feel so obligated, it is kinder to send announcements only to those close to the graduate.
- To announce a separation or divorce to family and friends (which is a personal decision), state the news briefly ("We regret to inform you that our divorce was finalized on December 1") or frame the news as a change of address, telling where each person and the children will live after a certain date. If the woman resumes her birth name, identify her that way. You are not obliged to explain what has happened; if people sense from your announcement that you are retaining some privacy, it will be easier to cope the next time you see them. Notify banks, businesses, charge accounts, and creditors of the changed circumstances.
- Deaths are announced in several ways: (1) a death notice is inserted (usually for a fee) in the obituary section of the newspaper; (2) a news article describes the person's achievements and contributions; (3) printed announcements are sent to out-of-town friends and acquaintances; (4) handwritten notes are sent to close family and friends who live out of town. The deceased person's address book will indicate who should be notified. The newspaper obituary notice includes: name of deceased, including a woman's birth name if she wasn't already using it; address; date of death; age at time of death; names, relationships, and hometowns of survivors; affiliations; personal or career information; date and place of services and interment; whether services are private or open to friends and relatives; suggestions for flowers or memorial contributions; name, address, and telephone number of funeral home. Since the death announcement appears

in the paper almost immediately, hand-deliver it or read it over the phone.

What Not to Say

- Don't include unrelated information or news. Although there are some exceptions (changes in company policy, for example), an announcement is not meant for lengthy explanations, instructions, or descriptions. An announcement can become diluted when it is part of a longer communication.

Tips on Writing

■ Send your announcement as soon as possible after the event. "The first rule of thumb about announcing an event . . . is that *your* announcement reaches the reader before the news travels by other means. If your announcement is old news, it has arrived too late." (Dianne Booher)

■ Ask someone to double-check your spelling and the general content. The announcement that contains errors is announcing something very different from what was intended.

Special Situations

■ Combine routine announcements (new type of billing statement, new address, or meeting notice) with goodwill or sales messages.

■ A news release announces information of interest to the general public (product recall; annual or quarterly financial report; business anniversary; fundraiser; new programs, policies, executives; company achievements, mergers, or acquisitions). Sent to newspaper editors and to radio and television station news directors, the news release includes, along with the announcement, your organization's name and address and the name and telephone number of a contact person. Address the news release to a specific person; call and ask for a name if you don't have one. Double or triple space, leaving wide margins, and answer the who-what-when-where-why-how questions in the first paragraph or two. Double-check accuracy of your facts and explain any unfamiliar terms. News releases traditionally have "more" typed at the bottom of each page except the last, which has "- 30 -" or "# # #" to indicate the end.

Format

■ Business announcements are made in traditional letter format typed on letterhead stationery. When sent to large numbers of people, form letters are used.

■ Use a memo format for interoffice announcements (new benefits package, change in flex-hours procedures). Sometimes e-mail is a good choice.

■ Formal announcements are printed or engraved in black ink on a white or cream-colored card (with matching envelopes). Stationery stores and printers have sample announcements ranging from traditional to modern in a variety of fonts, papers, inks, and formats.

■ Announcements made to close friends and family are handwritten on foldovers or personal stationery.

■ Postcards are appropriate for announcing changes of address, meetings, and special sales.

WORDS

announce	honor	pleased
celebrate	inform	report
delighted	introduce	reveal
gratified	mention	share
happy	notice	signal

PHRASES

announces the appointment of

are pleased/proud/happy to announce

give notice that

happily announce the merger of/ a new subsidiary

have the honor of announcing

it is with great pleasure that we announce

joyfully announce the birth/ adoption/arrival of

make known/public

notice is hereby given that

public announcement

take pleasure in announcing

wish to announce/inform/advise you

SENTENCES

A meeting of the Broadway-Aldine Community Council will be held October 3 at 7:00 p.m. in the NewBank boardroom to elect board members and officers for the coming year.

Ben Bowser announces that by permission of the court of Ramsey County, New Jersey, April 18, 2010, he will now be known as Benjamin Middleton.

Broadbent Civil Engineering, Inc., is proud to announce the opening of offices in Denver and Salt Lake City.

Dolores Haze (formerly Mrs. Richard F. Schiller) has changed her address to 155 Carol Avenue, Gilberts, IL 60136.

Important notice of change in terms: Effective January 1, 2011, your credit card agreement will be amended as follows.

Isabel Wahrfield and Frank Goodwin announce the dissolution of their marriage, effective July 15.

Mrs. Rachel Dean announces the engagement of her daughter Susan to Richard Tebben.

Nguyen Van Truy and Tran Huong Lang are proud and happy to announce the birth of their son Nguyen Van Tuân on March 11, 2010.

Please be advised that your payment due date has been changed to the sixteenth day of each month.

Vanderhof Industries, Inc. is pleased to announce the acquisition of the Connelly-Smith-Dulcy Energy Group, a Gordon-area company with ninety-seven employees that specializes in energy development services.

With great sadness we announce the death of our husband and father, Leon Gonsalez.

PARAGRAPHS

Fairford Corporation, Cooper City, announces that it has reached a distributorship agreement with Antoine-Lettice, based in Paris, France, granting them exclusive marketing rights for its Superbe! ultra-high-pressure waterjet equipment in France and Italy, with nonexclusive rights for the rest of Europe.

Averill Airlines will now serve Paris's Charles de Gaulle Airport (previously Orly). Airport transfers included in any of our vacation packages will provide convenient motorcoach transportation between Charles de Gaulle Airport and Port Maillot Station in Paris (formerly Montparnasse Station).

Miles and I have decided that we would make better friends than spouses. As of last week, we have canceled our engagement. We are both, I think, quite relieved, although we still think the world of each other. I know how happy you were for me when I wrote about our engagement, so I wanted to let you know right away that you can still be happy for me—but not because I'm engaged.

Carrie and Frederick Josser, New London, celebrated their twenty-fifth wedding anniversary on March 2. An open house was hosted by Cynthia and Ted Josser of Collins. Eight proud children and many friends and relatives were there.

I'm sorry to tell you that Mother died on July 11 of a heart attack. I know how much your friendship and your lively letters meant to her over the years. She spoke of you often.

We regret to announce that our Davy Jones Aquarium Pump, Model no. 686, has been found to be defective. It is possible that it could deliver a fatal shock. Please return your pump as soon as possible to the store where you purchased it or call the toll-free number below for instructions.

Eggerson Power Equipment Company is proud to announce the opening of a new store on County Road B and Highway 47. One of the largest power equipment sources in the state, the new store specializes in an exhaustive in-store stock and a forty-eight-hour "we can get it" guarantee.

Cornelia (Kay) Motford, George, and Gladys are now living at 1941 Knowles Avenue, Centralia, KY 42330 (502-555-4590). Henry Moulton Pulham is living at 332 Riverside Drive, Lexington, KY 40507 (606-555-2441).

Montford Estates is pleased to announce the expansion of its commercial construction division. The division offers cost-efficient, high-quality commercial construction with emphasis on interior detailing.

Georgina Gardner has been promoted to director of retail leasing for Pelham Development Properties. She will be responsible for leasing Pelham Mall in downtown Brandon.

Due to the rapid rise in labor and operating costs, Ames Fast Maintenance finds it necessary to increase service charges as of September 1. Service charge increases will vary, depending upon the type of service your company uses: on call, when needed, monthly preventive maintenance.

The Board of Directors of the Fiske Corporation will meet on Wednesday, December 3, at 10:00 a.m. at the company's central office in Harrington. New contracts for executives will be discussed, and such other business as may come before the meeting will be acted upon. If you cannot attend, please sign the enclosed waiver of notice.

Thanks to you, and the orders that have been pouring in for our special line of children's clothing, we are able to make greater bulk purchases of raw materials and thus manufacture at a lower cost. We are proud to announce that we are passing on these savings to you. Enclosed is our current catalog, but please note the new low prices printed in red.

Francis Getliffe, age 44, of Cambridge. Survived by wife, Katherine March Getliffe; son, Francis Jr.; brother Herbert; also nieces and nephews and good friends from C.P. Snow, Inc. Special thanks to the staff at Cambridge Lutheran Hospital. Memorial service Sunday at 2:00 p.m. at the Hillside Memorial Funeral Home. Family will receive friends one hour prior to the service. Interment Hillside, with reception following in the Hillside Community Room. Memorials preferred. Hillside Memorium, 555-1216.

SAMPLE LETTERS

Dear Friend,

We have moved! During the past fifteen years we were so crowded in our old location that sometimes customers had to stand shoulder to shoulder or squeeze through the aisles. Nowadays you'll find it much easier to shop at Taylor & Company.

Convenient parking facilities in our parking lot and pleasant offices will make it simple for you to meet all your printing needs.

Enclosed is a map showing the new location, along with a one-time 10 percent discount coupon. Come in and see us while the paint's still fresh!

Sincerely yours,

———

Brangwen International
is pleased to announce
that Lydia Lensky
has joined the firm
as a partner.
She will direct the
Southeast Asia Operations.

———

FOR: Immediate Release

Boorman, Inc. of Menzies announces the recall of its fresh and frozen sandwiches because of the discovery of bacterial contamination during a recent Food and Drug Administration (FDA) test. Some of the sandwiches were found to contain *Listeria monocytogenes*, a bacterium that can endanger fetuses, infants, pregnant women, the elderly, and people with weakened immune systems.

No illnesses have been reported.

Please destroy all Boorman QuickWich sandwiches from lot 480032 or return them to Boorman for a refund.

———

Paul J. Maggio, D.D.S.
and Matthew J. Maggio, D.D.S.
announce the opening

of their new office
at 1099 Kenyon Road
Fort Dodge, Iowa 50501
(515-576-1981)
and an open house
on July 15, 2011

Dear Bondholder:

This letter is to inform you that a portion of the July 1, 2011, debt service payment for the above-referenced bond issue was made with monies transferred from the Reserve Fund established pursuant to Section 4.09 of the Indenture of Trust dated December 1, 1997, between Simmons International and Herbert Banking & Trust, as Trustee. Use of such monies in the Reserve Fund does *not* constitute an Event of Default under the indenture. However, the Trustee considers this information may be of interest to bondholders and potential bondholders.

Sincerely,

Bonnie and Steven Goldsmith
are most happy to announce
the arrival of their daughter
Emily Virginia
born in Korea May 23, 1989
welcomed home October 11, 1989

Dear Customer:

As of May 1 of this year, your garbage hauling fee will be increased by $1.95 per month. We are always reluctant to raise prices, but are obliged to do so in this case by a recent ruling of the Silvius County Board of Commissioners.

In order to conserve landfill space, all garbage collected in Silvius County since July of 1999 has been required to be taken to the new recovery facility in Shepard rather than to landfills. However, it costs more to "tip" a load of garbage at Shepard than at a landfill, so the County agreed to subsidize haulers until April 30 of this year.

Although other haulers may be raising the householder's portion of the bill more than $1.95 (due to inflation and haulers' additional operating expenses), we are going to try to keep the price increase as low as possible.

It is only fair to warn you, however, that there may be more increases in sight. The current legislature is considering raising landfill surcharges and putting a sales tax on hauling fees, which could further increase garbage bills.

There are several ways you can lower your garbage bills. Enclosed are flyers with information on using a volume-based garbage hauler, recycling, composting yard waste at home or at one of the County composting sites, and disposing properly of household hazardous waste.

For further information, call 555-1567.

Sincerely,

———

See also: COVER LETTERS, GOODWILL, SALES, WEDDINGS

SEVEN

APOLOGIES

An apology is the superglue of life. It can repair just about anything.
—LYNN JOHNSTON

A letter is often better than a face-to-face or telephone apology because you can take your time getting the words right. It's also better to write when you don't know if the other person is willing to speak to you. A letter doesn't oblige them to respond immediately; there's time to absorb the message and decide how to react.

Whether you think of apologies as etiquette, ethics, justice, or even good business, they are an inevitable by-product of being alive. Because we all make mistakes, people are generally less bothered by your errors than you are; write your apology with dignity. "If you haven't made any mistakes lately, you must be doing something wrong." (Susan Jeffers)

Occasions That Call for Apologies

- belated response to a gift, favor, invitation, or major event in someone's life
- billing, credit, or financial errors
- business errors: incorrect information given, order mix-ups, contract misunderstandings, merchandise that is defective, dangerous, ineffective, damaged, delayed, or that is missing parts, instructions, or warranties
- children's misbehavior or damage to property/pet
- damage to another's property
- employee problems: rudeness, ineptness, dishonesty, poor service, unsatisfactory work

- failure to keep an appointment, deadline, shipping date, payment schedule, or promise
- insulting or insensitive remarks
- personal errors: giving someone's name and phone number to a third party without permission, forgetting to include someone in an invitation, betraying a secret
- pets that bite, bark, damage property, or are otherwise nuisances
- sexual harassment
- tactless, inappropriate, rude, or drunken behavior

How to Say It

- Briefly specify the fault and apologize for it ("I'm so sorry about the damaged book") or, in the case of a customer complaint, summarize the problem ("I understand you were twice given incorrect information"). In most cases, use the words "I apologize" or "I am sorry."
- Thank the person for writing or calling or for bringing the problem to your attention.
- When appropriate, convey understanding of the other person's position: "I can see how disappointing this must have been"; "You have every right to be upset."
- Tell what corrective action you're taking, if appropriate ("I will replace the shovel"; "A refund check is being sent"), or offer to make amends. Suggest several possible solutions and ask which the person prefers.
- Assure the person this won't happen again.
- In a business context, end the letter with a forward-looking comment about serving their future needs.

What Not to Say

- Don't apologize for more than the specific incident. Avoid generalizations about what a klutz you are or how these things always happen to you.
- Don't be overly dramatic ("You will probably never want to see me again after what I did." "I wish I were dead after the way I behaved last night." "I am very, very, very sorry." "This is the worst thing I've ever done in my whole life"). Apologize briefly once instead of apologizing many times in different ways.
- Don't defend or excuse yourself, justify your actions, or sidestep an apology ("I'm sorry, but I still think I was right"). If you are going to apologize, do so cheerfully and wholeheartedly. "A stiff apology is a second insult."

(G. K. Chesterton) Ethicist Jeremy Iggers says an apology must be made unilaterally. When we begin to stray into the area of what the other person did to us, we lose the ethical base of making an apology. Whatever anyone did to us is a separate matter from whatever mistake we made.

- Don't imply that the other person is at fault. Some people's apologies read like accusations. In business, it is probably better not to write than to insinuate that the customer is at fault. With some ingenuity, you can express regret without accepting responsibility for a situation that is not entirely your fault. When the other person is partly responsible, apologize only for your share of it. Don't mention anything else.
- Don't blame the computer. By now everyone knows that some human had its fingerprints all over the guilty computer; this patently untrue excuse only irritates people. And don't say that these things are bound to happen from time to time. Although this may be true, it makes you look careless.
- Don't admit negligence in writing. If negligence is a factor, consult with your attorney, who can suggest the best approach for your letter. In his article, "Saying You're Sorry in a Litigious Society" (in *The International Journal of Medicine and Law*, no. 7/8, 1992), Ralph Slovenko advises doctors to be careful about how they sympathize on a patient's death. An expression of sympathy at a funeral, for example, "could lead to an utterance which, in the hands of a skillful lawyer, might be turned into an admission of wrongdoing."

Tips on Writing

■ Write as soon as possible. Procrastination turns writing an apology into a major effort and you end up apologizing twice, once for the infraction and once for the delay.

■ Sometimes there are mitigating circumstances—for example, a shipment delayed because of a strike or flu outbreak. At other times, however, explanations weaken your apology—when, for example, you try to explain why you were rude or why a child said something tactless but truthful.

Special Situations

■ Parents of a child who annoys or hurts others or damages property write a note of apology. However, the child should also apologize in some age-appropriate manner. The adult's note might say, "Of course, Drusilla will want to apologize to you herself."

■ Employees apologizing to their boss for work-related errors or behavior provide a written, detailed account of what happened because their boss most likely reports to another higher-up and will need all relevant information.

■ The problem of sexual harassment has become increasingly visible and is no longer categorized as "just fooling around" or "having a good sense of humor." Making sexual remarks, threats, innuendoes, or passes is illegal. Anything that can be construed as sexual harassment requires a heartfelt apology that shows that the offender has some real (as opposed to expedient) understanding of what was done. The apology may not avert a company reprimand or even legal action, but then again it might. In any case, an apology is owed to anyone who has been sexually harassed. In addition to exhibiting contrition, the offender should promise not to repeat the behavior. Individuals being sued for sexual harassment are generally repeat offenders who still don't understand how unacceptable their actions were. Few people will pursue a first-time offender who didn't fully realize the harm done and who is now contrite and reformed.

■ The apology may have a special place in customer relations. "Two words will get you through many bad times in the business world: *I'm sorry.*" (Mary A. De Vries) A well-written apology for a business problem can make a satisfied customer out of an unsatisfied one. Sometimes you may add a refund, discount, free pass, or other material apology for your customer's inconvenience. When writing an apology to a customer, end with a positive statement: "We look forward to continuing to serve you" or "We value your patronage and your friendship."

Format

■ Use personal stationery or notecards for apologies dealing with social situations. A few greeting cards charmingly or amusingly say "I'm sorry," but you still need to add a handwritten message.

■ Use business stationery for all apologies to customers, clients, and suppliers. If, however, the situation has personal overtones (a manager has publicly slighted someone or a supervisor has unjustly docked someone's pay), the apology might be handwritten on business-personal stationery.

■ Routine apologies (shipping delays, out-of-stock merchandise) are handled with a form letter.

■ An e-mailed apology would probably not be the most persuasive, unless you needed to get the apology to the other person immediately and the telephone wasn't an option.

WORDS

absentmindedly	ill-advised	misleading	repay
accidental	imperfect	misprint	responsible
acknowledge	imprudent	misquote	restitution
admit	inaccurate	mistaken	restore
awkward	inadequate	misunderstanding	sheepish
blunder	inadvertent	muddle	short-sighted
careless	incomplete	negligence	slip
compensate	inconsiderate	omitted	tactless
distressed	inconvenience	overlooked	thoughtless
disturbed	incorrect	pardon	unaware
embarrassed	insufficient	rectify	unfortunate
erroneous	irresponsible	red-faced	unhappy
error	lax	redo	unintentional
excuse	miscalculation	regrettable	unsatisfactory
explain	misconception	reimburse	unsound
failure	misconstrued	remiss	unwarranted
fault	misinterpreted	repair	unwise

PHRASES

absolutely no excuse for

accept the blame for

admit that I was wrong

angry with myself

appreciate your calling our attention to

asleep at the wheel/on the job/ at the switch

avoid this in the future

breach of good manners

correct the situation

express my regret

feel sorry/terrible/bad about

how can I apologize for

I am most upset about

I am not excusing our/my errors, but

I am so sorry for

I don't know how it happened that

I have thoroughly investigated/ looked into the matter and

I'm sorry you were dissatisfied with

it was embarrassing to discover that

it was most understanding of you to

I was distressed to hear/read/ discover/learn that

make amends/restitution

make right with you

much to my regret

my apologies for any inconvenience

owe you an apology for

please accept my/our apology/
   apologies for

presumed where I shouldn't have
   presumed

prevent a recurrence

put to rights

reproach myself

sincerely regret/apologize

sorely regret

sorry for the inconvenience/
   confusion/mix-up/
   misunderstanding

the least I can do is

to compensate for

under the mistaken impression that

until you are completely satisfied

weighs on my mind

we regret to inform our customers
   that

you were entirely right about

SENTENCES

Although I apologized to you last night for our guests blocking your driveway, I want you to know how sorry we are and to assure you that it won't happen again.

As you rightly pointed out, a mistake has been made on your July bill.

I am extremely embarrassed about my behavior last night.

I am sincerely/very sorry.

I apologize for Jimmy's behavior.

I can only hope you will forgive this serious lapse of good taste on my part.

I don't blame you for being upset.

I don't like being on the outs with you, particularly since it was my fault.

I hope this situation can be mended to everyone's satisfaction.

I'm sorry for telling everyone in the office your good news before you could tell them—I don't know what I was thinking.

I'm sorry you were treated so disparagingly by the salesclerk.

I only realized later how insulting my remarks might have appeared.

I understand how disappointed you must have been to receive only half your order.

I've taken steps to ensure that it doesn't happen again.

I was totally out of line this morning when I insisted on knowing what your salary is—I can only hope you will forgive my poor taste and insensitivity.

My face gets red every time I remember that night.

Please accept my apology for the oversight.

Please excuse my inattention/shortsightedness/thoughtlessness.

Please forgive me.

Thank you for advising us of this error/for bringing the matter to my attention.

Thank you for your letter of July 15 telling us about the unfortunate remark made by one of the security guards.

Thank you for your patience and understanding.

This will not, of course, happen again.

We apologize for the delay—it is unfortunately unavoidable.

We are sorry/apologize for any embarrassment this has caused you.

We look forward to continuing to serve you.

We owe you an apology.

We were caught napping on this one.

You were right, I was wrong, and I'm sorry.

PARAGRAPHS

We are unable to deliver the spring fabric samples by the date promised. The product supervisor promises me that you will have them by January 5. If this is unsatisfactory, please telephone me. It isn't often we have to renege on a delivery date, and we're not happy about it. Please accept our apologies for the delay.

Please accept our apologies for what's recently happened at your house. We're all working hard to find other homes for the bunnies. When Hillel assured you that both bunnies were female, he relied on the green-striped ribbons they wore around their necks. None of us knew that a four-year-old neighbor had switched a green-striped ribbon for a yellow polka-dotted ribbon that the male rabbits were wearing. I know this doesn't make up to you for what you've been through, but I thought you should know that our intentions were good. Again, we're sorry and we'll let you know as soon as we've found ten good homes.

We were sorry to hear that the track lighting fixture you ordered was defective, as described in your letter of April 29. Please return it to us using its original mailing box and the enclosed label, and we will send you a replacement by return mail. All Midlothian merchandise is inspected twice before leaving the factory, but with a recent 45 percent increase in production, we have a few rough spots to work out yet. I'm sorry that you were inconvenienced, and hope that you will continue to use our fine Midlothian products—products that we proudly back with our full-service Midlothian guarantee.

It occurred to me in a dream, or maybe it was in the shower, that you had asked for the return of your baby books some time ago. I suppose the friend's child has gone off to college by now. I'm sorry for the tardiness—they're in today's mail.

We erroneously mailed you the same order you placed last month. This month's order has been sent this morning, and we've marked the box plainly with AUGUST written in large red letters. If you will please refuse acceptance of the first box, the carrier will bring it back to us. We apologize for the error.

We were sorry to hear that the last neon tetras you bought from us were infected with ich and subsequently infected your entire aquarium. As tropical fish enthusiasts ourselves, we appreciate how devastating this has been. I immediately spoke to our supplier about the problem, and she has assured me this was an isolated slip-up. In the meantime, please restock your aquarium at our expense. Thank you for your understanding. I hope you will continue to be one of our most valued customers.

SAMPLE LETTERS

Dear Dorothea,

I feel dreadful about ruining your lovely luncheon yesterday by arguing with Celia about Will Ladislaw. You certainly did everything you could to save the situation, and I apologize most humbly for ignoring good taste, old friendship, and common sense in pursuing a "discussion" that was completely inappropriate.

I spoke with Celia first thing this morning and attempted to mend my fences there, but I feel a great deal worse about what I did to you. The luncheon was delicious, and the first two hours were delightful. I hope you will someday be able to forgive me for blighting the last half-hour.

Your friend,

———

Dear Mr. Ravenal:

As editor of the Cotton Blossom newsletter, I want to apologize for omitting your name in the last issue. Captain Hawks asked me how I could have possibly forgotten to include our hottest new actor! In proofreading the copy, my eyes failed to notice that your name wasn't where my brain expected it to be. I'm sorry. A correction will appear in the next issue.

Regretfully,

————

Dear Hsiao-Wei,

I apologize for not showing up at the meeting this afternoon. Although there is no excuse for such a thing, I will say that I was involved in an automobile accident on the way to work and what with filling out forms, notifying my insurance company, and arranging for a rental car, I completely forgot about the meeting.

Can we reschedule for this Thursday, same time? Thanks—and again, I'm sorry.

Regards,

————

Dear Merton Denscher,

Thank you for your letter of March 19. I am sorry that the background research I submitted was unusable. A careful rereading of your instructions showed me at once where I'd gone wrong. I do apologize.

With your permission, I would like to resubmit the work—this time correctly. I believe I can get it to you by the end of next week since I am already familiar with the relevant sources for your topic.

Please let me know at once if you prefer me not to go ahead.

Sincerely,

————

Dear Annette,

I must beg your forgiveness for my outspoken and insensitive remarks last night about your religious convictions. I'm afraid I got carried away in the heat of the discussion. I certainly feel that each of us has a right to our own beliefs, and I in no way meant to belittle yours.

I would be happy if you would accept an invitation to dinner at my house on Saturday, August 3, at 7:00 p.m. I'm just having a few friends, most of whom you know.

Hoping to see you then, I am

Yours truly,

————

See also: ACKNOWLEDGMENTS, ADJUSTMENTS, BELATED, COMPLAINTS, RESPONSES, SENSITIVE

EIGHT

LETTERS OF APPLICATION

*The nearest to perfection most people ever come is when
filling out an employment application.*
—KEN KRAFT

There are three ways to persuade a prospective employer to invite you for an interview:

1. Fill in one of the company's application forms and submit it alone or with a cover letter (a brief letter stating that the application is enclosed and mentioning a point or two indicating you are a good candidate for the job).
2. Send a résumé (a businesslike and detailed summary of your work and educational history, your skills, and your career goals), also accompanied by a cover letter.
3. Write a letter of application, which is a combination cover letter and résumé—longer than a cover letter, shorter and less formal than a résumé. (The letter of application is also known as a broadcast letter or a letter of interest.)

Which approach is best? The clue comes from the prospective employer: "Fill out an application form"; "Mail or fax a résumé"; "Apply to the following department."

In addition to applications that are solicited (there is a definite opening being advertised), there are unsolicited applications (you know of no opening but you would like to work for that company). In the latter case, with no directions from the employer as to how to apply, a letter of application—a powerful one-page letter that includes résumé material—may be more effective than a conventional résumé and cover letter.

Some organizations continue to rely on letters of application to gauge an applicant's overall self-presentation and command of the written language.

The purpose of the application letter is to attract and hold the reader's attention long enough to get your letter placed in the short pile of those candidates who will receive an invitation to an interview. (The other pile is much, much taller.) A letter of application is thus a sales letter in which you are both seller and product.

Send an Application Letter to

- camps
- clubs and organizations
- colleges, universities, technical schools
- franchise companies
- internships
- private elementary and secondary schools
- prospective employers
- volunteer organizations

How to Say It

- Address your letter to a specific individual, after verifying the person's title and double-checking the spelling of the name (even if it's simple—"Gene" could be "Jeanne," "John" could be "Jon").
- Open with an attention-getting sentence or paragraph.
- Tell why you are seeking this position, why you have chosen to apply to this particular company, and why you believe you are qualified.
- List the skills, education, and experience that are most relevant to the opening. Leave the rest for the interview.
- Request an interview ("I will be in Burbank next week and would like to arrange an interview").
- Provide an address, daytime phone number, fax number, and e-mail address.
- Close with a pleasant or forward-looking statement: "I appreciate your time and consideration"; "I look forward to discussing this position with you."

What Not to Say

- Don't indulge in generalities or the vague "etc."; specify exactly what you can do or have done.
- Don't use gimmicks, fancy language that you don't normally use, a

"humorous" approach, or any attention-getting device that could backfire. Conservative (which is not the same as boring) is better here.

- Don't refer to yourself as "the writer" ("The writer has had six years' experience as a heavy equipment operator").
- Don't emphasize how much the company can do to further your career goals. Emphasize rather how your abilities can benefit the company. Instead of the message "Here is what I can do," fashion the message to say, "Here is what I can do for you."
- Don't mention negative aspects of your present or past employment.
- Don't belittle your qualifications.
- Don't base your request on your need for the job or on an appeal to sympathy ("I am the only support of my family"); focus on what you have to offer.
- Don't mention salary in your letter (even when an ad asks you to state salary requirements); save that discussion for the interview.

Tips on Writing

■ Don't use your present company's letterhead stationery for your letter of application.

■ Reread your letter before mailing to see if it sounds confident, professional, and persuasive. If you were the employer, would you want to interview the person who wrote this?

■ Be concise. The letter of application should be no longer than one page.

■ Use action verbs when describing your abilities and accomplishments (see RÉSUMÉS for a list of effective verbs).

■ Tailor your message to a specific company. Employers can spot a generic or boilerplate letter; it tells them you are more interested in a job, any job, than in a job with them. Personalize your letter. When prospective employers receive a letter that has been written especially for them, they will give it more than the sixty seconds most letters get.

■ The most critical factor in getting an interview is how closely you match the prospective employer's needs. You already know what you have to offer; you also have to know what the company needs from you. Call the company and ask questions; research the company at the library; speak to people who work there or who know the company. By presenting as clear a picture of yourself as you can, couched in terms of what the company needs, you make it easy for an employer to determine quickly whether there is a match.

■ It's not necessary to say "References available upon request." It is understood by both parties that references will be offered and checked.

■ Avoid spelling or grammar errors, low-quality paper, smudged or hard-to-read print, and poor spacing on the page. In the case of a fax, use the "fine resolution" setting to send as sharp a copy as possible.

Special Situations

■ To apply for a franchise, study FTC guidelines. You may want a lawyer to help you with some of the correspondence.

■ Most applications to colleges, universities, community colleges, or technical schools are routine and codified. If, however, you are a student at the very high or very low end of your graduating class or if you have special needs (for financial assistance, for example), seek help from your high school counseling office, private counseling services, or some of the numerous publications available. For some students, the process of applying for admission to college can take many months and require specialized information.

■ If you are on the other side of the desk and are asked to design a job application form, familiarize yourself with state and federal antidiscrimination laws. You may not ask applicants for such information as age, race, sex, height and weight, color of eyes, hair, or complexion; birthplace; dates of public school attendance; arrest record, type of military discharge, past workers' compensation claims; whether they own their own home, have ever been sued, or had a surety bond or government clearance denied; work transportation arrangements; non-job-related handicaps; activities, memberships, and hobbies not directly related to the job; how they heard about the job opening. Have a lawyer check the rough draft of your application form to ensure that it complies with state and federal laws.

Format

■ Letters of application are typed, preferably on letterhead stationery.

■ Some prospective employers suggest that applicants fax materials to them. Unless a résumé is specifically requested, you may fax a letter of application, either with a cover sheet or leaving space at the top of the letter for the faxing information (see FAXES).

WORDS

abilities	education	opportunity	skills
apply	experience	professional	suitable
background	goals	qualified	
credentials	objectives	responsible	

PHRASES

applying for the position of

arrange a meeting at your convenience

experience that qualifies me for

extensive experience with

good candidate/match for the job

in response to your advertisement

interested in pursuing a career with

may I have fifteen minutes of your time to discuss

meet and exceed your criteria

serious interest in

similar to my most recent position

skills that would be useful to

ten years' experience with

well suited for

SENTENCES

According to this morning's paper, you are seeking a storm restoration contractor.

After eight years as a senior analog engineer at Blayds-Conway, I am seeking a position in this area because of a family move.

At the suggestion of Wilhelmina Douglas-Stewart, I am writing to request an interview for the project leader position in your long haul fiber optic communications department.

Because I believe you would find me to be an efficient, experienced, and dedicated legal administrative assistant, I am applying for the position at Wilson & Bean.

Dr. Breuer has informed me that you are currently looking for a part-time veterinary technician.

I am applying for the position of credit research analyst that you advertised in today's paper.

I look forward to hearing from you.

I understand from Dr. Demetrius Doboobie that you have an opening for a medical records supervisor.

I understand that there is currently no opening in your office, but I would like you to keep my résumé on file and to consider me for any openings that occur.

I was happy to learn that there is an opening for an insurance underwriting coordinator at the Daffyd Evans Marine Insurance Agency.

I was pleased to see your advertisement in this morning's paper for a floral designer because I have just moved here and am looking for a position after having worked as a floral designer in Chicago for the past six years.

I will call you Thursday to discuss setting up an interview.

My eight years as a food microbiologist at Samuel Braceweight, Inc., make me eminently suitable for the responsibilities of the position you are currently advertising.

Please consider me as an applicant for your advertised part-time position as clerical assistant in your business office.

Roger Brevard told me that you are looking for a real-time software engineer.

Thank you for considering my application.

The skills and duties outlined in your advertisement in today's paper are almost a perfect match for the position I held until recently at Geoffrey Bentley Publishers, Inc.

PARAGRAPHS

I have held a position as head teller very similar to the one you are currently advertising. Employed for the past five years at Jethway State Bank, I was promoted to head teller last January. Because of a family situation, I am obliged to move to Swancourt. My immediate supervisor, Felix Jethway, said he would be happy to discuss my work with you if you would like to telephone him (515-555-1000).

As you know, I have been managing the Albany branch of your Woodstock Bookstore for three years. I understand that you plan to franchise several of your bookstores, and I would like to apply for the franchise for this store, if it is available.

Your neighbor, Gina Gregers, who is a friend of mine from high school, told me yesterday that you are seeking a lunch-hour delivery driver for your catering company. I have a valid driver's license, have never had a moving violation, and, as a twenty-year resident of Werle Heights, know my way around the city and suburbs.

My career accomplishments include: setting a fifteen-year collection record during the first two months of employment as a collector of delinquent medical accounts; being promoted to unit manager as a result of high achievement levels and later to office collection manager; maintaining my record as the leading collector at the Denver branch of the Montjoy Agencies.

I would like to be considered for your customer service representative position. You requested experience in the transportation industry: I was employed from 2001–2010 as customer service representative for Coldstream

Transport and from 1998–2001 as dispatcher for Steenson Intermountain Express.

SAMPLE LETTERS

Dear Mr. Hartright,

I heard about your internship through the film scoring department at Berklee College of Music, where I'm currently in my eleventh semester.

Although I will graduate next semester with requirements fulfilled for the four-year program with three majors (film scoring, songwriting, and jazz composition), I intend to specialize in film. I view this internship as one of a number of significant steps in bettering my skills and adding to my experience.

If selected, I can guarantee that you will be pleased with me as an employee. I've been a paid and unpaid composer, music director, and performer, and all my previous employers have been highly satisfied. I tend to work harder than anyone else in the vicinity, turn out twice whatever the goal or assignment is, and am perfectionistic, creative, responsible, and knowledgeable.

My experience with studio work is limited, but I thoroughly understand the function and use of the equipment involved.

Enclosed please find an unofficial transcript, work samples, and letters of recommendation.

I look forward to speaking with you about the internship.

Sincerely,

————

Dear Mr. Kringelein,

Please consider me as an applicant for your advertised part-time position as clerical assistant in your business office.

My word-processing and business computer skills, which you require, are excellent: I am completely conversant with the current versions of Windows, Office, and Microsoft Word.

Before my move here last month, I was employed for six years as assistant to the manager of Baum Office Products in Philadelphia on a part-time basis. My duties there included all office word processing, mailing list management, transcription, and such general office functions as telephone answering, faxing, and photocopying.

I look forward to hearing from you.

Sincerely,

————

Dear Mr. Artworth,

We are responding to your opening for a full-time resident manager team for your 100-unit townhouse community.

We have experience with all aspects of on-site management and maintenance: six years as caretaker of the Roland Arms Hotel (we shared the one position, which required more work than one person could do); eight years as resident managers of the Beaker Estates; and the last three years as resident managers of the Burkin-Jones Assisted Living Community, all in the St. Louis area (references are available).

We are moving here to be near a daughter and her family, and would like to find work and salaries commensurate with our work history.

We would enjoy discussing these positions with you.

Dinah and Roland Delacroix

Dear Mr. Brandon,

I am interested in your opening for a cargo agent. I meet or exceed all the qualifications given in your classified ad (I have a high school diploma and a perfect driving record, I am able to lift up to 75 pounds, and I can work well without supervision). I am also willing to work nights, weekends, and holidays.

I have been working for Dashwood Warehouse Inc. for the past eighteen months, unloading rail cars and being responsible for various other warehouse duties. However, Dashwood is downsizing and will be letting eight employees, including myself, go as of November 1. I expect to receive a very positive reference from Dashwood.

I am available for an interview at your convenience.

Sincerely,

Dear Ms. Chuffnell,

We have just moved to Seabury and have heard good things about the Seabury Fitness Center. My husband, three children, and I are interested in applying for membership.

I am enclosing an application and the one-time nonrefundable processing fee of $50. If you need any further information, please call me during the day at 555-2498 or in the evening at 555-9980.

We are looking forward to enjoying the Seabury Fitness Center for years to come.

With best wishes,

Dear Ms. Rondabale,

I would like to apply for the position of surgery scheduler for your ophthalmology practice.

I received a two-year degree in office administration from Beckford Business College in 2007. Since then, I have worked full-time for Alasi Surgical Associates as a surgery scheduler.

The work here has been more than satisfactory to me, but your clinic is half an hour closer to my home and I would like to shorten the commute.

I can come for an interview any Saturday, or any weekday during the lunch hour, or after 5:30. If you leave an interview date and time on my home answering machine (661-555-1234), I will call to confirm.

Thank you.

———

Dear Ms. Saverne,

As the result of a telephone call to your office this morning, I learned that Duval International is seeking someone to manage the security operations of its office complex, and that you are the person to contact about the position.

I have eleven years' experience as a security services supervisor and broad experience with access control and with most security systems, including CCTV alarms. I also have an AA degree in law enforcement.

I was employed by Stanislas & Sons from 2000–2005, and by Barr Associates from 2005 to the present. Favorable references are available from both companies.

I would like to set up an interview to discuss the position with you. I have 24-hour voice mail at 515-555-1234.

———

Dear Ms. Jocelyn,

I am looking for a position as an electrical engineer. Several people have mentioned your employment agency as being outstanding in placing people in this field.

I have an MS in Electrical Engineering and seven years' experience in the design of lighting and power systems; the last two years I was also project manager.

I believe my qualifications make me someone you can place, both to my satisfaction and to a future employer's satisfaction.

I will call next week for an appointment and can then bring in my résumé, list of publications, and references.

I look forward to meeting you.

Sincerely,

———

Dear Mr. Squales,

As someone with three years' telemarketing experience and two years' experience as office manager of a small business, I think I am a good candidate for your convention sales and marketing coordinator position.

My strengths include effective oral and written communication skills and an aptitude for interpersonal business relationships. I am considered a good team player and am precise and detail-oriented in my work.

I would like to bring in my résumé and references and discuss this opening with you.

———

Dear Margaret West,

Libraries have been a second home to me for years, and I will be majoring in library science. In the meantime, I would like to apply for the summer job opening in your children's room.

Although my work background is slight (see résumé), I think I can offer you a deep and genuine interest in library science, a strong desire to excel at this kind of work, and library skills that come from many hundreds of library visits. As the oldest of five children, I also have considerable experience and a high comfort level in dealing with young people.

Thank you for your time and attention.

––––––––

Dear Mr. Baillie:

The requirements for the branch manager position you advertised describe almost perfectly my own background.

As assistant manager of Gulliver Travel, I have been responsible for overseeing eight full-time agents. I am a travel school graduate (Charlson International) with a great deal of experience and a good working knowledge of the travel industry in all its phases—from issuing tickets and seat assignments and assisting with ticket assembly to PARS computer experience. I have two years of experience in domestic reservations, one year of experience working with corporate international travel operations, and a thorough understanding of international tariffs.

I would like to discuss this position with you and will be happy to come in for an interview at your convenience.

Sincerely yours,

––––––––

See also: COVER LETTERS, EMPLOYMENT, FOLLOW-UP, RÉSUMÉS

NINE

APPOINTMENTS AND INTERVIEWS

Showing up is 80 percent of life.
—WOODY ALLEN

Many appointments, interviews, and meetings arranged by telephone are confirmed by letter, fax, or e-mail.

Some appointment letters are simple: confirming or altering an appointment; reminding someone of an appointment; refusing or canceling an appointment.

When you want someone's time in order to sell your company's product or service, however, the letter requesting an appointment must be an outstanding sales letter, persuading the person that it is in their interest to see you.

To secure a job interview, send some combination of carefully crafted résumé, cover letter, or letter of application (see APPLICATIONS, COVER LETTERS, RÉSUMÉS).

Letters About Appointments Include

- accepting
- asking for/requesting
- canceling
- changing/postponing/delaying
- confirming/following up
- refusing
- thanking for

How to Say It

- When asking for an appointment: identify yourself if you're unknown to the person; explain why you want to meet with them; mention a benefit to them in meeting with you; suggest a length of time for the appointment ("fifteen minutes" or "no more than half an hour of your time"); offer possible dates, times, and places; mention others who will be present; give your address, phone number, e-mail address, and fax number; express your appreciation for the person's attention to your request. In some cases, tell when you will call for their response.
- When agreeing to meet with someone: say yes to the meeting; repeat the purpose, date, time, place, and length of meeting; express your pleasure or thanks (see also ACCEPTANCES, ACKNOWLEDGMENTS).
- When confirming arrangements made in person or by telephone: refer to your previous discussion; repeat the meeting specifics—date, time, place, purpose; close with an expression of pleasure ("look forward to discussing this").
- When changing or postponing an appointment: mention the original time, date, and place; state your alternatives; apologize for the inconvenience; ask for confirmation of the new time.
- When refusing a request for an appointment: thank the person for their letter or telephone call; say no politely and neutrally; if appropriate, offer an alternative way to meet the goals of the proposed meeting; if you wish, indicate why you cannot accept, although a simple "I am unable to meet with you" should suffice.
- When canceling arrangements: repeat the time, date, place; state that you must cancel; briefly explain why; apologize for the inconvenience; offer a substitute action, if appropriate.
- When sending a follow-up letter after an appointment: give the date of the meeting; state your pleasure at all that was accomplished; enclose promised information or materials; refer to your hope for future meetings/contacts/business.

What Not to Say

- Don't "postpone" or "delay" a meeting that you are actually canceling. If you have no intention of ever meeting with the person, use the word "cancel" and omit all references to the future.
- Don't over-apologize for canceling or changing an appointment unless the situation is special (you've requested the meeting and the company has invited upper-level management and arranged for refreshments and video

equipment). Usually all you need is a brief "I'm sorry to have to cancel/change/postpone . . ." For more complex situations, see Apologies.

Tips on Writing

■ Be assertive about making appointments; if you leave it to the other person ("I'd appreciate hearing from you") you may not get a response.

■ Thank the person who sets up the meeting when there are more than two people getting together.

■ Some people are persistent about wanting your time, from the neighbor who is determined to learn everything you know about genealogy or playing bridge to the sales representative who won't take no for an answer. When it's someone you will continue to deal with (the neighbor), write a note, using equal doses of tact and firmness: "I know you will understand, but I must say no." In the face of persistence, never give a reason for your no. The moment you say why you are unable to meet with them ("I'm really busy just now"), they will have a response ("It will only take a minute"). When you offer another reason, they will have another rebuttal. Engaging you in wearying debate is part of the strategy; you wouldn't be the first person to say yes just to avoid being harangued. A simple "I'm sorry, but no" repeated many times is most effective—and putting it in writing doubles its effect.

Special Situations

■ When requesting a sales or job interview, use your letter to pique the person's curiosity. Make them want to see you. Sell your product or yourself, but don't tell so much that the person thinks nothing more will be gained by an interview.

■ If you forget an interview, appointment, or meeting, write an immediate, sincere apology. Ask what you can do to make amends.

Format

■ Correspondence about business appointments, interviews, and meetings is typewritten on business letterhead or personal-business stationery.

■ Interoffice and some out-of-house communications about meetings are handled by memo or e-mail.

■ Letters regarding personal appointments can be either typed or handwritten. The more formal or personal the appointment is, the stronger the indication for a handwritten message.

WORDS

accept	consult	examine	pleasure	session
arrange	contact	interview	postpone	unable
confer	discussion	notify	review	

PHRASES

already committed/have plans

another engagement

an unexpected complication

can't keep our original date

convenient time

introduce you to

looking forward to seeing/
   meeting you

may I suggest

meet with you

move up the date to

of interest to you

previous commitments

set a time and date

unfortunately obliged to

when you are able

won't be free

would be convenient for me

SENTENCES

Can we change our meeting on July 15 from 2:00 p.m. to 4:30 p.m.?

I am unfortunately obliged to change the date we set earlier.

I don't believe a meeting would benefit either of us.

If you're unable to make the meeting on the tenth, please let my assistant know as soon as possible.

If you would like to discuss this, I could meet with you at a time convenient for you.

I'll give you a call in a couple of days to see if you can schedule a meeting with me.

I'm not able to meet with you for several months—please contact me again in late January.

I would be happy to meet with you in my office on Friday, November 8, at two o'clock to discuss your invention.

I would appreciate twenty minutes of your time this week.

I would like to meet with you to discuss Jackie's progress so far on the new medication.

I would like to review with you my current salary, which I believe no longer reflects my responsibilities and contributions.

Let me know as soon as possible if this is convenient for you.

May I stop by your office for a few minutes next week to drop off our latest samples and catalog and to explain how our new service contract works?

Mr. Patterne is seriously ill and will be unable to keep his appointment with you on June 23 at 1:30.

Thank you for your time yesterday—I enjoyed meeting with you.

This will confirm your appointment with Ms. Tucker on Tuesday, December 18, at 3:00 p.m.

We would like to discuss with you, either in person or over the telephone, our concerns about the academic progress of our daughter, May Bracknel.

PARAGRAPHS

After you have evaluated my application and résumé, I hope we can arrange an interview at a mutually convenient time. I note several areas where the company's areas of emphasis and my areas of expertise overlap, and I would like to discuss these aspects of the position. You will no doubt have questions for me as well. I look forward to hearing from you.

Charlotte Moulin, managing director of Hardy's Cycle Supply, will be in Alberta the week of August 4, and would like to tour Wheels Unlimited while she is there. Please let me know if something can be arranged.

I understand you are looking for acreage east of town. May I come in and speak with you sometime this week about the property I have for sale?

Thank you for the copies of the contracts, which we received October 31. As we review them with our lawyer, a few questions occur to us. We would appreciate being able to sit down with you and your lawyer to discuss a few of them. When would this be possible?

Did I have the date wrong? I thought we had a meeting scheduled for 1:30 yesterday. I'm afraid I won't be free again until late next week, but maybe we can arrange something then. Please let me hear from you.

May I have fifteen minutes of your time next week to show you some large colored photographs of what Office Greenery has done for other area businesses? Offices that use our services report increased customer and employee satisfaction, and I think you will be glad you investigated our unique, effective, and cost-efficient program. I will call your secretary on Monday to see if you are available for a brief meeting.

We are interested in replacing the decorative stone brick on our home and would like you to give us an estimate on your lightweight "cultured stone."

Please call either of us at work during the day or at home during the evening (see enclosed business cards) to set up an appointment. Thank you.

SAMPLE LETTERS

Dear Mr. Stobbs:

I've received your letter of June 16 requesting an appointment to see me about your Handley Cross computer software.

We have been using the Surtees line of software for all our business needs for the past three years, and we are very satisfied with it. I don't see a meeting benefiting either of us.

Thank you, however, for thinking of us.

Yours truly,

————

Dear Lionel,

I have to cancel the meeting we set up for Friday, September 3, at 2:30 p.m., as we've got a little trouble at the Valliscourt plant. I should be back on September 6 and will call you then to set up another appointment.

Thanks for understanding.

Sincerely,

————

Dear Ms. Vulliamy:

People with disabilities get hired for one very special reason: they're qualified.

I would like to tell you about some of the highly qualified people listed with the Ogilvy Employment Agency who could make a positive and energetic contribution to your organization.

May I meet with you sometime next week?

Sincerely,

————

Dear Laura Payton:

Our longtime supplier of plastic tubing has recently informed us that they are discontinuing their plastic tubing division. Our vice-president of purchasing will be visiting several plastic tubing manufacturers in your area next week.

Would it be possible for you to schedule a meeting and plant tour for him on Tuesday or Wednesday of next week? Enclosed are data on our projected needs for plastic tubing, our production schedules, and delivery requirements that may be helpful to you in preparing for his visit.

Thank you.

Sincerely,

————

Dear Ms. Green,

According to the article about you in last Sunday's paper, you are researching the Arapaho peoples for your new book. My great-grandmother was an Arapaho, and I have a number of papers, mementos, and other belongings that might be of interest to you. I am at home most evenings if you would like to call for an appointment to see if I have anything that interests you.

Congratulations on your most recent book, which I read with great pleasure.

With best wishes,

———

See also: ACCEPTANCES, ACKNOWLEDGMENTS, EMPLOYMENT, FOLLOW-UP, INVITATIONS, REFUSALS, REQUESTS, THANK YOU

TEN

LETTERS OF APPRECIATION

I have yet to be bored by someone paying me a compliment.
—OTTO VAN ISCH

Letters of appreciation are the easiest, most delightful letters to write. You are never obliged to write them, there is no deadline, and the only rule is sincerity. One of life's small pleasures is to be able to be kind and generous with little cost to yourself.

Letters of appreciation are related to letters of acknowledgment, congratulations, and thanks. In the latter cases, we are not surprised to hear from others, whereas a letter of appreciation is always unexpected. When Aunt Estrella gives you a gift, you thank her. When Aunt Estrella sends your son a graduation gift, he thanks her, but you write a letter of appreciation, saying how much her support of your children has meant to you over the years.

You don't need to thank someone for prompt payment, for turning in a report, for giving you a bonus based on performance, or for returning your lost wallet intact. In all these cases people are doing the expected thing. However, it is entirely appropriate to show your appreciation. As Abraham Lincoln said, "Everybody likes a compliment."

Letters of appreciation are sent to employees who do "ordinary" work, but do it well; to strangers you encounter who demonstrate above-average efficiency and service; to friends and relatives who go the extra mile for you; to people who have referred work or clients to you; perhaps to people you've read about in the newspaper who have contributed something to your community.

Write Letters of Appreciation for

- awards/honors
- commendations/compliments/encouragement/praise
- community service
- complimentary letters about company/employee/service/product
- customer referrals
- customers to whom you extend privileges in appreciation of their business/prompt payments/new accounts
- customers whose business you want to acknowledge
- employees for their good work
- employers for a bonus/raise/promotion
- financial contributions
- group efforts
- helpful advice/suggestions/tips
- introductions
- prompt payments
- public figures whose work you admire
- speeches/workshops/conferences
- sympathy (see also ACKNOWLEDGMENTS, THANK YOU)
- volunteers

How to Say It

- State what you appreciate (a talent, the business lunch, the plans for the new building).
- Use a key word early in your note: "appreciation," "congratulations," "gratitude," "admiration," "recognition."
- Be specific about the person's work, talent, or actions: "You're a delight to work with because . . ." or "Your work has meant a lot to the company because . . ." In some cases, relate an anecdote, a shared memory, or a reflection that bolsters your good wishes.
- Close with wishes for continued success or with some forward-looking remark about your future business or personal association.

What Not to Say

- Don't add information, a meeting reminder, or a sales message; for maximum impact your upbeat message should stand alone.
- Don't express more than you feel. People know when your sentiments are

insincere. Use language that feels genuine and comfortable to you; avoid effusiveness, exaggeration, and excessive flattery.
- Don't talk about "luck" when expressing appreciation; it implies that chance rather than talent and hard work was responsible for the person's achievements.
- Don't use letters of appreciation to customers as an excuse to solicit more business or for your future advantage; a meaningful letter of appreciation has only one purpose.

Tips on Writing

▪ Be brief, warm, and sincere. The "brief" part is easy, but if you have trouble being warm and sincere, you might want to think about why you're writing. Perhaps it is not a letter of appreciation that you need to send.

▪ Be slightly formal. Even when you know well the person to whom you're writing, a certain formality increases its impact.

▪ Be positive. Instead of writing, "I never thought you could do it," say "You've shown us what a person can do with enough energy and determination."

▪ When someone sends you a letter of appreciation, reflect on what pleases you about it. Remember this the next time you write one.

Special Situations

▪ Letters of appreciation sent to customers, present and potential, are more sales letters than letters of appreciation (see SALES).

▪ Enormous goodwill can be generated for your business by writing brief, sincere notes of appreciation to employees, customers, or suppliers. Once you start looking for ways to appreciate people, you will see them everywhere; make a habit of sending off appreciative notes several times a month.

▪ Sometimes you need to turn down something—a gift, an invitation, a membership—but you are flattered and pleased at the thought behind it, so you write a letter that is part appreciation, part refusal (see also REFUSALS).

▪ Letters of appreciation can be written to several employees at once—teams, divisions, branch offices, sectors, and other groups that have performed particularly well or solved a problem.

▪ "A fan letter is an enduring testament to excellence, which puts it in a category of its own—perhaps somewhere between a valentine and an honorary degree." (Jennifer Williams) When writing a fan letter to a movie star or public figure, be brief (no more than one page). There is little point in asking for the person to call you or see you—as they say, "only in your dreams." Requesting a photograph is acceptable, although not everyone will respond. Don't send a gift; it's unlikely that the person will ever see it (it will be donated to a nonprofit organization). Addresses for most celebrities can be obtained at the library.

■ If your company gives corporate gifts, attaching handwritten notes of appreciation will double their impact. Eighty-five years ago, Agnes Repplier wrote, "Letterwriting on the part of a busy man or woman is the quintessence of generosity." In today's fast-lane business culture, this generosity is even more highly regarded. Unlike the spoken compliment, this one can be read and reread.

Format

■ Use postcards for one- or two-sentence notes of appreciation. In just minutes you can dash off notes rich in public relations potential. Consider postcards featuring scenery from your area for people outside it, art postcards, reprints from old movies that might relate to your business or your interests, or even an especially attractive picture of your factory, office, building, or other installation.

■ Personal notes of appreciation are handwritten on foldovers or personal stationery.

■ Business letters of appreciation are typed on letterhead stationery if you have a somewhat formal relationship with the person. In more casual contexts, jot an appreciative message on memo paper.

■ E-mail, which wouldn't be appropriate for a standard thank-you note, is often useful for the quick note of appreciation. Some things seem too trivial to warrant notepaper and pen, but are just right for e-mail: "Great presentation!" (from a colleague; from a superior, a handwritten note would be preferable); "I noticed your rose garden when I drove by the other day—fabulous!"; "Heard you got another patent—way to go!"

WORDS

admire	engaging	generous	inspired
appreciate	enjoyable	gracious	kindness
commendable	fascinating	honor	knowledgeable
delightful	favorite	impressive	large-hearted

memorable	remarkable	stunned	triumph
one-of-a-kind	respect	superb	unique
overwhelmed	satisfying	thoughtfulness	valuable
pleased	sensational	thrilled	welcome
recommend	sincere	touched	
refreshing	special	treasure	

PHRASES

appreciate your contributions to	I want you to know how much we/I appreciate
as a token of our gratitude/ appreciation	job well done
delighted to learn about	let me tell you how much I liked
grateful to you for	offer my compliments
heard about your success	realize the worth of
held in high regard	set great store by
hope I can return the favor someday	think highly of
I am impressed by/with	we can point with pride
I appreciate the time and effort you expended on	wish you well
important contribution	without your dedication and expertise
it was thoughtful of you to	would like to compliment you on

SENTENCES

As principal of Jerome Elementary School, you might like to know that we think Miss Eurgain is an absolute treasure.

Can you stand one more compliment?

Customers like you are the reason we stay in business.

I'd like to express my appreciation for the knowledgeable and sympathetic care you gave me during my hospitalization for bypass surgery.

I don't know how I would have managed without your help.

If I can repay your kindness, let me know.

I'm impressed!

I sincerely appreciate your time and attention.

I want to express my appreciation to all of you for the extra hours and hard work you put in last week to secure the Gryseworth contract.

I want to tell you how much I appreciate what you are doing for the recycling program in our neighborhood.

My hat's off to you!

Thanks again for your clever and useful suggestion.

The Ridley County School Board would like to add its thanks and appreciation to those of the recipients of the scholarships you made possible.

This past year has been a banner year for the company, and you have contributed significantly to its success.

We are all happy for you.

Well done!

Your efforts have made this possible.

Your support is greatly appreciated.

You've done it again!

PARAGRAPHS

As Bette Midler once said, "People are not the best because they work hard. They work hard because they are the best." And you are the best! Know that we appreciate you!

You've been a valued cardmember with Stuyvesant Bank since 2000, and we thank you for the exceptional manner in which you've handled your account. To show our appreciation, we've preapproved you for our premier bankcard, the Gold 100. We think you will find it to be the ultimate in credit card performance.

Please accept the enclosed token of our appreciation for your five years as one of our most dependable and delightful volunteers. We don't know what we would do without you!

Thank you for your timely and excellent solution to the problem of tangled hoses. Only those of us who have struggled with this annoying and time-consuming inconvenience can appreciate what a delight the new boom system will be. You will be receiving an Outstanding Contribution award in May, but I didn't want to wait that long before telling you how pleased and impressed we all are.

All of us here at Legson Ltd. enjoyed your enthusiastic letter about the quality of our lace goods. We are proud to offer such a wide selection of fine handiwork from all four corners of the globe. Please accept with our appreciation the enclosed 20 percent discount coupon good on your next order.

Appreciation and thanks go to Angela Messenger and her Documentation Department for a successful transformation of the tracking system. The new equipment and its faster, more accurate method of record-keeping will help keep us in the forefront of the Stout, Old, Mild, Bitter, Family Ales market. Our success here at Marsden & Company is due to an exceptional group of talented employees.

SAMPLE LETTERS

Dear Dr. Rowlands,

Your suggestions for next year's technical forum are much appreciated. I've turned them over to the steering committee, although I suspect you'll be invited to join them. I hope you will accept—your ideas seem as workable as they are useful.

> Sincerely yours,

———

Dear Ms. Lees-Noel:

I'm told that you were the good-hearted soul who kept my desk from overflowing during my sick leave (while still keeping up with your own work).

Instead of the chaos I expected to return to, I was able to start back with a clear slate. I am most appreciative of everything you did. I don't know whether this is a compliment or not, but you did things just the way I would have!

Do call on me if I can ever return the favor.

> Sincerely,

———

Dear Mr. Fitzmarshall:

We were pleased to learn that you received such outstanding service from one of our employees. Be assured that we have passed on your compliments to Ms. Stretton. You will perhaps enjoy knowing that in recognition of her talent and managerial skills, Ms. Stretton has just been promoted to floor supervisor.

We appreciate your taking the time to write us.

> Yours truly,

———

Dear Mrs. Sixsmith,

Thank you for accompanying the fifth and sixth graders to Language Camp last weekend. I understand you chaperoned the group on your own time. Since Ronald arrived home, I've heard dozens of stories of your helpfulness, good humor, and ability to make the camp a home-away-from-home for these youngsters.

We felt a lot better knowing you would be with the group, and we appreciate Ronald's opportunity to spend time with a dynamic adult who's a good role model.

> With best wishes,

———

Dear Ms. Stanley,

The entire department joins me in thanking you for the superb workshop on hard disk filing systems. We all learned a great deal (I was fascinated by your introductory description of early Abyssinian slate files).

I am passing on your brochure to George Hickson in Building 201-BE in case he would be interested in having you speak to his department.

Yours truly,

––––––––

Dear Judge Whipple,

Congratulations on the editorial you wrote for Sunday's op-ed page. I have followed your career over the years and have been impressed by your passion for justice, especially for society's most vulnerable people: children, the homeless, and those with disabilities.

My best wishes to you for professional and personal happiness.

Sincerely,

––––––––

See also: ACKNOWLEDGMENTS, CONGRATULATIONS, GOODWILL, THANK YOU

ELEVEN

BELATED LETTERS

*People who are late are often so much jollier than
the people who have to wait for them.*
—EDWARD VERRALL LUCAS

One of the most difficult letters to write is the one that is overdue. Every day that passes magnifies our guilt and intensifies our resistance to writing; too often we end up not writing at all.

Centuries ago, Titus Livius advised, "Better late than never." In the case of a letter, "late" is inconsiderate. "Never" can be unpardonable. Your effort in writing, even though belated, will be appreciated.

"Whenever possible, respond to a letter immediately," says Pat Dorff. "The longer you postpone answering, the more lengthy the response needs to be." She is, in general, correct. The letter that might have been a simple yes or confirmation of an appointment or requested information now needs an apology, possibly a reason for the delay, and a little more warmth because of its tardiness.

Belated Letters Include

- letters dealing with sensitive issues (see also SENSITIVE)
- letters to family and friends who have written us such lovely, long, newsy letters that we don't know where to begin to answer them (see also FAMILY)
- refusal and rejection letters (see also REFUSALS)
- sympathy notes for which we feel we have no words (see also SYMPATHY)
- thank-you notes for gifts we didn't like or that were so generous we were overwhelmed by them (see also THANK YOU)

How to Say It

- Avoid the situation in the first place by organizing letters to be answered in order of importance. Don't respond to less difficult letters until you have taken care of those on top of the pile.
- Briefly acknowledge your tardiness and then go directly to the main message.

What Not to Say

- Don't go into a long song and dance about how sorry you are for your tardiness, or an even longer explanation of exactly why you couldn't write earlier. "Don't fill *more* than a page and a half with apologies for not having written sooner!" (Lewis Carroll) Egocentric agonizing about your shortcomings only takes the spotlight off the other person and focuses it on you.
- Don't imply the tardiness is somehow the other person's fault ("I'm always nervous about writing you because you write such beautiful letters" or "I didn't want to hurt your feelings with our rejection, so I put off writing").

Tips on Writing

■ Keep a selection of interesting postcards on hand. When you realize you're going to have trouble writing a letter, send a brief note on a postcard acknowledging the issue and saying you'll write soon. This does away with the sense of something hanging over you. The letter will be twice as easy to write when you get to it because you'll feel virtuous for having sent the postcard.

■ Knowing that "the path of later leads to the house of never" (Donald E. Walker), set yourself up for success. Address an envelope to the person. Open a computer file or pick up pen and paper. You'll feel the weight of a half-begun task pulling at you and you will find it easier to finish it, just to get that envelope off your desk.

■ Don't feel you have to write three times as much and four times as charmingly because you're late; this kind of pressure will keep you from ever writing. Write the letter you would have written had you written it earlier.

■ We aren't the only ones behind in our correspondence. Oscar W. Firkins (in Ina Ten Eyck Firkins, ed., *Memoirs and Letters of Oscar W. Firkins*, 1934) was often late:

> "I want to write a word to you this morning to thank you for the kind letter I received some months ago, and to assure you that my silence has meant neither forgetfulness nor indifference."

"Again delay has overtaken me in the matter of response to your letter. Examination time and the preparations for my trip must shoulder part of the responsibility, and the rest must be referred to that immemorial scapegoat, human nature."

"I have long had in mind a letter to you, postponed by the foolish wish we all have to write more and better tomorrow instead of less and worse today."

Sylvia Townsend Warner (in William Maxwell, ed., *Letters: Sylvia Townsend Warner*, Viking Press, 1982) did her share of apologizing:

"It is disgraceful that I have meant for so long to write to you, and put it off for equally long."

"I have begun many letters to you in my mind, and some even on paper, but never finished them."

"I have been a Hog with Bristles not to have written to you before—though I got back ten days ago I have not had a moment to turn around in since, not to turn around with any feelings of leisure and amplitude, such as I would want when I write to you."

"You must have thought me very ungrateful in not writing before to thank you for taking so much trouble about my poems. My time has been taken up with visitors."

Special Situations

■ Although in principle there is zero tolerance for business tardiness—late deliveries, unanswered letters, unfilled orders—it happens. Frequently. Advice in this chapter is useful, but for industrial-strength help, see ADJUSTMENTS and APOLOGIES.

■ When late with a "thank you," don't take more than a phrase or a sentence to apologize ("My thanks are no less sincere for being so unforgivably late"; "I am sorry not to have told you sooner how much we enjoyed your home-made chutney"). There are not many good excuses for being late with a thank-you note, so don't offer one—it's bound to appear feeble. It's better to say you have no excuse and you're sorry. Then continue with an expression of your thanks, which should probably be more fervent and well-crafted than if you'd written at once. "The obligation to express gratitude deepens with procrastination. The longer you wait, the more effusive must be the thanks." (Judith Martin, "Miss Manners")

Format

■ All belated letters take the format of the letter as it would originally have been written: a handwritten belated thank-you note; a typewritten apology on letterhead stationery for a business tardiness.

WORDS

absentminded	forgive	overlook	remiss
apologies	inadvertently	pardon	sheepish
distressed	negligence	regret	sorry
embarrassed			

PHRASES

accept my apology

asleep at the wheel/on the job/
   at the switch

delayed answering your letter
   because

embarrassing to discover that

excuse the delay

feel sorry/terrible/bad about

forgive my tardiness

I am upset about

I don't know how it happened that

intended to write immediately

much to my regret

no excuse for

not from any lack of

pardon my late response

reproach myself

slipped my mind

SENTENCES

I apologize for not having responded sooner.

I hope my tardiness in answering your question has not greatly inconvenienced you.

I imagine that everyone but me has written by now to congratulate you on your promotion and exciting move to Los Angeles.

I'm sorry for the delay in getting back to you—I've been out of town the past three weeks.

I'm sorry—this letter is badly overdue.

I've been writing you in my head for weeks—it's time to get it down on paper.

My delay in acknowledging the touching gift of your father's stamp collection is simply inexcusable.

My tardiness is due to bouts of extreme busyness and bouts of extreme laziness—I don't know which is worse.

Our best wishes for your 75th birthday are no less warm and heartfelt for being so late.

Our holiday greetings are late this year, frankly for no good reason.

Please forgive me for not writing sooner to thank you for the unique and useful fleur-de-lis letter-opener.

Please forgive the delay in responding to your letter of June 14.

PARAGRAPHS

Well, yes, it's me responding with my usual promptness. I wish that I had any kind of excuse (I've been hospitalized, I've been imprisoned, I've been on a secret mission, I'm a finalist with Publisher's Clearing House), but sadly I do not.

I might have to borrow Groucho Marx's explanation for his belated letter: "Excuse me for not answering your letter sooner, but I've been so busy not answering letters that I couldn't get around to not answering yours in time."

Many and fervent (but, alas, belated) good wishes to you on your birthday. I've got a bad sector in my brain, and can't remember if it was this year or last year that I sent you the birthday card with the warthogs on it. However, I'm betting on last year.

We apologize for the delay in scheduling your tree trimming. The cleanup after the May 30 storm left us shorthanded for everything else. A crew is available at 8:00 a.m. on the following dates: June 6, 9, 10. Please call with a day that is convenient for you.

SAMPLE LETTERS

Dear Ms. Lessways,

Cyril Povey passed on to me your request for information about buying a home in the Bursley area the same day he received your letter; the delay is entirely my fault and I apologize.

If you have not yet made other arrangements, I would be happy to show you some lovely homes. We currently list seven properties in your price range that meet or exceed your requirements.

I would be happy to help you find "your" house. If I am out of the office when you call for an appointment, please speak to Janet Orgreave, who will set something up.

Sincerely,
Edwin Clayhanger

———

Dear Mrs. Wix,

I am sorry to be so tardy thanking you for the extraordinary quilt. After studying each square carefully, I realized you had "written" the story of my life. No wonder you asked for any rags or cast-off clothing I might have! It is such a stunning gift that I have dithered for days about how to properly thank you for it, how to let you know that I am deeply touched and grateful. There is no way to do it adequately, so I hope you will accept my simple but heartfelt "Thank you, dear Mrs. Wix!"

Would you be able to come to dinner one night this week so that you can tell me all about the making of the quilt and we can admire it together?

Much love,
Maisie

Dear Ursula and John,

There is no adequate excuse for not having written sooner. We were stunned by the news of Muriel's death—please know that we are grieving with you. Any death is difficult to understand, but a child's death is simply not something we know how to accept.

The last time we visited you, I spent some time reading to Muriel and I was enchanted with her quick mind and her loving heart. I will never forget that moment at the door, when we were leaving, and she insisted on giving me her favorite book. I don't know that I've ever seen a child capable of that kind of generosity. And when I sent her a copy of the book, so that we could both enjoy it, she had you send me yet another from her personal "liberry."

If anything could comfort you at this time (which I doubt) it would be that you loved Muriel as few children are privileged to be loved, and you saw that her life was nearly perfect in every way. She was a thoroughly happy child.

Can you come to us for a weekend soon?

With all our love and sympathy,
Maud and William

Dear Walter Morel,

Please excuse the delay in sending you your copy of the signed contract. Mr. Lawrence will be calling you next week about the schedule.

Sincerely,
Gertrude Coppard

Dear Mr. Cuff,

You will receive the ten (10) hanging pedestals (model #233-1010) for your workstation modulars this week. We apologize for the delay in getting this part of your new workstations to you, especially since you received the other modulars some time ago. Our supplier had an unexpected shortfall of the hanging pedestal.

I hope the delay has not inconvenienced you too much. You are one of our four-star customers and we look forward to doing business with you for many more years to come.

Sincerely,
Rachel Verinder

P.S. Enclosed is a certificate good for $200 off on your next order—our way of saying, "Sorry for the delay."

Dear Mrs. Carthew,

Please forgive our tardiness in thanking you for your most generous and valued donation to the Community Affairs Treasure Chest. Because moneys received in our current fund drive are being matched, your contribution is a significant one for us.

Thank you for being one of our most consistent and openhanded supporters.

Dear Mala Tarn,

Six weeks ago you requested information about filing deadlines for the current round of state artist-in-residence grants.

I regret my delay in responding. You will know how much I deplore my oversight and how deeply sorry I am when I tell you that the deadline was August 1, two days ago.

I have no way of making my negligence right with you. I can only hope you will accept my apologies.

I have put your name on our mailing list so that from now on you will automatically receive all news of grants, and their deadlines.

Yours truly,

Dear Mrs. Tuke,

I apologize most sincerely for the delay in getting our estimate to you. You should have had it within days of our estimator's visit to your office. I'm sorry to say that it's entirely my fault (I put the estimator's notes in the wrong file). I hope I have not, by my delay, caused you to lose interest in Trevor Floor Coverings as the best company to install your hardwood flooring.

Attached please find an itemized estimate of all materials and labor plus information on installation services, site cleanup procedures, and our company lifetime guarantee.

Our policy is to match wherever possible any other estimates you might have received. To discuss this, please call Alban Roche, Manager of Trevor Floor Coverings at 555-1234.

Thank you.

Dear Sylvia and Austin,

My good wishes to the two of you for a long and happy married life are no less fervent for being so late. I hope you will accept my belated greetings (and an equally tardy package I'm mailing separately).

Knowing how kind you both are, I expect that you will overlook the fact that my habitual disorganization got the best of me (once again!).

Think about a trip to Florida. I have a lovely bedroom with a private entrance and your name on the door! (Well, it'll be on the door if you give me a couple of days' notice!)

> Love,
> Aunt Dorothy C.

_____

My dear Brenda,

Belated but loving birthday wishes to you! How can you stand me, with my laggard ways? I hope you give me credit, however, for the tasteful blending of my holiday greetings with your birthday. Subtle, no? It took me awhile to organize this, especially the little Santa tie-in on the birthday card—that was a nice touch, I thought.

I hope your day was lovely and I wish I could have been there as I feel sure you celebrated it in some offbeat and memorable way. I'll never forget the year you invited us to your birthday party and had a bus waiting out front. Your friends immediately divided into two groups: the one that leaped onto the bus, ready for the adventure, and the rest of us, who sounded like six-year-olds: "But where are we going? When will we be back? Is there a bathroom on the bus?"

Whatever you did, I hope it was grand!

> Love,
> Minna

_____

Dear Maurice Garcia,

Please accept our apology for not letting you know that the Carlist desktop organizer (#CL-5521) you ordered on February 11 is temporarily out of stock. You are correct: three weeks is a long time to wait for something billed for same-day shipping. In the normal way, you would have received a postcard asking whether you wished to wait until we had the item in stock or wished to change or cancel your order.

As you've ordered the organizer from another company, we will cancel your order with Wallace Office Supply. In the meantime, I am enclosing a coupon good for 20 percent off your next Wallace order. We regret the inconvenience to you and look forward to serving you more effectively in the future.

_____

From: "PT"<akadoc@email.net>
To: "Mary"<MMM@email.net>
Date: Tue, 15 Aug 2009 11:26:14 -0500

Hi, I have a good excuse for not writing. I've been thinking. For example, did you hear about the guy who collected paste jewelry? He was hooked on faux onyx! Ha, ha, ha . . .

_____

Dear Reverend Charwell,

I said I would notify you as soon as we made a decision on filling our associate position. I imagine that, not having heard from us, you assumed correctly that we had offered the position to another candidate. However, I am sorry to be so late letting you know myself.

We were impressed with your credentials, especially with your achievements in Porthminster and with the references from Hubert Conway and Jean Tasbrugh. In the end, however, we decided in favor of the candidate with more experience in homiletics.

Best wishes to you for continued good work in your ministry.

―――――

From: BJZG@email.net
To: RMK@email.net
Date: Fri, 7 Jul 2009 12:33:33 EDT
Subject: a major case of guilt—yea, a boatload

Oh, right. I neglect you shamefully and what do you do in return? You send me a present! I am scheduling hara-kiri for next Wednesday at 11:20. Be there.

―――――

See also: ACKNOWLEDGMENTS, APOLOGIES, SENSITIVE, THANK YOU

TWELVE

COLLECTION LETTERS

The object of collection letters is to get the money
without losing the customer.
—N. H. AND S. K. MAGER

When writing collection letters you have two goals that work against each other: you want the customer to pay the overdue account and you want to keep the customer's goodwill and business. Well-written, effective collection letters pay off handsomely, not only because of the retrieved income but also because of the delinquent accounts that become dependable accounts.

Collection attempts most often begin as past-due reminders from a company's billing office, accounting department, or credit division. When the account is thirty, sixty, or ninety days overdue, the first of a series of collection letters will be sent. Only when the company's series of increasingly aggressive collection letters is ignored is the account turned over to a collection agency. Many large firms use statistical models to predict which accounts need more aggressive action early on. Remember, too, that in some situations, the single most effective collection method may be a pleasant telephone reminder.

Collection Letters Include

- announcements that the account is being turned over to lawyer/collection agency
- letters to lawyer/collection agency
- personal collection letters: friend/relative
- reminders
- series of increasingly insistent letters
- thank you for payment

How to Say It

- Collection letters can reach levels of high art in their quest to collect on an overdue bill without losing the customer's goodwill. They are always courteous and in the beginning they assume that the customer intends to pay but has been forgetful. Each letter sent to an overdue account is written as though it is the last; you are optimistic, appreciative, confident. Include: customer, order, or invoice number; date and amount of purchase; items purchased; original payment due date; date by which you expect payment now; references to previous letters about the outstanding balance; suggested payment plan; other descriptive information. Leave enough time (two to three weeks between letters) to give the customer a chance to pay. End each letter with a definite request as well as a statement that if payment has been sent this letter can be ignored. Include a postage-paid reply envelope to encourage prompt response. A suggested plan featuring six collection letters is given below. Your own needs may be better met by a series of four or ten, or you may vary the messages.
- Collection letter 1: After sending several statements indicating the past-due status of the account (perhaps with a stamped message or reminder sticker that says "Past Due" or "Second Notice"), you send a gentle, friendly letter pointing out the overdue payment. Your letter is brief, saying simply that a stated amount is so many weeks or months overdue. You pleasantly request payment.
- Collection letter 2: You are a little more insistent and remind the customer that payment still hasn't been received. In a second paragraph, ask for explanations or suggest several face-saving reasons why the person hasn't paid (bill was overlooked, was lost in the mail, customer was away). Close with an expression of your confidence that the payment will be sent at once.
- Collection letter 3: Your tone becomes more urgent, your letter is longer, and you give the customer one or more good reasons to pay the bill: it will protect their credit rating and reputation; it is a matter of fairness/justice/ conscience; it is the responsible thing to do; it will make them feel good; it is a matter of their self-respect; it is in their own best self-interest. In this or the next letter, propose two payment schedules that are acceptable to you, and offer the customer a choice. Divide the past-due amount into weekly, semi-monthly, monthly, or two lump-sum payments.
- Collection letter 4: Your message is increasingly stern, and you present additional arguments for payment: you have carried out your obligations by providing the service or shipping the goods and now they must carry out theirs; the amount is too small to lose their credit rating over it; the customer

wouldn't want to be placed on your delinquent list; they wouldn't want to be reported to the trade credit bureau; they will not be able to place any future orders with you. For the first time, you mention the possibility of turning their account over to a collection agent or attorney for collection.

- Collection letter 5: By now you assume the customer is aware of the problem and is deliberately avoiding payment. In a strong message, you announce that you're obliged to take other action, to turn the account over to a collection agency for collection or to a lawyer for legal action. (If you opt for legal action, word your letter with your attorney's advice.) Even now, however, give the customer ten days in which to make arrangements to settle the account before taking action. Be clear that the action can be avoided if the customer responds at once.
- Collection letter 6: The final letter represents your belief that the customer will pay only if compelled. You say that the account is being transferred to a stated collection agency or to a stated law firm as of a stated date. This letter simply announces the action you're taking; you no longer try to get the customer to pay.
- When you write to the collection agency, give complete information: name, address, telephone numbers, account number, copies of all correspondence, statements, data sheets.

What Not to Say

- Don't threaten the customer with a collection agency or legal action unless you are prepared to pursue these avenues. If you say you are turning the account over to a collection agency in ten days, do so.
- Don't use words like "failure" ("your failure to respond," "failure to pay"); "ignore" ("you have ignored our letters"); "insist" or "demand" ("we insist that you send payment at once"). They make the other person feel small, which will not endear you to them.
- Don't use negative tactics (insults, name-calling, bullying, sarcasm, arrogance, and verbal wrist-slapping); they produce only negative results and tarnish your company's reputation.
- Avoid the arch, pseudo-puzzled, and ineffective tone sometimes seen: "We simply cannot comprehend why someone with such a good credit rating . . ." "We are at a loss to understand why we have not heard from you." "We've been scratching our heads . . ."
- Don't say anything that could be construed as libelous.

Tips on Writing

■ Be tactful. Even people with poor credit histories often feel they are doing a good job given their circumstances. A poorly written collection letter can inspire feelings of anger, self-pity, or helplessness, none of which leads to the writing of a check.

■ Space collection letters. In the beginning send them monthly, immediately after a payment date is missed. Allow enough time for the customer to respond or for delays caused by illness, busy periods, or vacations. Later, send letters every ten days to two weeks. The more stubborn the account, the closer together you space the letters. When the account has a good credit history, you don't send letters quite as often.

■ Credit and financial matters are, theoretically at least, confidential. Make every attempt to safeguard the credit information you give and receive.

■ Don't send collection letters to a person's place of business where others might open the mail. For the same reasons of privacy, don't use postcards to send collection messages. You don't want to embarrass your customer or leave yourself open to complaint or legal action.

Special Situations

■ When trying to collect from a customer who reports adverse circumstances (illness, unemployment, financial reverses), work out a feasible payment program even if it is a generous one. A background check will indicate whether the person is experiencing difficulties that merit special attention. Reducing a debt by even a small amount is a success for both creditor and debtor and is worthy of your best efforts.

■ To remind a friend or family member of an overdue loan, help the person save face by including an excuse ("I know how busy you are . . ."; "I wonder if you forgot about . . ."; "Am I mistaken, or did we agree that you'd repay the loan September 1?"). It will be helpful if you have drawn up a loan agreement or a letter stating the terms. When writing a second time, include a photocopy of your agreement.

Format

■ Collection letters are always typed on letterhead stationery.

■ Form letters are used for the first few collection letters in a series. The first can be a simple reminder with spaces to fill in the amount and due date.

WORDS

action	explanation	propose
advise	extend	reminder
arrangement	liability	repayment
balance	misunderstanding	request
circumstances	necessitate	require
collect	nonpayment	satisfy
concerned	notice	settle
cooperation	outstanding	statement
creditworthiness	overdue	terms
debt	overlooked	unpaid
disappointed	oversight	urge
embarrass	past-due	

PHRASES

account past due

accounts receivable

act upon

amount/balance due/owed

appreciate hearing from you

at least a partial payment

be good enough to/so good as to

behind with your payments

call/direct your attention to

clear your account before the next
   statement period

credit rating/standing/record

damaging to your credit record/
   standing/rating

delinquent status of your account

despite our notice of a month ago

did not respond

discuss this with you

easy payment plan

escaped your attention

final opportunity

friendly reminder

have heard nothing from you

how can we work together to

immediately payable

important to resolve this matter

in arrears

it is our policy

I understand and appreciate your
   position, but

just a reminder/to remind you

legal action/advice/steps

let us hear from you right away

mail today

must hear from you

mutually satisfactory solution

no activity on your account

not made a payment since

now due on your account

official notice

outstanding balance

overdue account

past-due amount

perhaps you didn't realize

please let us hear from you by

please mail/send us

pressing need for action

prompt payment/remittance

reasonable payment arrangement

recourse to legal action

reduce your balance

resolve this matter

review of our files/
your account shows

seriously delinquent

several statements and letters

since you haven't replied to our last
letter

so that you can maintain your credit
standing

special appeal

strongly suggest

suggested payment plan solution

to avoid additional expenses, delays
and unpleasantness

unacceptable delay

valued customer

we haven't heard from you

we would appreciate your
sending us

without further delay

SENTENCES

After 120 days, we normally/routinely/automatically turn an account over to
our attorneys for collection.

A postage-paid envelope is enclosed for your convenience.

Despite our last three reminders, your account remains unpaid.

Enclosed is a copy of your last statement, showing a balance of $457.89 that
is ninety days overdue.

I am sorry, but we are unable to extend you any more time for the payment of
your outstanding balance of $896.78.

If we do not hear from you at once/within the next ten days, we will be
obliged to pursue other collection procedures/we will have no choice but
to engage the services of a collection agency.

If you have already sent your check/paid your balance of $324.56, please ig-
nore this notice.

If you haven't already mailed in your payment, won't you take a moment to
mail it today?

If your financial circumstances make it impossible to pay the full amount at
this time, please let us know as I am sure that we can work out an acceptable schedule of installment payments.

If your payment is not received by June 1, we will be obliged to turn your account over to the Costello Collection Agency.

It is important that you take some action before this unpaid balance affects your credit rating.

Just a reminder: your account balance of $106.87 is thirty days past due.

May we have your check for $89.43 by return mail?

Our records show your account to be seriously in arrears.

Please call or write to make arrangements.

Please forward payment in the amount of $269.89 promptly.

Please mail your check by May 5 so that no future action will be necessary.

Thank you for your cooperation/attention to this matter/for taking care of this at once.

Thank you for your recent remittance, which has allowed us to reactivate your account.

There may be a good explanation for your lack of response to our requests for payment of your overdue account—won't you tell us about it?

This matter must be resolved without further delay.

Unfortunately your payment has not been received.

We are disappointed not to have heard from you about your overdue balance of $1,785.97.

We ask for your cooperation in paying the balance due.

We expect to hear from you by July 15 without fail.

We have sent a number of friendly requests for payment but have had no response from you.

We hope that you will take advantage of this last invitation to settle your account and to avoid further damage to your credit rating as well as the costs of any possible legal action.

We look forward to hearing from you.

We must know your intentions immediately.

We provide prompt service, and we expect prompt payment.

We resort to legal action with the greatest reluctance.

We would be happy to work with you to arrange an easy payment plan suited to your circumstances.

Why not take care of this matter right now?

You are a much-appreciated customer, and we hope there is no problem.

You may not realize that your account is ninety days past due.

Your account has been turned over to Darley and Havison, our attorneys, for collection and, if necessary, legal action.

Your payment of $876.23 will be appreciated.

Your prompt payment will protect your good credit rating.

You will want to mail your check today so that you can continue using your credit privileges.

PARAGRAPHS

Enclosed are copies of your statements, year to date. Please check them against your records, and let us know if they do not agree with ours. We show an outstanding balance of $1,236.90.

The nonpayment of your balance is expensive for both of us: it is costing you your excellent credit record as well as monthly service charges and it is costing us lost revenues and extra accounting expenses. We strongly urge you to make out a check right now for the balance due on your account (a self-addressed stamped envelope is enclosed for your convenience). If you wish to discuss some financial difficulty or arrange for a special payment schedule, please call 800-555-1331 today so that we can avoid reclassifying your account as delinquent.

The Locksley-Jones Collection Agency has been authorized by Elliot Lumber to collect the $980.54 past due amount on your account. According to information turned over to us by Elliot, you have not responded to requests for payment made over a period of eight months. This letter serves as your official notice that collection proceedings will begin ten days from the date of this letter unless you contact us to make some satisfactory arrangement for payment.

Thank you for your payment of $763.21, received today. We are happy to be able to remove you from our collection system and to reestablish your line of credit. We do this with the understanding that you will keep your account current in the future. We hope to continue to serve you with all your plumbing and electrical needs.

SAMPLE LETTERS

Dear Sarah Scally:

On September 15, your account (#3178-S) will be transferred to the Bowyer Collection Agency for collection of the past-due amount of $481.69. If we should hear from you before then, we would be glad to make other arrangements. Otherwise, however, you will be hearing from someone at Bowyer.

Sincerely,

_____

TO: Gombold Collection Agency
FROM: Van Allen Department Stores
DATE: February 3, 2010

We would like to engage your services to collect a past-due account in the name of:

Hermione Roddice
1921 Lawrence Parkway
Sunnybrook, OH 45043

Enclosed are copies of statements sent, the data sheet on this account, and all correspondence between us and Ms. Roddice to date.

_____

Dear Avery,

I'm enclosing a self-addressed stamped envelope along with the form below. I hope to hear from you by return mail.

– –

Please mark one of the responses below and enclose this form in the self-addressed stamped envelope along with your check, money order, or cash.

___ Whoops! I was just about to send you the $300. Here it is.

___ The kids need shoes and we don't have any food in the house, but, what the heck, I owe you!

___ Are you SURE it was $300? Let me check. Yup, I guess it was.

___ WHAT $300??!! Heh heh, just joking.

___ I don't know why you should get paid before the dentist, Sears, and the kid who cuts the grass, but, here, take it!

_____

Dear Ms. Phippard:

Your account is now ninety days overdue in the amount of $85.89. As you are one of our longtime customers with an excellent credit rating, we assume this is a simple oversight.

Thank you for taking care of this matter promptly.

Sincerely,

_____

Dear Mr. Landauer,

We would like to remind you once again that we have not received any payment on your account balance of $597.45. If you need additional time or would like to arrange a special payment schedule, please call the credit department today or tomorrow at extension 91. Otherwise, we will expect to receive a check in the mail.

We appreciate your prompt attention to this matter.

Sincerely,

_____

TO: Nolan Associates
FROM: Charney Office Supplies
DATE: March 6, 2011
RE: Past-Due Account

We have alerted you several times (see our statements of November 4 and December 7 and our letters of January 6 and February 5) that your account has a balance of $1,059.32 outstanding. Because your credit rating could be adversely affected by continuing nonpayment, we hope that you will send us something on account immediately.

We need to hear from you this week concerning your plans for repayment. Thank you.

Sincerely,

_____

Dear Ms. Seebach:

We are concerned about your past-due account of $473.23 and your lack of response to our inquiries about it. We would like to hear from you within the next ten days so that we are not obliged to seek other, more serious means of satisfying this debt.

Please consider protecting your credit rating by sending us a check promptly. You will be glad you did.

Sincerely,

_____

Dear Stephen Bracebridge:

Your account (#8103-484-2329) is seriously in arrears. As we have had no response to our reminders, we are obliged to consider collecting the past-due amount of $12,489.19 with the help of a collection agency.

We like to avoid this way of removing unpaid accounts from our books—both for your sake and ours. Your credit standing will be affected by such action, and we lose time and money trying to collect money that is, in all justice, owed to us.

We will transfer this account to a collection agency on April 3. We would, however, be happy to work out a payment schedule with you if you will call before then.

Sincerely,

_____

Dear Algy,

I dislike reminding you yet again, but it's now been six weeks since I lent you $200 "for just a few days." If I could just forget about it, I would, but as it happens I need that money myself—right away.

Shall I stop by after work to pick it up or do you want to drop it off at the house? Let me know.

Sincerely,

————

See also: CREDIT, FOLLOW-UP, REQUESTS

THIRTEEN

COMPLAINTS

If you don't write to complain, you'll never receive your order.
If you do write, you'll receive the merchandise before your
angry letter reaches its destination.
—ARTHUR BLOCH

If you're writing a letter of complaint, you're not alone. Millions write them every year. One multifoods corporation receives three hundred thousand complaining phone calls and letters per year.

Some complaints can be handled by telephone. In general, however, a letter of complaint (also known as a claim letter or consumer action letter) is more effective. First, you've put something tangible on someone's desk—eventually it must be dealt with. Second, you can be more tactful in a letter. Third, the details are conveyed in an accessible form (it's hard to imagine someone on the other end of the telephone taking down dates, names, and invoice numbers as carefully as you would spell them out in a letter). Fourth, you have a record of your complaint.

When you have a general, community-wide complaint, see LETTERS TO THE EDITOR. If you are responding to a complaint, see ADJUSTMENTS or even APOLOGIES.

Write Letters of Complaint About

- billing/collection/financial/ordering errors
- children: misbehavior/damage by
- community or neighborhood problems: adult bookstores/unkempt property/noisy parties
- delays: late shipment/refund/merchandise/supplies/payment

- employees: incompetent/rude/inappropriate behavior
- legislative problems: high taxes/unfair laws/pending bills
- merchandise: defective/damaged/dangerous/overpriced/missing parts, misleading advertising, bait-and-switch tactics
- mistakes, misunderstandings, personal errors
- neighbors (see also NEIGHBORS)
- pets: damage by/attacks by
- policies: unfavorable/restrictive/discriminatory
- schools: undeserved reprimands/undesirable programs

How to Say It

- State the problem: what it is, when you noticed it, how it inconvenienced you.
- Provide factual details. For a problem with merchandise: date and place of purchase, sales slip number, description of product, serial or model number, amount paid, name of salesperson, your account number or charge card number. For a problem with a rude or inefficient service person: date and time of the incident, name of person involved (if you know it), where it occurred, names of witnesses, description of behavior. For a problem with printed inaccuracies, misstatements, or incomplete information: date, section, page, column, and incorrect material; correct data; your phone number. For a problem with the airlines: flight number, dates of flight, points of origin and termination, description of problem or incident, where and when it occurred.
- Include relevant documentation: sales slips, receipts, warranties or guarantees, previous correspondence, pictures of damaged item, repair or service orders, canceled checks, contracts, paid invoices. (Send photocopies of your documents.)
- Tell why it's important to resolve your problem.
- State clearly what you expect from the person or company: refund, replacement, exchange, repair. If you want money, state how much. Request a reasonable solution.
- Suggest a deadline for the action.
- Give your name, address, and home and work telephone numbers.
- Close with your confidence in the other person's desire to do the right thing and ability to take care of the problem to your satisfaction ("I am sure you will find a solution for this problem"; "I am confident that you will want to replace this defective scanner"). Assume that the person who receives your letter will be helpful and let this assurance show.

What Not to Say

- Don't use subjective phrases like "I want," "I feel," and "I need." Figures, dates, facts, photographs, and documentation are more persuasive.
- Don't indulge in sarcasm, accusations, abuse, recriminations, blaming, smart remarks, exaggerations, or emotional outbursts—unless, of course, your only aim is to vent your anger on someone. If you want an adjustment, an apology, or other positive response, avoid antagonizing the person who is in the best position to help you. Negative letters are not only ineffective, they make you look foolish (and feel foolish later, when you think about it).
- Don't be negative ("I don't suppose you'll do anything about this"). Assume the other person wants to be helpful (at least until you find out otherwise).
- Don't threaten to sue. This is generally seen as a bluff; people who actually sue leave this to their lawyers. You might—if you mean this—say that you are going to take the case to small claims court. Sometimes this can lead to a quick, inexpensive resolution. (Note that there are time limits on certain legal actions.)
- Don't accuse anyone of lies, unprofessionalism, cheating, stealing, or misrepresentation. You may be creating legal problems for yourself.
- Don't hint for free products or compensation beyond what you are due.

Tips on Writing

■ Write your letter soon after the incident or problem; details are fresher in your mind, and your chances of getting a good response are greater.

■ Be brief: a one-page letter has the best chance of being read.

■ Be courteous: the person to whom you are writing may have had nothing to do with the error and will be more willing to help you if you are calm and reasonable. When appropriate, include positive remarks: why you chose that product, how long you've used the company's services or products, that you think this incident must be an exception to the rule.

■ Focus on one complaint or issue per letter. When you report in the same letter a rude salesperson, insufficient parking, a mispriced item, and a can opener too dull to open anything, you are likely to get (at most) a blanket apology and no particular action on any of the individual problems.

■ Place more emphasis on how the problem can be resolved and less emphasis on the details of the mix-up, your reactions and feelings, and what a disaster it has all been. Your letter should be oriented toward resolving the problem or arriving at a solution.

■ Help the other person save face. If you act as though only your threats and string-pulling are bringing about a settlement, you deny the other person their sense of themselves as decent, generous people.

■ If your complaint has several components (list of ordered items missing, series of events), set off these items in a numbered or bulleted list.

■ Keep a record of every phone call, letter, or other action you take, along with the dates, the names and titles of those you dealt with, and a summary of the results.

■ Keep the originals of all correspondence, canceled checks, sales slips, and supporting documents.

■ Don't send copies to third parties when you first write a company; give it a chance to settle the problem. If you receive no satisfaction, subsequent letters can be copied to regulatory agencies, trade associations, or consumer advocate offices. On your letter to the company, use "cc:" to indicate those who are receiving a copy.

■ "Complain to one who can help you." (Yugoslavian proverb) There's nothing less effective than writing a great letter to the wrong person. In general, send a complaint letter to a specific person. A letter addressed to nobody in particular ends up on nobody's list of responsibilities. When writing to lawmakers or government officials, check the library reference department for listings in *U.S. Government Manual* (new edition every year), *Who's Who in American Politics*, and state and federal handbooks and directories. *Federal Information Centers*, which lists contacts across the country when you need assistance from the federal government, is available free from Consumer Information Center, Pueblo, CO 81009. When writing businesses, obtain names and titles of company officials by calling the company or from directories of U.S. businesses in the reference section of your library or on the Internet. Addressing a letter to the company's consumer affairs department is a good choice; these departments specialize in problems like yours. If you receive no satisfaction from the company, pursue the matter with: your local Better Business Bureau; a local, county, or state consumer agency; the consumer division of the state attorney general's office; your state representatives; a relevant consumer group; trade association; the appropriate regulatory government agency. When appealing to one of these groups, include a description of the problem, a list of the steps you've taken, and the names and titles of those you've contacted. If you're involved in a disagreement with a professional, write the state board that licenses the person.

■ *The Consumer Action Handbook* is a useful 176-page publication updated yearly and available free by ordering online at www.consumeraction.gov. In addition to preventive advice (consumer tips on car repair, purchase, and leasing; shopping from home; avoiding consumer and investment fraud; home improvement and financing; choosing and using credit cards wisely), the handbook tells you where to direct complaints, listing contact information for national consumer organizations, corporate consumer relations departments, automobile manufacturers, better business bureaus throughout the country, trade associations, third-party dispute resolution programs, federal agencies as well as state and local consumer protection offices. You can also go to www.pueblo.gsa.gov/complaintresources.htm where the Federal Consumer Information Center offers a list of resources for consumer complaints about medicines, drugs, and medical devices; health clubs and exercise equipment; veterinary products; airline baggage and service; auto dealers; banking; on-line services, spam, or junk e-mail; telephone service.

■ If you write many complaint letters, you might like *Shocked, Appalled, and Dismayed! How to Write Letters of Complaint That Get Results* by Ellen Phillips.

Special Situations

■ In a dispute about a credit-card purchase, contact the credit card company to withhold payment while the problem is being resolved (read the information on the back of your statement for details). Most companies have forms for this, asking for your name, account number, credit card statement reference number, amount, store where purchased, and description of the item and the problem.

■ To protest an increase in rent or in auto, medical, or homeowner insurance, include: name, address, telephone number, apartment or policy number, years you have been renting or insured with that company, history of rates, reasons for your objection. Ask that someone call you to discuss the matter.

■ When there are issues with your child's school, assume nothing at the outset. Begin your letter with questions: "Can you tell me . . . ?" "Is it true that . . . ?" Too often, misunderstandings crop up somewhere between school and home. Clarify the issues before asking for changes or apologies.

■ When schools relay complaints to parents, phone calls are the first avenue of communication, but sometimes letters must be sent. In writing parents, the school official's points of reference will be "tact" and "fact." State what happened briefly and objectively. Suggest a date and time for a meeting or ask that the parent call you. Enclose a copy of the school regulations the child violated or refer the parent to the student handbook. State what action is being taken or may be taken by the school.

■ When you are one of a large group protesting an action, product, service, or corporate behavior, send individual, personalized letters rather than form letters or group-generated complaints. Organizations are more likely to respond to one well-written, original letter than to hundreds of boilerplate postcards. In some cases, the great number of complaints is persuasive, but in general you may be wasting time and postage on mass-produced complaints.

■ When writing to an elected official to recommend a course of action, mention the issue or legislation you're writing about in the first sentence or in a subject line ("Re: property taxes" or "Subject: HR4116"). State your opinion clearly ("I strongly disapprove of . . . /I urge you to . . ."). Give reasons for your position. If there are several, list them separately, set off by numbers, asterisks, or bullets. Indicate the course of action you would like the person to take or the response that you expect. Offer to serve as a resource if the issue is something you are particularly knowledgeable about. End with an expression of appreciation for their interest and time.

■ Sometimes apologies are necessary on both sides of a dispute. Even when you have a legitimate complaint, it's possible that you have in some small way aggravated the situation. Making your own apology is not only honest (if called for) but is often helpful in eliciting the response you want.

Format

■ Business letterhead, business-personal stationery, or personal letterhead are all good choices for a complaint letter.

■ Type the letter if possible. If you must handwrite it, be sure it is legible and neat.

WORDS

action	fault	lax	nonfunctioning
adjustment	flaw	misapprehension	off-putting
agreed-upon	grievance	miscalculation	omission
breakdown	ill-advised	misconception	overcharged
compensation	impolite	misconstrued	overestimated
concerned	inaccurate	mishandled	overlooked
damaged	inadequate	misinformed	oversight
defective	inappropriate	misinterpreted	regrettable
disagreement	incident	misleading	reimburse
disappointed	incomplete	misprint	remake
displeased	inconsistent	misquote	repair
dispute	inconvenient	misrepresented	repay
dissatisfaction	incorrect	missing	replace
embarrassing	inexperienced	misstatement	resolve
exasperating	inferior	mistake	restore
experience	insufficient	misunderstanding	shortsighted

slipshod	unfounded	unqualified	unsound
thoughtless	unjustifiable	unreasonable	untidy
uncooperative	unpleasant	unreliable	untrue
unfortunate	unprofessional	unsatisfactory	unwarranted

PHRASES

a mix-up in my order

appealing to you for help

are you aware that

as a longtime customer

call to your immediate attention

correct your records

deceptive advertising

defective upon arrival

does not meet our performance standards

expect to hear from you soon

expensive maintenance

has not met my expectations

high prices

hope to resolve this problem

I am concerned about

I feel certain you would want to know that

inefficient design

it has come to my attention that

it is with reluctance that I must inform you

it was disconcerting to find that

I was displeased/distressed/disturbed/ offended/disappointed by

I wish to be reimbursed for

I would like to alert you to

may not be aware that

not up to your usual high standards

register a complaint about

serious omission/problem

shoddy workmanship

slow delivery

under the conditions of the warranty

unpleasant incident

unresponsive personnel

unsafe product

unsatisfactory performance

warranty inaccuracies

we were unhappy with

with all possible speed

would like credit for

you have generally given us excellent service, but

SENTENCES

Anything you can do to speed matters up/resolve this problem will be greatly appreciated.

Here are the facts.

I am confident that you can resolve this.

I am expecting the courtesy of a prompt reply.

I am writing regarding my last bill, invoice #G4889, dated August 15, 2010.

I believe that an apology is due us.

I expect an adjustment to be made as soon as possible.

I hope you will take this complaint in the helpful spirit in which it is meant.

I know you will want to see that such an incident does not occur again.

I like your product but I object strongly to your advertising.

I'm concerned about Coach Ingelsant's angry, abusive manner with the junior soccer players.

I'm confident that we can resolve this matter to our mutual satisfaction.

I regret/am sorry to inform you of the following unpleasant situation.

I strongly oppose your position on this weapons system.

It is my understanding that it will be repaired/replaced at your expense.

I will send a check for the balance as soon as I receive a corrected statement.

I wish to receive credit on my account for this item.

I would appreciate a telephone call from you about this situation.

I would like a refund in the amount of $49.99.

I would like to clear up this misunderstanding as soon as possible.

Let me know what is being done.

Please call the principal's office to arrange a meeting with the principal, the school counselor, and myself regarding Christie's suspension.

Please contact me within three business days to make arrangements for rectifying the situation.

Please let me hear from you at your earliest convenience.

Please let me know what options are available to me.

Thank you for your prompt assistance with this situation/problem.

The following situation has come to my attention.

The most satisfactory solution for us would be for you to send us a replacement lamp and reimburse us for the cost of mailing the defective lamp back to you.

There was too little feedback to us during the design of the #2 unit.

This product has been unsatisfactory in several respects.

We experienced the following problem in your store/restaurant/hotel last week.

We would like to resolve this situation without delay/without having recourse to the Better Business Bureau or small-claims court.

Will you please check on this?

PARAGRAPHS

I received the leather patchwork travel bag today (copies of catalog page and invoice enclosed), but the matching billfold was not included. Please send me one as soon as possible, in burgundy to match the bag. Thank you.

Five weeks ago I mailed you my check for our stay at the Vörös Csillig in Budapest, and I have not yet received confirmation of our reservations. As the rest of my itinerary depends on whether we are able to stay in Budapest, I would appreciate an immediate phone call from you.

Channel 12's insistence on running inappropriate programming between 5:00 p.m. and 7:00 p.m., when many young people are watching, means that this family at least will no longer turn to Channel 12 for any of its news, entertainment, or programs.

Please find enclosed a bracelet, a necklace, and a pair of earrings. We would appreciate either repair or replacement of these items. The bracelet has a broken clasp, the gold on the earrings appears to be chipped, and the silver finish is overlaying the gemstone on the necklace. In each case, dissatisfied customers of our store returned the items to us. Your immediate attention to this matter will be greatly appreciated.

I'm enclosing a photocopy of a collection letter I received from your agency. This is the sixth letter I have received about this account. Although my first initial and last name are the same as the person responsible for it, we have nothing else in common. I marked each of the earlier letters "incorrect address" and returned them to you. Please verify the correct address of your correspondent. I will expect a letter from you stating that my name and address have been removed from your files and that my credit rating has not been affected by this error.

My order (#578942-E) for two dozen Shipley shortwave radios, placed three weeks ago, has not yet been received. I was told to expect them within the week. Will you please check to see if the order has gone astray? We need them immediately.

I object to the tactics used in your telephone sales efforts. Today a caller identified herself as someone from the credit bureau. After hearing the words "credit bureau" I stayed attentively on the line. It was only after several minutes of trying to understand what was wrong with my credit rating that I realized I was being asked to buy life insurance. I think your approach is deceitful. Enclosed is a copy of the letter I have written to the Better Business Bureau complaining of it.

Thank you for your fifty-six-page report on your department's activities over the past six months. The graphics are outstanding. However, while there is much to reflect on in the text, I find many questions unanswered and several important issues left unaddressed. I would like to discuss with you the kinds of information I need to see in a departmental semiannual report. Please phone my secretary to set up an appointment.

Imagine our embarrassment when we served one of your Paramount Hams for Easter, and none of our guests were able to eat it because it was excessively salty. I would like a refund for the inedible ham (label and store receipt enclosed). Also, can you give me any good reasons for ever buying another Trotter and Duff Paramount Ham? I don't like writing someone off on the basis of a single error, but one bad ham is one too many.

The Abbeville Faxphone 200 that I ordered from you two weeks ago receives documents but will not transmit them. Several phone calls to your service department (I was, of course, unable to fax them) about this serious problem have been unhelpful. The only information I was given was that I was not to return the machine without prior approval. Please send such approval immediately.

SAMPLE LETTERS

Dear Harter & Benjamin Jewelers:

We, the undersigned members of the Eustace College staff, object to the recent ads for Harter & Benjamin Jewelers that have appeared in the college newspaper. All of them advertise your jewelry with the word Intoxicating and show a young man and young woman obviously drinking alcohol. The artwork features champagne glasses and wine and liquor bottles.

Why are you using alcohol to sell jewelry? There must be many other symbols, appeals, campaigns, graphics that would better sell your product. By associating alcohol with "the good life," you are selling college students on the "joys" of booze. We believe this is undesirable and indefensible.

We've spoken to the newspaper staff and adviser about the wisdom of accepting any more of these ads and have also suggested they write an article explaining why such ads are refused.

We sincerely hope you will consider dropping this particular angle in your advertising, especially in periodicals aimed at young audiences.

Sincerely,

———

Dear Dean Higgs:

Last week the College hosted one of the most important international conferences on philosophy in many years—and virtually nobody knew about it.

The Public Affairs Office was briefed about the conference over a period of months: at a two-hour breakfast meeting in March, at three meetings in April, via ten pages of updated notes, details, and list of interview possibilities in May, and at a final one-hour meeting in June.

Despite this, no news releases were sent by the College's publicity department, no photographers were present at major events, the Nobel Prize–winning speakers were not interviewed, and neither of the metro-area newspapers carried articles or features on what was surely an event of local and international significance.

I ask that this situation be investigated, an apology be tendered, and some guarantees for future College publicity be spelled out.

Yours truly,

———

Dear Mr. Blowberry,

I would like to register a complaint about one of your employees, Albert Grope. When I was in your bookstore last week, Mr. Grope persisted in answering my questions in a very loud voice, using one-syllable words and enunciating in an exaggerated fashion. Although I have an accent, my English is correct enough to allow me to teach classics at the university level, and I feel his behavior was inappropriate. Between sentences he would archly eye the other clerk, obviously aware of how hilariously "funny" he was. Even if I had as little command of the English language as Mr. Grope assumed, and were dim-witted besides, I believe he owes every customer a certain respect.

I have spoken to you on several occasions and I felt you were the sort of person who would want to know this.

Sincerely,

———

Re: BankCard #2378-54-8970

My statement dated August 28, 2010, shows an entry for $59 payable to NewFit Shoes, Murray Road and Converse Boulevard, Chicago, dated June 30, 2010.

This charge does not belong on my account. I was in California at the time and, in any case, have never been in that particular store.

Please remove this charge from my account. Enclosed is my check for the balance of my account, $148.53. This amount does not include the $59 for the shoes.

Thank you for taking care of this matter.

———

Dear Governor Foyle:

Re: Susan Price

I am writing to protest most strongly and urgently the treatment of Susan Price, a pacifist prisoner, by the State—specifically for several assaults by prison guards that left her with bruises, lacerations, and possible head injuries.

This is unconscionable.

I urge you to have this situation investigated at once. Please let me know how you plan to handle it.

Sincerely yours,

————————

Dear Mr. Tallant:

As you know, a great deal of our work is coordinated with Harvey Crane Construction. They must complete their paving and other operations before the median work on Pearl Street can begin.

I have seen no progress on their part for about a month. Their delays mean that we incur such damages as loss of production, lower profits, winter protection costs, remobilization, accelerated schedules (overtime), and barricade rental—to name just a few items.

As these costs and damages will necessarily be passed on to you, you may want to check into the situation.

Sincerely,

————————

Dear Mr. Thornton,

This is the third time we have contacted you about your dog, Buck. The neighborhood children continue to be frightened of him, and refuse to play outdoors when he is in your yard. There have been several reports of him snapping at the children.

When would be a good time to discuss this situation with you? We would like to come to some agreement without going to the authorities.

I hope to hear from you very soon.

Sincerely yours,

————————

dear cummings writing machine company,

i would like an immediate replacement for this keyboard. i bought it on june 3 of this year from 'tulips' in cambridge, massachusetts (sales slip enclosed), but, as you can see, it will not produce capital letters.

the 'tulips' people tell me that the manufacturer is responsible for all defects. please let me know at once how you plan to supply me with a keyboard that types capital letters.

yours truly,

————————

Dear Mr. Abednego,

When I bought my first insurance policy with the Independent W. Diddlesex Insurance Company, I was told that buying my auto, homeowners, and life insurances from you would guarantee me a 20 percent reduction over the rates I would normally pay separately. Now that I have switched my life insurance to Diddlesex to obtain this complete coverage, I find that I am paying substantially the same rates as before.

Will you please check to see why I am not getting the lower rates, and let me know as soon as possible?

Sincerely,

————

Dear Mr. Bellman:

We have come to expect a high degree of judgment and integrity from the Calcutta Tape and Sealing Wax Office. It was therefore as surprising as it was distressing when the last shipment was found to be substandard.

Substitutions were made without our permission—invariably a substitution of an inferior product at the original price. In two instances, quantities were not the quantities ordered (they were smaller), with no equivalent adjustment made on the invoice. I am enclosing a copy of our order, a copy of your invoice, and a list of what we actually received. I would appreciate hearing from you immediately on what we can do not only to remedy the current shipment but also to ensure that this doesn't happen again.

Sincerely,

————

Dear Mr. Atterbury:

Before scheduling an appointment with you to discuss the incorporation of my business, I asked your secretary about your legal fees. He told me you charge $100 an hour. I was therefore very surprised to receive a bill for $350 when I spent no more than one hour with you.

I will appreciate an explanation of my bill. Thank you.

Sincerely,

————

Dear Ms. Scanlon,

We have been renting Apartment 206 at 1935 Chicago Avenue for the past four years and have been pleased with our situation until just recently, when new tenants moved into Apartment 306.

We have spoken to Mr. Lonigan and Ms. Branahan about the frequent parties, arguments, and loud noises after 11:00 p.m., and we have also asked the building manager to do what she could. However, we think you need to look into this situation yourself.

Please let us know what we can expect.

Sincerely yours,

————

Dear Wheatley Office Products:

On April 3, I purchased your four-drawer, self-locking EZ-Open File Cabinet, serial number 007800, from your Wheatley outlet on Broadway. I paid a sale price of $329.99 plus tax for the unit.

Unfortunately, the file cabinet does not function as claimed. It self-locks arbitrarily; half the time it does, half the time it doesn't, and no one is able to predict just when it will do which. The one-touch unlocking mechanism does not work at all, which means that usually the drawers have to be unlocked manually with the "emergency only" key. Even when the drawers are not locked, they are difficult to open because of a design problem with overlapping inside shelving.

Mr. Denny Swinton, who sold me the unit, informs me that because the unit was on sale I am unable to return it. I am certain, however, that, sale price or no, I have a right to expect that the unit will perform as promised.

I would like to hear within the next several days that a truck will be coming from Wheatley to pick up the defective unit and that my purchase price will be refunded.

Sincerely,

———————

Dear Dr. Blenkinsop,

As you know, we have been satisfied patients of yours for the past six years. However, I wonder if you are aware that the condition of your waiting room is off-putting. The carpet rarely appears vacuumed, the plastic plants are thick with dust, and the magazines and children's playthings are strewn about, apparently untouched from one of our visits to the next. Hygiene seems particularly important in a health care environment, and, although I know what an excellent physician you are, I can't help worrying about how clean everything else is.

I hope you find this letter helpful rather than unpleasant—it was written with the best intentions.

Sincerely,

———————

See also: ACKNOWLEDGMENTS, ADJUSTMENTS, APOLOGIES, NEIGHBORS, ORDERS, RESPONSES

FOURTEEN

CONGRATULATIONS

To hear how special and wonderful we are is endlessly enthralling.
—GAIL SHEEHY

Some of the most delightful words we receive—right up there with "I love you"—is the letter that begins, "Congratulations!" Because it is rarely obligatory and because its contents are wholly positive, the congratulations note adds a glow to any personal or business relationship. And you don't have to wait for big news to send one. Small landmarks and successes have a sweetness all their own, and the recipient of your note will long remember your thoughtfulness.

Occasions That Call for Letters of Congratulations

- achievements/awards/honors/prizes/speeches/publications/recognition
- adoption or birth of child
- anniversaries: business/years of service/wedding (see ANNIVERSARIES)
- birthdays (see ANNIVERSARIES)
- business: good business year, new store, new account, new contract, merger, opening own business, securing a franchise
- changes: new car/home/job
- customers: good news, major life events
- election to office: public/organization or club/professional society/social group
- employees' work

- engagement (see WEDDINGS)
- graduation
- jobs: new job, promotion, new title
- loan payment (see CREDIT)
- religious milestones: christening/circumcision/bar mitzvah/bat mitzvah/ first communion/confirmation/ordination/taking of religious vows
- retirement
- sales messages: being selected to receive special offer/credit limit raised (see SALES)
- wedding (see WEDDINGS)

How to Say It

- Use the word "congratulations" early in your note.
- Mention the reason (graduation, promotion, honor, baby).
- Tell how happy, pleased, proud, or impressed you are—and why. "The art of pleasing consists in being pleased." (William Hazlitt)
- If appropriate, tell how you learned about the good news. If you read it in the newspaper, enclose the clipping or a photocopy of it.
- Relate an anecdote, shared memory, or reflection that has some bearing on the occasion.
- In closing, wish the person continued success and happiness; express your confidence in a bright future; assure them of your affection, love, admiration, best wishes, interest, delight, pleasure, or continued business support.

What Not to Say

- Don't indulge in excessive flattery ("watch out, Corporate America—here she comes," "I can see that I'll soon be writing to congratulate you on the Nobel Prize"). It makes people uncomfortable. A simple "Congratulations!" and a few personal remarks bring quite enough joy.
- Don't make your congratulatory note do double duty: don't include questions, information, sales messages, or work matters that aren't relevant to the good news.
- Don't compare the recipient's news to something you once did or to something you read in the paper; let the person enjoy a moment in the sun—alone.
- Don't talk about "luck" when congratulating someone; it implies that chance rather than talent and hard work was responsible for the success.
- Beware of inadvertently putting a negative spin on your congratulations. Instead of "I never would have thought you could do it" or "After all this

time, you finally did it," say "I'm so impressed with your energy and determination" or "Congratulations on your hard work and perseverance."

Tips on Writing

■ Written congratulations are optional except when you have received an announcement of personal news (a graduation, for example).

■ Write soon after hearing the news. Congratulations are best served up warm. If you're late, apologize only briefly.

■ Even when you're close to the person to whom you're writing, make your congratulatory letter brief and somewhat formal; this increases its impact.

Special Situations

■ Sending notes of congratulations to customers, clients, colleagues, and other business associates about their good news (births, weddings, promotions, new business) is a thoughtful goodwill gesture.

■ When a branch office, department, or division has enjoyed a collective success, write to them as a group, naming each employee ("Congratulations on surpassing this year's collection goal/securing the new account/your speedy inventory reduction/a new sales volume record/a smooth departmental reorganization").

■ Your response to news of an engagement is pleasant and congratulatory. If you have reservations about the relationship, deal with them in person or don't write at all; cautionary or qualified congratulations are worse than none. Traditionally, "congratulations" were offered to the engaged man and "best wishes" to the engaged woman; you may properly use either expression for women or men.

■ The news of a divorce can elicit a simple acknowledgment, a letter of sympathy, or a letter of congratulations. The latter is sent rarely, and then only to someone you know well. You might, however, want to congratulate someone not on the divorce itself but on surviving the upheaval of a difficult period.

■ Baby announcements inspire some of the happiest congratulations. When the baby is premature, send congratulations, gifts, and good wishes in the normal way; do not wait to see how the baby does. In the event of multiple births, don't ask if the woman took fertility pills and don't say or imply, "You poor things!" Just say "Congratulations!" When a child is born with medical problems or a disability, write that you've heard they have a new little one, that you are thinking of them. Avoid commercial "new baby" cards and conventional congratulations on the one hand, and expressions of sympathy on the other. Some of the unfortunate remarks that these new parents hear include:

"You're not going to keep it, are you?" "I think you should sue the hospital." "Is one of you a carrier for this?" "Maybe the baby won't live; that would be best all around." "Whose fault was it?" "Did you drink while you were pregnant?" "I guess it could have been worse." "God only sends burdens to those who can bear them." Until you know how the parents are feeling (devastated, concerned but optimistic, happy to have the child at any price), don't reveal your feelings—they may be wide of the mark. Later, when you know how the parents are feeling, you can respond on a more emotional level. When congratulating someone on an adoption, do not write, "I'll bet you get pregnant now." People adopt for reasons other than fertility and adoption is not, in any case, a cure for infertility (pregnancies occur after adoption at approximately the same rates as they occur in couples dealing with problems of infertility). Don't ask about the child's background or biological/birth parents (never write "real parents"; you are writing to the real parents). Don't say that you "admire" your friends for adopting anymore than you would "admire" a biological parent for having a child. What *do* you write? Ask the parents to tell you about the child and the great arrival day. Say that you can't wait to come visit, and wish them much happiness.

■ Sometimes a "congratulations" approach is used in sales letters (see SALES).

Format

■ Most congratulations take the form of a note—on personal stationery, foldovers, or notecards.

■ Commercial cards are available for almost every occasion that calls for congratulations. However, use the inside or back of the card to add your own message.

■ In some contexts (business, politics, clubs and organizations), congratulations may be sent on business letterhead, business-personal paper, or memo stationery, depending on the degree of closeness between sender and recipient and the importance of the good news.

■ Some congratulations may be e-mailed, particularly in office settings among colleagues.

WORDS

accomplishment	appreciate	cheer	contribution
achievement	asset	commend	creative
admire	brilliant	compliment	dazzling
applaud	celebration	congratulate	début

dedicated	happy	peerless	talent
delighted	hero	performance	thrilled
dependable	honor	perseverance	tradition
distinguished	imaginative	pleasure	tremendous
effort	impressed	progress	tribute
enterprising	incomparable	prolific	triumph
esteem	innovative	proud	unforgettable
excellent	inspiring	recognize	unique
exceptional	invaluable	resourceful	unparalleled
exciting	inventive	respected	unrivaled
extraordinary	kudos	salute	valuable
feat	leadership	satisfying	victory
finest	legendary	sensational	vision
foresight	meaningful	skillful	vital
future	memorable	special	well-deserved
generous	milestone	success	winner
genius	momentous	superb	
gift	occasion	superior	
gratifying	outstanding	superlative	

PHRASES

accept my heartiest congratulations on

achieved your goals

all possible joy and happiness

an impressive record/achievement

another success

beyond all expectations

cheerful/cheering news

continued health and happiness/
success

couldn't let this happy occasion
go by without

delighted/happy/thrilled to hear/
read/receive the news

good/great/sensational/joyful/
thrilling news

high quality of your work

I especially liked the way you

impressed with this latest award/
honor/prize/achievement

in awe of all that you've done

joins me in sending best/good/
warm wishes

know that you're held in high esteem

many congratulations and much
happiness

offer my warmest/sincerest/
heartiest congratulations

red-letter day

rejoice with you

sharing in your happiness

significant/valuable contribution

sincere wishes for continued success

spectacular achievement

take great pleasure in sending
congratulations to you

take this opportunity to wish you
every happiness

were thrilled to hear about

wishing you all the best/much
success/continued success

with all good wishes to you in your
new venture

wonderful ability to get things
done—and done well

your important contribution

you've done a superb job of

SENTENCES

Baxter called this evening to tell us that the two of you are engaged to be married, and we wanted to tell you immediately how happy we are for you.

Best wishes from all of us.

Congratulations on opening your own chiropractic office!

Congratulations on the littlest Woodley—may she know health, happiness, and love all her life.

Good news travels fast!

Hear, hear!

I am almost as delighted as you are with this recent turn of events.

I couldn't be happier if it had happened to me.

I hear wonderful things about you.

I hope we will enjoy many more years of doing business together.

I just heard the news—congratulations!

I'm proud to know you/to be your friend!

I'm so impressed!

It was a splendid performance/great triumph/brilliant speech.

I understand that congratulations are in order.

I've just heard from Choi Nam-Sun that two of your poems will be included in the next issue—congratulations!

I very much admire your organizational skills/perseverance/many achievements/ingenuity/calm in the face of difficulties.

I wanted you to know how proud and happy I was to hear that your short will be shown at the Brooklyn Film Festival.

I wish I could be with you to share in this happy occasion.

My hat's off to you!

My heartiest congratulations to you both.

My thoughts are with you today as you celebrate.

My warmest congratulations on your graduation from Columbia!

This is the best news I've heard in a long time.

We are pleased with your work on ethics-in-government legislation.

Well done!

We've all benefited from your expertise and creativity.

What terrific news!

With best wishes for fair weather and smooth sailing in the years ahead.

You certainly haven't let the grass grow under your feet.

Your reputation had preceded you, and I see you intend to live up to it.

You've done it again!

You've topped everyone in the store in sales this past month—congratulations!

PARAGRAPHS

I was delighted (although not surprised) to hear that you won the Schubert piano concerto competition this year. Congratulations! I've watched you develop as a fine pianist over the years, and it is a thrill to see you rewarded for your talent—and, above all, for your hard work.

Please accept the congratulations of everyone here at Avonia-Bunn Title Insurance Company on your Outstanding Service Award. Your industry, your attention to detail, and your creative problem-solving have been an inspiration to all of us.

You remind me of something I read by Elinor Smith: "It had long since come to my attention that people of accomplishment rarely sat back and let things happen to them. They went out and happened to things."

I well remember your diffident début twenty-five years ago. Who would have guessed that your "awkward little offspring" would grow to be the successful business it is today?

In the past ten years, the company has grown beyond all recognition—a complete line of new products, computerization of all departments, financial growth beyond our wildest expectations—and wherever there has been innovation, development, progress, you've been in the front ranks. We wouldn't be the company we are today without you. Please accept the enclosed bonus as a sign of our gratitude and appreciation for ten wonderful years.

Aunt Evalina told us about your "dramatic" success. Congratulations on what was evidently a stunning performance! I'm so proud of you, not only for this latest accomplishment, but for all your hard work of the past four years.

SAMPLE LETTERS

Dear Raoul,

Felicitacións on being named the company's Man of the Year, Panza-Spain Division. Having recently visited one of your division branches, I know that you very much deserve this honor. (As Miguel de Cervantes once said, "By a small sample we may judge of the whole piece.")

I'm looking forward to seeing you at the May banquet when you accept your plaque. Until then, best wishes and hasta la vista!

Sincerely,

―――――

Dear Debbie and Jeff,

Congratulations on your engagement. Although our record on marriage is not very good as a society, I am optimistic about the two of you. Seldom have I seen such a hard-working, loving, sensible (yet wildly romantic) pair. I like the way you respect and support each other. I like the way you make difficult decisions together. Offhand, I'd say you've struck gold!

I'm looking forward to your wedding.

Love,

―――――

Dear Liz,

Congratulations on your new job in the animal research lab. I know this is something you've wanted for a long time. I also think they are lucky to have you, with your background and experience with animals. I hope it turns out as well for you as I think it will.

Love,

―――――

Dear Professor Arronax,

Heartiest congratulations on the recently published accounts of your discoveries. I have read them with the greatest fervor and admiration.

With all best wishes, I am

Faithfully yours,

―――――

Dear Briggs,

I was happy to hear about your promotion to division credit manager. Let's celebrate!

Your cousin,

————

Dear Governor Peck,

Congratulations on your landslide election. All of us who campaigned for you in this area are proud and pleased to have been part of your victory.

Please accept my best wishes for a distinguished, productive, and happy term of office.

Respectfully yours,

————

Dear Mr. Dodsworth:

Congratulations on the opening of your newest branch of the Revelation Motor Company. We have always appreciated doing business with you, and expect to enjoy it even more now that your new office is only two blocks from us.

Best wishes for happiness and success to all of you at Revelation.

Sincerely,

————

Dear Synnöve,

Congratulations on receiving the Granliden award! That's terrific. I was so happy for you when I saw the announcement in the paper.

I hope everything else in your life is going as well.

Best,

————

Dear William,

I've just heard from Katherine that you are finally a full-fledged chemical engineer—congratulations! I've admired you as I've watched your struggles these past few years to acquire an education. Katherine and I said some rather flattering things about you and concluded that you're going to go far in this world.

My best wishes to you for a bright and happy future.

Fondly,

————

Dear Mr. Rochester,

Congratulations on your election to the Thornfield School Board. I hope that after running such a vigorous and inspiring campaign you still have enough energy to carry out some of your sound and needed ideas.

Be assured of our continued support, and do not hesitate to call on us if we can do anything to help.

With best wishes,

———

Dear Ms. Hubbard,

Congratulations on an outstanding first year at Grattan Public Relations, Inc. A growing company like ours needs and appreciates people with your energy, expertise, and intuition. We are all predicting a brilliant future for you.

Congratulations and best wishes.

Sincerely,

———

Dear Helen and Arthur,

So little Laura has arrived at last. It has been such a long process, and I know it's been hard for you wondering if there would ever be an end to the red tape and waiting. But all that's over now, and the three of you can begin your life together.

From what I hear, this is definitely an adoption made in heaven. I know that Laura will add a great deal to the joy you two already find in each other.

With every good wish,

———

See also: APPRECIATION, EMPLOYMENT, FAMILY, GOODWILL, RESPONSES, SALES, WEDDINGS

FIFTEEN

LETTERS THAT SERVE AS CONTRACTS

The degree of miscommunication regarding what's been agreed upon in a business deal tends to increase in direct proportion to the amount of money involved.
—ROBERT J. RINGER

A letter can serve as a short, informal contract. Whether you need an attorney to check such letters depends on the complexity of the contract and the possible negative outcomes if it is poorly written.

Contract Letters Deal with

- agreements
- cancellations of agreements/contracts
- changes in terms
- leases
- rentals
- work orders

How to Say It

- Identify the nature of the contract in a subject line ("Re: Tuckpointing at 1711 Grismer Avenue").
- Begin with a phrase such as "This letter will serve as a contract between . . ."
- Give names and addresses of both parties to the agreement or contract.

- State what each party will give and receive.
- Specify dates by which the work must be completed and by which payment must be received.
- Mention whether and under what conditions the contract may be canceled.
- Specify date by which you expect the letter to be signed and returned.
- Leave lines and blank spaces at the bottom for both parties to sign and date the letter.

What Not to Say

- Don't include anything that doesn't bear on the contract; this is a focused document.
- Don't use legal-sounding terminology to make a contract look more legal (unless you are a lawyer). Use simple, standard English to avoid later charges that the other party "didn't understand" part of the contract.

Tips on Writing

■ Before writing, list all factors that will protect your agreement (for example, time limits, price ceilings, independent inspector). Have someone familiar with the situation double-check it for you.

■ Don't be afraid to write as though you were speaking. Use personal pronouns and ordinary grammar and sentence structure ("I promise to . . . in exchange for . . ."). On the other hand, maintain a businesslike tone to inspire confidence and to strengthen the letter's use as a contract.

■ The main body of the contract can be as short as a paragraph or long enough to be divided into many paragraphs. In the latter case, organize the information into clear, logical units.

Special Situations

■ If timing is important to your agreement, contract, or the cancellation of either, send your letter return receipt requested so that you can verify the date that the letter was received. If your lease requires you to give thirty days' notice, you will be glad to have a receipt stating that the notice was received within the time limit.

■ When submitting a proposal that you expect to be accepted, turn it into a contract or binding agreement by adding at the bottom, "Approved by [signature] on [date] by [printed name and title]."

■ When lending money to family or friends, all parties will benefit from having a letter contract spelling out amounts, dates, and responsibilities.

Format

■ All contracts and letters dealing with contracts are typed on business letterhead, personal letterhead stationery, or good bond stationery.

■ Forms are used when your business habitually contracts for the same kind of work.

WORDS

agreement	conditions	negotiation	transaction
arrangement	confirm	obligations	understanding
assure	conform	provisions	underwrite
bind	consent	settlement	verify
certify	endorse	stipulation	warrant
clauses	guarantee	terms	

PHRASES

agreed-to terms	mutual satisfaction
articles of the agreement	on condition that
as of the agreed-upon date	please sign and date
comply with	reach an understanding
considered complete when	return this letter by
effective as of/until	terms listed below
in return, you agree to	

SENTENCES

Enclosed is a check for $500, which will serve as earnest money for the purchase of apartment #37 in the 131 Park Drive building.

In the event of disagreement about the quality of the work, the dispute will be submitted to independent arbitration with costs being shared equally by both parties.

Note: This contract may be withdrawn by us if not accepted within 10 days.

Paragraph N of the contract is irrelevant to the matter at hand; please delete it and initial and return this letter.

The enclosed forward currency contract constitutes an agreement to deliver or receive a present stated amount of currency at a future specified date.

This letter serves as a contract between Madge Allen and Cain & Sons for sheetrock and plaster repair to the property at 35 James Court, with the following conditions and specifications.

This letter will serve as an informal agreement between us covering the period from January 1, 2010, to December 31, 2011, for the following services.

PARAGRAPHS

We will pay the mortgage payments on your town house from now until Simon graduates next June. Based on Hatty's job, the two of you will pay the Homeowners Association monthly fee, your utilities, and other housing-related expenses. When Simon becomes employed and your incomes stabilize, we'll discuss selling the town house to you on a contract for deed basis. When you eventually sell it, we expect to receive the $45,000 we have put into it plus a percentage of the appreciation of the town house's value (if it has appreciated 25 percent we will receive $45,000 + 25 percent of that amount).

I am happy to lend you the money to buy the truck. As we discussed, you will repay the $9,000 loan over a period of 36 months in the amount of $250 per month. There will be no interest. Please sign and date the second copy of this letter and return it to me.

I agree to translate your Moroccan contracts, letters, faxes, and other messages for the fee of $35 per hour. I further agree to complete the outstanding translations by February 10. You will pay messenger service fees between your office and mine, parking fees for consultations at your offices, and postage for mail or overnighting services.

Acceptance of contract: The above prices, specifications, and conditions are satisfactory and are hereby accepted. You are authorized to do the work as specified. Payment will be made upon completion. Date of acceptance: May 6, 2010. Authorized signature: Bernard Boweri

SAMPLE LETTERS

Dear Mr. Bowling,

As required by our lease, we hereby give you thirty days' notice of our intention to move from Apartment 2 at 619 Fourth Street.

Please call any evening after 6:00 p.m. to let us know when you need to show the apartment.

Our rent deposit of $450 will need to be refunded to us as we have not damaged the apartment in any way during our tenancy.

We have enjoyed our two years here very much, and will be sorry to move.

Sincerely yours,

―――――

Dear Ms. Hart:

Pryke Financial Services Inc. will be happy to act as Investment Adviser to the Collins Foundation and, as such, will assist with cash management and investment of foundation funds with the exception of the initial investment of the bond issue proceeds from certain bond issues.

We agree to provide the following services:

1. A complete review and analysis of the Collins Foundation's financial structure and conditions.
2. The preparation of written investment objectives outlining preferable investments, portfolio goals, risk limits, and diversification possibilities.
3. The establishment of preferred depository or certificate arrangements with banks or savings and loans.
4. Soliciting bids for guaranteed investment agreements.
5. Monitoring fund transfers, verifying receipt of collateral, completing documentation.
6. Working with a governmental securities dealer to execute governmental security transactions.
7. Meeting with your treasurer and financial adviser periodically and with your board of directors as requested.
8. Providing monthly portfolio status reports with sufficient detail for accounting and recording purposes.

Pryke Financial Services Inc. will submit quarterly statements for services. Our fees will be billed in advance and calculated by multiplying .000375 times the Collins Foundation's invested portfolio at the beginning of each calendar quarter (.0015 annually). Fees will be adjusted at the end of each quarter to reflect the rate times the average invested balance for the previous quarter. Adjustments will be included in the next billing.

Fees can be reviewed and adjusted annually on the anniversary date of this contract.

This agreement will run from June 1, 2010, through June 1, 2011, but may be canceled by either party without cause with thirty days' written notice.

Sincerely,
Grace Bloom
President

The above agreement is accepted by the Collins Foundation (blanks for date, signatures, titles).

Dear Mr. Golspie,

This letter will serve as an informal agreement between us. On Feb. 7 from 4:00–5:00 p.m. you agree to provide entertainers for my daughter's birthday party consisting of one clown, one magician, and one facepainter. I understand that the clown and magician portion of the entertainment will last about 20 minutes, and the facepainter will remain for the rest of the hour.

I agree to pay you a $50 deposit (check enclosed) and the remaining $200 on Feb. 7. As requested, a room will be available for your use. Also enclosed is a detailed map with directions to our home.

We're all looking forward to this, adults as well as children!

———

See also: ACCEPTANCES, ACKNOWLEDGMENTS, ADJUSTMENTS, ORDERS

SIXTEEN

COVER LETTERS

It is estimated that the average piece of business correspondence gets less than thirty seconds of the reader's attention. Even a truly great cover letter will not get much more.
—MARTIN YATE

Cover letters (also called transmittal letters) accompany résumés, application forms, manuscripts, documents, product literature, payments, charitable contributions, contracts, reports, samples, data, and other materials.

They may be as short as two sentences, telling what is enclosed and why, or as long as two pages, highlighting important points in the enclosures, explaining something that is not immediately obvious, or developing a sales message to accompany the report, sample, document, information, or package.

The main purpose of the cover letter is to direct the reader quickly and persuasively to the enclosed materials.

Distinct from a cover letter, the cover sheet accompanies a fax and lists the person sending the fax, the person receiving it, the fax number, and the number of pages being faxed (see FAXES).

Cover Letters Accompany

- application forms
- brochures/booklets/catalogs/pamphlets (see SALES)
- checks unaccompanied by statements or invoices
- contracts/agreements
- contributions to charitable causes
- documents

- faxes (see FAXES)
- information/instructions
- manuscripts
- product literature (see SALES)
- proposals
- questionnaires
- résumés
- samples (see SALES)
- surveys

How to Say It

- Address your letter to a specific person.
- State what is enclosed, attached, or mailed under separate cover. If there are several items, list them. Give number and type of items ("three brochures"), amount of payment, or other descriptive information.
- Mention why you're sending the material (in response to a request, to introduce the person to a new product, for their information).
- If necessary, explain what the item is and how to interpret or use it.
- Summarize the main points of the enclosure, highlight strong qualifications on your résumé, or otherwise orient the reader toward the most important issues of your material.
- Tell what response you're expecting from the other person or what future action you'll be taking.
- Include your name, address, telephone number, e-mail address, and fax number.
- Close with an expression of appreciation or a forward-looking statement.

What Not to Say

- Don't duplicate the enclosed material. Summarizing a document or mentioning the salient points of a contract is helpful, but repeating sentences and paragraphs may lead the reader to skip over those parts later.
- Don't close on a weak note. Words like "hope," "wish," "if," "should," "could," and "might" signal a lack of confidence ("If you wish, I could come for an interview at your convenience"; "Call me if you're interested").
- Don't try to attract attention with "cute" stationery, humor, multiple question marks or exclamation marks, smiley faces, or other gimmicks. You want to personalize your letter and make it stand out, but there's a fine line between an enthusiastic, confident letter and one that makes the reader wince. If

you're in any doubt as to which your letter is, ask someone to evaluate it for you.

Tips on Writing

■ Cover letters aren't needed for routine orders, payments, shipments, recommendations, references, or when the recipient has requested or is expecting your enclosure. Include a cover letter when the materials are not expected, do not speak clearly for themselves, or benefit from an accompanying persuasive message.

■ Double-check names, titles, and addresses for accuracy; this is crucial when applying for a position or sending a manuscript to an editor.

■ Be brief. Shakespeare's advice was to use "few words, but to effect." Except when the cover letter is a sales letter accompanying samples, product literature, or catalogs, it is only a side dish, not the main course. A good cover letter is usually not more than one page long (five or six paragraphs) and it will make the reader want to set it aside quickly in order to get to the enclosure.

■ Cover letters are exquisitely clean and attractive, with generous margins and no spelling, grammar, or usage errors. "The old aphorisms are basically sound. First impressions *are* lasting." (Jessie Fauset)

■ In *Cover Letters That Will Get You the Job You Want* (Better Way Books, 1993) Stanley Wynnett says, "The last two words of every cover letter I have ever written are *thank you*." Some authorities think that it is presumptuous to say thank you in advance, that it is trite, and that it signals the end of an exchange rather than an intermediate step. However, few people object to being thanked, so use your own judgment.

■ For more assistance with cover letters, see the excellent *Cover Letters That Knock 'Em Dead* by Martin Yate, 7th ed. (Adams Media Corporation, 2006) and *Cover Letters* by Taunee Besson, 2nd ed. (John Wiley & Sons, 1996). For cover letters that accompany résumés, see *The Perfect Cover Letter* by Richard H. Beatty, 3rd ed. (John Wiley & Sons Inc., 2003) and for cover letters that accompany manuscript submissions, see *How to Write Attention-Grabbing Query & Cover Letters* by John Wood (Writer's Digest Books, 1996).

Special Situations

■ A well-written cover letter for your résumé is a powerful selling instrument. "Very seldom will you write a letter more important to you than that accompanying a résumé." (Margaret McCarthy) Open by mentioning the person who referred you, the ad you're responding to, or something complimentary about the company you're applying to (and the more specific you are about what you like about the company the more effective it is). Identify the position or kind of work you're applying for. Emphasize how your qualifications match those the company is seeking (but don't repeat phrases or dates or specific material from the résumé). Don't focus on what you want, but generate interest in you by telling how you can contribute to the company. Don't write more than a page; you may want to include everything, but a long cover letter is off-putting to a busy person and your résumé may not get read at all. Don't send a one-size-fits-all cover letter. Tailor each letter to a specific company; recipients often look to see if there is anything related to their company; few are impressed by mass-produced letters. Close by requesting an interview, which is the purpose of your cover letter and résumé: "I will call you next week to arrange an interview appointment after you have had a chance to review my résumé"; "I look forward to meeting with you to discuss the match between your requirements and my qualifications." See APPLICATIONS for additional ideas for writing the cover letter.

■ When sending a cover letter by e-mail, you may want to include the résumé or other material in the body of the e-mail below the "cover" letter instead of appending it as an attachment. Some people distrust attachments because of the possibility of viruses. For this reason, avoid attaching photos, writing samples, or other materials. Indicate instead that they are available upon request. The subject line of the e-mail should state briefly and explicitly the main point: "Application for Human Resources Opening" or "Response to Ad for Mosquito Inspectors." Include your contact information in your cover letter as well as repeating it below your signature line. Busy people sometimes don't look any further for your telephone or fax number. Because e-mails tend to be more error-prone than letters, print your message and proofread it before hitting Send.

■ The cover letter you send to an editor with a manuscript is brief. Its main purpose is to introduce your submission (type of book or article, title, word count) and yourself (past publishing credits or credentials for writing the material). A good cover letter includes a tightly written paragraph that reads like catalog copy. Your best writing skills are used to describe or give the flavor of your book or article. Always (that's "always") include a SASE and close with a courtesy.

■ The cover letter that accompanies a report identifies the report by title; mentions why it was prepared, who authorized it, and who wrote it; provides a summary (based on the report's introduction, abstract, or summary). If the report is formal, the transmittal letter is placed after the title page and before the table of contents.

■ A note that accompanies a gift has a purpose similar to that of a cover letter. Identify the enclosure ("a little something for your birthday") and include your greetings and best wishes. To accompany a corporate gift, mention the occasion for the gift, if there is one (service anniversary, completion of a major project). Be specific about the person's work, talent, anniversary, or award: "I'm particularly grateful because . . ." or "You've been a delight to work with because . . ." or "Your work has meant a lot to the company because . . ." Relate an anecdote, a shared memory, or reflection that bolsters your good wishes. End your note with pleasant wishes for continued success or with some forward-looking remark about your future work association. The same type of note is written when the gift is being sent to the person from the shipper or from an Internet company, except that the writer mentions sending "a little something" or "something I thought you'd like" or "something for your desk" and, when possible, estimates when it will arrive. The impact of a corporate gift is magnified one-hundredfold when it is accompanied by a handwritten note of appreciation. Employees who receive such a note from a busy executive feel valued in a personal, memorable way.

■ A cover letter accompanying a sample or product literature is more properly considered a sales letter (see SALES).

Format

■ Except for notes accompanying gifts or the most informal transmittals, cover letters are typed on business letterhead or on memo paper (for in-house materials or for those outside people and firms with which you have a high-volume and casual correspondence).

■ When applying for a position, use plain white, gray, or beige letterhead or high-quality stationery. Avoid gimmicky paper, fonts, colors, and graphics.

■ When asked to fax or e-mail a résumé, you will also be faxing or e-mailing your cover letter. In the case of a fax, write it as you would a regular letter on letterhead stationery and use the "fine resolution" setting to ensure that it is as attractive and readable as possible when it arrives.

■ Use form cover letters to accompany requested information. To give them a more personal appearance, use good quality paper, address the person by name (instead of "Dear Friend" or "Dear Subscriber"), and sign each letter individually. For potentially important customers, write a personal cover letter.

WORDS

announce	enclosed	policy	provisions
attached	illustrate	project	report
deliver	notice	proposal	summarize
document	outline	prospectus	terms
draft			

PHRASES

acquaint you with	for further information
as promised	here are/is
at your request	I am sending you
brochure that presents/details/ describes/outlines/explains	if you need/want additional information
call with questions	I'm also enclosing
complimentary copy	in response to your advertisement
direct your attention to	please note that
enclosed is/are	rough draft

SENTENCES

After you have reviewed the enclosed proposal, please call me (or Bess Beynon if I'm out of town) to discuss it.

As a June graduate of Cleveland College with a BA in business, I am looking for employment and wanted to check first with you because I so enjoyed working for The Clement Group as an intern in your marketing department.

As you will see from my résumé, I have a great deal of experience in program development, administration, contract development, and budget planning.

At your request, I am enclosing three copies of the Empire State Film Festival program.

Complete medical records from the office of Dr. Anna Lakington for Mr. Barnabas Holly are enclosed.

Enclosed are copies of the recorded deeds and easements for the above-referenced properties.

Enclosed is a completed application form—please note my four years' experience as an installation technician.

Enclosed is a copy of the survey on equipment rental in the six-county metro area.

Enclosed is a quitclaim deed conveying the new Fort Road from Faulkland County to the City of Sheridan.

Enclosed is the requested report on the Heat Treatment Seminar, held July 14-17.

Here are the molding samples we'd like you to evaluate.

I am enclosing the damaged belt from my twenty-year-old Bannister vacuum in the hopes that you can locate a replacement for it.

I am interested in your part-time position for a truck unloader.

I am responding to your advertisement in Sunday's paper for a senior analyst programmer.

I am writing to introduce myself and inquire about openings for a Tae Kwon Do instructor.

I believe I am well qualified to apply for your opening for a water quality extension agent.

I'm sending you a copy of the article on the Minnesota Twins that we discussed last week.

In response to your ad for a website producer/editor, I'm enclosing my résumé, which details my considerable experience in this area.

I understand you are looking for a form tool grinder.

I will telephone your assistant Monday morning to see if you can schedule an interview next week to discuss the position.

I would like to bring my commercial interior design skills to work for Engelred Offices Inc.

Ms. DeGroot suggested I contact you about the development grant writer and board liaison position.

Please sign both copies of the enclosed letter of agreement and return them to us.

Prentice Page suggested I write you about the wallpapering specialist position.

Thank you for your patience—enclosed please find the replacement part for your Noyes Intercommunication System.

Under separate cover I'm sending you samples of our new line of Natural Solution products for the hair.

We are pleased to send you the set of deck plans you requested.

Will you please look over the enclosed rough draft of your will and let me know if it needs any changes or corrections?

I note that you are seeking a warehouse manager with five years of supervisory or managing experience and five years of experience in shipping, receiving, and inventory control. This almost precisely describes my qualifications.

Enclosed is a sample (ref. #4467-AB) of the film that Alwyn Tower and I discussed with you last Thursday. Please keep in mind that the sample was produced under laboratory conditions. If you have any questions about this material or variations of it, please call Alwyn or me.

Enclosed is an Agreement and Release between you and Lakely Associates, which gives the terms of the settlement for the redevelopment of your well. When you sign the Agreement and present written proof of the adjudication of the well to Lakely Associates, we will send you a check for the agreed-upon amount.

Our check for $15,223.92 is enclosed and constitutes full payment for all items listed on Invoice #68-331982. Thank you for your help in getting the air conditioners to us so quickly.

Today I am shipping approximately one square foot each of 0.090 to 0.100 inch thick sheets of Fe-3% Si (hot-rolled) and IF (niobium-containing interstitial-free; hot-rolled, one sheet, cold-rolled, one sheet). The rolling direction is marked on each sheet.

I am currently employed in an engineering environment by a large independent transportation firm, but I am interested in making a career change into the investment/financial services field. I have recently obtained my CFP designation and hope to find a position as a broker trainee. I am enclosing my résumé for your review and consideration for such a position.

Enclosed is the complete report on the foreign language survey conducted last fall. Vice-presidents and personnel directors of one hundred of the nation's largest corporations were asked which foreign language would be most important for a successful business career during the next twenty years. The results may surprise you!

Thank you for your interest in Griffiths Collar and Shirt Company. I'm enclosing a packet of materials that will describe our range of products and services. I will call you next week to see if you have any questions and to discuss how we might be of help to you. You are, of course, always welcome to visit our offices and factory here in Lycurgus.

You've been buying Ponderevo's Cough Lintus and our line of Mogg's soap for years. Now we proudly announce a new product that is sure to become a household word: Tono-Bungay! Enclosed are several samples. Try Tono-Bungay yourself and share some with friends. Our Order Line is available to you 24 hours a day, and orders are shipped within 48 hours.

The attached set of project plans covers work through the end of 2012. The plans have been generated in consultation with each of the key people involved. We expect to review progress the first of each month and to adjust the work accordingly. You will note that we are dependent on the work of others in the office and that they are in turn dependent on us. Please review the scheduled work and give me your comments.

SAMPLE LETTERS

Dear Ms. Lownie:

As an editor with eighteen years' experience, I think I may be well qualified for the position of Editor advertised in *Engineering Today*. You will see from the enclosed résumé that I have edited both technical and trade publications. In each case, I was able to raise the standards of the editorial content, increase ad sales (in one case by 120 percent), and attract new subscribers in significant numbers.

Having met and exceeded my goals in my present position and knowing that the assistant editor here is more than capable of taking over, I want to challenge myself with a more demanding position. *Engineering Today* appeals to me very much as this type of challenge.

Thank you for considering my application.

Sincerely,

————

Dear Customer,

Thank you for writing for your free sample of the "world's toughest disposable rubber gloves!" Please read through the enclosed flyer for the many ways you can use these gloves to save your hands from damaging liquids and abrasives. Then go ahead and try the last word in convenience, comfort . . . and toughness! You will never want to use any other glove again.

We would appreciate hearing your comments on the gloves after trying them. Enclosed is a postage-paid reply postcard.

————

Dear Isabella and John,

Enclosed are photocopies of the original Last Wills and Testaments that I have drafted upon your request. Please examine these copies carefully and then phone or write my office. If the contents of the Wills meet with your approval, make arrangements with my secretary, Judith Trevisa, to come to my office and formally execute the original Wills.

If there are any changes or corrections you wish to make to your Wills, please call or write me and I will be happy to discuss them with you.

Best regards,

———

Dear G. E. Challenger,

I was intrigued with the ad in Sunday's paper seeking someone experienced with high pressure liquid chromatography—first, because there aren't that many openings in this field and, second, because my experience and background match almost precisely what you appear to need.

I was further intrigued when I called the number given in the ad and discovered that this is your company. I have never forgotten several of your research papers that were required reading when I was in college.

After you have a chance to read my résumé, I hope you will agree that an interview might be interesting for us both.

———

Dear Kurt,

Enclosed is a copy of the letter of recommendation I wrote for you. I've sent the original on to the academic dean in the envelope you provided. I thought you might like a copy for your files.

I am so pleased you asked me to do this. I just hope I was of some small help. Let me know as soon as you hear the good news!

With best wishes,

———

Dear Dr. Cheesewright,

Your office manager, Ms. Sherriff, mentioned to me that you might soon have an opening for a dental hygienist. She suggested I send you my résumé.

You may not remember, but I was a patient of yours when I was growing up here, and even as a youngster I thought it would be "fun" to work in your office! I've been living in Chicago for the past ten years, but am planning to move back here because of my father's health.

After you've had a chance to look at my résumé, you can reach me at 312-555-1234 to schedule an interview.

———

Dear Maria,

I received the film sample (#18-1A) from Julian Silvercross and am impressed. We are excited about the performance improvement that we think this technology may offer us. As Nancy Sibley explained to you on the phone, we are interested in using it for our silicon detector assembly, which is an integral part of sensors used for various industrial purposes.

I'm enclosing three of these detector assemblies for your review. Feel free to dissect them.

We ask that you respect the confidentiality of our product and of our interest in your film.

Please give me a call after you have had a chance to look at the sensors.

Yours truly,

———————

Dear Mr. Oakley:

Enclosed is your copy of the contract between Sullivan Press and Eaglesham Publications. Several of the clauses are being revised, and I will see that you receive the amended version as soon as it is ready.

If you have any questions about your obligations under the contract, please check with our attorney, Mary Jane Reed, in the Legal Services Department.

Sincerely yours,

———————

See also: APPLICATIONS, QUERIES, RÉSUMÉS, SALES

SEVENTEEN

LETTERS ABOUT CREDIT

The world is a puzzling place today. All these banks sending us credit cards. . . .
Imagine a bank sending credit cards to two ladies over a hundred years old!
What are those folks thinking?
—SARAH AND A. ELIZABETH DELANY

Much of the paperwork involved in obtaining and granting credit has been standardized and codified into forms reflecting federal, state, or institutional rules and guidelines. However, nonroutine matters require carefully written letters.

Letters About Credit Include

- approving loans
- canceling an account
- collecting past-due accounts (see COLLECTION)
- congratulations: fine record/payment (see also SALES)
- credit bureaus: letters to and from
- delinquent account
- denying/refusing credit or loan applications (see REFUSALS)
- errors in credit history
- explaining credit/loan refusals/conditions
- extending payment deadlines
- family members and friends: lending/borrowing
- inviting new accounts/reviving inactive accounts
- obtaining one's own credit history
- requesting credit/bankcard/loan

How to Say It

- When asking a credit bureau for a copy of your credit report: give name, address, social security number, and telephone number. Use letterhead stationery or enclose a business card to substantiate that you are the subject of the check. When requesting a credit report on another person: supply the person's name, address, and social security number; give a reason for asking (you are renting property to the person, selling them a car, cosigning a contract for deed with them).

- When writing an individual or a business to ask for a credit reference, give the name and address of the person under consideration, request any pertinent credit information, explain briefly why you want it ("we are discussing a partnership"), state that you will treat the information confidentially, express your appreciation for the information, and enclose a self-addressed stamped envelope for their reply. In some cases, mention how you were referred to them (for example, by the person under consideration). Ask specific questions: How long have you known the person? In what capacity? What kinds of credit have you extended? What is the current balance? The person's payment pattern? How long have they been employed there? What is their income?

- When requesting correction of an inaccurate credit record, identify yourself by full name and address, state the incorrect portions of the record, and explain why they are incorrect. Include copies of documents (statements, loan papers, tax returns, paycheck stubs) substantiating your position. Ask that a corrected copy of the report be sent to you. Thank the person; they most likely were not responsible for the errors and can, in fact, be helpful to you.

- When denying credit or a loan: thank the person for their interest; express regret that you are unable to extend credit; assure them that you considered their request thoroughly; suggest an alternate course of action (layaway, paying cash, smaller loan) that will allow a continued relationship; encourage them to reapply later. If questioned further, list your credit criteria, mentioning the problems presented by the person's credit background, and telling what sources you used to determine creditworthiness. For smaller, more routine credit requests, use forms stating simply, "Your request for a loan has been denied," followed by a check-off list of possible reasons: length of employment, lack of information, excessive credit obligations, newcomer to the area with no credit record, poor payment record, garnishment. Leave a blank to fill in the name of the credit bureau where you obtained your information.

- When approving a loan application or granting credit, state that you've approved the request, indicate the amount approved and the effective date, and explain credit or loan payoff procedures. Enclose forms needing signatures along with instructions on how to complete them. Welcome new customers to your lending institution or business, express appreciation for their business, and suggest they bring all their credit needs to you.

What Not to Say

- Don't write anything that cannot be documented. Phrases like "misses payments" or "habitually late with payments" must be substantiated by records of such payment patterns.

Tips on Writing

■ Credit matters are confidential. Take every precaution to safeguard the credit information you give or receive.

■ Accuracy is essential when providing information on someone's credit history. Double-check your facts as well as spellings of names and account numbers.

■ Be tactful. Even people with poor credit histories want to hear good of themselves and often feel they are doing a decent job given their circumstances. In her 1923 book, Mary Owens Crowther writes, "Tactless credit handling is the most effective way known to dissipate good-will."

Special Situations

■ Loans between family members or friends often come with hidden financial and personal costs. When requesting a loan, be businesslike and factual: tell how much you need and why; suggest a repayment plan and the amount of interest you will pay. Always offer the other person a face-saving "out" ("You may have financial problems of your own, for all I know," "This may not be a good time for you," or "You may disapprove, on principle, of loans between friends"). Reassure them that there is no reason to feel guilty or uncomfortable about turning you down. Do not beg or play on their sympathies; pressuring a person who is not willing to lend you money won't get you the money—and it will lose you a friend. When refusing a request for a personal loan, be brief: "I wish I could help you, but it's not possible just now." Don't overexplain or apologize or hedge. If you like, close by asking if there is some other way you could help. When granting a request for a loan from a friend or family member, put it in writing: state the loan amount, the terms and dates of repayment, the interest, and any other information. Send two copies of your letter and ask that the person sign and date one and return it to you. To remind a friend or family member of an overdue loan, be gentle at first: "I know how busy you've been . . ."; "Did you forget about . . ."; "Didn't we agree you'd repay the loan December 1?" If you write a second time, include a photocopy of your original agreement letter and word your expectation of getting your money back more strongly.

■ If you can't make a loan or installment credit payment on time, write the company at once. Apologize for being overdue, tell them you intend to pay as soon as possible, and enclose whatever portion of the balance you can. If you have a good reason for being overdue (illness, layoff), mention it. Otherwise, don't go into lengthy excuses; your creditor is more interested in knowing that you are taking responsibility for the account.

Format

■ There are virtually no handwritten letters dealing with credit matters. Routine correspondence may be handled with form letters. Others will be typed on business letterhead.

WORDS

application	default	lessor	reimburse
approval	finance	lien	repay
arrangement	funds	loan	requirements
balance	guarantee	mortgage	verify
collateral	installment	nonpayment	
creditworthy	IOU	receipt	
debt	lender	regretfully	

PHRASES

after careful consideration

although you have only occasional payment problems

apply for credit privileges

as much as we would like to extend credit to you

cannot justify approval

cash basis only

consistently on-time credit payments

credit application/history/record/ standing/rating/limit

current/up-to-date financial statement

due to a rise in the number of uncollectable past-due accounts

due to cash flow difficulties

excellent credit rating

financial difficulties/needs/services

in checking your credit background

it is our policy

I understand and appreciate your position, but

late payments

must delay payment

one of our credit requirements is

pattern of late payments

pay in advance/in full

pleased to be able to accommodate you

poor payment history

preferred customer

regret that we are unable to

responsible use of credit

review of our files

steady credit payments

subject only to normal credit requirements

unable to accommodate you at this time

unpaid balance

we are happy/pleased to approve

will you please run a credit check on

SENTENCES

Because our inquiries disclosed a number of past-due and unpaid accounts, we are unable to extend the line of credit you requested.

Could you see your way clear to lending me $200 for approximately three weeks, until I receive my income tax refund (enclosed is a copy of my return, showing the amount I will be receiving)?

Cressida Mary MacPhail, 1968 Taylor Avenue, Bretton, IN 47834, has applied to the Maxwell Credit Union for a loan, and gave us your name as a reference.

Eileen Schwartz has had an excellent credit history with this company, and we recommend her highly as a credit customer.

I appreciate your courtesy in allowing me to pay off the balance of my account in small installments.

I'm writing to notify you of an error in our credit history and to request an immediate correction.

I would appreciate your raising my credit limit from $10,000 to $20,000.

Please close my Fortis-Pryde account, effective immediately.

Please keep us in mind for your other credit needs.

The credit bureau cites repeated credit delinquencies.

We are pleased to report that our credit dealings with Angela Crossby have been excellent.

We are puzzled that our application for a home equity line of credit has been refused—please send us a copy of our credit report, if that was the problem, or your explanation for this refusal.

We are unable to furnish you with any current credit information on Emerson-Toller—they have not been a credit customer of ours for over ten years.

We expect to be making large purchases of office furniture from your firm as well as routine purchases of office supplies and would like to open a credit account with you.

We have run into some difficulties checking the references you supplied.

We note a persistent pattern of nonpayment in your credit history.

We suggest you reapply for the loan once you have resolved some of these problems.

We will appreciate any credit information you can give us about Walter Tillotson.

PARAGRAPHS

Enclosed please find a check for $457.32, which will bring my account up to date. I am sorry that I let the account become past due. I expect to keep it current in the future.

I would like to see the credit record you currently have on me. I am applying for a second mortgage on my home next month, and would not want to be unpleasantly surprised by anything that may be on file. Thank you.

I am pleased to report that we were able to approve your loan request for the amount of $5,000. A check is enclosed, along with a payment booklet and a packet of payment envelopes. Please read your repayment schedule carefully.

We are sorry to report that your loan application has not been approved. Our decision was based primarily on information received from the Carnaby Reporting Services credit bureau. You may want to look at their record on you to verify that it is correct. If it is, we suggest working with a financial counselor, something that has been helpful to several of our customers. We will be happy to review your loan application at a later date if your circumstances change.

In order to set up a credit account for you with Copper Beeches, we need the following information: company name and tax identification number; a copy of your annual report; the names of banks with which you currently have accounts and those account numbers; names and phone numbers of at least three companies from which you have purchased materials in the past six months. We appreciate your business and look forward to serving you.

Because of an electrical fire at our main plant three months ago, we have been experiencing some temporary financial difficulties and have fallen behind on our payments to you. We expect to rectify the situation by the end of the year. In the meantime, please accept the enclosed check on account. We thank you for your understanding.

We must report that our business experiences with the Baroness de la Cruchecassée have been less than satisfactory. Over a period of eighteen months we have failed to collect anything on a fairly large outstanding balance. We trust you will keep this information confidential.

SAMPLE LETTERS

TO: Dudley Credit Data
FROM: Eustace Landor, Landor First Banks
DATE: September 3, 2010
RE: Edith Millbank

Will you please run a credit check for us on:

Edith Millbank
1844 Coningsby
Oswald, OH 45042
Social Security #000-00-0000

Ms. Millbank is taking out a loan application with us, and we wish to verify the information she has given us with regard to her credit history.

Thank you.

———

Dear Ms. Panzoust,

Thank you for your letter of March 16 requesting our opinion of the creditworthiness of Valmouth Fiber Arts.

We have had only the most limited business transactions with them and, since they have always been on a cash basis with us, we have no idea of their financial standing. I would not feel comfortable expressing an opinion on so little information.

I'm sorry I couldn't have been more helpful.

———

Re: Loan #211925
Dear Ms. Parry-Lewis,

We have reviewed your request for a renewal of your home equity loan, as required by Raine National Bank every five years. In addition to a pattern of late payments and frequent disagreements about interest payments, we find that your current financial obligations seem excessive for your stated income. As a result, we are unable to grant you a renewal.

We would be happy to serve your banking needs in the future. If you meet our criteria for a home equity loan renewal in six months, please reapply and we will waive the new-loan fees.

Sincerely,

———————

Dear Michael Dunne,

We noticed that you have not used your Pearson Charge Card for some time now. If you do not use it before it expires in March of 2011, we will be unable to issue you a new card for the following year.

We would be sorry to lose you as a good charge customer, but we think that you would lose too—lose out on such benefits as the $250,000 flight insurance that is yours every time you charge an airline ticket on your card . . . the twice-yearly newsletter that saves you money by offering discounts on motels, car rentals, and vacation packages . . . the low annual rate . . . the variable interest rate . . . and the flexibility of a card that can be used at over 15,000 places of business.

We hope that you will rediscover the many uses and benefits of the versatile Pearson Charge Card!

Sincerely yours,

———————

See also: ACKNOWLEDGMENTS, ADJUSTMENTS, ANNOUNCEMENTS, APOLOGIES, COLLECTION, COMPLAINTS, ORDERS, REFUSALS, REQUESTS, RESPONSES, THANK YOU

EIGHTEEN

LETTERS OF DISAGREEMENT

*Anyone who thinks there aren't two sides to every argument
is probably in one.*
—THE COCKLE BUR

There are people who thrive on conflict, and there are those who spend enormous energy avoiding it. If they live in the real world, both types will sooner or later have to write a letter about a disagreement. Disagreement is neither good nor bad, but the way you handle it affects subsequent events, feelings, and relationships.

Letters of Disagreement May Concern

- contracts
- decisions
- oral agreements
- payments
- personnel problems
- policies/programs/procedures/regulations
- property lines

How to Say It

- Refer to the previous correspondence or to the event responsible for the present letter.
- Outline the two opposing views or actions.
- Give clear (perhaps numbered) reasons for your stand, using statistics, quotations from an employee handbook, supportive anecdotal material,

or names of witnesses or others who agree with you (with their permission).

- If appropriate, suggest an intermediate stage of negotiation: a reply to specific questions in your letter; further research; a meeting between the two of you or with third parties present; visits to a lawyer, accountant, or other appropriate expert.
- If the disagreement has reached the stage where you can effectively do this, state clearly the outcome you desire.
- End with your best wishes for a solution acceptable to both of you and a reference to good future relations.

What Not to Say

- Don't put the person on the defensive. Use more "I" than "you" phrases ("you" statements tend to sound accusatory). Make sure your letter doesn't make the person feel bad, shamed, inept, or weak; people who have been made to feel small are not likely to give you what you want.
- Avoid language that escalates the situation ("ridiculous," "egregious," "brainless"). This is counterproductive as well as unconvincing. "Neither irony nor sarcasm is argument." (Rufus Choate) It also betrays vulnerability. "Strong and bitter words indicate a weak cause." (Victor Hugo)
- Avoid emotional statements. Concentrate on facts instead of feelings. For example, saying, "I don't feel this is fair" does not carry as much weight as saying, "I believe it is unfair that only one out of seven secretaries is consistently asked to work overtime—without overtime pay."

Tips on Writing

■ The tone of your letter can make all the difference between being heard and not being heard. Strive for a letter that is factual, dispassionate, considerate, and evenhanded.

■ Be clear about your goal. Before writing, think about the end of this sentence: "I want them to . . ." Do you want a rebate, an exchange, repairs? Do you want an apology, a corrected statement, a credit? Do you want to convince the person that their facts, statistics, opinions are wrong? Do you want something redone?

■ Help the other person save face. Set up the situation so that the person can do what you want in a way that makes them feel generous, gracious, powerful, and willing.

■ Although active voice is usually preferred to the passive voice, consider using the more tactful passive voice when involved in a disagreement. Instead of saying, "You did this," say, "This was done."

■ Examine your position for possible areas of negotiation. Can you trade one point for another? Can you accept anything less than what you originally wanted?

■ When writing to disapprove the passage of legislation, note whether the bill is state or federal and then write the appropriate lawmakers. Federal bills have numbers prefixed by HR (House Resolution) or SR (Senate Resolution). State bills are usually denoted HF (House File) and SF (Senate File).

Special Situations

■ You will handle most disagreements yourself or with the help of family or coworkers. However, in situations like the following you may want to consult with a lawyer: in marital separations where letters contain admissions, demands, or threats; where you need to reduce informal, oral agreements to written agreements; when family disagreements about an estate become heated; when you are being accused of something; when the disagreement escalates to threats of lawsuits.

■ Sometimes groups use letter-writing campaigns on controversial issues. A sample letter is distributed for proponents to copy over their own signature. When representatives are interested in the number of people on each side of an issue, such letter-writing campaigns have value. Most often, however, form letters do not get much attention. One well-written original letter will carry more weight with a lawmaker than a hundred form letters. Know when a group effort is effective and when it is not. "If you were the Establishment, which would you rather see coming in the door: one lion or five hundred mice?" (Florynce B. Kennedy)

■ When you write to lawmakers to inform them of your opinion on an issue, you often don't need to receive a three-page reply outlining their position—a position with which you're already familiar from the newspapers. In this case, end your letter with, "Please do not respond to this letter. I know your views; I wanted you to know mine."

Format

■ Letters dealing with business disagreements are typed on letterhead stationery.

■ When writing about personal disagreements, your letter will appear friendlier and a little more open to negotiation if you handwrite it. If you wish to appear firm and not open to negotiation, typing is best.

WORDS

argument	dilemma	friction	quarrel
break	disapprove	impasse	reconcile
conflict	displeased	incompatible	regrettable
contention	dispute	infuriated	rift
contradiction	dissatisfaction	irritating	stalemate
controversy	disturbing	misunderstanding	standstill
dead-end	estrangement	object	unfortunate
deadlock	faction	offense	unhappy
differ	feud	protest	

PHRASES

agree to differ/disagree

as I understand it

at cross-purposes

be at odds with

believe you should know that

bone of contention

bury the hatchet

come to terms

complicated situation

conduct an inquiry

difference of opinion

direct your attention to

disputed point

do a disservice to

fail to agree

I am convinced that

I assume/presume/think/have no doubt that

I have the impression that

in my estimation/judgment/opinion/view

in the best interests of

I take it that

it seems to me

matter/point in dispute/at issue/under discussion/in question

my information is

part company with

point of view

question at issue

register my opinion

strongly oppose

take into consideration

think differently

to my way of thinking

to the best of my knowledge

wonder if you are aware that

SENTENCES

Are we ready to put this to a vote?

Do you think it would help to call in an arbitrator?

Enclosed please find several abstracts that may be helpful.

I agree with the necessity of fundraising for the purchase and maintenance of band instruments, but I disagree with the fundraising program adopted for next year.

I am convinced that the passage of this bill would do more harm than good/ is not in the best interests of the state/would be a grave error.

I disagree with the store policy of filling prescriptions with generic drugs without notifying the customer.

I found the language and tone of your last letter completely unacceptable; please put us in touch with someone else in your organization who can handle this matter.

If you would like some background reading on this issue, I would be happy to furnish you with some.

I received your letter this morning and am sorry to hear that you cannot accept our terms.

Several of the points you mention are negotiable; some are not.

We are submitting this matter to an independent referee.

We still have one major area of disagreement.

What would make the situation more agreeable to you?

PARAGRAPHS

I realize that there is technically no more to be said about the Dillon-Reed merger, but I would like to state for the record that I strongly oppose the move. I refer you to the enclosed independent report that we commissioned from Elkus Inc. This is the classic situation where one owns a dog but persists in barking oneself. The Elkus people, acknowledged experts in the field, advised us against the merger. Do we have strong enough grounds for rejecting their conclusions? I think not.

I know we've talked about this until we're both blue in the face, but I feel strongly that Great-Aunt Elsie is not yet ready for a nursing home. It would make her unhappy and shorten her life to be placed in one prematurely. What changes would you need to see before you could feel comfortable about her remaining in her apartment?

My lawyer requested the addition of the following clause to the contract: "Clause S. This agreement will expire ten years from the date of execution." The clause does not appear in the final contract. I know this issue was in dispute at one time, but I understood that you had finally agreed to it. I am returning the unsigned contracts to you for correction.

We seem to be at an impasse on determining the boundary line between our properties. Would you be interested in sharing the costs of hiring a surveyor?

SAMPLE LETTERS

TO: Adrian Singleton
FROM: Herbert Fraide
DATE: November 3, 2011
RE: Reading for Young People Series

I am concerned about the narrow scope of our new series. Of the fifty stories to be included, fifty feature middle-class, white protagonists. All fifty are set in the United States. All fifty are domestic fiction dealing with fairly trivial school and neighborhood themes. I find the series unacceptably homogeneous—and, yes, boring. It cannot begin to respond to the varied experiences of our prospective readers. It also fails to conform to the company's stated guidelines on inclusiveness and global awareness.

Marianna Selby and I are 180 degrees apart on this issue, and find ourselves presently deadlocked. I told her I'd ask you to help us, either with a three-way discussion or by calling for a department meeting or with some other clarification procedure.

cc: Marianna Selby

———

Dear Senator Burrows,

I urge you to oppose the Television Soundtrack Copyright Reform Bill.

As you know, music performance rights for syndicated television programs are licensed in one of four ways: (1) a blanket license with a performing rights society; (2) a per program license; (3) a source license; or (4) a direct license. This bill would mandate that music performance rights for syndicated television programs be licensed in only one way, at the source in conjunction with all other broadcast rights for the program.

The current system has been used since the beginning of television and has been upheld in court challenges. It assures a fair return based on performance to composers and songwriters who create television music. The proponents of the bill have a heavy burden to demonstrate the need for Congress to interfere in the current system and mandate a single way of doing business.

They have not met their burden, and I oppose the legislation.

Sincerely,

———

Dear Ms. Burling-Ward:

I enjoy working for Stegner Publishing, and you in particular have been most helpful in introducing me to people and showing me around.

When I was interviewed for the job, Mr. Oliver consistently used the term "production editor," and the job duties he listed were those generally associated with the position of production editor.

During my three weeks on the job, I have done nothing but copyediting. After speaking with you yesterday and discovering that this was not just a training stage but my permanent position, I suspect there has been a misunderstanding.

I would like to meet with you and Mr. Oliver sometime soon to clarify this situation.

Sincerely,

———

Dear Nandie and Victor,

Our jazz trio has been so compatible and has had such a good time these last three years that I'm uncomfortable with our present disagreement. I think we're used to getting along and thus don't know how to handle it when we don't agree.

Here's my suggestion. Next Thursday night, instead of rehearsing, let's meet at Saduko's Restaurant for dinner. Each of us will bring three 3×5 cards with our reasons for changing the trio's name.

After a good meal and some nonwork conversation, we will exchange cards so that each of us is holding the three viewpoints. I hope we can then come to a good decision.

What do you think?

Angelo

———

Dear Mr. and Mrs. Archibald Craven,

Thank you for your letter of November 30, disputing the payment of interest charges on your "12-month interest-free" purchase of furniture from us.

When you purchased your sofa, chair, and ottoman last November 18, we offered to carry the full amount of the purchase, $1,574.97, interest-free for one year—and you accepted our offer. The terms of the offer were explained at that time.

Each month thereafter you received a statement from us, noting the amount of the original purchase, the accruing finance charges, and stating clearly, "If you pay the payoff amount by the expiration date listed below, you will be credited for the amount of interest accumulated on that purchase."

You did not pay the payoff amount by the expiration date of our agreement, November 19 of this year; thus you now owe the payoff amount plus the accrued interest of $272.61.

Please note that interest will continue to accrue until all charges are paid.

For further questions, call Mary Lennox in the Accounts Due Department at 800-555-1234.

———

See also: COMPLAINTS, NEIGHBORS, REFUSALS, SENSITIVE

NINETEEN

LETTERS TO THE EDITOR

It were not best that we should all think alike;
it is difference of opinion that makes horse-races.
—MARK TWAIN

Letters to the editor constitute some of people's favorite reading. Knowing this, almost every newspaper and periodical prints a limited number of letters in each issue. A daily newspaper publishes as many as 30 to 40 percent of the letters it receives; a national weekly newsmagazine publishes only 2 to 5 percent of its incoming letters. Fortunately, there are ways of increasing the chances of your letter being chosen for publication.

Write a Letter to the Editor When

- you agree or disagree with a story, article, news item, editorial stance, or other letter writer
- you have an opinion about a topic of current national or local interest
- you want to correct published information
- you want to reach a large number of people with information that you think would interest them

How to Say It

- In the first sentence, refer to the issue that prompted your letter ("the Nov. 1 editorial opposing a new hockey arena") so that readers know immediately what you're talking about.
- State your position ("I agree with," "I oppose," "I question").

- Briefly support, defend, or explain your position. Most publications have word limits for these letters; if you exceed them, editors may trim your letter in ways you don't like. Aim for around 100 to 300 words.
- Include facts (statistics, studies, articles, items of record, quotes) rather than feelings and impressions. If you have specific knowledge or a professional connection with an issue, mention it; this often makes publication likelier and your opinion more useful.
- Indicate what action, if any, you want readers to take (form neighborhood block watches, call legislators, boycott a product, sign a petition, stop littering).
- Close with a startling, memorable, or powerful sentence, if possible—something that makes the reader want to go back and read your letter again.
- Give your first and last name, or at least two initials and a last name, address, and daytime phone number. Sign your name. Almost all publications insist on this. When letters to the editor are signed by a number of people, usually only one or two of the names are published (followed by a note "and 16 others"); most publications prefer to use that space for opinions, not lists of names.

What Not to Say

- Don't begin your letter with, "You won't dare print this letter." Editors generally delete such sentences because, in fact, they dare to print a wide range of opinion, including letters critical of themselves.
- Avoid whining ("It's not fair," "It always happens to me"). It does not make interesting reading.
- Don't expect newspapers or magazines to print letters that are thinly disguised advertisements for your business or your group. If you want people to know about a nonprofit, community-wide event, editors are generally willing to include it in an events column.
- Avoid half-truths or inaccuracies. Letters are subject to editing for length, libel, good taste, newspaper style, and accuracy. Editors will check the facts in your letters.
- Don't write anything that can be proved malicious (even if it's true) and don't write anything that can't be proved (even if there's no intent to harm); publishers won't print anything libelous.
- Don't use threats, bullying language, pejorative adjectives ("stupid," "ridiculous," "redneck," "bleeding heart liberal"), or stereotypes ("what can you expect from a lawyer," "labor unions have always looked out for themselves first," "another anti-male feminist"). Certain readers will agree with your sentiments. Most, however, will see, quite properly, that such language

indicates a weak argument. Margaret Thatcher once said, "I always cheer up immensely if an attack is particularly wounding because I think, well, if they attack one personally, it means they have not a single political argument left."

- Don't end your letter with "Think about it!" One editor says this line shows up routinely in letters and is just as routinely deleted. If your letter appears on the opinion-editorial (op-ed) page, the implication is that you want people to think about it.
- Don't submit poetry, lost-and-found announcements, or personal messages ("I'm looking for descendants of Jenny Treibel").

Tips on Writing

■ Check the area near the letters-to-the-editor column for guidelines; most publications have requirements.

■ Address your letter "To the Editor," rather than to the person responsible for the article, cartoon, or letter you're writing about.

■ Although regional publications might accept letters commenting on a previously published letter, most national publications have policies against publishing letters about letters.

■ Your topic should be timely; editors rarely run letters about issues that are weeks or months old.

■ Limit yourself to one topic, to one main thought. If you don't stick to the point, your letter will probably be edited so that it does.

■ Your topic should be important to more than one person (you). Readers may not care how awful your neighbors are, unless you can tie their behavior to a larger issue (people who don't shovel their walks).

■ To get a letter accepted in a competitive market, aim for pithiness, humor, unusual information, or a twist on conventional thinking. Editors like letters of interest to other readers, opinionated letters on a controversy, letters reflecting a unique point of view on a broad topic, and letters that are clear, entertaining, and thought-provoking.

■ When you feel strongly about an issue, get others to write too so that the letters to the editor column reflects that many people feel the way you do.

■ Have others read your letter; oftentimes you are too close to the problem to see how your letter may affect others.

■ Most papers won't print letters from the same individual more frequently than every month or two, so if you've just had a letter published there's no point in writing again soon.

■ Some publications want letters original to them, not copies of letters sent to other publications. Check your publication's editorial policy.

Special Situations

■ Anonymous letters aren't often printed as most publishers believe their readers have a right to know whose views are being expressed. However, some circumstances (prospect of physical harm to the writer or loss of a job) justify anonymous letters. Editors will print such letters over "Name Withheld." Call first to be sure this is possible. When you write, specify that the letter is to be published only if your name does not appear.

■ Letters-to-the-editor columns become especially popular just before elections. Some publications print letters that support one candidate or criticize another; others ban election-related letters during a period immediately preceding an election or on Election Day in order to avoid being used to launch last-minute offensives. Blatant politicking usually never makes it to the printed page; editors have learned to spot letters that are thinly disguised publicity efforts or those that are part of an effort to create a bandwagon effect.

■ When asking for a correction or retraction of an inaccuracy, begin by identifying the erroneous article by date, section, page, and column. Be polite, factual, firm. Offer to supply correct data, proofs of your assertion, and phone numbers to call for verification.

■ Write letters to the editor commending civic groups or individuals who have contributed to the common good in ways that may not be known to everyone. Letters like these not only add welcome relief to the usual fare of the letters column, but they build positive community feelings and often engender more of the same productive activities. Note, however, that "nice" letters don't often get published; this kind of letter needs an extra dash of humor, wit, or color.

Format

■ Editors prefer typewritten letters. If you handwrite a letter, it must be legible.

■ Most publications accept e-mailed or faxed letters.

WORDS

advice	consensus	doctrinaire	insulting
aspect	consider	dogmatic	judgmental
assume	contradict	embarrassing	misunderstanding
attitude	controversy	examine	notion
bias	disagree	express	offensive
commentary	disapprove	impression	omission
conclude	dissatisfied	infer	one-sided
conjecture	disturbing	inflammatory	partisan

perspective	prejudiced	slant	surmise
persuade	premise	stand	unfortunate
position	provocative	suppose	view
posture			

PHRASES

after reading your Sept. 29 article on

a May 3 *New York Post Dispatch* article spoke of

an affront to those of us who

cartoonist Humphry Clinker should be aware that

did a slow burn when I read

difference of opinion

fail to agree

how can anyone state, as did Laetitia Snap (June 3), that

I agree wholeheartedly with

I am horrified by the Aug. 11 report

I am one of the many "misguided" people who was outraged by

I am puzzled by the reference to the long-term effects of

I am writing on behalf of

I disagree with the Reverend Septimus Crisparkle's premise (Feb. 7)

I found the short story in your September issue to be

I must take issue with

infuriating to see that

in response to a July 3 letter writer who said

I really enjoyed

I strongly object

I take exception to the opinions expressed by

I was disturbed/incensed/pleased/ angry/disappointed to read that

it seems to me

letter writer Muriel McComber's suggestion (Aug. 9) was intriguing, but

made me see red

neglected to mention

one side of the story

on the one hand/on the other hand

point in dispute

presented a false picture

read with great/considerable interest

recipe for disaster

regarding Senator Sam Blundel's new bill for the hearing-impaired

several letter writers have commented upon

the article on women in trades did much to

your editorial position on

your Sept. 17 editorial on

SENTENCES

A Dec. 9 writer is incorrect in saying that the Regional Transit Board was abolished several years ago; we are, in fact, alive and well.

I am writing to express my appreciation for your excellent coverage of City Council meetings on the local groundwater issue.

I commend you for your Aug. 11 editorial on magnet schools.

I disagree with Elizabeth Saunders' Apr. 5 column on city-supported recycling.

I look forward to seeing a published retraction of the incorrect information given in this article.

In Hennie Feinschreiber's Dec. 9 column on the living will, she uses statistics that have long since been discredited.

In his December 1 Counterpoint, "Tax Breaks for the Rich," Gerald Tetley suggests that out of fear of giving the rich a break, we are actually cutting off our noses to spite our face.

I was disappointed that not one of the dozens who wrote to complain about the hike in municipal sewer rates noticed that the rates are actually lower than they were ten years ago.

Many thanks for your unpopular but eminently sane editorial stand on gun control (July 2).

Please consider the cumulative effect of such legislation on our children.

Please do not drop Flora Lewis/Cal Thomas/Ellen Goodman/George Will from your editorial pages.

Several important factors were omitted from your Apr. 6 article on wide-area telephone service.

The writer of the Mar. 16 letter against triple trailers seemed to have little factual understanding of semi-truck traffic and professional truck drivers.

Your Aug. 3 editorial on workers' compensation overlooked a crucial factor.

Your June 29 editorial on child care failed to mention one of the largest and most effective groups working on this issue.

PARAGRAPHS

Has anyone noticed that the city has become overrun with dogs in the last several years? Most of these dogs have no collars and run in packs of five to eight dogs. If I had small children, I'd worry when they played outdoors. Where have these dogs come from? Whose problem is it? The city council's? The health department's? The police department's?

Letter writer Charles Shandon neglected to mention in his long, rather hysterical diatribe against mayoral candidate Hugh Desprez that he is running Mary Shandon's bid for the mayor's office. He is also her husband.

Your story on the newest technology in today's emergency rooms featured the views of hospital administrators, medical caregivers, and manufacturers' representatives. Nowhere was a patient mentioned. Is overlooking the patient also a feature of today's emergency rooms? (If it is, it's not new.)

To those of you who have been expressing yourself in these pages about the presence of wild geese in the city parks: Hello! A park is supposed to be natural. It is not meant to be as clean as your kitchen floor. It has messy leaves and gravel and bugs and, yes, goose grease. If you can't handle nature in the raw, there's always your backyard.

Count at least six women (the undersigned) who were outraged at your "news story" on the recently appointed Episcopalian bishop for our area. You devoted several lines early on in the story (thus implying their relative importance) to Ms. Dinah Morris's clothes, hairstyle, and even the color of her fingernail polish. Do you do this for new male bishops?

There was an error in your otherwise excellent article about the Lamprey Brothers Moving and Storage. In addition to brothers Henry, Colin, and Stephen (whom you mentioned), there is also brother Michael, a full partner.

A flurry of letter writers urges us to rally against the proposed congressional pay raise. I wonder if they understand the protection that such a raise would give us against special interest groups. Let's give this one a closer look. It may actually be a sheep in wolf's clothing.

I commend Meg Bishop for the use of "people first" language in her Jan. 2 column. By using expressions such as "people with severe disabilities" rather than "the severely disabled" and "people with quadriplegia" rather than "quadriplegics," Bishop helps change the way society views people with disabilities.

SAMPLE LETTERS

To the Editor:

So the tax collectors and money changers in rural Wayne County are persecuting Amish woodworker Sam Swartzendruber because he will not get a permit for his outdoor privy. They have fined him and charged him with over 100 offenses, one for each day he uses the privy without a permit. Now he will probably go to jail for his refusal to bend his beliefs to those of the bureaucrats who cannot come up with a reasonable way to regulate outdoor privies.

On my farm in a residential zone in Story County, I could build an unlined earthen sewage cesspool with more than 2 million gallons of liquid manure, taking in waste from up to 4,166 factory hogs, with no state or county permits. I could pollute the air for miles around, contaminate groundwater, and pile up my dead hogs daily out by the road with no permits. Not only would I not go to jail, but our governor, Legislature, and the Iowa Supreme Court would all congratulate me and tell me I was helping to build a better Iowa.

Be a good neighbor, go to jail. But build a hog factory, and you're a hero. Iowans ought to give Sam a medal for reminding us all what it means to stand up for our beliefs. We're jailing the wrong people. Let's pen up the mega-hog factory profiteers and turn Sam loose.

———

Dear Mr. Scott,

What happened to the ecclesiastical crossword puzzle you used to have every month in *The Abbot*?

———

To the Editor:

Several months ago, you announced a "bold new look" for the paper. Could we perhaps have the timid old look back?

Sometimes I find the financial pages behind the sports pages, sometimes in a section of their own, and occasionally with the classified ads. Usually the advice columnists and funnies are run together in their own section, but more often they are separated and positioned variously with the sports pages, the community news, the feature section, or the food pages.

I have tried to discern a method to your madness—perhaps on Mondays the sports have their own section, on Tuesdays they appear with the financial papers. No such luck. Somebody down there must just roll dice and say, "Ha! Let them try to find the foreign exchange rates today!"

Is there any hope for a more organized future?

———

Dear Mr. Burlap:

The excerpt from *Point Counter Point* in your June issue was excellent. I hope you will continue to offer us selections from lesser-known but high-quality literature.

———

Dear Business Editor:

An article in the Aug. 3 morning edition reported sales for our company in the billions. Naturally that would be nice, but it should have read millions. We would appreciate your printing a correction in the next edition of the paper.

Enclosed is our most recent annual report.

———

Dear Editor:

I read with interest the proposal to add four stories to the downtown public library building at a cost of $5.3 million.

I am concerned, however, that no provision has been made for user access. As it now stands, hundreds of thousands of books are all but useless since no one can get to them. There are a handful of metered street parking spaces, but you must be lucky to find one. And then you must not forget to run out every hour and insert four more quarters (the meter readers are particularly active in this area).

How many of you have driven around and around and around hoping for a parking place? How many of you have walked five or six blocks carrying a backbreaking load of books? How many of you have gotten $10 tickets because you forgot to feed the meter on time? It is utterly pointless to spend $5.3 million on a facility that no one can use.

———

To the Editor:

The front page of your Nov. 3 issue carried a full-color picture of a car accident victim who later died.

We, the undersigned, worked with Hilda Derriford—some of us for only two years, some of us for as long as sixteen years. To see our good friend and coworker displayed in her last moments for an unknowing and uncaring public was one of the most painful things we can describe. How her husband and children felt about the picture is another story, but we can't think they were any less devastated than we were.

What is the point of using a photo like that? Can you defend such a practice in any logical, compassionate way?

———

See also: APPRECIATION, COMPLAINTS, DISAGREEMENTS

TWENTY

E-MAIL

*Admitting you don't have an e-mail address these days is almost
like admitting you still listen to eight-track tapes.*
—TOM MCNICHOL

Less intrusive than the telephone and far simpler and quicker than writing a letter, e-mail has been embraced with enthusiasm by millions for their business and personal communications.

Precise figures are difficult to ascertain or verify, but it's possible that as many as 180 billion e-mail messages are sent every day and that some 70 percent of them are spam, or junk mail. (Fewer than 200 people are thought to be responsible for 80 percent of the spam.)

The hallmark of the e-mailed message is its conversational tone. Because questions and answers can be sent back and forth rapidly, it resembles a dialogue where a regular letter resembles a monologue. The relative effortlessness of e-mail has inspired a surge in communicating. People who haven't written a letter in years use e-mail because of its simplicity, directness, and speed. The savings to business in time, postage, and work hours has been incalculable. When contacting someone in another time zone or on another biorhythmic pattern, there is no fear of waking them with a phone call. When working late, you can send information to another person's electronic mailbox for retrieval first thing in the morning. E-mail is also useful when you have a thirty-second message to send someone who usually involves you in a fifteen-minute phone call.

Senders dash off e-mails, knowing that if they make a mistake or omit information, they can send another e-mail in seconds. The downside of the immediacy of e-mail is that it allows people to send notes, idle thoughts, jokes, forwards, chain letters, and trivia that they would never, in the old days, have taken the time, effort, and money (postage) to send anyone. Now we are privy to our friends' and coworkers' unhatched reflections and most recent thoughts. Just as cell phones tapped a hitherto unnoticed need to "reach out and touch someone" during most of our waking hours ("I'm just standing in line. What are you doing?"), so too has e-mail filled the desire to keep in touch 24/7.

Properly harnessed and used, however, e-mail is the most significant and useful new communication tool in centuries.

Instant Messaging (IM) resembles e-mail in some respects. For tips on IM, see the Special Situations section below.

E-Mail When Your Message Is

- brief
- informal
- sent to a number of people
- timely
- urgent

How to Say It

- Double-check every e-mail address before sending your message. The system is absolutely unforgiving. "Almost correct" doesn't cut it.
- Use a subject line, a word or brief phrase to tell your reader right away what the e-mail is about. Never leave this space blank. Your recipient needs to know, and deserves to know, immediately what the e-mail is about. Formats vary on e-mail servers, but all will have a space for this purpose. Examples of subject lines:

  Re: Welcome back!
  Re: newsletter error
  Re: benefits hotline
  Subject: the check's in the mail
  Subject: fundraising meeting
  Subject: new corporate library hours

- Start with "Hi" or "Hello," or the person's name followed by a comma or dash. The "Dear" convention of letters is generally too formal for e-mail.
- State your message briefly. Most people find e-mails longer than one screen annoying or intimidating, and often ignore them or put them off until later.
- If appropriate, tell what action you expect: a telephone call, an e-mail response, attendance at a meeting. When the e-mail is simply for their information, indicate this with "FYI."

- Close with a courtesy, if you wish. Formal closings ("Sincerely," "Truly yours") aren't necessary.
- Type your name; the person's system may indicate only your e-mail address. Especially in the workplace, all your e-mails should include your full name, title, telephone number, and e-mail address; it might also include your physical address and any pertinent company identification or information. This identifies you quickly and is useful if the e-mail is forwarded to a third party who needs to contact you.

What Not To Say

- Don't use e-mail to convey high-impact news (a death, new company president, serious illness).
- Don't write anything you don't want the whole world to know. E-mail is far from private and it is easily forwarded or misrouted. It was never meant for confidential messages. Etiquette maven Peggy Post says, "Work e-mail is a public document: If you wouldn't write it in a memo and hang it on the bulletin board, don't put it in an e-mail."
- Don't send an urgent message by e-mail unless you know the person is expecting it or you call to say it's coming; there's no guarantee it will be read immediately. Some people check their e-mail frequently and in many offices users are notified when e-mail comes in, but other people may not read an e-mail for days.
- Don't write angry e-mails; it's too easy to fire off our first thoughts and regret them afterward.
- Don't use all capital letters unless you want the recipient to understand that you are YELLING.

Tips on Writing

■ An e-mail address consists of (1) a name identifying the individual or group ("xyz"); (2) the "at" sign ("@"); (3) the name of the server (for example, "earthling"); and (4) a code that identifies the mail by type (domain): .com (commercial); .net (network); .gov (government); .edu (educational institution); .org (organization—usually nonprofit); .mil (military); .st (state government). Thus: xyz@earthling.com.

■ Be sure your e-mail address is professional. If you've had the same e-mail address for some time, give it another look to be sure it suits who you are today.

■ Include one topic per e-mail. You are more likely to get the responses you need if you send the same person three e-mails with three different questions than if you bundle them into one e-mail.

■ Use everyday language. In a letter you might write "I will" or, more formally, "I shall." In an e-mail you write "I'll." However, even though e-mails tend to informal language, use correct punctuation and grammar and standard spelling when writing to superiors.

■ Be careful of the "Reply to All" function. Your e-mail software may require you to manually toggle between writing only to the person who sent you the e-mail and to all those copied on their message. Sometimes you don't want the whole list to receive your reply.

■ Respond promptly. Especially in work situations, you probably need to reply within 24 hours. When you can't supply the answer or information immediately, let the sender know the message was received and you will write later. When you are away from your desk for a day or more, program an automatic "I'm away" reply.

■ Be careful about copying others on an e-mail you are sending to one individual (listing the copied recipients' names under "cc"). E-mail has made copying so easy that it is sometimes done unnecessarily and counterproductively. Does everyone really need to receive this? When you list other recipients under "bcc" (blind carbon copy), your principal recipient doesn't know that other people have also seen the message. Use this device sparingly and carefully.

■ E-mail services allow us to compile lists of groups (people in your department, your softball team, family members) so that you can e-mail all of them at once by simply sending it to "CommComm" (Communication Committee) or "MatSci" (Materials Science Group). Update these lists often and think twice about sending a message to the group when perhaps only one or two people need to receive the e-mail. Too many people have a list that might be called "Everyone I Know in the Whole Wide World and Then Some" and tend to copy the whole group on jokes, comments, news, and the like. None of us like mass mailings on paper; we don't like them any better on e-mail. Monitor your use of lists.

■ You may ignore chain mail, jokes, and petitions without being thought rude. Logically, it is the sender who is possibly being rude. Almost no one likes these unfiltered gleanings; resist forwarding them. You are of course free to enjoy them with like-minded friends and family—if you're certain of the "like-minded" part.

■ Before forwarding an e-mail, obtain the original sender's permission and delete the headers and extraneous material.

■ Do not pass on others' e-mail addresses without their permission. And never give your password or user ID to anyone you don't know very, very well.

■ Abbreviations are popular with some e-mailers. Others never use them and even find them annoying. Examples include:

ASAP = as soon as possible
BTW = by the way
FAQ = frequently asked questions
FYI = for your information
LOL = laughed out loud
OIC = Oh, I see
TIA = thanks in advance
TMI = too much information
TY = thank you
WTG = way to go

Avoid them in business communications unless you know the other person well. To see the full range of abbreviations, check with sites such as www. netlingo.com.

■ Emoticons are also used by some people, shunned by others. For example, :-) stands for a happy face (look at it sideways) and :(for an unhappy face; :) for a smile, ;-) for a wink, :-D for a laugh, and :'(for crying.

■ Be sensitive about sending very long files that may either jam a recipient's e-box, take a long time to load, or interrupt their work in another program.

Special Situations

■ If you use e-mail at work, familiarize yourself thoroughly with your company's policies on e-mail usage, monitoring activity, privacy, security, and archiving. The e-mail system is company property and most organizations have guidelines about its use by employees. Know the line between business use and any permitted personal use.

■ The American Management Association recommends documenting your business e-mail transactions so that you can retrace your steps if necessary. Deleting old business e-mails is not a good idea. Check company policy to see how long they must be kept.

■ Attachments (long files hooked onto your e-mail "cover letter") are iffy. If you work for a large company where your computers are effectively protected against viruses, you send and receive attachments worry-free. Individuals using computers in small businesses or at home may decide not to open an attachment because of the possibility of importing a virus. When you must send an attachment, check first to see if your recipient is willing and able (has the proper software) to open it. And remember that not everything has to be an attachment. When you can paste something in the body of the e-mail, it makes it easier for the recipient.

■ An estimated 70 percent of the e-mail received in the United States is spam. Unsolicited and generally unwanted e-mail sent to thousands of e-mail addresses, spam is the electronic equivalent of junk mail. Many are both spam and scam; do not bite. (Get used to checking with www.snopes.com and other myth busters to find out which of the amazing stories in your e-box are true, and which are not.) Completely eliminating spam has so far not been successful. Some software blocks certain addresses so that you don't receive their mail, but the e-mailers get around this by inventing random and unfathomable new e-mail addresses. Should you respond to their invitation to tell them you want your address removed from their files, they rejoice at having found a "live" one and send you more spam than ever. Just delete them. Don't even sigh, just delete. (Reputable Internet companies are good about removing your name from their mailings; usually you can simply click on "Unsubscribe.")

■ Sometimes a friend or acquaintance stuffs your e-box with jokes (that you've heard before), maudlin anecdotes, canned advice, virus scares, and notices of websites that you absolutely must visit. Letitia Baldrige, former White House social secretary, advises sending the person an e-mail saying, "I really appreciate your thinking of me and keeping me on your routing list, but I'm sorry to say I'm so darned busy, I can't read my necessary, urgent mail, much less amusing mail. I think it's time you substituted my name with someone else's because Father Time won't let me enjoy your e-mails." Peggy Post's suggestion is to say, "I love hearing from you, but please stop sending me jokes via e-mail. I'm so busy at work that I don't have time to keep up with personal e-mail."

■ Instant Messaging (IM) varies greatly in terms of hardware, software, and added features, but the content—the text—resembles e-mail in its brevity, speed, one-topic focus, and sense of immediacy. Because IM can happen in real time and by means of mobile phones, it is even more instant and more flexible than e-mail. However, when you IM someone who is offline, IM is almost exactly like e-mail. IM is used most often for quick questions and clarifications, scheduling and coordinating tasks and meetings, and keeping in touch with friends and family. To save time and keystrokes, texters use abbreviations, acronyms, slang, and "text speak." Most of the information in this chapter also applies to IM, particularly: (1) the strict line between business and personal use; (2) the importance of familiarizing yourself with company policies on security, confidentiality, viruses, archiving, and personal use (over 10,000 U.S. laws and regulations govern electronic messages and records retention, so there's a reason your company is fussy about IM use).

Format

■ The format will depend upon your server although you will have some choices (length of your lines, whether to include the other person's message in your e-mail).

■ Making a hard copy of an e-mail message (that is, printing it) gives it the same permanence and nearly the same legal validity as a letter or memo.

WORDS

announce	following	message	responding
answer	forwarding	notify	thanks
attachment	inform	reminder	
explain	inquiry	reply	

PHRASES

alert you to the possibility	in answer to your question
ask your help	just a note to let you know
do you know	please let me know ASAP
for your information	send me a copy of
here are	wanted to follow up
information you wanted/requested	will you please send

SENTENCES

Are you available to judge a race walk a week from Saturday?

Did you see the article about elder law in today's *New York Times*?

Feel free to forward the following to anyone who might be interested.

Forgot to ask—is it their 37th or 38th anniversary?

Here are this week's airfare bargains.

I had a note from Mrs. Hook Eagles asking about a vacancy in the 1330 building—do we have one, do you know?

I'll be gone the next two weeks—if anything comes up, e-mail me and I'll get back to you after the 3rd.

I'm trying to round up some people to hike through New England for two weeks this fall—are you interested?

I read about the tornado that went through your area—are you OK?

Is it my bookkeeping or am I missing a check for the last job?

Is there any news about Cressida?

I've just mailed you the material for your audio presentation—you should have it Monday or Tuesday.

I've lost Miriam Ephraim's address—do you have it?

Just a note to say I enjoyed your op-ed piece on hog confinements—have you had much feedback, so to speak?

Just a reminder about the conference call with Eusabio International Friday at 3:00 p.m.

New surge protectors are now available for anyone who needs one.

Subject: Nearby houses of worship

Tax forms are available in the lobby from now until April 15, thanks to Courtenay Brundit, who obtained them for us.

Thanks for forwarding the specs—I'm interested.

This is to let you know that your order (#08554) was received and will be shipped this afternoon.

We've been notified that Highway 36 will be closed from July 9-15; you may want to plan alternate routes to work.

When you have a minute, will you fax me a copy of your most recent patent application?

You asked if the company store currently has sandpaper seconds: yes, it does.

PARAGRAPHS

Please mark your calendars. William Denny, industrial engineer at our new high-tech data entry facility in Porter, will explain the latest technology on Thursday, Jan. 21 at 3:00 p.m. in Building 201B, Room 43. A question-and-answer period will follow.

You wanted to know who keeps my Harley in such great shape? I do! Okay, okay, I know what you mean. The greatest Harley repair and service east of the Mississippi is The Caloveglia Shop on South Douglas.

Thanks for the new programmable multifunction mouse that you sent over. I'm having a good time with it!

In response to your question about the community organizer position, yes, benefits are included. In addition, the deadline for applying has been changed to September 30.

Would you please let me know the name of the contractor who did your deck? We're inspired enough to get going on ours.

Can you give me some idea what would be necessary to develop the tooling and fixturing needed to form and laserweld small-diameter sleeve tools for use on the Bowen project and others?

Thanks for letting me know about the time change for the grant-writing meeting. Are we still meeting in 306?

SAMPLE LETTERS

FROM: burb@email.com
TO: realty@email.com
DATE: Fri, 16 Aug 2010 12:41:00

Yes, draw up a purchase agreement at the asking price and then fax me a copy at 651-555-1234.

———

FROM: info@ducksfordinner.com
TO: foxes@email.com
DATE: 20 Nov 2011 14:30:01
SUBJECT: Order confirmation #82654560

This is an automated message acknowledging acceptance of your online order. You may check your order status by writing to: info@ducksfordinner.com

———

FROM: clubred@aol.com
TO: juliagotrocks@email.com
DATE: Tue, 18 Jan 2011 16:53:31 EST
SUBJECT: Thank you!

Hello, Julia—I received your check. Thanks! I put $30 toward dues, and $50 as a contribution to our latest fundraising drive. You'll be getting a fundraiser letter but it will be fyi only—not to ask you to give again. Netty

———

FROM: sgk@email.com
TO: rmk@email.com
DATE: Wed, 29 Mar 2010 17:02:35 +0400
SUBJECT: Help—April 1

Hello from Russia! I'm planning my April 1 English class around the idea of practical jokes and I'd appreciate your help. (1) Could you describe this tradition as far as you know it from your own experience? (2) Do you remember a really successful April 1 practical joke? (3) In Russia the joke ends with the cliche "S pervym aprelya!" which means "Congratulations on April 1!" What do they say in the circumstances in your part of the world? Thanks!

———

FROM: hcalverly@email.com
TO: thewhitecompany@email.com
DATE: Tue, 29 Jul 2010 17:34:08 (EDT)
SUBJECT: ATTN: Doyle

I received the fax of the essay. It was above and beyond the call of duty, and yes, I still needed it. I owe you one. Best, Hugh

————

FROM: msadlier@email.com
TO: kcairns@email.com
DATE: 07 Apr 2010 13:01:21
SUBJECT: favor

Kitty, would you be willing to spend fifteen minutes or so speaking with a high-school senior in your area who's interested in the Fanny Gaslight School of Design? Thanks!

————

FROM: gordy@email.com
TO: cary@email.com
DATE: Mon, 30 Sep 2010 11:21:21
RE: amorphous metals symposium

Oct. 16 is fine with me. Sorry to be late with my response—I've been out of town. I hope all's well with you. Gordy

————

FROM: bc@email.com (Baldassare Calvo, PhD)
TO: ced@email.com (Members of Continuing Education Network)
RE: "Modern Business Writing: Creative Expressions"
DATE: April 3, 2010

"Modern Business Writing: Creative Expressions" is a series of weekly distance education classes available to your location via videotape or video teleconferencing. This series of four seminars will cover the main forms of business writing (letters, reports, proposals, e-mail) with guidelines and practical examples for each.

Each live teleconference is limited to the first 15 locations to register. Fees are $50 per videotape or free teleconferencing to member sites.

For detailed information, reply by typing INFORMATION in the subject line. To receive educational credit, a list of attendees' names and employee numbers must be faxed to 608-555-1234.

————

FROM: kmm@email.com
TO: bert@email.com
DATE: Tues, 26 Feb 2010 20:35:29 EST
SUBJECT: Thesaurus

I've been meaning to ask which thesaurus you recommend. I don't have any confidence in the one on my word-processing program, but I don't know much about thesauruses other than that they're in the dinosaur family. Thanks. Love, K

––––––––

FROM: slz3@email.edu
TO: krasinsky@email.com
DATE: Mon, 9 Dec 2010 15:48:00 -0500 (EST)
SUBJECT: WHM Contract

Hi. I'm filling out the contract for women's history month right now and I have a couple of questions. We've decided on an honorarium of $150—is that agreeable? Should we have books there for signing? My adviser is checking out how much the housing is here and I'll let you know as soon as I find out. Thanks, Samara

––––––––

From: nick@email.com
To: hartmore1@email.com
Date: Sat, 28 Sep 2010 19:26:34 EDT
Subject: Paris tomorrow!

Hey! I just got a job today as National Sales Manager for Oliphant Books, a trade publisher here in San Fran.

We're leaving for Paris tomorrow morning, for a week's stay. Hope to reside at a small hotel in the Marais. Any last-minute tips/advice?

Yes, this is the SAME trip we had planned when I got sick 50 weeks ago, and twice since then. The tix expire on 10/13, so the timing was a little too close on this one.

Hope you're well,
Nick

––––––––

FROM: hop@email.com
TO: maggie@email.com
DATE: Tues, 17 Sep 2010 09:03:35
SUBJECT: your layover on Oct. 12

Because of the parking situation, we won't meet you at the gate. Stay on the ticketing level and walk straight out the main doors. We'll be waiting out front to take you to dinner and we'll get you back in plenty of time to catch your connecting flight. See you!

––––––––

FROM: kenlake@email.com
TO: cl@email.com
DATE: Mon, 4 Mar 2010 18:25:23

Hi Colleen! I'm back at the office and have dug out from under mail, phone calls, e-mail—YOU know what it's like—and now I want to make good on whatever I promised to send you while under the influence of fresh mussels! I've completely forgotten. Let me know.

———

See also: ACKNOWLEDGMENTS, FAMILY, FOLLOW-UP, MEMOS

TWENTY-ONE

LETTERS DEALING WITH EMPLOYMENT

*It's strange how unimportant your job is when you ask for a raise,
and how important it is when you want a day off.*
—HOWIE LASSETER

Robert Orben said, "Every morning I get up and look through the Forbes list of the richest people in America. If I'm not there, I go to work." Most of us go to work.

While we're there, letters between employers and employees contribute to (or undermine) workplace morale, efficiency, and rapport.

The employee is affected, directly or indirectly, by letters that range from requesting a raise to asking for clarification of retirement benefits. The employer depends on well-written letters to maintain good employee relations and to resolve personnel problems that interfere with the company's goals.

Employment Letters Deal with

- acknowledgments: applications/proposals/suggestions (see also ACKNOW-LEDGMENTS)
- advice/complaints/reprimands (see ADVICE, COMPLAINTS)
- announcements: layoffs/changes/company policies (see ANNOUNCE-MENTS, INSTRUCTIONS)
- approvals: raise/promotion/projects/requests/changes (see also ACCEP-TANCES)
- congratulations/commendations (see also CONGRATULATIONS)
- getting a job (see APPLICATIONS, COVER LETTERS, REFERENCES, RÉSUMÉS)

- goodwill notes: thank you, welcome, appreciation (see also APPRECIA-TION, THANK YOU, WELCOME)
- interviews (see APPOINTMENTS, FOLLOW-UP, RÉSUMÉS)
- invitations: retirement parties/service anniversaries/awards ceremonies/speaking engagements (see also INVITATIONS)
- meetings: announcing/canceling/changing/postponing (see also APPOINT-MENTS)
- networking (see INTRODUCTIONS)
- references and recommendations (see REFERENCES)
- refusals: raises/promotions/proposals/requests (see REFUSALS)
- requests: raise/promotion/project approval/interview/meeting (see RE-QUESTS)
- resignations
- résumés and letters of application (see RÉSUMÉS)
- retirement (see also ACKNOWLEDGMENTS, ANNOUNCEMENTS, CONGRATULATIONS, INVITATIONS)
- terminations

How to Say It

- Date every memo or letter.
- When responding to job applicants: (1) If you are unable to make an immediate choice among applicants, acknowledge receipt of their materials or thank them for their interviews. If possible, say when you will notify them of your decision. Thank them for their interest in your company. (2) In the case of a rejection, express appreciation for the applicant's time and interest and state simply that you are unable to make an offer. If appropriate, briefly explain the decision. Close with positive comments on the person's application, an invitation to reapply at a later time (if you mean it), and your confidence of success in the person's search for a suitable position. (3) When offering someone a position, open with congratulatory and complimentary remarks. Include confirmation of the job description and the name and telephone number of someone who can answer further questions. Repeat a selling point or two about the company to influence the person's decision to accept the offer. Close with an expression of goodwill about the person's future with your organization.
- When announcing a change in company policies, procedures, or regulations, include: description of the new policy; reference to the old policy, if necessary for clarification; brief reason for the change; expected benefits of the change; deadline for the change implementation; instructions or enclosures that further explain the change; name and telephone number of

someone to answer questions or help with problems; expression of your enthusiasm about the change.

- When you arrange an in-house meeting by memo or e-mail: explain the purpose of the meeting, offer possible dates and times, and express your appreciation for the person's attention to your request. To change a meeting time, always mention the original date and time and ask for acknowledgment of the new time. To cancel a meeting, repeat the time and date, state that you must cancel (briefly explaining why), and apologize for the inconvenience. If you miss a scheduled meeting, write an immediate, sincere apology.

- When writing to request a raise, be brief and factual, supplying as much supporting material as possible (letters of commendation, sales records, copies of patents, research papers, evaluations, list of awards). No one ever has a "right" to a raise; do not let this attitude color your letter. Avoid threatening to leave unless you mean it. Don't compare your salary to others'; it is tactless, usually meaningless, and puts your reader on the defensive. Instead, show how your work has become more valuable to the company or speak of an "adjustment" to reflect additional hours, duties, or productivity.

- When writing a reprimand, begin with a positive or complimentary remark. Describe factually the employee behavior and, if necessary, tell why it is unacceptable. If appropriate, tell how this came to your attention. Suggest how the employee can change. State the consequences of continuing the behavior. Close with an expression of confidence that the situation will be handled successfully. A reprimand is brief, respectful, encouraging, and positive (instead of writing, "Do not make personal phone calls while patients are in the waiting room," say, "Please confine personal phone calls to times when the waiting room is empty."). Your goal in writing a letter of reprimand is not to get revenge or blow off steam; it is to change employee behavior. Avoid condemning, belittling, haranguing, preaching, scolding, or patronizing the employee.

- Notifying employees of layoffs or terminations has become codified—because of labor unions, because of legal ramifications, and because it is most effective for large organizations to follow a uniform manner in dealing with them. When a letter is written, it is brief and might include: a statement about the layoff or termination; an expression of regret at the necessity of taking this measure; the date on which the layoff or termination becomes effective; details on severance pay, profit sharing, retirement benefits, and medical coverage; in the case of a layoff, the possible length of the time, if known; details on company layoff and termination policies, career counseling, letters of recommendation, available public assistance, and other information that helps employees cope with the layoff or termination; the name and telephone number of someone who can answer questions. When the termination is due to the employee's poor work record or behavior, you will want to follow company and legal guidelines carefully. Tell why they're being fired and document previous warnings.

- When resigning, an oral notice may be all that is necessary. Generally, however, it is useful for both employer and employee to have a written record of the resignation. The common practice is to resign in person and follow up with a letter. Begin by writing something positive about the position, company, or organization you're leaving. Give the effective date of your resignation. In most cases, give a reason for resigning: poor health; age; family move; work-related health problems; greater opportunities for advancement, higher salary or more desirable location with another company; wish to change careers; recent changes that have affected your position. If you're leaving because of problems with management, coworkers, restrictive company policies, or other negative reasons, be vague: "For personal reasons, I am resigning effective March 1." Don't use your letter as a dumping ground for complaints. Take your leave in a polite, dignified manner—even if the truth lies elsewhere. For one thing, you may need a letter of reference. For another, despite confidentiality, angry letters have a way of following you about in your professional community. And you don't know when you might have dealings with the company in the future. If you're leaving because of illegal or dishonest practices, take your information (with as much documentation as possible) to outside bureaus or agencies. If you've been asked to resign, your letter doesn't refer to this; state simply that you are resigning, so that it appears that way in the official records. Offer to help find or train a replacement, if appropriate. End on a pleasant note, expressing appreciation for what you have learned, for your coworkers, for being associated with such a dynamic company, for being part of a new development. In some situations, write a one-sentence letter of resignation, giving no explanation.
- In responding to a letter of resignation, include a statement of acceptance "with regret," positive comments on the person's association with your organization, and an expression of good wishes for the person's future.

What Not to Say

- Don't write anything in letters to employees or prospective employees that could be considered actionable. Common sense will provide some guidance, but in questionable instances, consult an attorney on the phrasing of sensitive letters (reprimands and terminations, for example).

- Don't express negative emotions. Negative facts may have to be outlined, but your letter remains objective rather than angry, vengeful, irritated, judgmental, hurt, or contemptuous. When you are overly involved emotionally, ask another person to write the letter.

Tips on Writing

■ Be brief. Your memos and letters will be more popular (and more quickly answered) if they are concise. Check your correspondence for words, sentences, and paragraphs that can be cut without loss of clarity.

■ Be professional and courteous. Even when writing someone you know well, maintain a businesslike tone. Anything that gets put on paper can be saved and reread. Although a careless remark can be forgotten, a carelessly written sentence lives forever.

■ Use parallel name forms. If you begin a letter, "Dear Hazel Marston" your name at the bottom is "John Reddin." When she is "Hazel," you are "John." If you feel a first name is appropriate after a job interview ("Dear Henry"), sign your first name ("Ferris") over your typed full name (just as the other person's name is spelled out in full in the address block).

Special Situations

■ Send goodwill notes of congratulations and commendation to: employees who complete a project, obtain a new account, or otherwise contribute to the good of the company; coworkers and employees who are promoted or receive awards; workers marking service anniversaries; employees, coworkers, and managers celebrating personal milestones (birth of baby, marriage). These notes are the least obligatory and the most influential of office correspondence. Something as brief as "Thanks, Tom. You're terrific" can inspire people to new heights of accomplishment.

Format

■ Most in-house correspondence consists of memos. More official communications (promotions and resignations, for example) or letters that go in people's files are typed on letterhead stationery.

■ E-mail is useful for brief nuts-and-bolts communications. Nothing confidential or important is sent this way, however.

WORDS

accomplishments	cutback	policies	regulations
achievement	goals	position	success
behavior	morale	procedure	supervise
capable	objectives	process	training
competent	operation	recognize	
conduct	outstanding	regret	

PHRASES

accepted another position

after much deliberation

an opportunity has recently arisen

appreciate having had the
    opportunity to work

ask you to accept my resignation

cannot presently offer you any
    encouragement

company cutbacks/merger

considered for the position of

due to economic conditions

eliminate certain positions

expect to fill the vacancy

financial problems/difficulties have
    forced/obliged us

have no other option but to

highly motivated

must advise/inform you

not adding to/expanding our staff at
    the moment

proposed termination date of

submit/tender my resignation

under consideration

value your contributions

with great personal regret/great
    reluctance/mixed feelings

SENTENCES

According to the terms of my contract, I hereby give four weeks' notice that as of April 18 I am terminating my employment as freight transportation manager with Sweedlepipe Inc.

Although your credentials are impressive, we are offering the position to someone who also has the grain futures experience we are looking for.

Because Don Rebura Associates was not awarded the Marryat contract, we are obliged to consider employee layoffs.

I accept with pleasure the offer to join Potticary Dairy Products as institutional services manager.

I am proud to be part of such a creative and enthusiastic team—I hope you are too.

I'll be happy to recommend you highly to potential employers.

I'm concerned about the infractions of our safety regulations.

I'm looking forward to a long and challenging association with Willard Electronics.

I've seen your wonderfully creative and appealing display windows and want to congratulate you on your excellent work.

I would like to meet with you to review the circumstances leading to my termination notice.

On behalf of the management of Steenson Engineering, I am happy to inform you that you have been promoted to Senior Research Engineer, effective March 1.

Our decision in no way reflects on your excellent qualifications.

Thank you for applying for the position of commercial plant specialist with Calvert Tropical Plants.

The award properly belongs to the entire department.

The position for which you applied has already been filled.

This is to advise you that you are being laid off in compliance with Article XXXI, Section 6, of our current labor agreement.

This letter will give formal notice of my resignation from Toddhunter Associates as Media Specialist effective April 1.

Unfortunately we are not able to offer you a position with Roehampton Ltd. at this time.

We accept your resignation with regret, and wish you well in future endeavors.

We are pleased to offer you the position as warehouse attendant for Landor Textiles.

We are sorry to see you leave.

We have received a number of responses to our advertisement, and we ask your patience while we evaluate them.

We hope to be able to consider you for another position soon.

We hope you will be available for recall.

We will let you know/contact you/notify you/be in touch with you/write or call you about the status of your application sometime before June 1.

PARAGRAPHS

A one-hour presentation on workplace e-mail usage, covering such issues as privacy, monitoring activities, retention and documentation, and definitions and consequences of personal use will be offered Tuesday, June 6, every hour on the hour from 9 to 5 in the conference room. Please reply to this e-mail with your name and the hour you will attend in the subject line.

We have carefully considered your letter of application, résumé, and portfolio, and have been most favorably impressed. Please call the Human Resources Office at 719-555-6790 to arrange an interview with Enoch Emery, the Art Director.

Thank you for offering me the opportunity to work for Wedderburn Printers and Lithographers as manager of bindery services. I am delighted to accept this position with such a distinguished and forward-looking company.

We are seeing more travel expenses turned in after the fact, whereas company policy states that all travel expenses must be preapproved. If you have questions about how to handle travel expenses, call Michael Lambourne in Human Resources, extension 310.

We've received complaints that employee attempts to guard against receiving bad checks have become overly intrusive, hostile, and humiliating. Several customers have said they will not return to the store. While we encourage every effort to prevent the writing of bad checks, your actions must be tactful, courteous, and respectful. Please reread your employee handbook for specific acceptable measures and for suggested phrases and actions for handling this situation.

Last month, we lost $3,780 worth of clothing to shoplifters. There is an informational seminar on shoplifting scheduled for June 16 at 3:00 p.m. In the meantime, we ask all employees to be especially vigilant.

I am obliged to resign my position with the Van Eyck Company because of ill health. I appreciate the good employer-employee relationship we have enjoyed over the years and will be watching the company's growth with much interest. If I can be of any assistance to my successor, I will be glad to help out.

We are sorry to announce that Jeanne Beroldy has resigned from the firm effective July 1. She has accepted the position of Managing Director with Christie Packaging Corp. Although we will miss her, we wish her every success in her exciting new position.

It is with much regret that we advise you that we are unable to continue your employment after September 1. As you are no doubt aware, the company is experiencing severe—but temporary, we hope—difficulties. We believe the layoff will also be temporary, although for the moment it is not possible to promise anything. In the meantime, please check with Personnel for information on letters of reference, company layoff policies, public assistance available to you until you find other employment, and career counseling.

With regret we accept your resignation, effective March 1. You have been one of the company's strongest assets for the past five years. Please accept our best wishes in your new position.

SAMPLE LETTERS

Dear Frank,

Welcome to Pierpont Industries! I hope you have a good first day on the job, and that it only gets better after that. We're very pleased to have you on our team, and hope that you're equally glad to be here. If any of us can make these first weeks smoother for you, don't hesitate to let us know.

————

Dear Marcus,

As you are no doubt aware, I recently received a raise, and I am of course grateful not only to have a job that I enjoy so much but to be appreciated in this very practical way.

However, I am not sure how the raise was determined. As I look back over my five years here, I see a fairly quick rise from the position I originally accepted (word processor) to my current position as department manager. All performance reviews have been particularly favorable, including the last one. Despite these outstanding reviews, and three successive promotions within the last two years, my recent raise was just 1.5% above the company average.

As my immediate supervisor, you are perhaps in the best position to tell me (1) if this is consistent with policy throughout the company; (2) if there is something I should be doing to let others know my achievements, qualifications, and general worth.

If you have time to discuss this in the next couple of days, I'd be grateful for your time.

Sincerely,

————

TO: Tracy Tupman
FROM: Sam Weller
DATE: June 3, 2010
SUBJECT: Resignation

Dear Tracy,

The past year and a half has been difficult. My wife and I have discussed in depth her health and the direction of our lives together. John, I need to be home.

It's with a heavy heart that I submit this written notice of resignation effective July 1, 2010. This was not an easy decision to make as I have thoroughly enjoyed working with you, Doug, and many others over the years. My experience here at Pickwick-Snodgrass has been rewarding and productive, and I wish the very best for you and the company.

I will be happy to help find or train a replacement—or do anything else you think will make the transition smoother.

Thank you so much for your friendship and trust.

Respectfully yours,

Dear Mr. Karkeek:

Thank you for your letter seeking employment with our firm.

You have an interesting background. However, we feel your qualifications and experience do not match the needs of the account executive/trainee position presently available in our Chicago office.

We thank you for your interest in Lessways International and wish you success in the attainment of your career objectives.

Sincerely yours,

Dear Elizabeth Firminger,

Thank you for applying for the position of insurance adjustor with the Raybrook Adjusting Service. Your work history is outstanding, and you made a good impression at your interview. As you know, however, we were looking for someone with experience in the inland marine area, and we did find a candidate with that qualification.

We appreciate your interest in our company, and would like to suggest that you reapply to us in six months when we expect to have several other positions open. We will keep your application on file until then.

It is clear that you will be an asset to the company that eventually hires you—good luck in finding the right place.

Sincerely,

Dear Marguerite Lambert,

Thank you for your application for the position of litho stripper, your résumé, and your work samples. They are being carefully considered by our Human Resources Department.

We received a number of other applications, so it may be three or four weeks before we can make a decision. You will be notified either way as soon as we do.

Thank you for your interest in Greatheart Printing Company.

Sincerely yours,

Dear Ms. Moncada:

As you know, I just celebrated five years with Tresham Paper Products. In that time, I've been stimulated by my work, supported by coworkers, and encouraged by management. I've enjoyed being part of the Tresham team.

The recent reorganization has changed things for me, however, and I question whether the next five years will be as fruitful for me as the last five and whether I'll be as useful to the company in my new situation. Because of this, I am accepting a position with Walter & Co. Inc. where I am assured of opportunities for advancement as well as exceptional laboratory support.

Please accept my resignation, effective November 1, along with my appreciation for a satisfying and rewarding five years.

Sincerely,

————

TO: All Employees
FROM: Lawrence Mont, Head Librarian
DATE: August 14, 2011
RE: Library usage

As of September 1, all library books will be due one month from the checkout date (the previous loan period was two months). For the first several months, we will be calling this change to your attention as you check out books.

————

TO: Dr. Betti Lancoch
FROM: Caradoc Evans
DATE: February 3, 2010
RE: Biodegradable plastics technology

We continue to be very interested in your biodegradable plastics technology, which appears to be the cornerstone for several new products. I understand you're pursuing patents for this technology. We'd like to see your patent applications filed by May 1, 2010, so that we could begin customer contact to clarify performance criteria for several of the products.

I want to emphasize our need for your technology along with appropriate patent protection. If you require additional support, please call. Thanks.

————

See also: ANNOUNCEMENTS, APPOINTMENTS, APPRECIATION, CONGRATULATIONS, COVER LETTERS, FOLLOW-UP, REFERENCES, REFUSALS, RESPONSES, RÉSUMÉS, THANK YOU, WELCOME

TWENTY-TWO

LETTERS TO FAMILY AND FRIENDS

Do let me hear from you even if it's only a twenty-page letter.
—GROUCHO MARX

Although inexpensive long-distance dialing has replaced some letters to family and friends, millions are still sent every year. E-mail has probably fueled writing among family and friends like nothing since the pony express.

Start talking about the joy of personal letters and people will tell you about their family round-robin letter, about the grandmother who returned years of correspondence to each of her children and grandchildren, about the couple celebrating their anniversary who read aloud their first letters to each other, about high school friends who saved their letters for twenty-five years.

And there are serious letters: the man whose friends flood him with letters before each chemotherapy appointment; the young woman who chooses her baby's adoptive parents by reading letters written to her from each candidate couple; the weekly letters that are read with such pleasure by a ninety-year-old uncle who can no longer hear.

"How eagerly in all times and all places, have people waited for mail from home! How wistfully have they repeated, over and over again, that old familiar question: 'Any mail for me?'" (Lillian Eichler Watson)

Letters to Family and Friends Include

- annual form letters (see HOLIDAYS)
- correspondence with friends and relatives

- Father's Day, Mother's Day
- letters to young people: birthdays/congratulations on an achievement/away from home
- love letters (see LOVE LETTERS)
- pen pals
- special-event letters (see CONGRATULATIONS, HOLIDAYS, SYMPATHY, WEDDINGS)
- welcoming prospective or new in-laws (see also WELCOME)

How to Say It

- Open with a cheerful remark indicating you're happy to be writing the other person.
- Ask questions about the other person's life, without, however, sounding like an interviewer.
- Write about what you've been doing lately; books you've read; movies or plays you've seen; sports events you've participated in or attended; local or national politics and issues you care about; news of mutual friends; something that made you laugh; an item you just bought; plans for summer, fall, next year; the weather; changes at work; pets' behavior; hobbies or collections. Or, choose a recent event (it needn't be terribly important) and tell it like a story.
- Close with an expression of affection or love and with a forward-looking statement about seeing or hearing from the person.

What Not to Say

- Don't begin with "I don't know why I'm writing, because I don't have anything to say," or "You know how I hate writing letters," or "I'm sorry for not writing sooner"—unless, of course, you can say it with wit and originality. Start your letter with a cheerful, positive, interesting remark.
- Don't write only questions and comments on the other person's life and last letter ("Your remodeled kitchen sounds fantastic!"; "The new car sounds great." "Your party must have been a lot of fun." "I'll bet you were proud of Cicely."). Mark Van Doren says, "The letter which merely answers another letter is no letter at all." And Sigmund Freud said, "I consider it a good rule for letterwriting to leave unmentioned what the recipient already knows, and instead tell . . . something new." D. H. Lawrence added, "I love people who can write reams and reams about themselves: it seems generous."

- Don't complain or be negative, unless you can do it entertainingly. A cheerful, positive tone is welcome (except when you or your reader have been facing difficulties).
- Don't end with "I've bored you long enough" or "I'd better quit before you fall asleep." Instead, say how much you'd enjoy hearing from them when time allows or how much you miss them or, again, how happy you are about their news.

Tips on Writing

■ Write when it is a pleasure and not a chore (unless, of course, this is never the case for you). The casual guideline about letters to family and friends is that short and frequent is better than long and infrequent. However, this is a matter of temperament. The general feeling is that it is delightful to get personal mail at all, and never mind whether it is short and infrequent, or otherwise.

■ When months pass between letters, we exhaust ourselves reporting everything we've done during that time. Skip most of it and focus on something you're doing, reading, or enjoying now. It's shorter and feels more immediate to your reader.

■ Remember your writing teacher's advice to "Elaborate! Elaborate!" Instead of merely reporting that you went camping, tell a story or describe something you saw so that the other person can visualize it. Almost any sentence lends itself to some kind of elaboration.

■ Include cartoons, newspaper clippings, snapshots, bookmarks, or other materials that are satisfying to receive and make your letter look like more than it is.

■ Postcards help you keep in touch when you haven't time for a letter. Keep a stack of colorful, funny, or old-time postcards near your letter-writing area and get in the habit of sending off a couple a week. This will make you popular and will relieve you of the guilt that unanswered mail produces in most people.

■ If you have trouble getting started, use a quotation that expresses your feeling and then build on it. For example, Dorothy Thompson wrote, "Children want to feel instinctively that their father is behind them as solid as a mountain, but, like a mountain, is something to look up to." You could go on to give examples of how your father makes you feel secure and the reasons you look up to him. Or, if you and your dad share an interest in sports or you do things together, you could use Solar Forst's "The good father never stops being a child" and recall some of the best times you've had with him. Other quotations:

My heart is happy, my mind is free
I had a father who talked with me.
—HILDA BIGELOW

I am many things besides, but I am daddy's girl too and so I will
remain—all the way to the old folks' home.
—PAULA WEIDEGER

When Father smiled, it was like the sun coming out, and spring and
summer in your heart.
—GLADYS TABER

All the feeling which my father could not put into words was in his
hand—any dog, child or horse would recognize the kindness of it.
—FREYA STARK

A daughter's love for a kind father . . . is mixed with the careless happiness
of childhood, which can never come again.
—CONSTANCE FENIMORE WOOLSON

Special Situations

■ One of the best letters to family doesn't even need postage: the notes or drawings put in children's lunchboxes; the note in a traveling spouse's luggage; the letter of congratulations to a hardworking student; the simple "I love you" pinned to a bedspread. These are worth many times their weight in the gold of family harmony.

■ Mother's Day and Father's Day allow you to say what might feel uncomfortable or excessive at another time. Take the opportunity—you'll be glad you did. Whether you write a letter or add a message to a commercial greeting card, include at least one anecdote, happy memory, or compliment ("I love it when you tear an article out of the newspaper that you think will interest me"; "I'll never forget your Sunday morning pancakes"; "I wouldn't have gotten into basketball if it hadn't been for you"; "I like the way you discuss your work with me as if I actually knew what you were talking about!"). For ideas, try finishing these sentences: "I'll never forget when you . . ."; "You were so funny when you . . ."; "Thanks for the time you . . ."; "One of my best memories is . . ."; "I like watching you get excited about . . ."; "I've never forgotten what you once told me . . ." When expressing your feelings, keep them simple: "I love you"; "I say 'thank you' for you every day"; "I've looked up to you all my life"; "Thank you for all you've done for me and given me and been to me." After a mother of eight died, the cards, letters, and photos from her children filled an appliance carton—and each was annotated in pencil with dates and comments about her love for that child. (On Mother's Day or Father's Day you can also send special notes to people who've done dad-ly or mom-ly things for you—a grandparent, older friend, teacher, neighbor.)

■ When children are in the care of adults other than their parents or guardians, they should have with them a letter authorizing emergency medical help. In the case of summer camps or day-care providers, a form for this purpose is generally provided. But if you leave your children with someone for the weekend, write: "I [name] give permission to [name of person caring for your children] to authorize any necessary medical emergency care for [name of child or children] from [date] to [date]." Sign and date the letter and give a telephone number where you can be reached.

■ When the families of an engaged couple do not know each other, there is often an exchange of letters expressing pleasure in the engagement of their son and daughter and perhaps arranging a visit. A courteous and graceful gesture is a note written before the visit by the prospective son- or daughter-in-law expressing appreciation for the invitation and pleasure in the forthcoming visit.

■ While it is rarely a good idea to write to unknown individuals who are incarcerated, it is generally a good idea to remember family and friends who are in jail or in prison—and with whom you have a close relationship. They appreciate mail. The first several letters will be awkward, but if you can establish some neutral subjects (books, interests, hobbies, mutual friends, social issues), the letters will become easier to write with time and practice.

■ When dealing with strong feelings, letters are effective because they distance people from each other and from the problem while obliging them to think clearly enough to put their thoughts down on paper. However, letters can also worsen a problem. Written words are not as easily forgotten as words spoken in the heat of anger; they can be reread many times by a grudge-holder. Words without accompanying gestures, smiles, and apologetic looks are colder and more inflexible. Think carefully about the temperament of the person to whom you are writing and determine an approach that the person will be able to "hear"; do not write in the heat of your strongest feelings—that is, it is good to write then, but do not mail it; reread and rewrite your letter several times over a period of days.

■ When writing to children: Print or type your letter; it's easier to read. Include a stimulating, challenging, or curious statement. Relate a bit of trivia, thought problem, word puzzle, anecdote. Children enjoy being let into the adult world; tell them about something important to you—a job problem, your garden, the next election. Share your thoughts, discuss ideas, ask questions. Avoid the word "kids" ("I'm so proud of you kids!"). For their reply to you, enclose a few postcards or a self-addressed envelope with an unattached stamp (so the stamp isn't wasted if they don't write back). Or, construct a letter for the child to return to you that consists of boxes to check off with various made-up statements and "news." This technique will probably net you a letter at least once. Very young children appreciate mail even if they can't read. Keep in mind that a parent will be reading your letter aloud; things sound different that way. Include a colorful drawing or cut-out picture along with the child's name (which many youngsters recognize early on), a picture of you, a fancy pencil, a small toy.

■ When writing a child who is away from home for the first time, you can say lightly, "We miss you!" but don't emphasize how empty the house seems; some children feel responsible for their parents' feelings. Don't detail what everyone at home is doing; that too can make a child sad. Instead, ask questions that will provide something to write back about: What time do you get up? What do you usually eat for breakfast? Do you have a swimming class? Who else lives in your cabin? Are there any animals there? Have you been in a canoe yet? What is your favorite activity? Who is your counselor? Have you made new friends?

■ To help your children become letter writers: see that they receive mail themselves; supply them with small sheets of wide-lined paper and interesting pens; sit with them during the writing of their first two dozen brief notes— being with you is part of the fun; make the writing of a thank-you note a requirement for using the gift or spending the money, but let them do it at their own pace and, whenever possible, make a mini-party out of it, writing thank-you notes of your own at the same time.

■ Although the term "pen pal" suggests youthful letter writers, it includes not only dedicated young correspondents but thousands of adults who write with great enthusiasm to people they've never met. A better term might be "pen friend." In the beginning, be discreet about giving personal information; start with facts that most people know about you and reserve more private details for later in the correspondence. The main "rule" for pen friends is to be yourself. Where one person is put off by a ten-page letter from a new correspondent, another person is delighted. The person who talks only about self-centered news fascinates one person, bores the next. The letter writer who never tells anything personal is considered discreet by some, too uptight by others. When you are being yourself you'll end up with those who like you just as you are. To find a pen pal, contact one of the following organizations. International Pen Friends, P.O. Box 156, Suffolk Park NSW 2481, Australia (www.ipf.net.au), has members of all ages, was established in 1967, and charges fees for lists of pen pals. World Pen Pals, P.O. Box 337, Saugerties NY 12477 (www.world-pen-pals.com) was founded in 1950 and offers a limited free membership to letter writers of all ages. The Student Letter Exchange, 211 Broadway, STE 201, Lynbrook, NY 11563 (www.pen-pal

.com/student.php) offers four names and addresses for no charge. The International Friendship League, 55 Mount Vernon Street, Boston, MA 02108 (www.iflworld.org), was founded in 1931; they select an appropriate pen friend for you.

Format

■ Letters to family and friends can use any format you like. Acquaintances are a little different; the less well you know a person, the more formal (personal stationery, handwritten) the letter or note will be.

WORDS

activities	friendship	news	tell
affectionately	funny	pleased	vacation
announce	goings-on	proud	weather
busy	happy	recently	
events	healthy	satisfying	

PHRASES

a warm hello	missing you
did you know	remember the time
good to hear from you	sympathize with
have you ever thought about	thinking of you
have you heard	we were so happy to hear that
how did you manage to	we wondered if
I enjoyed hearing about	what did you think of
I hope that by now	whatever happened to
I meant to tell you	what would you say to
in your last letter you didn't mention	when are you going to
I thought you might like to know	

SENTENCES

Are you planning to travel this summer?

Have you read any good books lately?

I can't tell you how much I appreciated your letter.

I'll be counting the minutes till I see you.

I'm wondering how your finals went.

I think of you every day/so often.

I've never written to anyone I didn't know before, so let's see how this goes!

I was so glad to see your handwriting again.

Please write and tell me all the news.

We'd love to see pictures of the new house.

We thoroughly enjoy your letters—you can't write often enough for us.

What a dear letter!

Write when you have time, will you?

You must send the quickest of moral support notes to me because I'm having an absolutely dreadful time at the office.

You're in my thoughts every minute of the day.

Your last letter was priceless/delightful/a pleasure to receive.

Your letters always brighten my day.

Your letter was such fun to read—thanks!

PARAGRAPHS

Hello! My name is Henry Earlforward and in addition to being your new pen friend I'm a bookseller by vocation and a bibliophile by avocation. I hope you like books as much as I do.

I can hardly wait for summer to get here. What's that you say? Summer has come and gone? The kids are back in school? But . . . but . . . I really don't know where the time goes.

Please say hello to everyone and tell Audrey thanks again for taking us out. We had a great time! Your family is so warm and fun to be around—so much energy and self-assurance! I miss you all!

I'm sorry about this one-size-fits-all letter, but my negligence in corresponding with all of you finally got so oppressive that I had to take immediate steps. These immediate steps have taken me almost three weeks. Meanwhile, my brand-new personal computer was crying out, "Use me! Use me!" Then . . . Poof! Voilà! Eureka! Hoover! . . . this letter was conceived and executed.

Will wonders never cease? Hannah is finally sprouting some teeth—believe it or don't. I mean she's only seventeen months old! I was beginning to wonder if kids need teeth to get into first grade. Well, those teeth may have been slow in coming but at least they brought out the monster in her for four months. Actually she's been pretty good considering how sore her mouth must be.

This evening we're having our first interview with a private adoption agency—at home, in my natural habitat. Next week we start paying them money and attend a two-day workshop. Then the following week there's another two-day workshop, then more interviews—all this to complete a home study. After that the search begins and could take anywhere from one day to eighteen months. It makes me nervous in the service because it's such a big step, but I think we're ready for it. Keep us in your thoughts!

SAMPLE LETTERS

Dear Angela and Tom,

Parlez-vous français? That means "Sorry I haven't written lately." It all started when I ran out of lined paper at my office. I hate trying to write on this blank stuff, it's like trying to drive on a snow-covered road, only a little safer.

So how's the world treating you these days? We are winding down from another busy summer and hoping for a beautiful and serene fall. Whoever coined the phrase "lazy days of summer" ought to have their vital signs checked. I mean, who are we kidding here?

Both Kalli and Lauren are taking a gymnastics class, so we spend a lot of after-dinner time in the yard practicing what they are learning, with me as their "equipment." But it's fun, at least until the mosquitoes begin setting up their derricks.

I had a busy summer at the office, but September is slow as usual. The kids are back in school, the farmers are busy, and bow-hunting season is here. It's actually a nice pace although hard on the budget. I think I would enjoy dentistry a lot more if I didn't have to make money at it.

I'm manager of our softball team this season. It's one of those things that doesn't sound like much, and shouldn't be, but is. I'd rate it about a 9.8 on the headache scale (of 10). We are winning at 11-3 and tied for first in our twelve-team league, but, honestly, the manager has nothing to do with that. Now if we were losing, then it would be my fault. The hardest part is collecting money from people for various things and making a lot of phone calls.

Well, that's all for now. Say hello to the kids for me.

With love,

———

Dear Mrs. K.,

It was so nice to hear from you. I wish we could have had a longer visit at Easter. This semester has gone by so quickly—there are only three weeks left. Maybe we can get together when I come home for the summer.

I know you don't watch TV, so I'll tell you what Oprah Winfrey said. The average cost of a wedding is $13,000. Can you believe that? Mom tried to break the news to Daddy. He guessed the average wedding cost was $700 to $1,000. Poor Daddy.

Because there *is* going to be a wedding! We think next year. Can you believe I've written a whole page and haven't mentioned the love of my life? Jeff is fine, and sends his love too.

With a hug,

_____

SUBJ: Just keepin' in touch
DATE: 04-05-05 13:43:52 EDT
FROM: md@email.com
TO: rm@email.com

Hi mom. Of course I'm alive. Had you doubts? I hardly think that three days without hearing from me justifies using capital letters.

_____

Dear Fritz,

And how is my favorite uncle? Your letter came the other day and it was one of the nicest I've gotten in a long time. It was great seeing you over Christmas break.

Baseball is now in full swing (get it?), and we're running sprints every morning by 6:00 a.m. By 10:00 we're hitting off the machine. I can't wait for the weather to clear up so we can go outside to do all this.

Tell everybody "Hi" for me, and if Liz has any questions about college, she can write me. I can't answer them all but tell her the first quarter of the first year is the toughest, and it's all downhill after that!

Love,

_____

Dear Lettie,

We all enjoyed your last letter, and have taped the cartoons up on the refrigerator.

Somewhere I read that life, to a five-year-old, is full of alternatives. Tommy is forever asking, "Mommy, would you rather have me get eaten by an alligator, bonked on the head, or fall out of a skyscraper window?"

I went bargain hunting at some rummage sales last weekend. I guess you could say I got my limit. The Lamberts were here for two days along with their poodle, Muffy (French for "lint ball," isn't it?).

I bought a generic fruit punch that says one of its ingredients is "natural punch flavoring." What is a punch? I assume it grows on trees, and I'm guessing it needs a warm climate.

We're having a party Friday night—twenty-two people. It's been the best way I've discovered to get the spring cleaning done.

This letter is more disjointed than most. I guess I don't try often enough to harness a thought, and now that I'm trying, my fingers are too weak to hold the reins. You like my metaphor? I ought to be a writer.

Give my love to everyone!

––––––––

SUBJ: Friday morning
DATE: 11-02-23 13:24:46 EST
FROM: mdk@email.com
TO: rmk@email.com

I will medley for you when I plane in to the Cities. Who's going to car me home from the airport? I'm going to go CD now.

––––––––

Dear Wu Sung,

This is my first experiment with writing to someone I've never met. It's a good thing that you speak (and write) English or this wouldn't be possible. Unfortunately I don't speak any other languages, not even Spanish, which I took for two years in high school.

To help us get to know each other, I'm sending you a few things that show my little corner of the world: a road map, postcards, a small travel book about Chicago, some pages from this morning's newspaper that tell what's going on in Chicago these days, and some pictures of my family, my apartment, and our cat, Mulch.

I work in a bank, so in my next letter I'll send a picture of the bank, some brochures describing its features, and tell you a little about what I do there.

I look forward to hearing about you and your corner of the world!

––––––––

Dear Christopher,

Congratulations on doing such a good job on your term paper. I read it through twice and learned so much. I'm not surprised you got an A+ on it. I especially liked the way you paced yourself on this long drawn-out project. I remember you starting your note cards back in February, and then working on it steadily all spring. I'm impressed!

Love,
Mom

––––––––

See also: ADVICE, ANNIVERSARIES, APOLOGIES, CONGRATULA-TIONS, "GET WELL," HOLIDAYS, LOVE LETTERS, SYMPATHY, THANK YOU, WEDDINGS, WELCOME

TWENTY-THREE

FAXED LETTERS

With the only certainty in our daily existence being change, and
a rate of change growing always faster in a kind of technological leapfrog game,
speed helps people think they are keeping up.
—GAIL SHEEHY

The fax (short for facsimile machine) has become indispensable to many individuals and businesses, increasing the speed of communication and changing our idea of "response time" from days to minutes. It scans letters, converts the words and graphics to signals that can be sent over telephone lines, and transmits them to a machine at the other end, where the process is reversed. Like a photocopying machine, it works only with already prepared documents.

A letter sent by fax is like any other letter. However, once it's been typed or printed and signed, it's inserted in the fax machine. No folding it, addressing an envelope, putting the letter in the envelope, sealing it, stamping it—and waiting several days for it to reach your addressee. The appeal is obvious.

However, the virtue of the faxed page is its speed, not its good looks. Some fax paper is not appealing aesthetically. The print can be blurry or smudged or at times illegible, depending on the quality of the original document and the machines used to transmit it.

Fax Letters When

- communicating overseas
- someone is difficult to reach by phone
- speed is the principal factor
- the appearance of the document is not an issue
- you've been requested to

How to Say It

- Determine whether faxing is indicated. If you and your addressee agree you need a speedy transferal of data or information, it is the best choice.
- Write your letter as carefully as you would if you were putting it in an envelope and sending it by mail.
- Include on a cover sheet or the first page of your fax: the recipient's name, department, and fax number; your name along with information on how to contact you (fax number, e-mail address, company name and address, phone number); the number of pages being faxed (include the cover sheet in your count).

What Not to Say

- Don't send thank-you letters by fax unless you know the other person well; doing it this way parcels out the cost of the thank you between sender and recipient. It's also not very heartwarming.
- Don't send confidential or sensitive information by fax, unless you're certain your intended recipient will collect it on the other end. Anyone can read your letter while the fax machine is printing it or while it waits to be picked up by your recipient. Ads may say, "Please fax confidential résumé," but it is better to assume that confidentiality is not absolute.

Tips on Writing

- ■ Handwritten letters or notes don't make satisfactory faxes; printed copy is the norm.
- ■ Use a readable font. A 10-point size is the minimum; 12-point is better.
- ■ When the page being faxed is important, send the fax for instant reception but mail the hard copy at the same time so the other person has a decent-looking original. (You may want to note at the bottom of the letter that this is a confirmation of a fax sent on such-and-such a date.)
- ■ Read over faxes before sending; they can constitute legally binding documents.
- ■ Don't fax something that has been faxed several times; each transmission reduces its sharpness, making it hard to read and unappealing. Any fax that looks a little fuzzy when you get it is going to look worse after you send it on. To see what your letter will look like when faxed to the recipient, run it through your fax machine on copy mode. The result is about what they'll get.
- ■ When faxing letters or documents with small, dense print, adjust your

resolution to "superfine." The document will be easier to read and the transmittal time will be increased only slightly.

■ Keep in mind that the fax machine reads everything. Heavy fonts, graphics, borders, icons all increase transmission time and, on the other end, gobble up ink.

■ If you rely heavily on the fax machine, it is thrifty and efficient to design letterhead stationery that will accommodate information needed for faxing. Experiment with different ink colors, letterheads, fonts, and logos in order to find the ones that look best after being faxed. You can then do away with the cover page, saving yourself and your recipient time, paper, and phone costs.

■ For fine-tuning your faxed letters, see Audrey Glassman's *Can I Fax a Thank-You Note?*

Special Situations

■ Faxing is useful for correspondence with people in other time zones. Many foreign hotels now routinely request that reservations be made by fax. Faxes have all the immediacy of a telephone call but are less expensive.

■ Faxes are being used for sending routine information quickly: receiving/confirming/changing orders, invoices, shipping information, specifications, quotes, and corrections to contracts or proposals in process. When faxes are legible, this has proved to be convenient and cost-effective.

■ Faxing has made possible long-distance business transactions where documents are sent to someone to be signed or initialed and faxed back. In many cases an original signature is eventually needed, but this allows the transaction to proceed in a timely manner.

■ Faxing unrequested sales messages is not appreciated. Theoretically someone could fax a sales letter to all the fax numbers they find. However, this means recipients pay to receive something they didn't request. Although most of us have learned to live with unsolicited third-class mail, we would not be pleased to have to pay to receive it. Because it costs the recipient to receive a fax, be sure the person welcomes it.

■ Faxing résumés and application letters has become acceptable to many companies and actively solicited by others. Faxing a résumé or letter of application in such cases is appropriate and probably necessary since other applicants will be faxing theirs. However, at this stage in the technology of fax machines, your résumé won't look as professional as a mailed original.

■ Faxes can be sent to anyone who has a fax machine—and to anyone who doesn't. People without a machine of their own send and receive faxes at photocopy centers. To send, bring in the letter or pages to be faxed while you wait. Don't take stapled items; this annoys copy shop personnel since pages are sent one at a time. To receive, notify your correspondent of the store's fax number and advise them to put your name and phone number at the top of the fax so the store can call you when it arrives.

Format

■ A faxed letter uses standard letterhead or memo stationery.

■ Small preprinted fax information forms are available to stick onto the first page of your letter or memo, thus making the cover sheet unnecessary. This only works, however, when there's room on the page for the form.

WORDS

attached	forward	quickly	speedy
confirm	immediately	request	transmittal
correction	instructions	rush	urgent
following	prompt	send	

PHRASES

additional instructions	please acknowledge receipt
as soon as possible	price quotation
as you requested/at your request	prompt reply
because of the tight deadline	the information you requested
by return fax	to advise you
by this afternoon	to speed your application
happy to be able to send	transmittal problems
I need a response by	via facsimile transmission and U.S. mail
pass along	

SENTENCES

Below are the figures you need for the meeting this afternoon.

Here is the missing paragraph for my newsletter piece.

I authorize you to debit my credit card in the amount of $4,000 (card number, signature, and date below).

I'd appreciate a call at 661-555-4234 when you receive this.

I'm sorry about the rush, but I'd appreciate it if you could look over this press release and let me know by noon if it's all right with you.

In response to your ad for an estimator at your headquarters office, I am faxing you my résumé.

Let me know if you have any problems reading this.

Please have the current owners and the buyers sign below to indicate that they have received this disclosure, and then fax it back to this office.

Please read and initial the attached rider to your contract #007945.

This will confirm the arrangements for delivery of order #C18803 made on the telephone this morning.

We were ready to start printing when Itzik Landsman pointed out that these figures don't make sense—will you check them and get back to us right away?

You may use this form to respond.

Your Peterkin Turkeys will be delivered today between 2:00 p.m. and 4:00 p.m. Please check the delivery against the attached order, sign to acknowledge receipt, and return the signed order form to us.

PARAGRAPHS

Your good faith estimate of closing costs is attached. Please read it and call me with any questions. I'd like to get a final copy typed up this afternoon. Thanks.

Bettina Vanderpoel has provided us with the necessary figures and documents. Please check the attached statement for errors or inconsistencies and fax it back with your corrections as soon as you can. Before 3:00 today would be helpful. Thanks!

O. A. Pardiggle Termite Inc. Wood destroying pests and organisms inspection report for 2405 Cedarwood. Please read, sign, and return ASAP.

Can you let us know by this afternoon if you can supply us with one hundred (100) pool-testing kits from stock? We need them immediately. Is there a possibility of one- or two-day delivery? I assume this purchase would fall under your bulk-rate (10 percent) discount.

I'm faxing both you and your lawyer a copy of the revised contract. If you leave a message on my voice mail or fax me back with an okay, I can overnight the original copies of the contract to you for your signature first thing Monday morning. I'm looking forward to working with you.

Please complete the attached Uniform Commercial Loan Application, responding to all fields marked with an X. Sign and return by 9/23.

TO: Faith Paleologos
FAX: 515-555-1999
FROM: Hervey Allen
TEL/FAX: 515-555-8365

I've just learned that you have an immediate opening for a counselor in your short-term high-adventure program for adolescent boys.

As indicated on the résumé on the next page, I've worked with both adolescents and wilderness adventure programs, and I have my B.A. degree in human services.

I would like to set up an appointment to discuss this position with you.

Thank you for your time and attention.

––––––––

TO: Customer Service, Fielding Furniture
FROM: Bridget Allworthy, Allworthy Mfg.
DATE: July 10, 2010
RE: Floor Mat #4A-668

The second sheet of this fax is the page from your catalog that describes the floor mat we recently ordered. Whoever wrote the copy for this item had never met the mat. This floor mat is NOT slip resistant, it is not forest green (we don't know what color it is, but we are certain it is not forest green), and it is impossible to vacuum, as suggested in the description. Most important, it is quite a bit shy of the 4' × 8' dimensions promised.

Please send instructions on how we can return the mat at your expense and obtain a refund. Thank you.

––––––––

Kim Cameron
Fax # 307-555-7777
August 31, 2010

Dear Kim Cameron,

While putting the final touches to our 40th Annual Investment Banking Convention brochure, I realized we don't have a professional bio for you. Will you fax us one (about a paragraph in length) as soon as possible? Thank you.

––––––––

Magnolia Hawks
I.B.C. Committee
Fax # 718-555-2222
Tel 818-555-3241
ATTN: Anthony Benson
Van Dine Printing Co. Inc.

Tony,

I'm relieved you haven't printed the booklets yet. Please substitute the paragraph below for the last paragraph on page 4.

All submitted technical papers must be publication-ready, printed on one side only, be accompanied by an abstract, summary, and bibliography, and not have been published previously elsewhere. Submission of a paper implies permission to publish.

Alvin

Fax 818-555-2314

———

FROM: Valentine Wannop
Security Systems
Fax # 212-555-1443

TO: Christopher Tietjens
Fax # 212-555-4877

PAGES SENT: 2

Chris, I need to turn in the attached meeting announcement this afternoon. Is everything correct? Thanks. Val

———

TO: Lambert Strether
     Strether Medical Supply
     Fax 612-555-2566
FROM: Chadwick Newsome
     Newsome Mfg. Co. Inc.
     Fax 715-555-2534
RE: Order #LSX-655-12211
DATE: Oct. 12, 2010

The above-referenced shipment should have arrived before noon today and did not. Are we scheduled to receive it this afternoon? Let me know. We were assured we would have it today. Thanks.

———

See also: MEMOS

TWENTY-FOUR

FOLLOW-UP LETTERS

*Bulldogs have been known to fall on their swords
when confronted by my superior tenacity.*
—MARGARET HALSEY

Writing a follow-up letter on the heels of an earlier letter, conversation, or meeting is a graceful way of tying up a loose end, reminding someone to carry through on a promised action, or building on something that went before. Sometimes you need to write several follow-up letters. Combine your bulldog tenacity with charm and originality, and you will achieve your goal.

Letitia Baldrige, the New York writer of etiquette books and former White House social secretary, encourages following up meetings and lunches with letters. "This little personal touch, which takes three minutes, makes an enormous impression," she says. "The ones who do it regularly in business are such standouts. They're the ones who jump ahead."

Write a Follow-Up Letter to

- amplify material in your original sales letter after it brings a response (order, expression of interest, request for more information)
- confirm a meeting date, a telephone or other oral agreement, a message left with a third party
- express appreciation and acknowledge what was accomplished at a business lunch, dinner, or meeting
- express appreciation and the hopes that they are interested to someone who has visited your school, university, college, or organization as an applicant
- express your appreciation and impressions after a visit to a school, university, or college or after attending a meeting as a guest or potential member

- inquire whether your unacknowledged gift arrived
- reinforce sales visits or demonstrations
- remind someone of an appointment, meeting, favor, request, inquiry, invitation, payment, or work deadline
- remind someone that you are waiting for answers, information, confirmation, or merchandise that you wrote about earlier
- send omitted or supplemental material or to revise an earlier correspondence
- someone who has not responded to a sales letter or product literature
- someone who hasn't returned your telephone call
- sum up what was accomplished in a meeting or interview so that there is a record and so that your view of what went on can be verified by others
- thank someone for a job interview
- verify with a customer that a shipping problem or missing order has been settled to their satisfaction

How to Say It

- State why you are writing ("I haven't heard from you"; "I wanted to remind you").
- Refer to the key idea (the meeting, your last letter, the unacknowledged gift).
- Thank the person for the interest shown or tie your purpose in writing to your last contact with them. If necessary, remind the person who you are ("We met last week at the performance boats trade show") or what your telephone discussion was about.
- Tell what you want the person to do: acknowledge receipt of merchandise, telephone you, send payment, reply to an earlier letter.
- Close with an expression of appreciation for the person's time and attention, or with a forward-looking statement about further business or contacts.

What Not to Say

- Don't imply your reader is thoughtless or negligent when writing about an unanswered letter or unacknowledged gift. Although the possibility of mail going astray is slim, you must allow for it. Even if the recipient is at fault, it is neither good manners nor good business to point this out.
- A follow-up letter should not simply repeat earlier information (except in the case of confirming an oral agreement or discussion). You need an identifiable reason for writing, such as sending new information, requesting a

response, making a special offer, thanking for a previous order or meeting.

Tips on Writing

■ When writing a follow-up letter to an unanswered request, query, or letter, repeat your original message (or include a copy of it). Go into a little more detail on the importance of the person's response.

■ Some offices maintain a tickler file. When sending a letter (inviting someone to speak at the awards banquet, for example), make a note on the calendar a week or two later to verify that you've heard from the person. Letters awaiting responses can be kept together, arranged by the date when a follow-up letter should be sent.

■ When sending a follow-up letter to an unacknowledged statement or invoice, include the necessary information (amount, account number, date due, days past due) with a simple notice, "A brief reminder." This is often all it takes since some late payments are oversights. (If this letter brings no response, see COLLECTION.)

Special Situations

■ After interviewing for a job, send a follow-up letter immediately, before a decision has been reached. "A follow-up letter after a job interview can often be the extra push that gets you the job." (Harold E. Meyer) State that you enjoyed the interview and restate your abilities and your interest in the position. Emphasize a particular strong point. If there were any misunderstandings or any points you failed to clarify during the interview, you can remedy the situation in this letter. Close with your thanks and a courtesy such as "I look forward to hearing from you."

■ If, following an interview, you are not offered the position, write a follow-up letter anyway. Thank the person for their time, tactfully express your disappointment, ask that they keep your résumé on file, and close with an appreciation of the person and the company.

■ When someone fails to acknowledge your gift, write a follow-up letter (about eight weeks after sending the gift). Describe the gift. Business gifts are often opened by staff rather than by the intended recipient and wedding gifts can be easily misidentified. Adopt a neutral tone, emphasizing your concern about receipt of the gift rather than negligence in acknowledging it.

■ When a meeting or event has been scheduled months in advance, it's helpful to send follow-up notes reminding people. Repeat all the information along with a pleasant remark about hoping to see them.

■ Follow-up sales letters are essential. Write promptly, while the customer is still thinking about the presentation, earlier sales message, or visit from a sales representative. Write after a customer requests a brochure, stops by your booth at a trade fair, calls with a question, or responds to an ad. Follow-up letters are also sent when you receive no response to a sales letter. Refer to the earlier contact ("I wrote you several weeks ago to tell you about . . ." or "Did you receive the certificate we sent you, good for . . . ?"), thank the person for their interest or the time they gave you, add something new to the overall message, emphasize the one or two features the person seemed most taken with during your presentation, reinforce your original strong selling points, and suggest an action: place an order, call you, call a toll-free number, accept a trial subscription, use the enclosed discount offer. If this is a second letter, emphasize a different benefit or aspect of your product or service. This letter is also shorter or longer than the first and perhaps different in tone. Although all these can be called follow-up letters, they are primarily sales letters.

■ Successful businesses keep in touch with customers after they purchase products or services, sending follow-up letters to see how things are working out, to inform customers of new product lines, to remind them that you appreciated their business in the past and hope to serve them again.

■ After a meeting or conference call, write a follow-up letter to the other participants. Outline the issues discussed and decisions made in order to provide a written record of what was said. In *The 100 Most Difficult Business Letters You'll Ever Have to Write, Fax, or E-mail*, Bernard Heller recommends writing a follow-up letter or memo when you want to be certain the ideas you contributed in a meeting are credited to you. He suggests saying that you've had some further thoughts on the ideas you submitted and that you think it's a good idea to get all of them down on paper: "This is the gist of the ideas I offered. A detailed explanation of each one is on the pages that follow." Patricia King (*Never Work for a Jerk!*) suggests giving a written summary of meetings and conferences to your boss and keeping one in your own file.

Format

■ Most business follow-up letters are typed on letterhead or memo stationery. Social letters or brief reminder-type notes can be handwritten.

■ Although not widely used, "to remind" cards can be sent to follow up a telephone invitation. Handwrite the information in regular invitation format on printed cards, foldovers, or personal stationery: "This is to remind you that Mr. and Mrs. Louis Rony expect you on . . ."

WORDS

acknowledge	mention	remind	review
confirm	notify	repeat	suggest
feedback	prompt	reply	summarize
inform	remember	response	

PHRASES

about a month ago, we sent you/ wrote you about

a little/brief reminder

am writing to remind you that

appreciate your interest in

as I have not heard from you

as I mentioned on the phone this morning

as mentioned in your letter

as we agreed yesterday

beginning to wonder if you received

I am still interested in

if you want further documentation on

I know how busy you are, so

in reference/reply/response to

jog your memory

just a note to remind you

make sure you're aware of

now that you've had time to consider/review/familiarize yourself with

prompt you to

since we haven't heard from you

thank you for your letter telling us about

thought you might like to be reminded

SENTENCES

After visiting with you at the textile trade convention last week, I telephoned Yvonne Dorm, our representative in your area, and asked her to call on you.

Did you receive the Blake River catalog and discounted price list that you requested?

I am writing to follow up on our conversation about the three-party agreement among Clara Hittaway, Amelia Fawn, and Georgiana Fawn.

I appreciate the time you gave me last week to demonstrate our unique Lammeter Integrated Phone Service System.

I enjoyed visiting with you last week when you stopped in to pick up some brochures at Spina Travel Consultants.

If you did not receive my materials, I would be happy to send you another set.

I'm wondering if you received my telephone message last week.

It occurred to me that I haven't received confirmation that you received the report mailed on June 4—could you let me know on the enclosed, self-addressed postcard?

It's so unlike you not to have responded that I suspect you didn't receive the wedding invitation.

I wanted to follow up on our phone conversation of yesterday.

I wanted to make sure you're aware of the service warranty on your new microwave.

Just a note to see if you received the message I left for you Friday.

Now that you have had a chance to tour the proposed site, I'd like to set a date to discuss our options.

On February 7, I sent a questionnaire to you on the departmental reorganization.

Reminder: staff meeting 3:30 p.m. Thursday in the teachers' lounge.

Thank you for letting me help you with the purchase of your new home, which I hope you are enjoying—I'm enclosing my business card in case I can be of further service to you or to anyone you know.

Thank you for taking the time this morning to describe the media buyer position, to show me around the complex, and to introduce me to other members of your staff.

PARAGRAPHS

I was delighted to meet with you at your home and hear your thoughts about our community. The best part of running for the Bonville City Council is the opportunity to talk with neighbors like you about our future. Please call my office with your concerns, and remember to vote on November 7!

On October 26, I submitted to you a letter of application in response to your advertisement for a moldmaker. I hope you have not yet filled the position and that you are considering my application. Could you please let me know where you are in this process? Thank you.

I'm looking forward to having dinner with you Friday evening. I'll be waiting in the lobby of the Rosalba Hotel at 7:00 p.m. See you then!

Several weeks ago we sent you a packet of informational materials on Topaz Island Resort. Now that you've had a chance to look over the color photographs of our unique vacation paradise, would you like to reserve vacation time in one of the ultramodern cabins? Our spaces fill up quickly after the first of the year, so make your choice soon!

Thank you for the courtesy and interest you showed me yesterday when I stopped in to inquire about the opening for a child care advocate. I didn't expect to do more than pick up an application form, so it was a pleasure to discuss the job with you. As you could probably tell from our conversation, I am very interested in the position and believe I am well qualified for it. I'll have my references and résumé in the mail to you by the end of the week.

As you know, the Norrington Trolley and Lunch Tour will begin its expanded summer schedule on June 2. Please let me know if we are on schedule to have the new seat covers installed by the May 25 date we agreed on. Thank you.

I know you've been especially busy these last few weeks trying to settle into your new home, but I'd like to make sure that you received a package I mailed you a month ago. It was a housewarming gift, of course. I did insure it, so if it's lost I can have a tracer put on it. Do let me know, won't you, if it hasn't shown up?

SAMPLE LETTERS

Dear Arnold,

You asked me to let you know John Culver's thoughts about the sample of shielding film I'd sent him. He said it was just what they'd had in mind. He had a few questions about the electrical connection and the wiring pattern. He explained what they are currently doing and said they'll send me a sketch of the preferred pattern.

I promised to send him some mesh samples as soon as Hildegarde has prepared them, and we agreed to set up a date to further discuss their needs.

Yours truly,

———

Dear Professor Fansler,

As one of the contributors to *The Handbook of English Studies*, you will want to know that there have been two changes: (1) the handbook is scheduled to appear in early December of this year, not in May, as previously planned; (2) it will be published in four volumes rather than two.

Many authors exceeded their space allocations, making a two-volume set unmanageable (it would have run nearly 1,300 pages per volume). Also, a smaller size per volume and thus a lower volume price will result in a larger sales potential (each volume is available individually).

All authors who contributed to the original volume I will still receive complimentary copies of volumes I and II, and those who contributed to original volume II will receive both volumes III and IV as complimentary copies.

Sincerely,

_____

TO: Johannes Rohn
FROM: Oren Cornell
DATE: February 10, 2010

We have not yet received your year-end report. I'm enclosing a copy of my original letter and another copy of the report form. Please complete it and turn it in as soon as possible. We now have all the evaluations but yours, and need to process them before the winter recess.

_____

Dear Ms. Collen:

We hope you are as pleased with your Safe-Home Security System as we were pleased to install it for you. Let us know if you experience any problems in these first few months. Very few of our customers do, but we're available if anything should come up.

You did not choose to purchase our Monthly Inspection Service at this time. However, if you change your mind, we can easily arrange it for you.

It was a pleasure doing business with you!

Sincerely yours,

_____

Dear Mr. Ayrton,

Just a note to remind you that I still haven't received my copy of the Brodie contract. It's probably in the mail, but with December being such a busy month, I thought I'd mention it.

Sincerely,

_____

Dear Julia Avery:

I'm wondering if you received my letter of January 14 asking you to speak at the Society of Professional Engineers meeting to be held May 3. We are still interested in having you present your recent work to the group.

If you did not receive my letter or if you would like additional information, please call me at 612-555-6613. We expect to send the program to the printers by the end of the month.

Sincerely yours,

_____

Dear Ms. Edelman:

On September 16, I sent you my résumé and reprints of several articles I have authored in response to your classified ad for a career services specialist.

As I have had no response, I wonder if you received my materials. Enclosed is a self-addressed stamped postcard. Would you please indicate whether my materials were received by you and, if not, if you are still interested in seeing them?

Thank you.

Sincerely,

See also: ACKNOWLEDGMENTS, APPRECIATION, CREDIT, EMPLOYMENT, RESPONSES, SALES, THANK YOU

TWENTY-FIVE

FUNDRAISING LETTERS

In the end, raising money is basically a matter of going out there and asking. There are no shortcuts.
—GEORGETTE MOSBACHER

Intense and growing competition for the charitable dollar means that your fundraising letter has to pack the maximum of persuasion and appeal in the minimum of words. In the average home mailbox, fundraising appeals will outnumber every kind of letter except sales letters. How do you convince readers to set *your* letter aside for a contribution?

It helps if you are writing on behalf of a long-established organization with a good reputation. Beyond that, your best strategy is vigorous writing: compelling anecdotes, easily grasped and persuasive statistics, thought-provoking metaphors, testimonials from familiar public figures, dynamic verbs, and well-worded appeals to heart and purse. One way of learning to write strong fundraising letters is to study effective sales letters.

Fundraising Letters Include

- asking for volunteers to help fundraise
- follow-up letters after initial appeal (see FOLLOW-UP)
- invitations: benefits/balls/banquets/fundraising events
- political campaign fundraising
- requests for contributions
- responses to fundraising letters (see ACCEPTANCES, REFUSALS, RESPONSES)
- thanks for contributing (see THANK YOU)

How to Say It

- Excite the reader's interest with an attention-getting opening.
- Clearly identify the organization.
- Describe the organization quickly and colorfully enough to retain the reader's interest: what it does and for whom, how it is unique, what its most impressive achievements are.
- Establish a compelling and urgent need for the reader's help.
- Appeal to the heart by the use of anecdotes, quotations, testimonials, case histories, descriptions.
- Appeal to the head by use of facts, statistics, information.
- Tell specifically how the person's contribution will be used ("With your help, we want to offer college scholarships to an additional twenty students this year").
- Mention the benefits of contributing (personal satisfaction, alleviation of suffering, improving the community, bettering someone's prospects, offering a tax deduction, providing entry to a select group of givers, resulting in recognition or publicity, allowing them to share some of their surplus, responding to a cause they believe in).
- Establish the credibility of the organization and assure readers that their contributions will be used effectively.
- Thank readers for their interest, attention, time, concern.
- Make it easy to give by including a postage-paid reply envelope or a toll-free number where contributions can be made by credit card.
- Have the letter signed by the highest-ranking member of your organization or by a well-known public figure.
- Add a postscript emphasizing a new or strong point.

What Not to Say

- Don't ask questions or suggest that your reader think about something. Build from one strong message to another without interrupting your sequence to give the reader a chance to reflect, "argue back," or rationalize.
- Don't allow a subtly harassing or moralizing tone to creep into your letter. People who feel strongly about a cause often think others "should" contribute, and this attitude colors their message. Potential contributors cannot be shamed or manipulated into giving; they prefer to believe their contribution is a freewill offering springing from their own higher impulses, not from your pressure.
- Don't use clichés if you can help it: "We need your help"; "Why read this letter?"; "You don't know me, but . . ."; "Send your check today!"; "Please

take a few minutes to read this letter." You can distinguish clichés only by reading hundreds of fundraising letters, but it is worthwhile to do so to see what works and what doesn't.

- Don't use gimmicks such as unusual typefaces, extensive underlining or capitalization, colorful inks, or odd page layouts. A strong message is key, and gimmicks will not help a weak one and will undercut a strong one. Fundraising appeals today, however, are using strategies such as what appears to be a handwritten note on the envelope, a smaller enclosed letter, or an incentive that is either enclosed or offered.

Tips on Writing

■ Be positive. Rather than describe how bad the situation will be if the reader doesn't contribute, describe how much improved the situation will be if the reader does contribute.

■ Be specific. Your support evidence is specific (instead of "Every night in this country children go to bed hungry," write, "Every night in this, the richest country in the world, one child in four goes to bed hungry"). Make a specific request ("Visit our website today") or ask for a specific amount ("Your $100 will plant four new trees").

■ Be as brief as possible. You have only seconds to make an impact.

■ Convey a sense of urgency. The reader must not only give, but give *now*. The letter that gets set aside to be dealt with later often doesn't get dealt with at all. Ask for an immediate response and include at least one good reason for doing so.

■ Establish a bond between you and your reader or between your organization and the reader ("As a parent/teacher/physician, you understand what it means to . . .").

■ Herschell Gordon Lewis, author of *How to Write Powerful Fund Raising Letters*, says, "The strongest word in fundraising is 'you.'" Check your letter to see which occurs more often: "you" or "we" (or "I").

■ Divide your message into two parts. First, give the reader a vivid picture of what is possible: healthy, well-nourished children; an active community center; eradication of a disease; a new library. Second, tell the reader exactly how you plan to arrive at the previously painted picture. Your vision statement has an emotional, subjective appeal; your mission statement is factual and objective.

■ A fundraising letter can begin by asking the reader to take some action (sign a petition, call a legislator, vote on an issue, participate in a letter-writing campaign) and then later in the letter ask for a contribution as well.

■ Most serious contributors are interested in how organizations use their money. Enclose an annual report or fact sheet telling what percentage of funds go to administrative costs and what is spent on the organization's main activities. Credibility and accountability are serious issues for fundraisers.

■ The P.S. is more likely to be read than any other part of your letter, and letters with a P.S. have higher response rates than those without. The attention-getting P.S. is brief (less than five lines) and urges the person to take action immediately, expresses appreciation for the person's help and interest, or adds one more persuasive bit of information. More is not better in this case; two postscripts are weaker than one.

■ A series of fundraising letters, each with a different emphasis, is often effective because when one angle doesn't rouse an individual, another might.

Special Situations

■ When inviting people to benefits and fundraising events, use the appropriate invitation form (see INVITATIONS), but be clear about what is expected of those who accept ("$100 donation suggested" or "Tax-deductible contribution of $500 per couple suggested"). Your wording may be limited by the allowable meanings of "tax deductible" and "donation."

■ When writing to ask someone to be part of a fundraising committee, spell out exactly what you expect of the person as well as a description of the fundraising efforts and the overall campaign goals (financial and publicity).

Format

■ The vast majority of fundraising letters are form letters. Although one might not expect people to respond to a generic request, these letters do in fact raise large sums for their organizations. Well-written form letters are not only acceptable but effective. The audience you target with this form letter is important to your success, however. Direct mail solicitation will be less effective than letters directed to members of specific groups or personal letters written to individuals.

■ Personal letters of appeal on business letterhead are effective but questionable. They should be written only with the express approval of your employer.

■ Fundraising letters are not sent by e-mail or fax.

WORDS

advocate	cooperation	help	request
aid	donation	humane	rescue
appeal	donor	necessity	share
ask	encourage	need	solicit
assistance	endow	offer	sponsorship
auspices	essential	openhanded	subsidy
backing	favor	participate	supply
befriend	foster	partnership	support
benefactor	furnish	patronage	tribute
benefit	generous	petition	unsparing
bequest	gift	philanthropic	urgent
charity	give	promote	
compassionate	grant	public-spirited	
contribution	grateful	relief	

PHRASES

a campaign to stop/protect/
   encourage/support

acquaint you with

adopt the cause of

all you have to do is

as generous as possible

as soon as you can

be good enough to

broad program of services

call upon you for

can bring comfort to those in
   need of

champion of

come to the aid of

consider carefully

continue our efforts

counting on your contribution

deserves your thoughtful
   consideration

direct your attention to

financial backing

for the sake of

give assistance

good/guardian angel

have the goodness to

helping hand

humanitarian interests

I am confident that we can

in order to provide the necessary
   funds

it can make all the difference for

join forces

make room in your heart for

make this possible

on account/behalf of

our immediate needs are

please join your friends and
   neighbors in supporting

pressing need

rising costs

shaping the future

special cause/program/need

struggling with a worldwide shortage of

there are no funds presently available for

the time has never been better to/for

this program really works because

those less fortunate than you

urgently need you to

welfare of others

with open hands

without your contribution

working together, we can

your contribution will enable

your donation will make it possible for

your past/unselfish generosity

your tax-deductible gift

SENTENCES

Almost all the money we need to help preserve the Bradgate River Valley comes from people like you.

Any amount/contribution is most welcome/appreciated.

Before we can begin raising funds for the new annex, we need volunteers to help with the mailing—will you consider giving several hours of your time to help out?

But without your help, it cannot be done.

Do it now, please!

Help us work for a solution to this most tragic disease.

Here's how you can help.

I am troubled by the growing incidence of violence in our society, and I know you are too.

If each family gave only $7.50 we could meet our goal of $5,000.

I'll call you next week to see if you can help.

I'm writing to ask you to join our campaign.

I need your immediate help to make sure our legislation continues to progress despite a fierce lobbying campaign against it.

In order to take advantage of bulk prices, we need to raise $10,000 before May 1.

It can be done!

I thank you from the bottom of my heart.

It is people like you who make the world a better place.

I want to share a story with you that illustrates for me what heroism is all about.

I want to tell you about the progress you have made possible.

I will truly appreciate whatever you can give, and I know these young scholars will too.

Join us today.

Last year, your contribution helped more than 3,000 students come closer to their dream of a liberal arts education.

Not a dime of your contribution will be wasted.

Now, more than ever, your continued support is needed to help keep the doors open.

Only by working together can we make a difference.

Our deadline for raising $50,000 is April 1—could you please send your gift by then?

Please be as generous as you can.

Please encourage your friends and neighbors to call legislators, sign a petition, contribute funds.

Please mail your tax-deductible check in the enclosed postage-paid envelope.

Please respond quickly and generously.

Please take some time to read the enclosed brochure.

P.S. Write your check and make your phone call today.

Thanks for whatever you can do.

The Cypros Food Shelf presently faces a crisis.

The people of Port Breedy are counting on you.

The Raybrook Foundation is at a financial crossroads this year and we critically need your generous giving to sustain the important work we've begun.

We are looking to people like you to help us provide the dollars we need to continue our hospice program.

We invite you to become part of the Annual Giving Campaign.

We've accomplished a great deal, but much more must be done.

Whatever you decide to send, please send it today—the situation is urgent.

When you contribute to the Belknap Foundation, you invest in the future.

You don't have to give until it hurts—just give until it feels good.

Your contribution will help us expand our resources and do a far more extensive job of protecting our vulnerable waters.

Your donation is tax deductible.

Your generosity to the Boyle County Library Fund will ensure not only that we can preserve existing books, manuscripts, and archives, but also that we can continue to supplement the rising acquisitions budget for new books and periodicals.

Your generosity will be recognized in *The Anchor*, the monthly organization newsletter.

Your telephone calls, letters, and checks have made all the difference.

PARAGRAPHS

All quality nonprofit organizations need financial resources to help achieve their goals. The Argante Human Services Agency has three basic means of financial support: foundations and corporations; fee services (based on ability to pay); and individuals. Your contribution is, and always has been, critical to our success.

You are cordially invited to the Holiday Open House, to be held Saturday evening December 12, from 7:00 p.m. to midnight, at the Bildad Mansion on Melville Avenue. This annual fundraiser for Pequod Elementary School is open to the public and will feature Victorian carols and refreshments, old-time vaudeville entertainment at 10:30 p.m., and "Nutcracker" characters circulating all evening long. Join us for a delightful and unforgettable evening of holiday magic. The suggested donation of $20/person is tax-deductible.

As you know, district school budgets are limited and cannot cover many items we want our students to have. A group of your friends and neighbors wants to raise $3,000 to provide the items on the attached list. Can you contribute to this fund to provide additional learning opportunities for our children? Every cent we receive will go directly to school supplies and services.

Many alumni and friends have "shared the wealth" of their Jarrett education by contributing to the tuition aid fund. Some of these tax-deductible gifts have been given directly to the development office, while others have been donated in memory of a loved one. This funding is available for students who are unable to pay all the necessary tuition fees and is a satisfying way of feeling that you have passed on some of what you have received.

I'm asking you to do two things. First, write your congressional representatives and senators and tell them you want a change. Second, help us meet the rising costs of lobbying and publicizing this issue with a gift of $10, $25, $50, or more.

Please indicate if your gift will be matched by your employer. (Your personnel office will provide the necessary information and forms.)

Will you be breathing cleaner air next year, or not? It's up to you. A bill currently before the state legislature (SF1011) will set new, lower levels of tolerable pollution for rural and urban areas. To convince lawmakers of the importance of this bill, I need you to sign the enclosed petition and return it to me at once. Time is running out—the bill comes out of committee later this month. A successful petition drive requires your signed petition . . . and your dollars. Along with your signed petition, I'm asking you to return a contribution of $25 or $50 to support lobbying efforts for this important measure. But please hurry!

Because the School Enrichment Council is organized for the purpose of lobbying and influencing legislation, your gift or donation is not deductible under current IRS guidelines as a charitable contribution. It may, however, be deductible as a business expense. If you have questions, please contact the SEC or your tax accountant.

The challenges we face this year are substantially greater than those of the past. We need your support, and you need the benefits of our important work.

Please try to send at least $15. Our only source of support is the voluntary dollars of those like yourself who are concerned about our vanishing wildflowers.

A sizable percentage of Clara Hibbert's campaign funding consists of small individual contributions from people like you who live in the Fifth Ward. She is not the candidate of special interests. She is the candidate of the people who live and do business in your ward.

SAMPLE LETTERS

Dear Mrs. Ogmore-Pritchard,

> *One can do much. And one and one and one can move mountains.*
> —JOAN WARD-HARRIS

Will you be one of the ones who will help us move mountains? We have one particular mountain in mind—the mountain of unconcern, neglect, abuse, and wrongful use of many of our wilderness areas.

The enclosed copies of recent newspaper articles will give you an idea of the problems facing us today. Also enclosed is an invitation to become a member and support our efforts to move this mountain!

―――――

Dear Fred and Aline,

I deeply appreciate your contribution. Thanks to the outstanding people who have worked on the campaign, we have accomplished a great deal. My commitment to public education is stronger than ever. I am pleased to have your confidence and support.

The campaign has grown in scope and intensity. In the remaining days, we are reaching out to large numbers of voters in a variety of ways. There is still much to be done. Please remember to tell your friends and neighbors to vote on November 7.

After the election, I will have eight weeks before the important School Board work begins. I will continue to prepare myself for the issues and problems facing our schools. I look forward to your continued input now and in the future.

Thank you again, Fred and Aline, for your help.

Sincerely yours,

————

Hello!

You might call this letter a "Newgate Update"—we wanted to get in touch with you who have donated vehicles to us within the past few years to let you know what's new at Newgate.

You may already know that we moved. We're located three blocks west of Highway 280 at 2900 E. Hennepin Avenue. This move brought Newgate to a bigger and better facility in which to provide more disadvantaged people with auto body repair training. We're training twenty students now and want to increase that to forty over the next two years, so we currently have openings for many new trainees in the program.

We're trying some new methods (newspaper articles and radio ads) to let people in the community know about Newgate's training program and our need for donated vehicles.

But what's been most important to Newgate in the past has been "word of mouth" referrals: people like you telling others about us. And so we'd like to remind you that we still need donated cars and they're still tax deductible. I've enclosed a brochure that you may want to pass along to a friend. We'd be glad to give an estimate of fair market value over the phone—just call us at 612-555-0177.

We thank you for your donation in the past, and hope you'll keep us in mind in the future.

Sincerely,

————

Dear Adelaide Culver and Henry Lambert:

I would like to invite you both to become members and supporters of Citizens for the Arts, the only statewide advocacy group working to enhance all the arts at all levels.

As a political action group, Citizens for the Arts has been highly successful during the last sixteen years in its efforts to build support for the arts throughout the state.

Through our efforts, state appropriations to the arts increased from $500,000 in

1975 to over $8 million last year. We also successfully lobbied for increased funding to individual artists through the regional arts councils and for the establishment of public art as a component in newly constructed state buildings. On the national level, we lobbied to exempt artists from the tax capitalization requirements of the 1986 Tax Reform Act.

Citizens for the Arts can continue to work for a healthy arts environment only with your support. Many of our successes are currently being challenged, and most of our state arts programs are insufficiently funded.

As a member and supporter of Citizens for the Arts, you will receive monthly newsletters on arts-related legislation and various arts events throughout the state as well as a pass entitling you to discounts at over seventy-five state arts organizations and events.

Please join us today. Your support is needed by Citizens for the Arts and the arts community.

Sincerely,

————

Dear Mrs. Farrinder:

The Board of Directors of the James Area Community Councils recognizes your invaluable help to the J.A.C.C. in various capacities over the years. We also note with great interest your successful fundraising efforts last year on behalf of the public library system.

We are asking for your support for the J.A.C.C. in a special way this year: Would you consider chairing the 2011 fundraising campaign?

This is of course a major commitment and you may have questions about it. Last year's chair, several members of the committee, and the Board of Directors will be happy to meet with you at your convenience to discuss what this position might involve.

We think you would be an effective and inspiring campaign chair, and we hope very much that you will say yes.

Sincerely,

————

Dear Monty Brewster:

On behalf of the Board of Directors of the McCutcheon Foundation and all those who benefit directly and indirectly from its work, I thank you for your most generous contribution. I think I can safely say we have not seen its like in all the years we have been asking individuals to help us with this important work.

Hundreds of people's lives will be materially and positively affected by the kindness and charity we have witnessed today.

Thank you, and may you reap one hundredfold the goodness that you sow.

Sincerely,

————

Dear Mr. and Mrs. Claggart:

You may wonder if people with severe disabilities really can live independently. Isn't it easier for a disabled person to be taken care of rather than to struggle with the day-to-day decisions about how and where to live? Isn't institutional living cheaper for the taxpayer? The answer is a resounding NO to both questions!

Consider Eva, a thirty-three-year-old woman with developmental disabilities who has lived with her parents all her life. She came to the Denver Center for Independent Living last March and asked for assistance so she could live in an apartment in the community. She *wanted* to be independent. And her parents were concerned about what would happen to Eva when they could no longer care for her.

DCIL staff went to Eva's home, evaluated her situation, and helped her decide exactly what special help she needed to live independently. One-on-one training in laundry, cooking, cleaning, money management, and job interviewing skills was provided. Additionally, Eva participated in our recreation program and found a great buddy to do things with.

Today Eva has a job washing dishes, her own checking account, a best friend, and a roommate with whom she will be sharing an apartment as soon as she has saved up her share of the rent deposit. Her family is delighted with the self-confidence and independence Eva has developed through her work with DCIL.

DCIL provides training and support services to any person with a physical, emotional, or developmental disability who wants to live in the community or who is liable to be placed in an institution. A recent study by the Colorado Department of Social Services shows a 40 percent savings to the taxpayer when severely disabled people live independently in the community. DCIL services help make that independence possible.

With your help, many more people like Eva can live productive lives. Please consider a tax-deductible end-of-year gift to DCIL to continue this important work. Your contribution directly enables persons with disabilities to become independent, contributing members of our community.

Thank you for your generosity, and happy holidays!

Sincerely,

―――――――

See also: ACCEPTANCES, ACKNOWLEDGMENTS, COVER LETTERS, FOLLOW-UP, GOODWILL, INVITATIONS, REFUSALS, REQUESTS, RESPONSES, THANK YOU

TWENTY-SIX

"GET WELL" LETTERS

I work for myself, which is fun. Except for when I call in sick.
I know I'm lying.
—RITA RUDNER

Most of us rely on "get well" cards, but if you've ever received a card with nothing but a signature below the commercial message, you know how disappointing it is. You're grateful for the kindness, but you would have loved a personal, handwritten message.

Some "get well" messages are easy to send—the illness isn't serious or we know the person only casually and aren't too involved emotionally. At other times, however, our feelings of helplessness, anxiety, and even pity either keep us from writing altogether or produce letters we feel are awkward.

The main purpose of "get well" letters is to remind people that they are not alone in their trouble, to offer them the undoubted power of love and friendship as a force for healing. Your "encouraging word" does not have to be lengthy, literary, or memorable; a few warmhearted sentences will do.

Send "Get Well" Letters to

- business customers, clients, and colleagues who are ill or who have an illness or accident in the family
- family members, friends, coworkers, neighbors, or acquaintances who are ill, hospitalized, recovering from an accident, undergoing tests, or having surgery
- friends or relatives in chemical dependency treatment or in treatment for depression, eating disorders, or other conditions

How to Say It

- State simply that you are sorry about (or sorry to hear or learn about) the illness, accident, surgery, hospitalization.
- Express concern for the person's well-being ("I want you to be comfortable and on the mend").
- Be pleasant, positive, optimistic.
- Offer to help in a specific way: to make the person's most critical sales calls the next week, finish a project, sit in on a meeting, bring in library books, take children for the weekend or chauffeur them to school events, make calls canceling a social event, provide meals for the family, bring mail to the hospital and help answer it, read aloud to the person, run errands. A vague "Let me know if there's anything I can do" isn't helpful. Someone who is ill often can't even think how you can help or muster the energy to call you. Check with a family member or neighbor to see what needs doing. "People seldom refuse help, if one offers it in the right way." (A. C. Benson)
- In some cases, offer to visit if the person is laid up for a long time or if you think they would welcome company. Generally it's better not to visit those who are hospitalized or seriously ill at home. The point of a "get well" message is to stand in for you when someone isn't well enough to see you. Make it easy for the person to refuse your visit in case they aren't feeling up to it.
- Assure the person of your affection, concern, warm thoughts, best wishes, love, or prayers.
- End with your hopes for less discomfort, speedy recovery, rapid improvement, better health, a brighter tomorrow.

What Not to Say

- Avoid being unnecessarily and tactlessly specific about the illness or accident. Say "your car accident" instead of "that horrible accident that took two lives," or "your surgery" instead of "your ileostomy."
- Avoid such words as "victim," "handicapped," and "bedridden" with their unnecessary overtones of tragedy, helplessness, and self-pity. Also avoid dramatic words such as "affliction," "torture," "nightmare," or "agony" unless the situation truly calls for them. Take your cue from the patient and do not jump to conclusions as to how they might perceive their situation. Be sympathetic without overstating the facts or dramatizing your own reaction to them.
- Don't resort to empty phrases, clichés, and false cheeriness like "It's

probably for the best" (it doesn't feel "best" to the patient); "I know how you feel" (no, you don't); "God only gives burdens to those who can carry them" (this is arguable); "Every cloud has a silver lining" (not when the cloud is hovering over *your* bed); "At least you don't have to go to work" (the person might prefer the office to the sickbed); "You'll be up and around again in no time" (the patient is sure of no such thing, and the time passed in bed does not feel like "no time"). Reread your letter to see how you, in the same situation, would feel about it.

- Don't criticize or question the patient's care or medical choices unless there is a good reason for doing so. Most people already have doubts about whether they are being cared for as effectively as possible; it's upsetting when friends add to these doubts.

- Don't compare the person's situation, illness, or surgery to anyone else's. Even if you have gone through something almost identical, wait until the person is fully convalescent and distanced from the present discomfort and danger to bring it up. Each person's experience is unique and generates its distinctive woes.

Tips on Writing

■ Write as soon as you hear the news. Although "get well" letters are welcome at any time, prompt ones carry a stronger message.

■ Focus more on the other person's situation than on your own feelings of inadequacy. If you feel helpless and upset, say so, but don't dwell on it. The situation is more about the patient's feelings than about yours.

■ Address the person in the same manner you did before the illness. Jean Kerr once wrote, "One of the most difficult things to contend with in a hospital is the assumption on the part of the staff that because you have lost your gall bladder you have also lost your mind." It is wounding when friends and family treat the patient as someone who is not quite what she or he used to be. The recipient of your letter is still a person, with all the usual human hopes, interests, relationships, and emotions.

■ Be brief if the person is seriously ill; later you can send a longer note or letter. Your note shouldn't be a chore to read; someone just out of surgery may not be up to deciphering illegible handwriting. The person convalescing at home, however, usually welcomes a long, newsy letter. Consider enclosing a few amusing or intriguing clippings from the paper ("What do you think about THIS?!"), photographs, a pressed flower, a cartoon, a sachet of potpourri, a quotation, a child's drawing, or colorful postcards or pictures. Enclosures are also a good idea when the usual words don't come easily—in the case of the terminally ill, for example.

Special Situations

■ Reassure hospitalized or ill employees that their jobs are secure and that their work is taken care of. If appropriate, reassure them about sick-leave policy and medical benefits. People often don't read the small print until they are too sick to do anything but worry about it. The person's immediate supervisor or someone from the human resources office can send information about insurance, sick leave, and company policies. If you know the person well, your simple assurance that there is nothing to worry about may be sufficient. "Get well" messages from managers or executives—even when the employee is not personally known to them—inspire loyalty and are a good idea on both the personal and business levels.

■ When writing to a sick child, say you're sorry to hear about the sickness and enclose something colorful, entertaining, and age-appropriate: a word puzzle, riddles, a cartoon or clipping from the paper, a story you made up or found in a magazine, a sticker book. Hand-letter a "coupon" good for a stack of library books that you will bring over and pick up several weeks later, a carry-in meal from a favorite fast-food place (if parents approve), thirty minutes of being read to, chauffeuring of friends to and from the patient's house or the hospital. If you think the child will write back, help them along by asking a few questions: What's the hospital room like? Who is the doctor? What is the best thing about being sick? The worst thing? What is your day like, from morning to night? What is the first thing you're going to do when you get well?

■ Don't send a get-well message to someone who isn't going to get well. And don't write to say how sad you are. Instead, send your love along with an upbeat note ("I'm glad you're resting comfortably now" or "It sounds as if you're getting excellent care" or "I see your grandson's math team is going to the finals"). Don't mention death until the other person brings it up. Some people do not want to discuss it; others do. Follow their lead. Reread your letter to see that you have not subconsciously written a "sympathy" card to the person about their anticipated death. An appropriate letter says you are thinking about your friend and (if this is true) that you are praying for them. Include a shared memory, but avoid telling it as an epitaph ("I will never forget . . ." "I will always remember you as the one who . . ."). You might say instead, "I'm still thinking about your giant pumpkin. I'll bet it would have won first prize at the State Fair." Focus on those pleasures that are still possible for the terminally ill patient, for example, letter writing, visits with family and friends, reading, old movies, card games, dictating memoirs.

■ Those who are living with AIDS are your friends, neighbors, and relatives first, and only second are people with a usually terminal illness. Write as you would to anyone with a serious illness, and don't assume the person's time is short; medical advances are adding years of high-quality life for some people with AIDS. Being supportive and sending a card is more important than saying exactly the right thing. Focus on the person, rather than on the illness. You might also suggest a visit. Because of the false perception of the nature of AIDS, some people distance themselves from friends living with it, adding another hardship to the illness.

■ When writing those in treatment for chemical dependency, eating disorders, and other such diseases, choose commercial cards that say "thinking of you" rather than "get well." Add a handwritten note that says in your own words "I care about you" or "You are important to me."

■ When a friend or relative is injured or ill enough to need constant care, write not only to the patient but to the person responsible for their care—spouse, parent, child, relative—and offer your emotional support as well as some practical help (running errands, chauffeuring, bringing meals, spending time with the patient so the caregiver has some free time).

Format

■ Commercial cards are appropriate for many different "get well" situations and their use is almost standard today. Some recipients skip the printed verse to read your handwritten message, but others read every word of the commercial message as though you had written it for them; for this reason, select your card with care. Always write something personal on the card—either a brief message at the bottom of the inside right-hand page or a longer message on the (usually blank) inside left-hand page.

■ Use personal stationery, notepaper, or engraved note cards for handwritten notes.

■ For business contacts or close friends, a typed message on business letterhead, personal-business stationery, or memo paper is as welcome as a handwritten note.

WORDS

accident	disheartening	painful	treatment
affection	disorder	recovery	uncomfortable
cheer	distressed	relapse	undergo
comfort	heal	saddened	unfortunate
concerned	health	sickness	unwelcome
convalescence	hope	sorry	
diagnosis	illness	support	
discomfort	optimistic	sympathy	

PHRASES

be up and about

bright prospects

clean bill of health

devoutly hope

early recovery

encouraging news

felt so bad to hear

fervent/fond hope

good prospects

greatly affected by the news that

have every/great confidence that

quick return to health

rapid/speedy recovery

regain your health

restore/return to health

sorry/very sorry/mighty sorry to hear

thinking of you

unhappy to hear about

wishing you happier, healthier
    days ahead

SENTENCES

Although we'll miss you, don't worry about your work—we're parceling it out among us for the time being.

Best wishes for a speedy recovery.

Don't worry about the office—we'll manage somehow.

Fawnia says you're doctoring that troublesome shoulder again.

From what I understand, this treatment will make all the difference/will give you a new lease on life.

Hearing about your diagnosis was a shock, but we're hoping for better news down the road.

Here's hoping you feel a little better every day.

I am concerned about you.

I hope you'll soon be well/back to your old self/up and around/up and about/back in the swing of things/back on your feet.

I hope you're not feeling too dejected by this latest setback.

I'm glad to hear you're getting some relief from the pain.

I'm sorry you've had such a scare, but relieved to know you caught it in time.

It's no fun being laid up.

I was so sorry to hear about your illness/that you were in the hospital.

Knowing your unusual determination and energy, we are anticipating a speedy recovery.

The news of your emergency surgery came as quite a shock.

The office/this place is not the same without you!

We expect to see you as good as new in a few weeks.

We're all rooting for you to get better quickly.

We're hoping for the best of everything for you.

We're thinking of you and hoping you'll feel better soon.

What a bitter pill to come through the heart surgery with flying colors and then to break your hip!

You're very much on my mind and in my heart these days.

PARAGRAPHS

I'd love to hear from you when you feel up to writing. Until then, be patient with yourself and don't try to do too much too soon. I'm thinking about you every day.

We're relieved you came out of the accident so lightly—although from your point of view, it may not feel all that good at the moment. I hope you're not too uncomfortable.

I was sorry to hear about your arthritis. I hope you don't mind, but I made a contribution in your name to the Arthritis Foundation and asked them to send you informational brochures.

Can I help with anything while you're out of commission? Because of my work schedule and the family's activities, I'm not as free as I'd like to be. However, some things I would be delighted to do are: pick up groceries for you on my way home from work (about 5:30), run the children to evening school events, have them over on Saturday or Sunday afternoons, make phone calls for you, run errands on Saturday mornings, bring over a hot dish once a week. I'd really like to help. You'd do the same for me if our positions were reversed. I'll be waiting for your call.

I'm sending you some old *Highlights for Children* magazines and one new scrapbook. I thought you could cut out your favorite pictures and stories and paste them in the scrapbook. It might help pass the time while you have to stay in bed.

SAMPLE LETTERS

Dear Damon,

What a shock to get to work this morning and have Harry the Horse explain that the only reason I punched in earlier than you for once was that you'd been in an accident. It was pretty gloomy around here until Little Isadore got some information from the hospital. Your doctor evidently thinks the general picture looks good and you shouldn't be laid up too long.

Last Card Louie has divided up your work between Society Max and Good Time Charlie Bernstein, so don't worry about anything at this end.

Best wishes,

Dear Uncle Mordecai,

We all felt bad to hear that your tricky hip has landed you in the hospital. Here's hoping that surgery is effective in clearing up the problem and that you aren't uncomfortable for too long.

I went over yesterday and cleared the leaves out of your gutters. I was afraid you'd be worrying about that.

We'd like to stop by the hospital some evening to see you, but I'm wondering if it isn't more important for you to get all the rest you can. If you feel up to company some evening, give us a call. Otherwise, we'll see you when you get home. Take care of yourself. You're pretty important to a few people around here.

With love,

Dear Horace,

We were all distressed to hear of your heart attack. Leo says you're doing well and all of us here at Giddens are looking forward to your full and speedy recovery.

You'll be happy to know that even in your absence, it's business as usual; your nephew Ted has been a quick study, and things are going smoothly. We loaded the last shipment of the big Hellman order yesterday, and so far all schedules have been maintained.

It must be difficult to be away from a business you raised from a baby, but you need have no fears about it. I hope you can instead spend your energy regaining your health and strength.

Very best wishes to you and Regina.

Sincerely,

Dear Mrs. Gummidge,

We were sorry to learn that you have been hospitalized. I took the liberty of stopping your newspaper and mail delivery for the time being (the mail is being held at the post office). Since I had a copy of your house key, I went in to make sure the faucets were off and the windows shut (except for leaving one upstairs and one downstairs open an inch for air). I've been going in at night and turning on a few lights so it doesn't look empty.

I wasn't sure you were up to a phone call, but I thought you'd want to know that the house is being looked after.

We're praying for your speedy recovery.

With best wishes,

Dear Ms. Melbury,

The staff and management at The Woodlanders join me in wishing you a speedy recovery from your emergency surgery. We are relieved to hear that the surgery went well and that you'll be back among us before long. For one thing, you are the only one who can ever find the Damson files.

Don't even think about work. Giles Winterborne is taking over the outstanding projects on your desk, and Felice Charmond is answering your phone and handling things as they come up. Marty South will send you a copy of company policy on sick leave and hospitalization costs (both are generous, I think).

Sincerely yours,

––––––––

Dear Jay,

I hear you've been under the weather lately. As soon as you feel up to it, let me know and I'll call Daisy and Tom and Nick—there's nothing like a party for lifting the old spirits.

Best,

––––––––

Dear Eliza,

Grandma and I were so sorry to hear that you've got the chicken socks. We didn't know chickens wore socks, so we were surprised. What's that? You say you have the chicken fox. What kind of an animal is a chicken fox anyway? What's that? You say you have a chicken box. Are you going to raise chickens in it? Oh, excuse me, you have the chicken rocks. We've never heard of them. Are they the latest fad, like pet rocks? Oho! We've got it now. You've got the CHICKEN POX. Maybe by the time you've read this long letter, you will be feeling a little better.

Grandma said to tell you to be sure not to scratch, but I'm sure you won't.

In a few days when you feel better we'll give you a call and you can tell us yourself how you're feeling.

Love,

––––––––

Dear Olivia,

You realize, of course, that there will be no further bridge games until you are well! None of us is willing to invite a substitute—"Replace Olivia? As Sam Goldwyn put it in two words: Im Possible."

Don't worry about the homefront. George has things under control, and we are all taking turns entertaining your house guest, that nice Mr. Pim.

Give us the high sign when you are ready for phone calls or visits—or a game of bridge!

Love,

––––––––

Dear Goldie,

I was sorry to hear about Abraham's accident yesterday. Your daughter seemed to think that although he was facing some surgery and was fairly uncomfortable, the outlook was good. I hope all goes well and that he can look forward to coming home soon.

You have taken no compassionate leave in the eight years you have been with us, so there is no problem with your taking as long as you like to be with Abraham. Patsy Tate assumed responsibility for your station; she may call you from time to time with a question, but otherwise the situation is well in hand.

Although our hospitalization insurance is based on a pre-admit system, this doesn't apply in the case of an emergency, such as Abraham's hospitalization. However, there are a few steps you should take in the next several days to regularize the situation. I've asked someone from Human Resources to call you about this.

If there is anything we can do to make things easier for you, let us know. In the meantime, you are very much in our thoughts.

Sincerely,

——————

See also: ACKNOWLEDGMENTS, BELATED, FAMILY, SENSITIVE, SYMPATHY, THANK YOU

TWENTY-SEVEN

GOODWILL LETTERS

*It is not enough to collect today's profits, for your competitor
is collecting tomorrow's goodwill.*
—THE SYSTEM COMPANY, *HOW TO WRITE LETTERS THAT WIN*, 1906

Goodwill letters are sales letters, but you aren't selling a product or service directly. You "sell" the recipient on your company's worth, reputation, friendliness, integrity, and competence. You want the reader to think well of your company and to keep you in mind for future purchases and services.

Although sales are generally based on price, color, dimensions, length of service contract, and other measurable properties, many other sales are based on feelings or attitudes. Goodwill letters appeal to the nonmaterial aspects of customer choice.

Kinds of Goodwill Letters

- anniversaries: service/wedding
- announcements: change in prices/personnel/policies/address (see also ANNOUNCEMENTS)
- appreciation: good payment record/past business/customer referral (see also APPRECIATION)
- congratulations (see CONGRATULATIONS)
- customers' and employees' life events (see appropriate topic)
- holiday greetings (see HOLIDAYS)
- special events and offers: open houses/sales/discounts/gifts/samples/certificates/coupons
- surveys/questionnaires

- thank you: previous business/current purchase/suggestions/assistance/good work (see also THANK YOU)
- welcome/welcome back (see also WELCOME)

How to Say It
- Open with a friendly or complimentary remark.
- State your main message (congratulations, thank you, keeping in touch, happy holidays, "just want to see how you're doing"). Almost any occasion is reason enough to show interest in your customers or employees.
- Expand on the message ("I'm particularly grateful because . . ." or "You've been a delight to work with because . . ." or "I hope the New Year is a happy and healthy one for you and your family").
- When possible, focus on the other person's situation, interests, concerns; this is a "you" letter.
- Close with pleasant wishes for success and a mention of future or continued contact.

What Not to Say
- Don't include a strong sales message in a goodwill letter. Mention your products or services only lightly or not at all.
- Don't dilute the impact of a goodwill letter by asking for business, or for a favor, or for higher work outputs, or by including business news or comments. Save them for another letter.
- Don't be too effusive. Use a natural, informal tone that conveys a genuine friendliness.

Tips on Writing

■ Send goodwill letters within your organization. Although it is never mandatory to congratulate an employee on a service anniversary, for example, you encourage good morale and company loyalty by doing so. Holidays are an excellent occasion for goodwill letters written to employees on behalf of company management, firm officers, or board of directors.

■ Take advantage of routine announcements (new type of billing statement, new address, meeting notice) to develop a goodwill letter (thanking customers for their business or employees for a good year).

■ The end-of-the-year holiday season is an excellent time to send a goodwill letter, but mail it early so that it doesn't get lost in the other December mail and so that customers haven't already spent their gift budget elsewhere.

Special Situations

■ A survey or questionnaire about the customer's use of your products or services is helpful to you; it also serves as a goodwill letter as most people like being asked for an opinion and thanked for their help. To ensure that it is a pleasure instead of a burden, the survey must be brief, easy to complete, and returnable with a postage-paid envelope.

■ Goodwill gifts—samples, trial sizes, the first in a series, something the customer can keep whether they purchase anything or not—are accompanied by a cover letter. The sales message is not too strong as the free product is theoretically the message. However, follow up this mailing with a letter a few weeks later. At that time you can intensify the sales message. (See also COVER LETTERS, FOLLOW-UP, SALES.)

Format

■ All goodwill letters are typed on letterhead stationery, except for brief congratulatory notes to employees and colleagues that may be typed, or possibly handwritten, on memo paper.

■ When sending holiday greetings to employees, or customers, or other general-message letters, a well-written form letter is customary and acceptable.

WORDS

appreciate	kindness	sensational	unique
delighted	memorable	special	valuable
enjoyed	pleased	superb	
grateful	remarkable	terrific	
inspired	satisfying	thoughtful	

PHRASES

happy/pleased to hear	look forward to your next
how are you getting along with	pleased to be able to
just thinking about you	show our gratitude for
just to let you know	wanted you to know
keep us in mind	wishing you all the best
let us know if	would be glad to have you stop in again when
like to keep in touch with	

SENTENCES

All of us here at Larolle International send you warmest holiday greetings and our best wishes for a happy, healthy new year!

As one of our longtime customers, you may be interested in our new, faster ordering procedures.

Because we appreciate the responsible handling of your account, we are raising your credit limit to $15,000.

Congratulations on your ten years with us—you're a key player on our (thanks to you!) successful team.

Enclosed is an article on retirement savings that we thought you'd like to see.

I heard something pretty special is going on over there!

Sawbridge Training Services Inc. now has a special customer hotline—at no charge to the calling party—for all your questions and concerns.

The Pig and Whistle invites you to a customer appreciation sale, but bring this card with you as the sale is "invitation only."

PARAGRAPHS

You used to order regularly from us, but we haven't heard from you for some time now. To help you remember how easy it was to order and how much you enjoyed our high-quality camping merchandise, we're enclosing a "welcome back" certificate good for 15 percent off your next order. We hope you use it—we've missed you!

I noticed the handsome photograph of you and your husband in Sunday's paper—congratulations on twenty-five years of marriage! Do stop by the office the next time you're in the store so I can congratulate you personally.

Thank you so much for referring Stanley Purves to us. It is because of generous and appreciative customers like you that Dorset Homes has been growing by leaps and bounds. We will give Mr. Purves our best service—and we are always ready to help you in any way we can. Thanks again for passing on the word!

You are cordially invited to an Open House on January 29 from 5:00 to 8:00 p.m. to celebrate our fiftieth anniversary. We are taking this opportunity to show our appreciation to our many fine customers. Do come—we will have a small gift waiting for you!

Dear Chung Hi,

We thank you—as always—for choosing Levi-Ponsonby Office Products for all your business office needs. You regularly receive our big catalog, the one that puts 20,000 office products at your fingertips.

We're proud of being able to supply every office product made. But we began to wonder if we weren't offering almost too many products!

Today I'm sending you a smaller catalog containing only our bestselling items. A select group of customers is receiving this special catalog. If it seems to be helpful to our customers, we may begin publishing smaller catalogs every few months while reserving the big catalog for once a year.

I hope you enjoy seeing what other businesses consider the most essential office products.

> Sincerely,
> Peter Levi
> Levi-Ponsonby Office Products

Dear Mr. Purdie,

We are pleased to have you enrolled at Okinawan Karate ("The Ultimate in Self-Protection and Self-Perfection") for the fall season. Welcome back!

For your convenience, we're enclosing a bookmark with our hours and telephone numbers. You might note on the back our standing invitation to take any other class on a trial basis, free of charge!

Stop in at the office any time and say hello!

Dear Jules,

I see that the bank is celebrating an important birthday—congratulations! You must be proud to see what a success Mignaud et Fils has become one hundred years after its founding by your great-grandfather.

All of us here at Philips Deluxe Checks wish you continued success and prosperity.

> Sincerely,

Dear Mr. and Mrs. Charles:

It has been three months since your new floor tiles were installed. I hope you've been enjoying them. We have customers who still rave about floor tile they bought from us thirty years ago.

If we can be of service to you in the future, keep us in mind. We're planning a store-wide three-day sale on all floor coverings in late January in case you're interested in doing any other rooms.

Thanks again for choosing a fine floor product from Geiger Tiles.

Yours truly,

————

Dear Joanna Pryke,

We are delighted to note that Warner Maintenance Experts have been cleaning your office carpets four times a year for six years now. As a business executive yourself, you know the value of faithful, longtime customers.

To show our appreciation, we'd like to pass on to you a sample of an effective carpet spot cleaner that we recently discovered. Note that we are not selling this product nor do we make any recommendation for it other than that we ourselves like it. When we had a chance to buy some samples, we thought of our favorite customers and decided to share them.

Enjoy the spot cleaner, and I hope you continue to look forward to our thorough, deep-cleaning process that leaves your carpeting like new!

————

Dear Hilda Cherrington:

Over the years, you have ordered a number of our fine products. You're one of the reasons that Lee Gifts is the premier mail-order house that it is.

To thank you for your business and to introduce you to a completely new line of Christmas ornaments, we are enclosing the "Christmas Star" for your enjoyment. We think you will admire the fine craftwork that went into this delicate ornament. It makes a wonderful keepsake gift for friends and relatives. Also enclosed is a copy of our current catalog, which shows all twenty-five of the new "Memories" series of ornaments.

We hope you enjoy your ornament!

Sincerely,

————

See also: ANNIVERSARIES, APPRECIATION, CONGRATULATIONS, "GET WELL," HOLIDAYS, NEIGHBORS, SYMPATHY, THANK YOU, WELCOME

TWENTY-EIGHT

HOLIDAY LETTERS

A holiday gives one a chance to look backward and forward,
to reset oneself by an inner compass.
—MAY SARTON

With the proliferation of commercial greeting cards and holiday-oriented retail sales events (Memorial Day Sale! July Fourth Sale! Presidents' Day Sale! Labor Day Sale!), we are now conscious not only of such traditional holidays as New Year's or Thanksgiving, but also of dozens of others.

Businesses wanting to send goodwill letters to customers, colleagues, and employees can choose any holiday as a reason for writing. Family and friends generally send holiday greetings and newsy letters no more than once or twice a year, most often around the end of the old year or the beginning of the new one. Fundraisers know that people are more willing to give during the holidays and therefore schedule some of their most important appeals in late fall. It is not surprising that first-class canceled mail peaks substantially in December.

The United States Postal Service likes us to "mail early" to equalize the flow of holiday mail and reduce the expense of overtime hours for carriers. During the holiday season extending from November 23 to December 31, USPS customers bring 20 billion pieces of mail to post offices across the country.

Of all personal mail, 43 percent is accounted for by holiday cards (other greeting cards make up 21 percent and letters the remaining 36 percent).

Holiday Letters Include

- Christmas
- Columbus Day
- Easter
- Election Day

- Father's Day
- form/annual letters
- goodwill letters
- Halloween
- Hanukkah
- Independence Day
- Labor Day
- Martin Luther King Jr.'s
  Birthday
- Memorial Day
- Mother's Day
- New Year's
- Pesach
- Purim
- Rosh Hashana
- St. Patrick's Day
- Thanksgiving
- Valentine's Day
- Veterans Day
- Yom Kippur

How to Say It

- Begin with an expression of the appropriate holiday greeting.
- Inquire about the other person and relate your own news if it is a personal letter. For a business letter, express appreciation for the other person and the hopes of being of service in the future.
- Wish the person happiness, success, health, prosperity.

What Not to Say

- Don't let a greeting card do all your speaking for you. If you have nothing to say to the person beyond the sentiments of a mass-produced card followed by a preprinted or signed name, your gesture may be meaningless; most people are disappointed to open a card and find no personal message.
- When sending a goodwill letter to employees, don't use it to "get a point across," to chide the group, or to transmit office news.
- Don't send an aggressive sales message in a holiday letter (which is essentially a goodwill letter). An exception is a logical connection such as florists and Mother's Day or candy and Valentine's Day.

Tips on Writing

■ Not every household is a happy one. Among your friends, coworkers, and customers are people who have lost loved ones, who have financial worries, illnesses, or other burdens. Except for mass-produced business holiday letters, of which no one expects great sensitivity, choose seasonal greetings that are low-key and can convey your good wishes without an insistent and perhaps offensive cheeriness.

■ Because some holidays are also holy days, businesses try to respect customers' beliefs. This means avoiding religious cards and sentiments unless your audience is well known to you. Do not casually bring religious elements into your goodwill letters; it may be perceived as hypocritical and self-serving. Consult with adherents of different faiths to see how your message appears to them. Since the majority of holiday letters are mailed in December, a reference to the New Year is appropriate. Mention the year ("to wish you success and happiness in 2011") to avoid confusion with religious year beginnings. Otherwise, use terms such as "the holidays," "this season," "at this time of year."

■ When sending holiday letters to family and friends, you can piggyback other news onto your greetings: the announcement of a new address, an engagement, a baby, or a new job. In the case of a divorce, for example, it is convenient to append the news to year's-end letters. Be sure to mail your greeting early to save friends the minor embarrassment of sending their good wishes to you as a couple.

■ When one member of the household writes the messages and signs the greeting cards for all, it doesn't matter if they put their name first or last.

Special Situations

■ Send holiday greetings to employees on behalf of company management, firm officers, or board of directors to generate goodwill and company identification. Wish the employees personal and professional happiness, offer congratulations for the good year just past, and express appreciation for the employees' contributions.

■ The most common customer goodwill letter is probably the year-end greeting. If your message is a general calling-to-mind letter or card (insurance agent, publisher, bank), send it anytime. But if December is an important sales or fundraising month for your organization, mail your greeting early in the month or even in November, before people shop or spend their donation dollars.

■ Some people (and letter-writing authorities) find holiday form letters unacceptable, while others (including yet other letter-writing authorities) enjoy writing and receiving them. Whatever one thinks of them, they are unlikely to disappear. After years of printing letters pro and con, Ann Landers polled her readers and then wrote, "The verdict is clear—100 to 1" in favor of the holiday newsletters. They are practical for those who must either send a form letter or not write at all. People used to live and die in the same town; their pool of friends and acquaintances was small and didn't require written communications. Today's family might have hundreds of names in its address file. Form letters don't have to be boring, and many aren't. In the polycopied part of your letter, tell your general news: the year's highlights, changes in your lives, travels, work and school happenings. You can organize your letter chronologically or by topic or by giving each family member a paragraph. A letter is more interesting if you discuss ideas as well as activities: your concerns about the environment, a good book you recommend, a lecture you attended, the state of television today, your political views. You can also include anecdotes, quotations, photocopied clippings of interest, or snapshots. Be specific. Instead of saying something was "wonderful" or "beautiful," give details. In the handwritten part of your letter (which is a "must," even if it's only a line or two), address the interests of that particular person, commenting on their last letter, asking about their life. If you receive a number of photocopied letters in your year's-end mail, you are probably safe sending one yourself. If none of your correspondents use this form, it's possible that you are marching to a different drummer—which may also be why they like you.

Format

■ The tremendously popular greeting card is always acceptable, but add a handwritten message to it. If your name is printed or engraved on the card, add a personal note. Don't use social titles when having your name printed. For example, "Eddie Swanson," "Goldie Rindskopf," "Bill and Sarah Ridden" (not "Mr. and Mrs. William Ridden") or simply "Bill and Sarah." Children's first names are usually listed on the second line. In the case of a single parent with a different name ("Grace Larkins"), the children's last name is given ("Annie, Miriam, and Minnie Wells").

■ Business letters conveying seasonal greetings are generally typed, although some companies send greeting cards, postcards, or specially printed letters with colorful graphics. A letter can be made more personal than a greeting card and can carry more information. Investigate the cost differences between greeting cards and letters. The latter are generally less expensive even if you use special effects, decorations, and a colored envelope. Keep an idea file of some of the clever seasonal creations other businesses have used over the years. Eye-catching letters are not, of course, appropriate for all purposes; banks, legal firms, insurance companies, and others are not helped by overly "creative" letters.

■ E-mail is becoming more popular for exchanging holiday greetings, helped along by readily available and appealing e-cards that do everything but serve hors d'oeuvres. However, e-greetings are most appropriate for people with whom we generally correspond by e-mail (or who have sent us a holiday e-card).

WORDS

blessings	health	prosperity	serenity
celebration	joy	rejoice	success
gratitude	peace	remembrances	wishes
happiness	pleasure	season	

PHRASES

all the best of the season	magic of the holiday season
at this time of year	much to look forward to
compliments of the season	season's blessings/greetings
during this season and always	sincere wishes for
great/happy/festive time of year	this festive season
happy memories	warmest regards/wishes to you
have appreciated your patronage over the past year	wishes for a joyous season
	wishing you love
holiday greetings	with warm personal regards
in commemoration/celebration of	wonderful holiday season

SENTENCES

As we at the Bennett Company look back over 2010, we remember with appreciation our friendly, faithful customers.

Best wishes for a bright and beautiful season/for a New Year of happiness.

Everyone here at Taunton-Dawbeney sends you best wishes for happiness, health, and prosperity throughout the coming New Year.

"Here's to your good health, and your family's good health, and may you all live long and prosper." (Washington Irving)

Holiday greetings and best wishes for the New Year.

I hope that 2010 was a good year for you and that 2011 will be even better.

I hope the New Year brings you health, happiness, and small daily joys!

May the beauty and joys of this season stay with you throughout the year.

May you be inscribed and sealed for a happy, healthy, and prosperous year.

May your shadow never be less!

On Rosh Hashanah it is written . . . On Yom Kippur it is sealed.

Our best wishes to you for a Merry Christmas and a prosperous New Year.

Skip this part if you are allergic to form letters, if you don't care what we've been doing, or if you can't remember who we are.

The best part of this beautiful season is keeping in touch with special friends like you.

This is just a note to say we're thinking of you at Thanksgiving/Hanukkah/Christmas/Passover/Easter.

This time of year inspires us to count our blessings—and good customers like you are chief among them!

Though we can't be with you at the Thanksgiving table, our hearts are there.

Warm wishes to you and your dear ones this holiday season.

We're remembering you at Passover and wishing you happiness always!

We send our warmest wishes for health and happiness—and to borrow my Irish grandfather's blessing: "I hope we're all here this day twelve-month."

We wish for you the gifts of love, friendship, and good health.

We wish you all the best in the coming year.

PARAGRAPHS

Anaïs Nin once wrote, "Each friend represents a world in us, a world possibly not born until they arrive, and it is only by this meeting that a new world is born." We're grateful for the worlds in us that you've made possible, and the New Year seems a good time to celebrate this.

They don't call them Easter "bonnets" anymore, but the idea is the same! Come in and see our chic selection of spring hats: delicate straws from Italy, smart little toques from France, wacky and colorful sun-skimmers from Haiti, elegant felts from England, and much more! Buy a hat before Easter and receive a free stuffed bunny (wearing the latest in bunny bonnets) for the special child in your life.

Eileen spent a month in Germany this summer, surviving a no-show on her luggage, a tick bite that required serum treatment, and a bomb threat on her return flight. As for me, I've been working with a local group to promote a recycling program here—we can talk trash, even in front of the children. Now you're thinking, "Great! I didn't have to hear about their latest remodeling project." Sorry. This year we turned the pantry into a bathroom, and . . .

To start the New Year off right and to show our appreciation for your patronage last year, I'm enclosing a certificate good for one free meal with the purchase of another of equal or greater price.

Mother's Day is coming soon, and Rowley Floral Shops (with twenty-three metro-area locations) are offering a Mother's Day special you'll want to consider. Choose from one of six stunning floral arrangements (and six surprisingly low prices) to tell that very important person in your life how much she means to you. Included in your one low price is delivery anywhere in the metro area and a special Mother's Day card with Anne Taylor's charming verse:

> Who ran to help me when I fell
> And would some pretty story tell,
> Or kiss the place to make it well?
> My Mother.

Come in today and see which of the six arrangements will bring a smile to YOUR Mother's face!

This Thanksgiving, as you reflect on your blessings, take a minute to consider those who have been overwhelmed by adversity. Help us provide traditional home-cooked Thanksgiving dinners with all the trimmings for the hungry and homeless during this Thanksgiving season. You can feed ten hungry people for $13.90, twenty for $27.80, or one hundred for $139. Won't you help?

SAMPLE LETTERS

Dear Carol and Cecil,

We're remembering you at Passover and wishing you happiness always!

Alison, Jordan, Rebecca, and Jeremy will be home next week and both sides of the family will be coming here for the Seder.

When are you coming to visit? We miss you!

———

TO: All Norton employees
FROM: Marda Norton, President
RE: Martin Luther King Jr. Day

Beginning this year, Martin Luther King Jr. Day will be a paid holiday for all employees. This day has particular significance for us as I believe Norton represents in many ways the lived-out reality of the dream for which Martin Luther King Jr. lived and died.

We urge employees to devote at least a part of the day to some community service. Bob Gates in Personnel has a list of suggestions if you are interested.

Also, for this, our first holiday, you are invited to a potluck dinner in the upper cafeteria at 6:00 p.m. on January 16. Please call Bob Gates, ext. 42, with your reservation, and bring a covered dish. Depending on the interest shown in this year's potluck, we may continue the tradition.

————

Dear Homeowner,

It's not too late! If you haven't put in your shrubs and trees and perennials yet, Verrinder Garden Center's big Memorial Day sale will make you glad you didn't get around to it!

Enclosed is a checklist of our complete tree, shrub, perennial, and annual stock (helpfully marked to show sun/shade requirements) so that you can walk around your yard and note what you need. Bring the list with you and you won't forget a thing! Not only that, but when you check out, show your checklist and you will receive a 10 percent discount on your entire order!

Have a safe and happy Memorial Day weekend!

————

Dear Mr. and Mrs. Burdock,

Will you be entertaining family and friends over the Fourth of July weekend?

How about inviting just one more to the celebration? Galbraith Catering—a full-service, licensed, insured caterer—can provide you with box lunches, a full multicourse buffet, or anything in between. If you want to make the main course, we'll bring salads, breads, and desserts. Or vice versa!

Feel like a guest at your own party! We provide servers, cleanup crew, tables, chairs, linens, dishes, and expert advice and assistance.

We are glad to supply references, and as a concerned member of the community, we recycle all papers and plastics, and we donate extra food to the Vane County Food Shelf.

For special events, you may want to make an appointment to come taste some of our specialties and choose the ones you think your guests would like. For simpler events, you are only a phone call away from trouble-free hospitality!

Happy Fourth of July! And, remember, we can help with everything but the fireworks!

————

Dear Parent,

What perfect timing! Just as you're worrying about getting the children outfitted for the winter months, along comes Columbus Day! The children have a free day, and we're having our lowest-prices-ever children's outerwear sale!

During our big Columbus Day sale (special hours 9:00 a.m. to 9:00 p.m.) we'll have free balloons and cookies for the children . . . and great prices and selections on over twenty name-brand children's coats and jackets.

Did we say it already? What perfect timing!

————

Dear Mrs. Gorsand,

If you're a kindergartener, Halloween can be scary. If you're a homeowner, it can also be scary—if you've gotten that far into fall without finishing your yard chores!

The MORGAN RENTAL BARN has everything you need to prepare for winter: leaf blowers, power rakes, lawn vacs, aerators, trimmers, chippers, shredders, drop spreaders, tillers—even lawnmowers if yours didn't make it through the season and you don't want to give a new one house room over the winter!

(And if you do finish your chores in time and want to celebrate Halloween with the kids, check out our rental party supplies!)

———

December 2010

Greetings Dear Family and Friends,

Seasonal salutations to you! We hope this finds you in good health and spirits.

The year 2010 has been especially noteworthy for our family. We saw Kalli play the clarinet at Carnegie Hall, Lauren's soccer team win the World Cup, Leah awarded the Nobel Prize for Literature, and Paul discover the cure for cavities. Not bad for a year's efforts.

Wait a minute! Wait a minute! Just testing to see if you were really reading this. Actually, it has been a fine year, mostly filled with all of the usual family business—school, soccer, piano lessons, soccer, gymnastics, soccer, clarinet, soccer, and softball. Favorite activities included skiing, hiking, swimming, camping, golfing, eating in, and eating out.

As the wonderful holidays approach, we want to take this opportunity to send you our best wishes. Even though in miles you may be far away, in spirit you're close to our hearts.

All the best to you and yours in 2011!

Lots of love,
Paul, Terry
Kalli, Lauren, and Leah

———

See also: CONGRATULATIONS, FAMILY, FUNDRAISING, GOODWILL, SALES

TWENTY-NINE

LETTERS OF INSTRUCTION

Most of us would rather risk catastrophe than read the directions.
—MIGNON MCLAUGHLIN

Individual letters of instruction have been replaced by form letters, package inserts, owners' manuals, product brochures, drugstore medication printouts, and other computer-generated or preprinted materials.

Such instructions include equipment or appliance operating instructions, safety instructions, assembly instructions, and installation instructions as well as instructions on how to dispute a credit card charge, apply for admission, sign an enclosed contract or lease, return merchandise, obtain a refund or exchange, or order replacement parts. Because commercial instructions deal with matters involving possible injury, loss of money, damage, and of course customer goodwill and repeat sales, they must be precisely crafted. "Read the manufacturer's directions with care. . . . This is one of the hardest kinds of prose in the world to write. It must be factual, accurate, and crystal clear." (Virginia Graham)

Businesses occasionally write letters of instruction, generally in response to a customer query. Letters of instruction are also written inside a company, most often as a memo.

Written instructions are given to the couple staying with your children while you are out of town, the patient following a specific care regimen, the neighbor child who waters your garden, the day-care provider, the carpenters working on your house.

Write Letters of Instruction for

- agreements/contracts/leases
- babysitters/day-care providers

- changes to your will and other legal issues
- forms/applications/surveys
- house/plant/garden/pet care
- new policies/procedures/regulations
- operating instructions: appliances/tools/equipment
- payments
- product registrations/use/care
- return, repair, or replacement of merchandise
- samples
- shipping instructions

How to Say It

- Thank the person (if you are responding to a letter, phone call, or in-person query) or state the purpose of your letter ("To help you get the most out of your new software, we offer the following suggestions for use"; "These instructions will help you care for your instrument so that it will give optimum performance pleasure").
- Number or otherwise set off each step in the instructions.
- If appropriate, give a phone number, contact person and address, or other resource where further help can be obtained.
- End with a pleasant statement of appreciation or with a mention of future business or enjoyment of the new product.

What Not to Say

- "Don't give instructions in the negative" is a negative statement. "Word your instructions positively" is a positive one. Use the positive form. When you see "don't," "never," and "should not" in your instructions, rephrase the sentence to read positively.
- Don't use words like "simple" and "obvious." Invariably, these words preface something that is neither simple nor obvious to readers, and they feel rebuked for not understanding something that apparently everyone else does.
- Don't use a condescending tone. For example, sometimes a "broken" appliance is simply not plugged in. The first in a list of troubleshooting instructions generally advises seeing that the appliance is plugged in. State this neutrally so that the customer doesn't feel too stupid if that's the problem.

Tips on Writing

- Be brief. After writing the instructions, pare them down to the essentials. "Explanations grow under our hands, in spite of our effort at compression." (John Henry Cardinal Newman)

- Be specific. If you say "soak contacts overnight," give the desired number of hours in parentheses. "Overnight" means different things to different people. When advising that an appliance be cleaned regularly, describe products and procedures that work best and tell what "regularly" means. Explain or graphically identify parts, in case readers are not familiar with industry terminology.

- Be intelligible. When preparing a form letter that will be used thousands of times, ask people outside your department to read it for clarity. Some of the worst instructions have been written by experts; because they know their field so well they cannot understand the mind of the uninitiated well enough to adequately explain anything. In her 1923 book, Mary Owens Crowther counsels, "It is well to remember that motion pictures do not accompany letters and hence to take for granted that if a way exists for getting what you mean wrong that way will be found."

- Be diplomatic. Some requests for instructions may appear inane to you and the answers so obvious you hardly know how to phrase your response. But people's brains work in wonderfully odd and divergent ways, and the person may actually be looking at the situation in a way very different from the way you see it. Then, too, even if it is a "stupid" question, good public relations demands that you treat it as politely and helpfully as any other question.

- When possible, explain *why* as well as *how*. For example, "Do not use this compound when there is danger of rain followed by temperatures below 32 degrees." Many people will accept this instruction without question. But others will wonder what rain and cold have to do with anything, and still others will ignore it, thinking it unimportant. If you add, "because the compound will absorb the moisture, freeze, expand, and probably crack," users are far more likely to follow the instruction—and you will receive fewer complaints. "I can never remember things I didn't understand in the first place." (Amy Tan)

Special Situations

- Cover letters often contain instructions. When sending someone a sample, a contract, or a product, for example, explain how to interpret or use the item.

- Any document that must be signed (contract, lease, stock transfer) is accompanied by a letter explaining where signatures or initials are needed, if the signatures need a medallion or notarization, which copy to retain for the person's files, where to send the other copies.
- Assembly, installation, operating, and safety instructions are generally included in an owner's manual. However, you might like to send a cover letter with the manual emphasizing special cautions ("Please particularly note the section on fire hazards").

Format

- Instructions to customers are typed on letterhead stationery.
- Memos are used for in-house instructions and are typed except for the briefest and most casual instructions.
- Form letters are used for routine letters of instruction.

WORDS

advice	explanation	method	simplify
carefully	guidelines	operation	steps
caution	how-to	policy	system
demonstrate	illustrate	precaution	warning
description	indicate	procedure	warranty
details	information	regulations	

PHRASES

alert you to	much more effective to
always check to see	note that
as the illustration shows	once you are familiar with
before you use your appliance	point out
commonly used to	recommend/suggest that you
important safety instructions	standard operating procedure
it requires that you	you will find that

SENTENCES

Caution: please read the rules for safe operation before plugging in your Villamarti "Thinking Bull" table lamp.

Follow the illustrated instructions to trim hair at home quickly and professionally with your Clavering Clippers.

I am not sure which model of the Thursley Electric Toothbrush you have, so I'm enclosing instructions for all of them.

If you have more questions, call our hotline at 800-555-5379.

If you plan to deliver your baby at Malmayne's Old St. Paul's Hospital, please note the following instructions for preadmittance.

Please note the following guidelines.

We are happy to be able to clarify this matter for you.

You don't need special tools to install this fixture, but follow the steps in the order given.

Your Aldridge electric knife will provide you with a lifetime of use if you follow these care instructions.

PARAGRAPHS

Enclosed is the final version of the contract, which constitutes the complete and entire agreement between us. Please read it carefully and consult with your attorney before signing all three copies on the bottom of page 5. Please also initial clauses C1 and D3 to indicate your awareness of the changes we have agreed upon. Return all three copies to me along with a check covering the agreed-upon amount. One copy of the contract will be countersigned and returned to you.

Thanks for taking care of the hamsters while we're away. If you can stop by once a day, that'd be great. Give everybody one-quarter cup of hamster food. Fill their water bottles. Give Furball an apple slice and Marigold a banana slice from the fruit in the plastic box (they don't care if it's old and brown). The others don't need any special treats. We'll be back before the cages need cleaning, so don't worry about that.

To obtain a credit card for another member of your immediate family, please complete the enclosed form, making sure that both your signature and the new cardholder's signature appear on the indicated lines.

Thank you for agreeing to complete the enclosed survey. It will take only a few minutes. Use a #2 pencil and carefully fill in the circles corresponding to your answer. Do not write in the white box in the upper right-hand corner. Fold the form along the dotted lines and seal by moistening the flap. Do not use staples or transparent tape. Your name and address are optional. Thank you!

Please give Caddy a bottle around 8:30 (or earlier if she seems hungry). If she falls asleep with the bottle in her mouth, take it out. Be sure the intercom is on so you can hear her from any room in the house. We can be reached at 555-2405.

Dear Mrs. Dollery:

We were sorry to hear that your AutoAnswer communication system is unsatisfactory. All our equipment is carefully checked before leaving our Chicago factory. However, in rare cases, an intermittent problem may have been overlooked or something may have happened to the equipment during shipping.

Please return your system to us, following these steps:

1. Use the original carton and packing materials to ship the system back to us.

2. Address the box to: Customer Service, P.O. Box 1887, Woodlanders, IL 60031. (The California address is only for placing orders.)

3. Enclose a letter describing the problem (a copy of the letter you originally sent us would be fine) and mention whether the trouble occurred immediately or after use. The more information you can give us, the more quickly we can locate the problem.

4. Fasten the enclosed RUSH label to the top right-hand corner of your letter. This will ensure that you receive a fully functioning machine (your present system or a new one) within ten working days.

Thousands of satisfied customers are experiencing the delight and time-saving features of the AutoAnswer communications system every day; I want you to be one of them very soon.

TO: Estabrook County Residents
FROM: Estabrook County Board of Commissioners
DATE: October 2
RE: Yard Waste

The amount of garbage each of us produces is enormous, and so are the problems and costs of disposing of it. During the summer months, grass clippings make up 24 percent of residential garbage.

Legislation passed earlier this year requires us to separate grass clippings and leaves—yard waste—from regular trash after January 1.

How do we do this?

1. Leave grass clippings on the lawn. This is the most cost-effective and environmentally sound way to deal with grass clippings. They decompose, returning nutrients to the soil, and never enter the waste stream.

2. Bag grass clippings and take them to one of the six County compost sites (list of compost sites is enclosed). Empty your bags of grass clippings and fill them with free compost for your garden.

3. Use grass clippings as mulch around trees and shrubs (if your grass has not been chemically treated).

4. Bag grass clippings and pay a trash hauler to collect them separately.

For additional information call 661-555-2117, Estabrook County's Compost Center.

P.S. We've had a number of calls asking if grass clippings will ruin the lawn if left on it. You can leave grass clippings on the lawn and still keep it healthy by (1) not letting the grass get too long before mowing (clippings should be no more than one inch long in order to filter down into the soil); (2) using a sharp mower blade (the sharper the blade the finer the clippings and the faster they decompose); (3) avoiding overfertilization (dense grass doesn't allow clippings to reach the soil to decompose); (4) removing excessive thatch ($\frac{1}{2}$ inch is ideal); (5) mowing the lawn when it's dry.

––––––––

Dear William D. Carmichael,

Beginning January 1, we will be adopting an exciting new program of flexible benefits. To become part of this program, we ask that you:

1. Read the enclosed brochure, which explains the program.

2. Sign up for the informational meeting that is most convenient for you (list enclosed).

3. Schedule an appointment with one of the Human Resources staff to discuss the program and to ask any questions you might have. At that time you will be given a confidential record of your personal benefit program and an enrollment form to fill out specifying the way you want to "spend" your benefits.

4. Return the form by October 1. This date is important. If you fail to send in your enrollment form by October 1, you will automatically be enrolled in the "no choice" plan (see brochure for description).

If you have questions about this process, call Human Resources at ext. 43.

––––––––

TO: All employees
FROM: Buildings and Grounds
DATE: July 6, 2010
RE: Parking lot resurfacing

The north parking lot will be resurfaced beginning July 15. This means the lot will be unavailable for employee parking July 15–17. We ask that, if possible, you share rides to work on those days. For those three days only, parking will be allowed along the east side of the access road and in the visitor parking places in the east lot (visitors will be able to park around the entrance circle). The Lerrick Mall management has also agreed to let us use the row of parking along its east side (that is, next to Morgan Road) July 15–17. We ask that you do not use any other spaces in the mall parking lot. As a last resort, use the Lerrick parking ramp and take city bus #78 (there is a bus every 12 minutes) or plan to walk (about 7 minutes). Thank you.

––––––––

Dear Mr. and Mrs. Gauss:

Enclosed for your review is a Contract to Buy and Sell Real Estate for your property located at 1946 Storm Road, Jameson, IN 47438.

The contract requires your acceptance on or before July 1. Both of you must sign the contract in each of the highlighted spaces before a notary public.

If you have any questions regarding this contract, please call me at 800-555-3369.

———

See also: ADVICE, RESPONSES

THIRTY

LETTERS OF INTRODUCTION

Why is it that the person who needs no introduction usually gets the longest one?
—MARCELENE COX

Letters of introduction are not as common as they were. The telephone has largely replaced them as a means of putting two people in touch with each other. Then, too, most people have enough social and business contacts to last several lifetimes. They are reluctant to suggest additional ones to friends unless they're sure the proposed introduction will be genuinely beneficial to both parties.

Although letters introducing people to each other are still seen, today's letter of introduction is more commonly used to introduce a new sales representative, new product, or new service to customers.

Letters of introduction are related to references and recommendations in that A is vouching for B to C. However, a letter of introduction is more like the superficial introduction that takes place at a large party, whereas the recommendation is more like a serious talk about someone your friend wants to employ.

Write Letters of Introduction for

- business associates/employees
- friends moving/traveling to a city where you know people
- introducing business/product/services to newcomers in the area (see WEL-COME)
- job seekers (see also REFERENCES)
- membership in clubs/groups/organizations
- new address/office/division/outlet/company (see also ANNOUNCEMENTS, WELCOME)

- new billing procedure/statement/payment schedule
- new employees/associates/partners/programs/policies/prices (see also AN-NOUNCEMENTS)
- new products/services (see also SALES)
- requesting an introduction to someone from a third party
- researcher working in the other person's field

How to Say It

- Begin by stating your reason for writing: to introduce yourself, to introduce someone to your reader, to suggest that your reader meet with someone visiting or new in their area.
- Give the person's full name, title, position, or some other "tag" to situate them for your reader.
- Tell something about the person being introduced—whether it is yourself or a third party—that will make your correspondent want to meet them ("she has collected paperweights for years, and I know this is a great interest of yours"). Mention people they both know, work or school connections, interests they have in common.
- Tell how you and the other person are related or acquainted.
- Explain why contact with this person is desirable.
- Suggest how the meeting can take place: the reader contacts the other person (include address and phone number); the other person calls your reader; you are inviting them both to lunch.
- Close with an expression of respect or friendship, and your thanks or appreciation ("I will be grateful for any courtesies you can extend to Chadwick").

What Not to Say

- Don't organize introductions lightly. They set in motion responsibilities, demands on time and energy, and consequences involving several people. Reserve introductions for special cases.
- Don't insist that two people meet or predict that they will like each other. No one can tell who will take to whom. By emphasizing what they have in common, your reader can decide how much interest there might be in meeting the other person.
- Don't make the person feel obligated to accommodate you. Unwilling hospitality or grudging meetings do not have good outcomes. Allow the person room to maneuver and provide a way to save face if they must refuse you ("I realize you may not be free just now").

Tips on Writing

■ There are two ways of providing a letter of introduction. One is to give the letter to the person you're introducing; the person then calls upon the third party and presents the letter. The envelope is left unsealed, which means your letter will be tactful. The second way is to write directly to the third party, asking if they would be able to meet with, entertain, or help the person you're introducing.

■ Be specific about what you would like the other person to do: invite your friend to dinner; make introductions in the neighborhood; explain work opportunities in the area.

Special Situations

■ It used to be that the letter of introduction had to be offered, unlike a letter of reference or recommendation, which is requested. In their 1942 book, *How to Write Letters for All Occasions*, Alexander L. Sheff and Edna Ingalls write sternly, "The note of introduction is often requested for a friend, never for one's self." This still applies to social introductions, but networking has changed the rules in the business world. You may tell someone you plan to be in a certain area or that you're job-hunting and wait for the other person to suggest introducing you to friends or colleagues. But you may also actively seek introductions.

■ When you want A to offer hospitality to B, write A directly and ask that they respond to you. This spares B the embarrassment of presenting a personal letter of introduction only to be rebuffed because of lack of time or interest. It also spares A the awkwardness of being caught off guard and pressured into doing something they don't really want to do.

■ Write a letter of thanks or appreciation to anyone who has written a letter of introduction on your behalf. You also write to thank the person to whom you were introduced for any courtesies extended to you.

■ Introduce new employees, business associates, or personnel to those with whom they'll be working with a paragraph or two: their names, new positions, starting dates, responsibilities and work relationships, highlights of their professional backgrounds, and a request for others to welcome them.

■ Introducing a new sales representative to customers before the first visit smoothes the representative's way. It also serves as a goodwill gesture, letting customers know that headquarters takes a personal interest in them. Express your confidence in the person's abilities.

■ When introducing a change in billing procedures (new due date, automatic deposit, windowed reply envelopes, new statement format), explain why you instituted the change and, if possible, enclose a sample procedure. Focus on the value of the change to the customer, not its value to you. When you express appreciation for the customer's business and say that the change will improve service, your letter of introduction becomes a goodwill letter or even a sales letter.

■ Letters introducing new products and services have strong sales messages. Only a phrase like "we are pleased to introduce" qualifies it as a letter of introduction (see SALES).

Format

■ Business introductions (requests for them, the letters themselves, and thank yous) are typed on business or personal-business letterhead. A personal touch is commonly added by a handwritten note on your business card to be included with the letter or given to the person requesting the introduction.

■ Handwriting social introductions used to be required, but it is not necessary today.

■ Form letters are useful when the same message of introduction must be conveyed to a number of people and the message is not particularly personal. For example, introducing a new slate of officers to a far-flung membership, or introducing a new product line or new payment schedules to thousands of customers.

■ E-mail is used for very informal introductions.

WORDS

acquaint	contact	meet	receive
announce	coworker	notify	sponsor
associate	greet	pleasure	suggest
colleague	hospitality	present	visit
connections	introduce	propose	welcome

PHRASES

acquaint you with	I think you'll like
bring together two such	known to me for many years
bring to your attention/notice	longtime friend
get together with	please don't feel obliged to
I'd like to introduce to you	present to you
if you have time	shares your interest in
I'm happy to introduce you to	similar background

the bearer of this letter

this letter/note will introduce

we'd like to tell you about

we're pleased to introduce

you've heard me mention/talk about

SENTENCES

Dr. Roselli plans to be in Rome for the next two years, so if you feel able to offer him any hospitality during that time, I would be most grateful—and I think you'd enjoy meeting him.

I'd appreciate any consideration you can extend to Mr. Chevenix.

I feel sure you would not regret meeting the Oakroyds.

I'll appreciate any hospitality you can offer Harriet.

I think you and Nathan would find you have a great deal in common.

I've always wanted to bring you two together, but of course it will depend on whether you are free just now.

I've asked Adela to give you a call.

Thank you for whatever you may be able to do for Ms. Ingoldsby.

There is little that Ms. Trindle does not know about the field; I suspect that you would enjoying talking to her.

This letter will introduce Nicholas Broune, president of our local professional editors network, who will be spending several weeks in New Orleans.

This will introduce a whole new concept in parent-teacher conferences.

We are pleased to introduce the Reverend Duncan McMillan, who will be serving as weekend presider as of June 1.

PARAGRAPHS

Hello! May I introduce myself? I'm Flora Mackenzie, and I'm running for city council from Ward 4. I'd like to give you a few reasons to vote for me on November 7.

Sarah Purfoy of Clark Machinery will be in San Francisco February 3, and I've given her my card to present to you. I wasn't sure if you knew that Clark is working on something that may solve your assembly problem. If you haven't time to see her, Ms. Purfoy will understand.

Dear friends of ours, Ellen and Thomas Sutpen, are moving to Jefferson later this month, and I immediately thought of you. They've bought one hundred acres not far from you, and their two children, Henry and Judith, are almost the same ages as your two. I know you're busy just now, so I'm not asking you to entertain them or to do anything in particular—I just wanted you to know that the Sutpens are delightful people, and I think you'd enjoy them. Remember us to them if you do meet them.

I would like you to meet Rachel Cameron, as I think she would be a wonderful person to run the Good Samaritan program. I'm having a small cocktail party Friday night, and I thought I could introduce you to her then. Will you come?

A friend of mine whom I admire very much, Dodge Pleydon, will be visiting various galleries in Atlanta this next week, and I suggested he see you. I think you would be interested in his work. He is rather shy, so if you do not like what he is doing, he will take the hint quickly. He is not at all like the artist you described who camped outside your office for days at a time trying to get you to change your mind!

I've just learned that our favorite babysitter has moved next door to you. Not only is it a small world but are you lucky! Bob Vincy is dependable, resourceful, and full of fun. I wish I could introduce you to him personally, but I hope this note will inspire you to go over and sign him up immediately.

I would like to arrange a meeting with Rosamund Redding to discuss setting up small investors' groups in rural areas. I know the two of you are good friends, and I thought it might mean something to her if I were to mention that you and I have been in the same investors' group and on the New Beginnings Center board of directors for several years. May I use your name when I write her for an appointment?

I don't often do this, but I'm going to stick my neck out and say that I think you ought to see an engineer named Alec Harvey. The man can do anything, and I think he may be just the person to unsnarl your transportation department. I've asked him to give you a call, but do feel free to tell him you're busy if you don't want to see him. It was I who urged him to call because I'm convinced it might be worth your while.

SAMPLE LETTERS

Dear Monica,

I've just received your letter asking for a letter of introduction to Herbert Pelham. As a matter of fact, I'm leaving tomorrow for San Francisco and will visit Herb while I'm out there. I'll sound him out about him seeing you. He is, however, something of a recluse and may not agree to it. I hope that when I explain your idea, he will be persuaded.

I'll be in touch sometime after the fifteenth.

Sincerely,

———

TO: All employees
RE: Avisa Pomeroy, Director of Global Strategy
DATE: August 1, 2010

The board of directors and the management of Vixen Tor International are pleased to introduce to you the new Director of Global Strategy, Avisa Pomeroy. She has been with Vixen Tor since 1995, bringing her talents and energy to the advertising and sales departments before being named Director of Overseas Sales, in which capacity she has spent the last four years in our Bonn office. She attributes the successes of the Global Strategy department to the retiring director, Ives Brown, and says she hopes to consolidate and build on the gains he has made.

––––––––

Dear Robert,

This letter will introduce Ethel Ormiston to you. Since you are younger than I, you won't remember her. She's Grandma Nell's cousin, and the two of them were raised like sisters. She approached me about our family genealogical records, but I told her that Mother had given everything to you.

I hope you won't mind letting her look at what you have, and possibly photocopy them. Thanks.

––––––––

FROM: hisp@email.com
TO: rls@email.com
SUBJECT: A little competition
DATE: Mon, 14 Jul 2002 16:31:31

Hi R.L.! A friend of mine, Tom Redruth, is being transferred to your office, and I think you'd enjoy looking him up. All you need to know about Tom at the moment is that his last marathon time was 3:19! I think he could give you a run for your money!

––––––––

Dear Eleanor,

Thanks for the letter and all the latest news. As for your colleague's visit to the Windy City, I'm sure I would find him interesting, particularly because of the work he's currently doing on alkanes. I will call him, but can't promise too much as I'm booked solid the next two weeks and his free time may not coincide with the little I have. However, I'm looking forward to meeting him and will do all I can to show him around, time permitting.

With best wishes,

––––––––

Dear Phil,

I ran into your old coach, Mr. Pope, the other day. I'm not sure you ever met his son, Ted, but it turns out he has just transferred to the University for the second semester. If it's hard to go to a new school where you don't know anybody, it's even harder to do it mid-year.

I know you're tremendously busy but I also know you've got a kind heart. Will you give him a call, meet him for coffee, or just in general see how things are going for him? He's living off-campus at 1912 Wells St., Apt. 3F. His phone number is 555-1234.

Thanks!

Dear Ms. Cardross:

The account you have established with us has been reassigned within our Telemarketing Department. I would like to introduce myself as your new representative at Chambers Office Supply and take this opportunity to ask if we can be of any service to you at this time.

You are currently set up with account AB 40021, and you receive a 15 percent discount on list prices.

I notice that the printer ribbons that you normally buy are on sale this month (25 percent off).

If you have questions regarding your account, or need assistance in any way, please contact me.

Thank you for your continued business. I look forward to working with you in the near future.

Sincerely,

Dear Edwin,

I'm going to be in New York for three weeks in June, trying to find a publisher for my book. I know that you have extensive publishing contacts there, and I wonder if you might know anyone in particular I ought to see and, if so, if you would be so kind as to provide me with a letter of introduction.

I hope this is not an imposition, and I wouldn't want you to do anything you're not comfortable with, so I'll understand perfectly if you don't feel you have any information that would be useful to me.

In grateful appreciation,
Henry

Dear Henry,

Congratulations on finishing the book! I'm so pleased for you. And, as a matter of fact, I do know someone I think you ought to see while you're in New York. Maud Dolomore has her own literary agency and she deals almost exclusively with biographies.

I'm enclosing a brief letter that will introduce you to her. In this case I feel that I am doing both you and Maud a favor by putting you in contact with each other—I suspect your book is something she would be pleased to handle.

Let me know how things turn out.

> With best wishes,
> Edwin

Dear Henry,

I'm pleased to hear that you've finished the book! Unfortunately, I've looked through my files but don't see anyone who would be particularly useful to you or to whom I'd feel comfortable writing a letter of introduction.

Most of my contacts are now older and retired, spending their limited time and energy on their own projects. I hope you understand.

> Sincerely,
> Edwin

Dear Edwin,

I am grateful for the letter of introduction you wrote to Maud Dolomore on my behalf.

I had lunch with her, and she decided to represent my book. From finding an agent to finding a book contract is a long way, but I am pleased that the manuscript is in good hands.

The next time you are in town for a conference, would you let me know ahead of time so I can take you to lunch?

I will let you know immediately if Maud manages to find me a book contract. Thanks again.

> Yours truly,
> Henry

Dear Mr. De Fontelles,

Thank you for your letter of August 16 asking me to introduce your son to my grandfather. Although I am sympathetic to his project, I must say no to your request. My grandfather is in very poor health.

I wish you luck interviewing some of the other former members of the Resistance.

> Sincerely yours,

Dear Gordon and Madeline,

Some good friends of ours, Nina and Charles Marsden, will be in Seattle August 18 to September 1. I usually hesitate to put strangers in touch with each other because it doesn't seem to work out. But in this case, I have a feeling you would enjoy meeting them. They are both officers of the Midwest Appaloosa Conference and are interested in arranging reciprocal shows with groups from outside the Midwest.

I've mentioned that I'd be writing you, but added that you are busy and may not even be in town during the last part of August, so there is certainly no obligation to call them. If, however, you have time and think you'd like to meet them, they'll be staying at the Horseshoe Inn on Murray Road.

All our best,

———————

Dear Homeowner,

Let me take this opportunity to introduce you to Irmiter Contractors and Builders. Founded in 1921 by my great-grandfather, our ninety years of experience have firmly established us in the home renovation, restoration, and remodeling industry.

We base our professionalism on the principles of old-world craftsmanship and customer service. We are members of, actively participate in, and meet the requirements of the National Association of the Remodeling Industry (NARI) and the National Kitchen and Bath Association (NKBA). Our six decades and four generations of experience in the building trades assure you, the homeowner, of the best return for your home improvement dollar. We are dedicated to creating the perfect living space for you and your family. Irmiter Contractors does this by combining state-of-the-art products and up-to-date management techniques with time-honored traditions of quality workmanship and attention to your needs. We recently received a Regional National Kitchen Design Award from NARI and offer complete design and drafting services for any type of project. In short, we are the problem solvers for the modern family living in an older home environment.

We invite you to compare, to talk to our customers, visit our jobs in progress! You'll see what we've done, what we're doing, and what we can do for you!

Please fill out and mail the enclosed card or give us a call today, and let's get started on our most important project this year—YOUR HOME!

Sincerely,
Tom Irmiter
President

P.S. We will accept invitations to bid on blueprints.

———————

See also: ANNOUNCEMENTS, APPLICATIONS, REFERENCES, REFUSALS, REQUESTS, THANK YOU, WELCOME

THIRTY-ONE

INVITATIONS

Invitation is the sincerest form of flattery.
—MARCELENE COX

All major and many minor life events are marked by occasions to which we invite family and friends. Being gregarious animals, we also celebrate nonevents for the pure fun of it. Social gatherings offer friendship, entertainment, and relaxation. Invitations can range from the casual "Come visit!" scrawled on a postcard to engraved, highly codified invitations to dinner-dances.

In the world of business, banquets, lunches, cocktail parties, receptions, and open houses offer opportunities to conduct business, to improve employee morale, and to encourage or solidify relationships with clients, customers, suppliers, and others.

Write Invitations to

- exhibitions/fashion shows/new equipment or product shows/trade shows/ book fairs
- fundraising events
- hospitality: lunches/dinners/teas/receptions/open houses/cocktail parties/ buffets/brunches/parties
- meetings/workshops/conferences
- open a store account/credit card account or to accept trial membership/ subscription/merchandise
- overnight/weekend hospitality
- recitals/performances
- religious ceremonies

- reunions—class, family
- sales (see SALES)
- school events
- showers: baby/engagement/wedding (see also WEDDINGS)
- speaking engagements: conference/banquet/workshop
- tours: factory/office/plant
- weddings (see WEDDINGS)

How to Say It

- State the occasion (open house, awards banquet, anniversary celebration, dinner-dance, retirement party).
- Give the date and time: month, day, year, day of week, a.m. or p.m. (In formal invitations, the time is written out: "Seven o'clock in the evening"; "a.m." and "p.m." are never used.)
- Give the address. If necessary, include driving instructions or a map.
- Mention refreshments, if appropriate.
- Include the charge, if any (for fundraisers and certain other nonsocial events).
- Enclose an engraved or printed reply card and envelope for a formal invitation ("RSVP" is noted on the invitation). Slightly less formal invitations may have in the lower left corner of the invitation "RSVP," "Rsvp," "Please respond," or "Regrets only," followed by an address or phone number. Informal invitations may also request a response and furnish a phone number. If appropriate, give a date by which you need a response.
- Indicate the preferred dress (black tie, white tie, formal, informal, casual, costume) in the lower right corner, when appropriate.
- Let overnight guests know when you expect them to arrive and leave, what special clothes they may need (for tennis, swimming, hiking), whether they will be sharing a room with a child, will need a sleeping bag, and whether there will be other guests. Ask if they can tolerate animals, cigarette smoke, or other potential nuisances.
- Additional information might include parking facilities, alternate arrangements in case of rain, and an offer of transportation.
- Express your anticipated pleasure in seeing the person.

What Not to Say

- Don't use "request the honour of your presence" except on wedding invitations.
- Don't use abbreviations in formal invitations except for "Mr.," "Mrs.," "Ms.,"

"Dr.," "Jr.," and sometimes military rank. Avoid initials in names. In formal invitations, write out "Second" and "Third" after a name, although you may use Roman numerals: Jason Prescott Allen III. There is no comma between the name and the numeral. States should be spelled out (Alabama, not Ala. or AL) as is the time ("half past eight o'clock").

Tips on Writing

■ Invitations are issued in the names of all those hosting the event. Women use whatever name they prefer (married name, business name, birth name) on invitations. The invitee responds using that name. When unsure how to address the woman, call her office or home and ask. For business invitations, hosts often use their titles and company names. Friends issue invitations together. Even groups issue invitations ("The Castorley Foundation invites you . . ." or "The Central High School senior class invites you . . .").

■ The phrase "request(s) the pleasure of your company" is suitable for any invitation but the most casual.

■ When you need to know who is coming, include a reply card. Of the same paper, style, and format as your invitation, this card is enclosed with a small envelope (at least 3½"×5" inches to meet postal requirements) printed or engraved with your address and with postage on it. The card says, "M———— [Ms., Mrs., Miss, Mr. Name to be filled in]————regrets————accepts [one is checked] for Saturday, November 20." In some cases, "accepts" and "regrets" stand alone, and the guest crosses out the word that doesn't apply or circles the one that does. The "M" is a puzzle to some people and contemporary usage often omits it. Printers have samples and can advise you on the format that fits your situation.

■ When inviting a single person or someone whose personal life is unfamiliar to you, indicate whether the invitation (1) is intended for that person only; (2) includes a friend; (3) can be taken either way as long as you are notified ahead of time.

■ When issuing an invitation to a family with young children, list each child by first name on the envelope on the line underneath the parents' names; never add "and family." Adults living in the family home should not be included in their parents' invitation but should receive their own. Children approximately thirteen and up also receive their own invitations.

■ In an invitation, it is wholly inappropriate to suggest the kind of gift one wants (mentioning where one is registered or specifying that money is the gift of choice, for example). Sometimes, however, people want to specify that gifts not be given (for example, the person celebrating an eightieth birthday who has no need of gifts and no room for them). Ann Landers approved two of the solutions suggested by readers of her column: "Your friendship is a cherished gift. We respectfully request no other." Or: "We request your help in compiling a book recalling memories from our parents' first fifty years of marriage. On the enclosed sheet, we ask that you write one memory or event that you have shared with them and return it to us by April 26. We believe that the loving memories they have shared with you, their friends, would be the most treasured gift they could receive; therefore, we request that no other gift be sent."

■ Some sit-down dinner invitations specify the time guests are to arrive and the time dinner will be served. These are usually sent by people whose previous dinner parties have been spoiled by late arrivals.

■ When dress is indicated, the following formulas are used. White tie is the most formal dress: men wear a white tie, wing collar, and tailcoat while women wear formal gowns. Black tie or formal means, for men, a tuxedo with soft shirt and a bow tie (a dark suit is not acceptable) and, for women, dressy dresses, cocktail-length dresses, or long evening wear. Semiformal means sports jackets or suits for men and dresses (but not long gowns) or dressier tops and pants for women; jeans and T-shirts are never appropriate as semiformal wear.

■ Mail invitations to an important event involving out-of-town guests as early as six months ahead. Guidelines for mailing invitations include: four to six weeks before a formal dinner, ball, dance, charity benefit, reception, or tea; two to four weeks before a reception or cocktail party; three weeks before a bar mitzvah or bat mitzvah; two weeks before a casual dinner or get-together.

Special Situations

■ When issuing invitations to a casual in-house business event, send a memo or e-mail that includes: type of occasion (retirement, going-away, service anniversary, guest speaker); time, date, place; if refreshments will be served; if a collection is being taken up; an extension number to call for confirmation or information.

■ Invitations to religious ceremonies include: date, time, place, type of ceremony, information about reception or gathering afterward. Invitations to a bar mitzvah or bat mitzvah can be engraved, printed, or handwritten, and should include: the young person's full name; time, date, place; details about reception or celebration afterward.

■ Invitations to a daughter's début are issued by the parents, whether married, widowed, divorced, or separated: "Sir Arthur and Lady Dorcas Clare request the pleasure of your company at a dinner-dance in honor of their daughter Millicent on Saturday . . ." When simply receiving, the invitation can read: "Mrs. Sybil Fairford and Miss Elizabeth Fairford will be at home Sunday the second of June from five until half past seven o'clock, One Cooper Row."

■ Invitations to a fundraising event should be clear about what is expected of those who accept ("$100 donation suggested" or "Tax-deductible contribution of $500 per couple suggested"). Your wording may be limited by the allowable meanings of "tax deductible" and "donation." Enclose a postage-paid reply envelope to make it easy for people to respond; if you don't, tell where to send the check and how to obtain tickets. Some fundraisers fail because potential donors are busy people who can't take the time to read the small print or guess how they should handle the request; make it easy for them. Invitations to benefits, public charity balls, and other fundraisers need no response; purchase of tickets constitutes acceptance.

■ When inviting a guest speaker include: the name of the event and sponsoring organization; the date, time, and place; the type of audience (size, level of interest, previous exposure to subject); the kind of speech wanted; the length of time allotted and the approximate time the speech will begin; equipment available for use; accommodation and transportation information or directions to the meeting site; whether there will be a question and answer session; a description of the program; meals available; name of the contact person; details of the honorarium; an offer of further assistance; an expression of pleasure at having the person speak to your group. At this time you also request biographical information from the speaker to use in the program.

■ Sales letters are sometimes phrased as invitations to a special showing, sale, open house, or demonstration or to become a member, account holder, or subscriber.

■ Annual meetings are usually announced with the formal notice required by corporation bylaws, but invitations may also be sent, especially if there is a banquet or dinner following. No reply is necessary to attend the meeting, but a reply is usually requested for the dinner.

■ When your invitees fail to "RSVP" and you need to know how many will be attending your event, the written word is no longer useful. You will have to telephone and ask. A recently married woman wrote "Dear Abby" (Abigail Van Buren) that of the one hundred printed wedding invitations she and her fiancé sent, only three self-addressed, stamped response cards were returned, yet most of their invitees showed up at the wedding. "Dear Abby" suggested the preventive measure of replacing "RSVP" with plain English: "Please let us know if you are able to attend—and also if you are *not*." Except for formal or large events, you are probably better off inviting your guests by telephone (or at least inviting their voice mail) and then following up with an invitation in the form of a reminder.

■ To cancel or postpone an invitation, follow the original invitation in format, style, and quality of paper. If there's time, the announcement is printed or engraved as the invitation was. Otherwise, handwrite the note, using the same style as the invitation: "Mr. and Mrs. Hans Oosthuizen regret that it is necessary/that they are obliged to postpone/cancel/recall their invitation to dinner on . . ." or "We must unfortunately cancel the dinner party we had planned for . . ." Urgent situations, of course, require the telephone.

■ To cancel an invitation that you have already accepted, call your host at once and then follow up with a note apologizing for the change of plans. Stress your regret and offer a believable excuse. When you cancel at the last minute or when your cancellation is an inconvenience, you may want to send flowers with your note.

Format

■ Formal invitations are engraved or printed on fine-quality notepaper, use a line-by-line style, and are phrased in the third person ("Terence Mulvaney requests the pleasure of your company at a dinner-dance in honor of his daughter . . ."). Printers, stationery stores, and large department stores offer a number of styles, papers, inks, and designs. Invitations may also be handwritten, using the same format and phrasing. The expression "requests the pleasure of your company" is appropriate for all invitations except formal weddings. Each invited person is mentioned by name and honorific (Ms., Mrs., Miss, Dr., Mr.) either on the envelope or in the invitation itself. All words, state names, and numbers less than 100 are spelled out. Abbreviations are not used. Telephone numbers and ZIP codes are never given on formal invitations. The ZIP code is usually available in the return address or on the reply envelope. Business formal invitations (awards banquet, for example) are issued in standard formal invitation format.

■ Informal social invitations are handwritten on informal stationery or foldovers in usual letter style (first person, run-in format). The invitation is usually written on the first page of a foldover or, if this page has your name on it, you can add the details of the invitation below your name. Commercial fill-in-the-blank invitations are available; there is nothing wrong with using these for casual gatherings. Some of them are even quite cheerful and clever.

■ Informal business invitations may be sent on letterhead stationery; in-house invitations may be issued via memo, even sometimes by e-mail.

■ Invitations that are actually sales letters use a form letter format.

■ If you entertain regularly you may want to order engraved or printed invitations with blank spaces to be filled in as needed: "Mr. and Mrs. Desmond Mulligan request the pleasure of [name's] company at [event] on [date] at [time] o'clock, 1843 Thackeray Street."

WORDS

attend	début	occasion	salute
cancel	fête	pleasure	solemnize
celebration	honor	postpone	welcome
commemorate	installation	rejoice	

PHRASES

accept with pleasure

be our guest

bring a guest

cordially invites you to

have the honor of inviting

in commemoration/celebration of

in honor of

invite you to

kindly respond on or before

looking forward to seeing you

obliged to recall/cancel/postpone

owing to the illness/death of

request the pleasure of your
    company

we are celebrating

we would like to invite you to

you are cordially invited

SENTENCES

A revolutionary new service is now available to valued customers—and you're among the first invited to enroll.

Are you free after work on Friday to join a few of us for dinner?

Business attire is suggested.

Come hear noted Reformation scholar and professor of history Dr. Margaret Heath speak on September 12 at the 8:30 and 11:00 services at Gloria Dei Lutheran Church, 1924 Forster Avenue.

Horseback riding will be available; dress accordingly.

I'm pleased to invite you to acquire the Golden American Bank Card.

It will be so good to see you again.

I urge you to look over the enclosed materials and consider this special invitation now.

Mr. and Mrs. Alex Polk-Faraday regret that it is necessary to cancel their invitation to brunch on Sunday, the sixteenth of August, because of the illness of their daughter.

Please confirm by June 6 that you can attend.

Please join us for a farewell party in honor of Veronica Roderick, who is leaving Wain International to pursue other business interests.

We invite you to apply for an account with Oxenham Leather Warehouse Inc.

You are invited to a special evening showing of our new line of furniture from European designers.

PARAGRAPHS

Please plan to attend the Hargate Open House this Thursday, September 26, at 7:00 p.m. You will have the opportunity to meet the school staff, sit in on each of your student's classes during a simulated (but greatly shortened) school day, and talk to other parents during the social hour that follows. (A contribution for the refreshment table will be greatly appreciated.)

The Jervis family invites you to help Laura and Frank celebrate their Golden Wedding Anniversary. An Open House will be held at the Russell Eagles Hall, from 1:00 to 4:00 p.m. on Sunday, March 10, 2010.

You are invited to attend the Fall Family Festival this Tuesday evening from 6:00 to 9:00 p.m. at Temple Beth Shalom, 14 Burnsville Parkway. There will be puppet shows, activity booths, games, and refreshments!

Kindly respond on or before
September 18, 2010

M————————————

accepts/declines
Number of persons————

You are invited to hear the National Liturgical Choir under the direction of Maugrabin Hayraddin at 4:00 p.m. Sunday, September 28, at Quentin Methodist Church, 1823 Scott Avenue. The sixty-voice chorus will sing Russian liturgical music by Gretchaninof and Kalinikof and selections by Bach, Shaw, and Schutz. The cost is $5 ($3 for seniors and students).

You are invited to join the Henderson Film Club for one month—at absolutely no cost to you. Tell us which four selections you want, and they will be sent the same day we receive your order.

The tenth annual Public Works Open House will be held on Tuesday, October 3, from 4:00 to 7:00 p.m. at the Evans Street yards, a block south of Owen Avenue. The whole family will enjoy it. Get your picture taken on a Public Works "cherry picker." Car buffs can tour the biggest maintenance and repair shop in the city. There will be drawings for prizes, music, food, and entertainment. Some lucky winner will take home an actual traffic signal used for fifty years on the corner of Blodwen and Marquand Streets.

SAMPLE LETTERS

Mr. and Mrs. Seymour Glass
joyfully invite you
to worship with them
at the Bat Mitzvah of their daughter
Muriel
Saturday, the tenth of July
Two thousand ten
at ten o'clock in the morning
Mount Zion Temple
1300 Summit Avenue
Colorado Springs, Colorado

———

You are cordially invited
to an open house celebration of
Hmong Language and Culture
sponsored by the Neighborhood Alliance
Coffinkey Community Center
1818 Scott Street
Friday, April 16, 7:00–9:00 p.m.
Refreshments
Exhibits
Entertainment
For more information, call 555-1234

———

The Addison-Steele Company
cordially invites you to an
open house
celebrating
its Fiftieth Anniversary
Friday, the tenth of November
two thousand eleven
from five to half past eight o'clock
Fourteen Sealand Boulevard
Bevil, Indiana

———

Owing to the illness of a family member
Blanche Hipper and Loftus Wilcher
are obliged to recall their invitation
for Saturday, the seventeenth of April
two thousand eleven

Lucas-Dockery Importers Inc.
cordially invites you to a
cocktail hour and reception
in honor of their merger with
Sheridan International Associates
Friday, the tenth of November
from five to half past eight o'clock
Mansfield Gardens
One Mansfield Commons

Dear James Ayrton,

You are invited to become a member of the Brodie Community Anti-Crack Coalition. Formed eight months ago, this coalition of three community councils and six community organizations was formed to oppose the activity and effects of illegal drug use and trafficking in Easdaile and especially in the Brodie neighborhood.

The Brodie Community Council already has two delegates to the coalition, but we believe it would be helpful to have one more. Your name has been mentioned several times as someone with the necessary experience and enthusiasm.

I'll call later this week to discuss the possibility of your participation.

Agnes Leslie Graham and Robert Graham
request the pleasure of your company
at a dinner-dance
on Saturday, the twenty-first of May
at seven-thirty o'clock
Harcourt Inn

RSVP

Dear Dr. Denny:

It is with great pleasure that I invite you to the 43rd Annual Engineering Society Conference. This year's Conference will be held at The Citadel Hotel in downtown Dallas from September 23 through September 27.

We are offering a valuable program with industry-wide applications, speakers who are recognized experts in their field, and topics with many implications for the future (see enclosed brochure). Ample time is scheduled for discussion periods. In addition, tours to two outstanding instructional materials centers have been arranged.

We have obtained special meeting rates from the management of The Citadel. Information on accommodations, transportation, and registration is enclosed.

If you have questions, please call the session coordinator, A. J. Cronin, at 214-555-1889.

Houghton-Maguire Marine
cordially invites you to its
First Annual Marine Electronic Equipment Exhibit
1:30 p.m. to 6:30 p.m.
Saturday, May 2, 2011

Highway 32 and County Road C

Refreshments
Drawings

Dear Mrs. Lucas,

We are having a reception on Sunday, May 5, from 1:00 p.m. to 4:00 p.m. to celebrate our joy in the adoption of our new son, Philip. It would mean a great deal to us to have you join us.

Sincerely,

Haidée Czelovar Power and Raoul Czelovar
cordially invite you to a reception
celebrating the
Golden Wedding Anniversary of
Simone Rakonitz Czelovar and Karl Czelovar
Sunday, the second of April
at eight o'clock
Wyatt's Village Inn
Indianapolis

RSVP   Formal Dress
555-1980

Special Savings Invitation!

Dear Martin Lynch Gibbon:

As one of our Preferred Customers, you are invited to save 10 percent on every purchase you make at Murdoch Jewelers on July 14 and 15. This discount applies to both sale-priced and regular-priced merchandise, and includes our line of dazzling Iris diamonds, the ever-popular Headliner watches for men and women, and our complete selection of wedding gifts.

You deserve the best, and for two days this month, "the best" comes with a discount just for you!

Note: The discount does not include labor or service charges.

––––––––

Dear Major and Mrs. Caswell,

We are planning to celebrate Mother and Dad's fortieth wedding anniversary with dinner at The Azalea Gardens on September 16, at 7:00 p.m. We would love to have you celebrate with us.

Please let me know if you can join us.

Fondly,

––––––––

The Board of Directors
of the Finsbury United Aid Society
requests the pleasure of your company
at a wine and cheese reception
on Saturday, the fourteenth of May
at half past seven o'clock
Finsbury Community Ballroom
for the benefit of
The Finsbury Children's Home

Suggested Contribution $50   Black Tie

––––––––

See also: ACCEPTANCES, ACKNOWLEDGMENTS, ANNIVERSARIES, ORGANIZATIONS, REFUSALS, RESPONSES, SALES, THANK YOU, WEDDINGS

THIRTY-TWO

LOVE LETTERS

*If valentines are the equivalent of a gentle rain, love letters have
all the power and unpredictability of a tropical storm.*
—Jennifer Williams

The love letter is one of the most difficult and frustrating letters to write because
we want it to be perfect. Stunning. Memorable. Touching. Thrilling. Witty. Tender.
Intelligent. And—did we say?—perfect.

Nothing is too good for the person we love. We pick up the pen, imagining
the letter that will say it all, the letter that will do everything but sing. But are our
expressive skills equal to the grandeur and fineness of our love? We fear not.

There are two kinds of love letters. One is written to someone who returns
your love. This letter carries an automatic guarantee of success; your reader thinks
everything you do is wonderful. In this chapter you can pick up a few more high
cards to go with the ace you already hold.

The second kind of love letter is written to someone you're courting, someone whose love you want to win. "Special Situations" offers assistance for this type
of letter.

Write Love Letters to

- a man
- a woman

How to Say It

- Open with something simple, preferably your main thought ("Dearest Leslie, I miss you" or "Dear Jack, This has been the longest week of my life!").

- Expand on your thoughts and feelings about the other person.
- Recall happy times you've spent together in the past and mention future plans that include both of you.
- Tell what you've been doing, thinking, feeling. The other person is hungry for news of you. Self-revelation is appealing and will usually elicit similar revelations from the other person. "I have never told you this, but . . ."; "When I was little, I always dreamed that . . ."; "One thing I'm really looking forward to (besides seeing you again!) is . . ."; "My favorite way of spending a Sunday afternoon is . . ."
- Use the person's name—not too often, but several times anyway. There's nothing quite as wonderful as reading our name in our lover's handwriting (or typing).
- Say the words: "I love you." No one can hear it often enough, and lovers—especially new ones—have fears and doubts that crave reassurance.

What Not to Say

- Don't be brief. "Brevity may be the soul of wit, but not when someone's saying, 'I love you.'" (Judith Viorst) The other person wants you to never stop talking or writing or saying how wonderful they are. Don't stint yourself.
- Don't use language that isn't natural to you. While you may be tempted to dress your letter in flowery or high-flown words, they will not sound like you, and you, after all, are the person your reader loves.
- Don't write a letter that requires a note at the end: "Tear this up as soon as you've read it." Recipients seldom do this. If it's a simple matter of your embarrassment, it won't make much difference, but if the letter falls into the wrong hands (as in the case of a romance involving infidelity), you may regret putting anything on paper.
- Don't ask another person to read your letter before you send it to see if it is "okay." The only people who know if the letter is good are you and the one you love. In 1901, Myrtle Reed wrote, "A real love letter is absolutely ridiculous to everyone except the writer and the recipient." This is still true.

Tips on Writing

■ Before writing the letter, jot down ideas that will lead to sentences or paragraphs in your letter: What is special or unexpected about being in love? What is it about the other person that is endearing? What touches you deeply? What do you miss? What would you do if she walked into the room right now? When do you think about her most often? What things remind you of him? What would you like to give him if you could give him anything? Why do you admire her? Be specific. Give examples of times you were filled with love.

■ Write from the heart. The most important quality of a love letter is its sincerity.

■ Keep the other person in mind as you write. Try to imagine what she is thinking, feeling, and doing at this moment and to picture her later as she reads your letter.

■ Fatten the letter with newspaper clippings or cartoons, a dried leaf or flower, bookmark, photographs, a half-completed crossword puzzle for him to finish.

■ If expressing yourself is difficult, invest in some commercial "to the one you love" greeting cards with carefully chosen messages. Add a handwritten line or two ("This is exactly how I feel"; "I can hardly wait to see you Friday") and perhaps a little drawing or enclosure. Cards don't replace personal letters, but they provide some variety and a break between letters.

■ Include a new "why I love you" reason in each letter.

■ If you expect to write more than a few love letters, buy a book of quotations on love. They can inspire you while supplying quotations that express your feelings. Some are good for discussion: "Do you agree with Antoine de Saint-Exupéry that 'love does not consist in gazing at each other but in looking outward together in the same direction'?" Bess Streeter Aldrich once wrote, "Love is the light that you see by." Aldrich probably wouldn't mind if you wrote, "You are the light that I see by," and then tell why that is.

■ For inspiration, read letters from the world's great lovers.

• For passion and fire, read Juliette Drouet writing to Victor Hugo (in Louis Gimbaud, ed., *The Love Letters of Juliette Drouet to Victor Hugo,* 1914):

"A fire that no longer blazes is quickly smothered in ashes. Only a love that scorches and dazzles is worthy of the name. Mine is like that."

"I see only you, think only of you, speak only to you, touch only you, breathe you, desire you, dream of you; in a word, I love you!"

"I love you *because* I love you, because it would be impossible for me not to love you. I love you without question, without calculation, without reason good or bad, faithfully, with all my heart and soul, and every faculty."

"When I am dead, I am certain that the imprint of my love will be found on my heart. It is impossible to worship as I do without leaving some visible trace behind when life is over."

• For a deeply sincere but lighter touch see Ogden Nash's letters to Frances Rider Leonard (in Linell Nash Smith, ed., *Loving Letters From Ogden Nash: A Family Album*, 1990):

"I couldn't go to bed without telling you how particularly marvelous you were today. You don't seem to have any idea of your own loveliness and sweetness; that can't go on, and I shall see that it doesn't."

"Both your letters arrived this morning. Thank you. I had sunk pretty low in the eyes of the elevator man, to whom I have been handing a letter to mail nearly every night and who has evidently noticed that I have been getting nothing in return. I could sense his thinking, 'You have no charm, sir.' But now it's all right again—his attitude today is as respectful and reverent as I could wish."

"I've been living all day on your letter. . . . Have I ever told you that I love you? Because I do. I even loved you yesterday when I didn't get any letter and thought you hated me for trying to rush things. It ought to worry me to think that no matter what you ever do to me that is dreadful I will still have to keep on loving you; but it doesn't, and I will."

"I've been reading your letter over all day, it's so dear. . . . Haven't you a photograph or even a snapshot of yourself? I want to look at and touch it, as I read and touch your letters; it helps bring you a little closer."

"Do you know what is the most delightful sound in the world? I'm sorry that you'll never be able to hear it. It's when I'm sitting in your library, and hear you cross the floor of your room and open the door; then your footsteps in the hall and on the stairs. In four days now—."

• For insight on a long-lasting, evergreen love, read Winston and Clementine Churchill's letters to each other (in Mary Soames, *Clementine Churchill: The Biography of a Marriage*, 1979):

Winston to Clemmie: "I love you so much and thought so much about you last night and all your courage and sweetness." "You cannot write to me too often or too long—my dearest and sweetest. The beauty and strength of your character and the sagacity of your judgment are more realized by me every day." "The most precious thing I have in life is your love for me." "Do cable every few days, just to let me know all is well and that you are happy when you think of me." "This is just a line to tell you how I love you and how sorry I am you are not here." "Darling, you can write anything but war secrets and it reaches me in a few hours. So send me a letter from your dear hand." "Tender love my darling, I miss you very much. I am lonely amid this throng. Your ever-loving husband W." "My darling one, I think always of you. . . . With all my love and constant kisses, I remain ever your devoted husband W." "Another week of toil is over and I am off to Chartwell in an hour. How I wish I was going to find you there! I feel a sense of loneliness and miss you often and would like to feel you near. I love you very much, my dear sweet Clemmie."

Clementine to Winston: "I miss you terribly—I ache to see you." "I feel there is no room for anyone but you in my heart—you fill every corner." "My beloved Winston,

This is a long separation. Think of your Pussy now and then with indulgence and love. Your own, Clemmie." "My darling. My thoughts are with you nearly all the time and though basking in lovely sunshine and blue seas I miss you and home terribly. Tender love, Clemmie." "I'm thinking so much of you and how you have enriched my life. I have loved you very much but I wish I had been a more amusing wife to you. How nice it would be if we were both young again."

Special Situations

■ When writing to someone who doesn't (yet!) love you as you love them, be brief rather than long. Retain some emotional distance. While you might tell an amusing anecdote about something that happened at work, you wouldn't tell a story from your childhood that has high meaning for you. Don't move too quickly. Instead of inviting the other person to go camping with you, ask if they've ever done much camping, what they thought of it. Instead of sprinkling your letter with "you" and "I" (and especially "you and I" as if you were already a couple) keep it neutral. Your goal is much like that of a letter of application: you don't aim to get the job, you want to get the interview. You present yourself as a warm, bright, funny, interesting person so that you can keep the person's interest long enough to present yourself as a candidate for their love.

Format

■ Anything goes. However you choose to write (type of paper, envelope, stamp, fountain pen, felt-tip, computer, e-mail, even fax) will be an expression of who you are. You can write longhand on lined paper, on scented stationery, or on the back of your movie rental receipt. You can use the same pen, ink, and paper every time so that your letters have a recognizable look even from a distance. Or you can vary your letters, sometimes on one kind of paper, sometimes typed, sometimes filling in the spaces on a greeting card. Use colorful postage stamps and rubber-stamp art on your envelopes. Or use perfectly decorous, conservative #10 envelopes and say wild things in the letter inside.

■ Is it a love letter if you send it by e-mail? Sometimes. In general, however, even the most romantic e-mailed words don't have the impact they have in a letter. A letter has come straight from the loved one's hands. It is personal, physical, an artifact. Rereading a printed-out e-mail doesn't do quite the same thing for us. Use e-mail for short "thinking of you" messages.

WORDS

attractive	fascinating	inspiring	promise
bliss	fate	intensely	remember
boundless	feelings	lasting	soulmate
charming	fiercely	lonesome	sweetest
cherish	forever	lovable	tenderness
dearest	handsome	lucky	treasure
delight	happy	memories	unceasing
desire	heart	miracle	undying
dream	heaven	paradise	unforgettable
endless	immeasurable	passionately	unique
eternal	incomparable	pleasure	

PHRASES

from the first moment
hardly wait for the day when
how I long to
how much you mean to me
if I had only one wish
if only you knew
in my heart
I often think of
make life worth living
memories that keep me going
miss you so much
one of the happiest moments of my life

only love of my life
on my mind
remember the time
reread your letter
so happy to get your letter
wait for the mail every day
want to hold you
whenever I think of you
when we're apart
without you, I feel
you make me feel

SENTENCES

I couldn't sleep last night—and you know why.

I'd give anything to be able to touch you right now.

I had to tell you how much I enjoyed being with you yesterday.

I'll never forget the first time I saw you.

It's too lonely without you!

I've been carrying your last letter with me everywhere and it's getting limp—will you write me another one?

Just when I think I know everything about you, there's a new and wonderful surprise.

Two more days until I see you—I'm not sure I can wait.

We're some of the lucky ones—our love is forever.

You are my whole world.

You're the answer to my prayers and my dreams.

PARAGRAPHS

You are the first thing I think of in the morning. You are the last thing I think of at night. And guess who's on my mind every minute in between!

There is nothing I want more to do and feel less able to do than write you a beautiful love letter. When I try to write, I'm wordless. I've been sitting here, pen in hand, for half an hour trying to express what you mean to me. Will you accept some borrowed words? Jeremy Taylor once said, "Love is friendship set on fire." I feel them both, the fire and the friendship. Bless you for bringing them into my life.

Why do I love you? It's going to take the rest of my life to tell you, so I'd better get started now. For one thing, your unswerving calm is both soothing and exciting to me. For another, with your smile we could enter you in the Smile Olympics—and win! For another . . .

I feel more intensely alive, more intensely real, more intensely myself since I met you. As if a dimming filter had been removed, the world suddenly shouts with bright colors, sharply outlined shapes, evocative scents, intriguing textures, music, laughter, flashes of joy. You.

SAMPLE LETTERS

Dear Nance,

Because of you, I find myself filled with love for the whole world. Ruth Rendell wrote in one of her mysteries, "It is not so much true that all the world loves a lover as that a lover loves all the world."

Yes! I do! I now pat grubby children on their grubby little heads. I no longer kill mosquitoes. I straighten up crumpled weeds in the sidewalk cracks. I let dogs sniff my ankles (and, well, you know). I line up the bars of soap on the shelves at K-Mart. The world is mine, and I am its, and I love it. Maybe this is a way of saying that I love you a whole world's worth!

Kisses from me

———

Dearest Oliver,

There's only time for a quick postcard between flights, but I wanted to tell you how I treasure my last sight of you waving at the window. All I have to do is shut my eyes and I see you again.

Three more days and I won't need to shut my eyes! Until then, all my love!

———

Dear Sophy,

Scientists seem unable to measure love. I—you will not be surprised to discover this, knowing how talented I am!—have found a way to do it.

When you go to your seminar in Denver next week, I am going to keep Traddles for you. Now you know that I am not, and have never been, a dog person. If I were a dog person, my tastes would not run to Mexican hairless dogs with bat-like ears, rat-like tails, wrinkled snouts, and, in this case, a cast on its leg.

Not only will I keep Traddles (we haven't taken the full measure of this love yet!), but I will let her sleep in my bed, I will be faithful to her finicky feeding schedule, and I will even—once or twice a day—kiss her on the lips. Or near the lips anyway. I will pet her, I will let her watch football with me and follow me around. I will take her for her daily walks, even though everyone who sees us will look at her cast, then look at me and think, "Ah, a man who abuses dogs!"

And all this because I love you. So, what do you think? Have I found a way to measure love?

> Tom

———

Dear Carol,

Today I found one more reason to be grateful for you.

You don't want to hear the whole sorry tale but my day involved things like oversleeping and then running into Mr. Valborg while trying to sneak into the office; losing irreplaceable data to the computer gremlins; dripping spaghetti sauce on my white shirt (while having lunch with, of course, Mr. Valborg); having to deal with two incredibly irate clients; and finding, when I finally left the office, that my battery was dead.

Thinking about you was the only pleasant thing in my life today! Thank you for being so wonderful that all by yourself you make up for everything that goes wrong.

> Love,
> Will

———

See also: APPRECIATION, FAMILY

THIRTY-THREE

MEMOS

Talk of nothing but business, and dispatch that business quickly.
—ALDUS MANUTIUS

Memos may be an endangered species.

The memo (short for memorandum—plural is memos, memoranda, or memorandums) grew out of a need to streamline correspondence—to communicate swiftly, directly, and concisely—among employees of the same company. There was little point in using letterhead stationery, "Dear," "Sincerely," and other complimentary openings and closings with coworkers, managers, and executives with whom you communicated constantly and who were well aware of what company they worked for.

E-mail meets the same criteria and has the advantage of being faster and easier.

The memo is still useful: in a small office where not everyone has access to e-mail; when the information is too confidential for e-mail; when you attach it to a report with too many pages and graphics to be easily sent electronically; when you want a message routed and signed or initialed or commented upon; for routine out-of-house communications with customers or suppliers (orders, transmitting material, acknowledgments, confirmations, inquiries).

In *How to Survive From Nine to Five*, Jilly Cooper writes, "The memo's chief function, however, is as a track-coverer, so that you can turn on someone six months later and snarl: 'Well, you should have known about it, I sent you a memo.'"

Write Memos About

- announcements
- changes in policy/procedure
- in-house events
- instructions
- meetings
- reminders
- reports

How to Say It

- The memo heading has four items. The most common arrangement stacks all four lines flush left:

      TO: Blanche Challoner
      FROM: Francis Levison
      DATE: Nov. 20, 2010
      SUBJECT: employee stock purchase

  Or, capitalize only the initial letter:

      To: Blanche Challoner
      From: Francis Levison.
      Date: Nov. 20, 2010
      Subject: employee stock purchase

  You may also line up the information like this:

          TO: Blanche Challoner
        FROM: Francis Levison
        DATE: Nov. 20, 2010
          RE: employee stock purchase

  Or, arrange them in two columns:

      TO: Blanche Challoner   DATE: Nov. 20, 2010
      FROM: Francis Levison   RE: employee stock purchase

- Select a phrase for the subject line that will immediately tell the reader the main point of your memo: "new flexible tubing"; "personal telephone calls"; "medical benefits enrollment"; "change in library hours."
- Begin the body of your message two to four lines below the subject line and flush left. All paragraphs in the body begin flush left and are separated by one line of space (text is otherwise single-spaced).
- Close with a request for the action you want, if appropriate, and a date by which it should be carried out: "Please call me before Tuesday"; "Please

inform others in your department"; "Send me a copy of your report by Oct. 13."

- Sign your name at the bottom of the memo or put your signature or initials next to your name in the heading.
- Reference initials and enclosure notation (if any) are typed under the memo flush left.

What Not to Say

- Don't include salutations or complimentary closings or any of the wind-up or wind-down sentences used in a standard business letter. You are courteous, but you get straight to the point.
- Don't use the memo for official communications (promotions and resignations, for example); type those on letterhead stationery.

Tips on Writing

■ State the purpose of your memo in the first sentence.

■ Be concise. Use short, simple sentences with present tense and active verbs. Although memos can technically be any length, the one- or two-page memo is the norm, except for report or issue memos. The shorter the memo, the more likely it is to be read immediately.

■ Informality is the hallmark of memos. They are shorter and less complicated than letters. They use plainer language. Jargon and acronyms familiar to those in the company may be used. "We" is used instead of "Lamprey-Wutherwood Telecommunications Inc."

■ When sending a memo to more than one person: (1) list each name, if you have only a few, after the word "To:"; or (2) list the principal recipient after "To:" and the others at the bottom of the memo after "cc:"; or (3) list all the names in a distribution list on the last page of your memo. After "To:" type "See distribution list on page 2." Names appear without courtesy titles (Ms., Mr.) but occasionally with professional titles (Dr.). When managers are listed, their names are often given in order of corporate rank. In some companies, alphabetic order is used.

Special Situations

■ An issue memo is a fact-oriented report that summarizes important information so that policy decisions can be made. An efficient organization of material includes some or all of the following: (1) stating what the issue is, putting it in context, providing history or background information; (2) listing available or suggested options or solutions, along with their pros and cons; (3) detailing the costs, fiscal impact, and effects on other programs of each of the options; (4) if appropriate and welcome, naming steps necessary to implement the various options; (5) offering your recommendations; (6) suggesting the next step in the process (further study, meeting, vote, management decision).

■ Employees can be invited to in-house events by memo, which is more "inviting" than an e-mail message. (See INVITATIONS for guidelines.)

Format

■ Memos are not sent on company letterhead. Some organizations have memo stationery with the company name or simply "Memo" at the top or forms preprinted with the headings. The use of computers (with a macro for memo headings) and e-mail, however, mean that dedicated memo stationery is less commonly seen today.

WORDS

announcement	information	policies	report
attachment	instructions	procedures	request
deadline	listing	progress	status
feedback	notice	proposed	summary
guidelines	outline	reminder	

PHRASES

appreciate your comments on	route this message to
background information	see below for
clarify recent changes in procedure	summarize yesterday's discussion
effective immediately	would like to announce the following
pleased to report	
request a response by	

SENTENCES

Attached is a "get well" card for Ethel Ormiston—sign it if you like and pass it on to the next name on the list.

I've had phone calls from the following people about the new hook lifting devices—will you please return their calls and let me know what the problem is?

Please initial this memo to indicate that you've read it.

Please read the attached proposal before tomorrow's meeting.

Please sign up below for staff lounge cleanup duty and route this memo as indicated.

The attached outline covers projected work through the end of the year.

There's been some confusion about the new procedures for travel reimbursements—please note and file the following guidelines.

This memo will serve to authorize the preparation and filing of a patent application in the United States Patent and Trademark Office for a Quick-Drying Colorless Gessu Substitute.

We are pleased to announce that last week's sales figures as reported by the branch offices (see below) constitute a record for us.

We suggest you keep these fire drill instructions posted near your desk.

PARAGRAPHS

The attached outline covers projected work through the end of the year. The outline was generated in consultation with department heads. We will review progress on the first of each month and adjust the work and timelines accordingly. We are highly interdependent in this company and we need the interlocking pieces to fit comfortably. Please review the scheduled work and let me know your opinion, particularly of the feasibility of project goals and deadlines.

As of January 1, all customer 612 area code numbers given on the attached sheet will be changed to 651. Please correct your files. Note that 612 area codes not on this list remain 612. Also attached is a list of the three-number prefixes that take 612 and those that take 651 so that you can verify the correct area code for any new numbers.

Devizes Inc. will be selling company cars that are more than two years old. Employees will be given priority. Please see the attached list of vehicles with descriptions and prices.

The Pudney Summer Soccer Camp has approached Potter Commercial Development Corp. to ask if some of our employees would be interested in volunteering at the Soccer Camp this summer. Attached is a brochure describing the camp and an application form for volunteers. Thank you for considering their request.

Those of you who work with Priss Hartshorn will want to know that her husband of eighteen years died suddenly last night. No other details are known at present. Funeral services will be held on Saturday; for time and place, please check the newspaper. Those who want to send a note or sympathy card can write to her home address: 1963 Vassar Street, 50501.

TO: All employees
FROM: Raymond Berenger, Building Services
DATE: November 15
SUBJECT: Building maintenance

Please be reminded that the building custodian was terminated a week ago, on the day of the merger announcement. I ask that all employees cooperate by keeping your areas clean. Thanks.

TO: Delina Delaney Deli counter clerks
From: M. De Maine, Manager
Date: June 15
Re: Soliciting from the homeless/vendor safety

The presence of homeless people in this area of Manhattan is a fact. Occasionally, as you know, a homeless individual will venture into our shop and ask for handouts of food. Sometimes he or she will simply take a loaf of bread or a muffin without asking.

Now that summer is here we see more of this activity and all staff must adhere to our policy: Never say no to a homeless person's request for food. Some of these visitors are mentally unstable, some may carry weapons. Give them the food they want and politely escort them to the door. The cost of the food involved is not worth the risk to your safety.

There is always the possibility that we will thus get a reputation on the avenue for having free food. If interference with regular business escalates, we will reevaluate our policy.

TO: All employees
FROM: Staffing
DATE: February 5
SUBJECT: Half-time employees

Following is the full list of half-time employees (continuing with, however, full benefits) during the merger transition with Half Moon Press for a period of half a year effective February 8. HALF a good day!

Anne Frith, editorial
Eden Herring, editorial
Maria Lousada, production
Luke Marks, production
Hope Ollerton, order fulfillment

TO: Olive Chancellor
FROM: Varena Tarrant
SUBJECT: Patent authorization for:

    "Three-Dimensional Blueprint Acrylic Viewer"

DATE: June 16, 2010

This memo will serve to authorize the preparation and filing of a patent application in the United States Patent and Trademark Office.

The invention provides a method for viewing blueprints that allows ready discrimination of varied elevations.

The inventors and I will provide additional information and any experimentation necessary to file the application. We suggest that this application be filed by outside attorney Basil Ransome (Ransome & Birdseye) who is familiar with the inventors and technology.

Varena Tarrant

Senior Patent Liaison Specialist

————

To: See distribution list below
From: Norman Rivers
Date: Nov. 10
Re: gas and arc welding lab proposal

A meeting was held on Nov. 2 with Harvey Anderson and Cherry Elwood of Arnott-Bracy Enterprises to discuss Arnott-Bracy's preliminary proposal for the new gas and arc welding lab. Several changes were made and Mr. Anderson sent the first revision of the proposal to me on Nov. 8. I am forwarding copies of this proposal to all team members. We will review it on Nov. 18 at 2:30 in Room 201. I would particularly like Blanche May, Alan Ernescliffe, George Larkins, Tom Ward, and Mary Cheviot to be available for this meeting. If you have a conflict, please let me know. Arnott-Bracy Enterprises is expecting a response from us by Nov. 23. They will then provide a final proposal on Nov. 30.

————

TO: See routing list
FROM: Beck Knibbs
DATE: June 10
SUBJECT: Department picnic at Talbothays Farm

Listed below is everything we need for the picnic. Please pencil in your name after the item you're willing to bring and keep this memo moving! The last person should return it to me. Thanks.

————

TO: Dick Phenyl
FROM: A. W. Pinero
DATE: March 3, 2011
SUBJECT: Internet training session on March 10

So far the following people have signed up for the class. Will you please arrange with their supervisors for their absence that day? It also looks as though we're going to need a larger room and a few more computers. Can you arrange it? Thanks.

––––––––

TO: See distribution list
FROM: Human Resources
DATE: August 28
SUBJECT: Design department/reduced schedule

Elfine Hawk-Monitor will be working a reduced schedule in the design department for the next three weeks. She will be here on Mondays and Tuesdays only as she is preparing for her gallery exhibit of sculptures made solely from scrap metal. (See the current newsletter for dates and the location of her show.) We all certainly wish her weld . . . I mean well. This schedule is effective as of August 25 and I'll keep you posted on any changes. We will welcome Ms. Hawk-Monitor back full-time in mid-September and hope she won't have gotten rusty in the interim.

––––––––

See also: ACKNOWLEDGMENTS, ANNOUNCEMENTS, E-MAIL, INSTRUCTIONS, REPORTS, REQUESTS, RESPONSES

THIRTY-FOUR

LETTERS TO NEIGHBORS

*While the spirit of neighborliness was important on the frontier
because neighbors were so few, it is even more important now
because our neighbors are so many.*
—LADY BIRD JOHNSON

The search for harmony among neighbors is as old as human society. And there's been no dearth of advice on how to achieve it. In a much-consulted etiquette book written in 1902, *The Correct Thing*, Florence Howe Hall writes, "It is not the correct thing to take offense if a neighbor states civilly that he would prefer your children should cease from breaking his windows." Of course! Why didn't we know that?

Most troublesome issues between neighbors can be handled with common sense and goodwill. In *Miss Manners' Guide for the Turn-of-the-Millennium*, Judith Martin says, "The challenge of manners is not so much to be nice to someone . . . as to be exposed to the bad manners of others without imitating them."

Write Your Neighbors to

- alert them to neighborhood problems
- announce personal or business news
- complain (see COMPLAINTS)
- congratulate them
- express appreciation
- introduce your local business to them
- invite them to a neighborhood gathering (see also INVITATIONS)
- offer help

- send birthday or anniversary wishes (see ANNIVERSARIES)
- thank them for assistance or cooperation

How to Say It

- Be certain that writing is the appropriate road to take. If you've already had several unproductive in-person or telephone discussions about the issue, it probably is. Dealing with a problem face-to-face keeps it smaller; once the discussion escalates to a letter, the situation becomes complicated.
- State your message ("thank you," "congratulations," "we invite you," "have you heard"). If you're asking something, be specific: stay off our new grass, trim trees that extend onto our property, contribute toward repairing a common fence.
- When appropriate, offer to reciprocate or in some indirect way express your desire to be a good neighbor.
- Close with a pleasantry, compliment, or forward-looking remark.

What Not to Say

- Don't accuse. This will put your neighbor on the defensive, a position that rarely apologizes or changes. Use an indirect construction. Instead of "You never put the lids on your garbage cans properly—no wonder it all ends up here!" say, "I'm finding garbage in the alley every Thursday morning." Instead of "Your wind chimes are driving us crazy," say "We are having trouble sleeping at night because of the wind chimes."
- Don't generalize ("you always park in front of our house" or "you never shovel your walk"). It undercuts your position and angers the other person who can think of lots of times they shoveled their walk.

Tips on Writing

■ If you are in the habit of sending your neighbors notes of thanks, appreciation, congratulations, or just saying "I'm thinking about you," you will have a good basis on which to build when problems crop up.

Special Situations

■ Apartment living is grand when the owner and neighbors are. For letters about problems, see COMPLAINTS.

■ Noisy, aggressive, or trespassing pets are a common sore spot. In all but the most egregious cases (obvious animal abuse, for example), you will not get much help from police or other authorities. Know from the outset that the solution to the problem most likely depends on how well you deal person-to-person with the pet's best friend. At the least, try honey before you go for the vinegar.

■ Unruly, unsupervised, or otherwise troublesome children are a neighborhood perennial. "Give the neighbors' kids an inch and they'll take the whole yard." (Helen Castle) A letter is written only after you have spoken kindly with the child and, if that is not successful, with a parent. Describe how the situation appears to you, using "I" statements (not "you" statements, as in "you let her run wild"). Offer to help resolve it or show yourself willing to compromise, if possible.

■ In a dispute, attempt to see the issue from your neighbor's point of view. The more clearly you see the other person's side, the more effectively you can frame the discussion so that your neighbor derives some benefit or saves face in some way, thus opening the way to a solution.

■ Build a sense of community with invitations to an annual block party, picnic, or ice cream social. Prevention of neighborhood problems is much more fun than most cures.

Format

■ Handwritten or typed notes can be hand-delivered or sent by mail or even by e-mail.

WORDS

admire	concerned	helpful	share
agreement	considerate	kindness	socialize
appreciate	cooperation	neighborly	solution
attention	coordinate	respect	troubling
careful	generous	responsibility	upkeep

PHRASES

affecting the neighborhood	did you know
ask your help/cooperation	get together to discuss
block watch	happy to help with
combined action	hope you are willing to
community council	important to all of us
coordinate our efforts	inform you that

not really my business but

on behalf of the neighbors opposite
   you

reluctant to write

wanted you to be aware that

what would you think of

would you consider

SENTENCES

Could you speak to the tenants on the first floor about the strollers, bicycles, and skateboards they keep in the entryway?

Here is a key to our back door—I'd really appreciate your keeping a copy in case I get locked out again.

I am going to be the "Safe House" this year, for children walking to and from school, and I wanted to explain how it works.

Thanks so much for taking care of things while we were away—we look forward to doing the same for you.

Would you have time to come over some evening for coffee and dessert—and to discuss what kind of a common fence we all might like?

Your daughter is the most dependable newspaper carrier we've ever had—I'm writing her a note, but I also wanted you to know what a delight we think she is.

PARAGRAPHS

Hi, Neighbors! We have corn coming out of our ears (and, oddly enough, ears coming out of our corn)—if you can use some, please help yourselves.

As you know, the fire last week at Alice and Roddy Wicklow's was pretty destructive. Their most urgent needs right now are warm school clothes for the kids, blankets and bedding, and kitchen utensils. If you have anything you think would be useful, give me a call—I have a list of their sizes as well as a sense of what they most need.

This is to let you all know that Ajax is having a graduation party for about twenty of his friends Friday night. Bill and I will be home all evening, but if it gets too loud for you give us a call (I'm hoping you won't need to do that).

I've just heard that Rosa Klebb is in the hospital with a broken hip. Would the seven families on this block want to buy a plant for her—perhaps something she could later plant in her garden? I'll be glad to buy it and take it to the hospital. I'll stop by tomorrow to see what you think and to have you sign the card.

I'm ordering trees to replace the ones we lost in the storm. I've found a great nursery in Wisconsin with the healthiest trees and the lowest prices of any place I've checked. There's a discount for bulk orders so if any of you are also thinking of buying trees now, check out the attached list of trees and prices available. If some of you ordered the same time I do we'd all save on delivery charges plus we'd get a more favorable rate.

I'd like to ask Olivia and Kate to feed the rabbit and play with her a little while we're gone. Would this be okay with you? I'd leave a key with them and they could come and go when they liked. I feel sure they'd be good about locking up behind them.

I wonder if you're aware of zoning regulations prohibiting small businesses in this area. I'm guessing it wouldn't be a problem for the neighbors if your students didn't take up all the street parking three nights a week.

SAMPLE LETTERS

Dear Jeremy and Alice,

We've been so delighted to have you for neighbors that it's difficult to write this letter. It's because we do value your friendship that we're hoping to settle something that's become a problem for us. In a word, Cleo.

This probably comes as no surprise to you since we've called several times about Cleo's early morning, dinnertime, and late evening barking. We understand that she has to be put outside sometime, but it is difficult to understand why she barks every minute she's outside. The early morning barking has been disturbing as we are often up all night with the baby. I can't imagine all the neighbors are up by 5:30 so it must waken some of them too. Cleo tends to bark an average of six hours a day, which is really too much given how close together the houses are.

We appreciate your apologies and goodwill, but we are hoping that this time you can figure out some way of actually solving the problem.

On behalf of my family and several of the neighbors, I am writing to ask you to make other arrangements for Cleo when you are at work during the day. As I have mentioned several times on the telephone, when you leave Cleo on a leash in the backyard she barks and howls almost without interruption all day long. Knowing what a good neighbor you are in other respects, I felt that you would want to resolve this without us having to resort to more official means of restoring peace and quiet to the neighborhood during the day.

Cordially,

———

Dear Ms. Abbott,

This is a long overdue note of appreciation to you for arranging the alley-plowing each winter. Short of taking over for you, is there anything I can do to help out? Deliver the fliers? Contact those who haven't paid yet? Make phone calls? Let me know.

Sincerely,
Jervis Pendleton

———

Dear Friends,

Samson and I feel so bad about Dan cutting your flowers. It seems somehow worse that his goal was a Mother's Day bouquet for me.

By the time you get this, Dan should have been to see you with his own apology, four-year-old style. We have thoroughly explained to him how wrong this was, and why. I just wanted you to know that we take this seriously, that he has been spoken to, and that I would be surprised if he ever touched anything on your property again. I think he has learned something, but I'm sorry it was at your expense.

Mali

———

Dear Mr. Tsi-Puff,

I've been asked to approach you about your nightly routine of riding your exercise bike while watching videos. It appears that in order to hear the movie over the noise of the bike, you have to turn the volume way up.

You're popular with the other tenants, so nobody wanted to complain, but apparently the problem is severe, especially for those who retire early, for renters on either side of you, and for those one floor up and one floor down. The general thinking is that you do not realize how loud the sound is.

Nobody wants to curtail your admirable exercise program, but there is a simple solution: headphones.

Let me know what you think of this. I'm particularly eager to see if this works because the sense I got was that a number of your neighbors were quite taken with the idea of exercise bikes and old movies!

———

Dear Neighbor,

You are probably aware that the City is planning to add two lanes to Turner Road and turn it into a link between the two metro-area interstate highways. What this will mean for our neighborhood in terms of increased traffic, pollution, and noise is almost incalculable.

Oddly enough, the EIS (Environmental Impact Statement) seems to think the environment would best be served by converting this quiet road to a heavily trafficked one.

It's going to take a concerted effort to defeat the City's proposal. If you are also concerned about this new direction for our neighborhood, please come to an informational and organizational meeting Friday evening, September 3, 7:00 p.m. in the Bates Junior High auditorium.

———

Dear Polly,

Thanks for your comments on our new sod last week—it's about time we did something about the yard!

I have a small sod-related problem. I need to water it almost constantly these first few weeks, so I've got the sprinklers going most of the time. Johnny and Emma have discovered how much fun it is on these hot days to ride their bikes through the sprinklers. However, that means they are riding on the new sod, which can't take the activity.

By the time I get outside, they're off and away, and anyway I hate to be the Bad Guy here, so I was wondering if you could say a word or two to them about how fragile new sod is.

Thanks!

––––––––

Dear Neighbor,

The list of items missing from our neighborhood is growing: 3 bikes, 2 car CD players, 1 electric drill, 2 aluminum ladders, 2 lawnmowers, 6 lawn chairs, 1 glider, 1 well-stocked toolbox, 6 garden hoses, 1 birdbath. For a number of reasons, the police—and most of us—feel the responsible person is someone in this area. There are a few steps we can take to protect ourselves against further thefts. If you're interested, you're invited to our place Saturday afternoon at 4:30 for lemonade and fresh-picked raspberries—and a little discussion.

––––––––

Hello Neighbor!

The Darnel-Greaves Community Council (District 14) is celebrating its 10th anniversary in the green space Saturday, July 15, from 1:00 p.m. to 4:00 p.m. We invite you not only to enjoy the refreshments and some good conversation with your neighbors but to consider joining us in making our neighborhood a better place to live. (The only "cost" of belonging is to attend monthly meetings when you can.)

In the last ten years the Darnel-Greaves Community Council has organized a recycling program, offered free radon checks of your home, bought bulk quantities of longlife light bulbs, lobbied for three new "Stop" signs, AND saved the green space from development!

See you Saturday!

––––––––

Hi Imogen and Jack!

I offered to take care of Winifred Forsyte's sidewalks this winter (oh, the pride and energy of the owner of a new snowblower!) but I've got to be out of town next week. Would you mind clearing her sidewalks when you do your own? Knowing you, you will generously say yes, but if there's a problem, give me a call before Friday, will you? Thanks!

––––––––

Dear Mr. Ancrum,

My name is Dora Lomax and I live around the corner from you at 1892 Ward Avenue. I noticed that you have a large pile of red bricks and a stack of old picket fence sections in your backyard. If you have no use for them and are planning to get rid of them, I'd love to take them off your hands and use them for my own backyard and garden.

I will tap on your door and introduce myself in the next day or two. Otherwise I would be happy to hear from you (555-6755). You may have your own plans for the bricks and picket fencing or they may already be spoken for. Perhaps you had planned to sell them? But if not and if I may have them, I would be grateful.

Thank you very much!

Sincerely,

———

See also: ANNIVERSARIES, APOLOGIES, CONGRATULATIONS, IN-VITATIONS, REQUESTS, SENSITIVE, THANK YOU

THIRTY-FIVE

LETTERS DEALING WITH ORDERS

If it is good and I want it, they don't make it anymore.
—ELIZABETH C. FINEGAN

Standardized order forms, purchase forms, and requisition forms, along with 24-hour toll-free order lines and the convenience of buying and selling on the Internet, have almost entirely done away with letters dealing with orders. However, as long as human beings are ordering and filling orders, there will be errors, exceptions, special requests, and problems to write about.

Write Letters About Orders When

- acknowledging/confirming receipt of order/telephone order/delivery date (see also ACKNOWLEDGMENTS)
- asking for additional information (see also REQUESTS)
- canceling/changing an order
- complaining about an order (see COMPLAINTS)
- explaining procedures/policy changes/overpayments
- inquiring about order/delivery date/how to return merchandise
- instructing how to order/return goods (see INSTRUCTIONS)
- making adjustments (see ADJUSTMENTS, APOLOGIES)
- payments are late (see COLLECTION, CREDIT)
- placing an order
- refusing/returning an unsatisfactory order

How to Say It

- When ordering without a form, give: description of the desired item, quantity, size, color, personalization/monogram, and price. Include your name, address, ZIP code, daytime phone number, e-mail address, and method of payment. If you pay by bank card, include number, expiration date, and signature. When buying from a company in your home state, add sales tax to the total. Include stated handling charges and specify shipping directions or any special considerations.
- Indicate the date by which items must be delivered. You can thus generally cancel the order without forfeit if you don't receive it in time; the letter serves as an informal contract.
- To respond to orders received, use an all-purpose form for problems. Begin with "Thank you for your order. We are unable to ship your merchandise at once because . . ." and list possible problems so that one or more can be circled, underlined, or checked off. For example: "Payment has not been received." "We no longer fill C.O.D. orders. Please send a check or money order." "We cannot ship to a post office box. Please supply a street address." "We are currently out of stock—may we ship later?" "We no longer carry that item. May we send a substitution of equal value and similar style?" "Please indicate size (quantity, style, color)." "We must receive shipping and handling charges before processing your order."

What Not to Say

- Don't include other business (request for new catalog, complaint about a previous order, request for preferred-customer status) when ordering. It may delay your shipment.

Tips on Writing

■ When ordering, arrange your request so that it can be deciphered at a glance. Instead of phrasing an order as a sentence ("I would like to order six pairs of size 11 men's white sports socks and four pairs of size 11 men's black dress socks, at $7.95 per pair . . ."), type the information in columns or units of information, each on a separate line. Use Arabic numerals ("12 Menaphon harmonicas") instead of writing them out; they are more quickly read.

■ Don't forget the niceties. In the nuts-and-bolts world of ordering it's easy to forget that real live people are on the other end. Buyers close their letters with, "Thank you for your prompt attention." Suppliers always say, "Thank you for your order" and indicate their readiness to be of service to the customer and an appreciation of their business; helpful, courteous responses serve as goodwill letters.

Special Situations

■ If your first order wasn't received and you order the same items again, emphasize that it's a duplicate order. The first order may turn up later and also be filled.

■ When canceling a prepaid order or asking for a refund, include: order, invoice, or reference number; date of order; description of merchandise. Specify whether the amount of the merchandise should be credited to your account, credited to your charge card, or returned to you as a check.

■ To return merchandise, include in your cover letter: your name and address; item description; copy of sales slip, invoice, or shipping label; why you're returning it; request for a refund, credit to your account, or replacement merchandise; an expression of appreciation. If returning the merchandise is difficult because of its large size or fragility, write first and ask how it should be returned. Request (although you may not get) reimbursement for your shipping costs.

Format

■ Orders were made for forms, and vice versa. Simplify dealing with orders by creating standardized forms for the original order, problem orders, refunds, returned merchandise, and any other routine correspondence. Include such items as: customer's name, business name or title, address, ZIP code, telephone number with area code, e-mail address, fax number; customer's account number; description of merchandise, page where it appears in catalog, quantity, size, color, type; monogram or personalization; price per unit; total price for each item; shipping and handling chart; sales tax information; amount enclosed; shipping information (options available plus shipping time); space for bank card number, expiration date, and signature; spaces for signatures from purchasing department or other authorization.

■ Individualized letters dealing with orders are typed on letterhead or memo stationery.

■ If writing about a personal order from your home, a handwritten note is acceptable if clearly written.

WORDS

billed	expedite	items	stock
cancel	freight	merchandise	underpayment
change	goods	overnight	urgent
charge	handling	overpayment	warehouse
confirm	immediately	receipt	
deposit	invoice	rush	

PHRASES

as soon as possible/at once	next-day delivery
being shipped to you	please advise us/let us know
confirm your order	please bill to
delivery date of	prompt attention
enclosed is my check for	retail/wholesale price
hereby confirm	return receipt requested
I would like to order	ship C.O.D.
must cancel my order of	shipping and handling charges

SENTENCES

Along with your order I'm enclosing our spring catalog as I think you'll want to know about our new lower prices (many are lower than last year's!) and our completely new line of Strato work clothes.

If you cannot have the storage cabinets here by October 3, please cancel the order and advise us at once.

Please bill this order to my account #JO4889 at the usual terms.

Please cancel my order for the Heatherstone china (copy of order enclosed)—the three-month delay is unacceptable.

Please charge this order to my Carlyle First Bank Credit Card #333-08-4891, expiration date 11/10 (signature below).

Please check on the status of my order #90-4657 dated March 1.

Please confirm receipt of this order by fax or telephone.

Please include your account number/invoice number/order number on all correspondence.

We acknowledge with thanks your order of August 19 for one Pumblechook self-closing, self-latching chain-link gate.

We are pleased to inform you that both your orders were shipped this morning.

We are sorry to advise you that we will be out of that particular piano tuning kit (#P11507) indefinitely.

We are unable to fill your order dated June 3 because your account is currently in arrears.

We hope you enjoy your personalized stationery, and will think of us for your other stationery needs.

Your order #KR45G is being processed and should be shipped by August 1.

PARAGRAPHS

This is to confirm receipt of your order #104-1297 dated June 17, 2011. It will be shipped on or about June 26. Please allow two to three weeks for arrival. If you need to contact us again about this order, use our reference number, 442-48895.

We appreciate your order #GR3315 for the exposed aggregate. However, we no longer ship C.O.D. Please send a check or money order for $782.11 so that we can expedite your order.

Please note that you received a special price on the sheet protectors. Your refund check for the overpayment is enclosed.

We are trying to match exactly the interior folders we use for our hanging files. The ones shown in your current catalog, page 217, look very much like ours. Could you please send us samples in several colors so that we can be sure before ordering?

With one exception, your order is being shipped to you from our Gregsbury warehouse this week. The six desktop calculators are coming from our Chicago warehouse, and we've been experiencing some delays from that warehouse recently. You may not receive the calculators until approximately March 8. Please let us know if this is acceptable.

Thank you for your purchase order (#K12291944) of July 9 for the Bascomb stairway elevator. Your order has been forwarded for fulfillment, and your Purchasing Department will be contacted with information about terms and shipping dates.

It was my impression that we agreed upon a delivery date of May 15. The confirmation I have just received gives June 15. This will unfortunately be too late for us. Please let me know at once if this was a clerical error or if we have a serious problem on our hands.

To: Order Department

Enclosed is your standard order form, which I have completed.

I would like to call your attention, however, to the fact that the glass block windows I'm ordering have the same catalog number as one of the chandeliers on p. 167.

Will you please check into this and make sure I receive the glass block windows and not a chandelier?

Thank you.

————

To: "On the Road" Travelogues

I would like to order the following travelogues:

Thailand

China

Japan

Korea

Enclosed is a check for $41.80, which includes shipping and handling.

Your ad offered a free bonus CD on Russia to customers who ordered by phone. I tried your 800 number hundreds of times over a period of four days (using the automatic re-dial feature of my phone). It was always busy.

I am interested in receiving the bonus CD. Do you expect the 800 number to be available or is there some other way I can obtain it?

————

Dear Home Fittings Inc.,

I am ordering your garage door opener, catalog #A6774 or #A6775 (order form at-tached).

Although the catalog copy discusses both chain-drive openers and screw-drive open-ers, I can't tell which catalog number is for which. I want the screw-drive opener. I am assuming it is the more expensive opener and am enclosing a check in that amount, but would you please double-check this for me?

Thank you.

————

Dear Ritson Projectors:

We have just received the front- and rear-screen slide projector we ordered from you on November 3 (copies of order and invoice enclosed). One of the lenses appears to have been broken in transit.

Please let us know whether we should return the entire projector to you, take it to a service center if you have one in the vicinity, or have it repaired and bill you.

Yours truly,

————

Dear Dr. Sturmthal:

Thank you for your purchase order #H459991, which we received on June 3, for the TEM-500 Transmission Electron Microscope. Your order has been sent to our Administration Department and your Purchasing Department will be advised directly as to the confirmation of terms and shipping dates.

Teresa Desterro, Manager of the Sales Department, located in our Gillespie office, will advise you of confirmed delivery dates and can provide you with answers to questions on order processing or shipment expediting. Alec Loding, National Service Manager, also located in our Gillespie Office, will send you complete information on the installation requirements of your new TEM-500. Both Ms. Desterro and Mr. Loding can be reached directly by calling 212-555-1212.

We appreciate your order and the confidence you have shown in our company and in our instruments. We look forward to hearing from you either now or in the future if there is any way in which we may be of assistance to you.

Sincerely yours,

————

TO: Conford Confections
FROM: Alexander Trott
DATE: June 3, 2010

I have been buying your Conford Confections for family, friends, and business acquaintances twice a year (Easter and Christmas) for many years. I will be traveling in Europe this summer and would like to take along Confections to offer friends and business acquaintances there.

My questions:

1. Do Confections need to be refrigerated, either to maintain good quality and appearance or to ensure that there is no product spoilage?

2. Do you have outlets for your product in Europe? (I would not like to cart them along as a "special treat" and then find them being sold everywhere over there.)

3. Is there any other reason that would prevent me from taking Confections with me? (Do they melt easily, for example?)

If you can reassure me on the above points, please place my order for:

| 6 boxes | 8 oz. Gift Box | $7.95@ |
| 10 boxes | 14 oz. Supremes | $12.95@ |

My check for $197.83 (including sales tax and shipping and handling) is enclosed. Please ship to the letterhead address.

If you think the Confections won't travel well, I'll appreciate your saying so and returning my check.

————

See also: ACKNOWLEDGMENTS, ADJUSTMENTS, APOLOGIES, COLLECTION, COMPLAINTS, CREDIT, INSTRUCTIONS, REFUSALS, RESPONSES

THIRTY-SIX

LETTERS RELATED TO ORGANIZATIONS AND CLUBS

*Please accept my resignation. I don't want to belong to
any club that would accept me as a member.*
—GROUCHO MARX

Over 35,000 nonprofit membership organizations are listed in the *Encyclopedia of
Associations* (Thomson Gale), and many other clubs, societies, and groups function in less formal ways to provide people with ways of sharing interests, goals,
professional information, and recreational activities.

Most club or organization correspondence is brief, routine, and easily written.
But every announcement, invitation, or letter also represents the organization to its
members and to the public and thus needs to be accurately written and attractively
presented.

Write Letters Dealing with Clubs/ Organizations for

- announcements: meetings/changes/reminders (see also ANNOUNCE-
  MENTS)
- invitations: organization events/speaking engagements (see also INVITA-
  TIONS)
- meetings: canceling/changing

- recommending new members (see also REFERENCES)
- recruiting new members
- requests: membership/sponsorship/applications/volunteers/information/copies of agenda or minutes
- resignations
- welcoming new members (see also WELCOME)

How to Say It
- When announcing a meeting, include: the name of your organization; date, time, and place of the meeting; a phone number for further information; at least one reason why a person would want to attend the meeting (celebrity guest speaker, special election, panel discussion, book signing).
- When inviting a speaker, include: your organization's full title; an estimate of the audience size; a description of the group's interests so the speaker can tailor the talk to them; available equipment (overhead projector, microphone); directions or map; name and phone number of contact person.
- When recruiting new members, an attractive brochure describing the group and its goals and activities may best "sell" you to others. Send it along with a friendly cover letter that emphasizes the group's strong points and tells why your organization would be appropriate for this person.

What Not to Say
- Avoid putting anything negative on paper. Personality conflicts, disagreements and disputes over policies, and shifting allegiances give groups their dynamism and distinct character, but they are best handled face-to-face. Committing delicate situations to letters that end up in public files is unwise.
- Avoid paternalistic, top-down language in letters. Most groups today have a collegial rather than hierarchical spirit. Although there may be officers or leaders, everyone in the organization feels some ownership of it.

Tips on Writing

■ Unless you write on behalf of a small, casual group, keep letters to members dignified, businesslike, and somewhat formal. Spuriously intimate letters are offputting to some people, whereas a reserved letter appears less warm but certainly not offensive.

■ Spell members' names correctly. The mutilation of our names on mailing labels has become routine, but no one likes to see it from their professional or social group.

Special Situations

■ You may be asked to do a favor or write a recommendation for someone in your club or society whom you don't know well. By virtue of association and club kinship, there is a subtle pressure to respond positively. But you are no more obliged in this case than in any other (see REFUSALS).

■ The word "chairman" has generally been replaced by "chair." (Other choices include moderator, committee/department head, presiding officer, presider, president, convener, coordinator, group coordinator, discussion/group/committee leader, head, organizer, facilitator, officiator, director, administrator.) Some people use "chairwoman" and "chairman," but "chairwoman" is perceived as a less weighty word and it is seldom used as an exact match for "chairman." "Chairperson" is a self-conscious term used mostly for women. The short, simple "chair" was the original term (1647), with "chairman" coming into the language in 1654 and "chairwoman" in 1685. Using "chair" as both noun and verb parallels the use of "head" for both noun and verb. (People who are upset about being called "a piece of furniture" apparently have no problem with the gruesome picture of a "head" directing a department, division, or group, nor is there evidence that anyone has confused people chairing meetings with their chairs.)

Format

■ Type all club or organization business correspondence. An exception might be a social club in which the members know each other well and handwrite notes to each other.

■ E-mail messages and postcards are wonderfully useful in getting out meeting notices, announcements, invitations, and short messages.

■ For an organization of any size, your mailing list should be computerized; combining such a list with the merge function of most word processing systems simplifies correspondence.

WORDS

action	coalition	heritage	practical
affiliation	committee	ideals	principles
agenda	constitution	improve	procedures
allegiance	contribution	league	program
alliance	establish	legacy	progress
association	generous	nominate	project
benefit	guild	policies	qualifications
bylaws	headquarters	positive	regulations

rules	support	valuable	worthwhile
society	unwavering	welcome	

PHRASES

a credit to the organization	join forces
affiliated/associated with	minutes of the meeting
all-out effort	service to the community
board of directors	slate of officers
committee chair	take pride in nominating
common goal	unfortunately must resign
cooperative spirit	worthwhile cause
credit to us all	would like to nominate you for
have been elected a member of	

SENTENCES

Enclosed please find names of hosts, meeting dates, and topics for the next six months.

I am sorry to inform you that family illness obliges me to step down from the club vice-presidency, effective immediately.

It is with great pleasure/regret that I accept/decline your nomination to the Board of Directors of Montmorency House.

I would be happy to discuss any questions you have about the Club over lunch some day next week.

I would like to recommend/wish to propose Brander Cheng for membership in the Burke Orchestra Society.

Join now and take advantage of this limited offer to new members.

Our annual fundraising meeting to plan events for the next year will be held August 3 at 7:00 p.m.—all are invited.

Please accept my resignation from the Rembrandt Society.

To join the Frobisher Society today, simply indicate your membership category on the enclosed form and return it with your check.

Would you be willing to staff the Club's concession stand at the High-Lake Street Fair?

Would you please place the following three items on the agenda for the November meeting?

PARAGRAPHS

The Belford Area Women in Trades Organization invites you to attend its next monthly meeting, Thursday, June 14, at 7:30 p.m. in the old Belford Union Hall. Get to know us. See what we're trying to do for women in trades in this area. And then, if you like what you see, join up! Introductory one-year membership is $45, and we think we can do as much for you as you can do for the Organization!

This is to acknowledge receipt of your membership application. You will hear from us as soon as we have received all your references and evaluated your application. Thank you for your interest in the Society.

I understand you and some other employees have formed several noon-hour foreign language clubs. I would be interested in joining your Italian-speaking group. Can you put me in touch with whoever is in charge of it? Thanks.

Congratulations to our new officers, elected at the September 12 meeting: Truda Silber, president; Martin Lynch Gibbon, vice president; Andrew Davies, secretary; Maria Eleonora Schoning, treasurer. They will be installed at the beginning of the October 15 meeting. Our most sincere gratitude is extended to last year's officers, who saw the Club through a remarkable expansion and a rewriting of the bylaws. Thanks, Fran, Leo, Rose, and Dennis!

Notice: The Professional Educators Network will not hold its regularly scheduled monthly meeting on February 10 at 7:30 p.m. We regret any inconvenience this cancellation may cause you. The next meeting will be held March 8 at 7:30 p.m. in the Schley Library meeting room.

We are all, of course, very sorry to see you resign, but we understand that you have many other obligations at this time. We will be happy to welcome you back whenever your circumstances change. It's been wonderful having you with us.

Thanks so much for helping to clean up after the dance last Saturday. It's certainly not a popular job, which makes me appreciate all the more the good-hearted folks who did pitch in. The next time you're on the cleanup committee, you can put my name down!

SAMPLE LETTERS

TO: Admissions Committee
FROM: Paul Dombey
DATE: April 16, 2011
RE: Recommendation for membership

It is my pleasure to propose Louisa and John Chick for membership in the Granger Social Club. I know Louisa and John both personally and professionally; he is a fellow merchant, owner of Chick Book & Stationery, and she is Louisa Dombey, my sister. I recommend them to you highly.

They are both graduates of Walter Gay University, members of Trinity Lutheran Church, and hosts of a weekly book club. In addition, Ms. Chick is currently president and part owner of the Women's Collective and Mr. Chick has served as vice president of the local merchants' group.

They are charming people, committed and accomplished tennis players, and assets to the community. I think the Club would benefit from welcoming them as members.

Sincerely,

Dear Hugh,

As a member and current secretary of the Merrivale Philatelic Society, I'm always on the lookout for other stamp collectors. Someone happened to mention yesterday that you have been collecting for years. Would you be interested in joining us?

Because some of the members have quite valuable collections, we are careful to accept newcomers only on the basis of three references in addition to the recommendation of a member.

I would like to propose you for membership, if you think it's something you would enjoy. I'm enclosing some information that will tell you a little more about the group and its activities.

Let me know if you're interested, because I'd be pleased to sponsor you.

Sincerely,

To: Board of Directors

It is with much regret that I resign my position as Secretary of the Macduff Drama Club. Family complications oblige me to withdraw from any evening activities at least for the foreseeable future. If I can be of any help to my successor, I am available by telephone.

I have thoroughly enjoyed my association with the Macduff Club. Best wishes to all of you. I look forward to joining you again as soon as possible.

Dear Friend,

There is something remarkable and unique about the Tropical Fish & Aquarists Club. For one thing, it really is a club, not an organization whose "membership benefits" amount to little more than having your name on a mailing list and receiving a monthly magazine.

When you join the Tropical Fish & Aquarists Club, you don't belong to it—it belongs to you. You have the option of meeting with other hobbyists in large, small, or special-interest groups as often as you and your co-enthusiasts want. You are entitled to four free five-line ads per year in a magazine that reaches thousands of other hobbyists. We'll extend your subscription to the magazine for one year if you contribute an article for publication. And, at the end of each year, we share any profits from membership fees and magazine revenues with members.

You don't belong to the Club; it belongs to you!

Yours truly,

———————

See also: ANNOUNCEMENTS, FUNDRAISING, INVITATIONS, REFERENCES, REFUSALS, REQUESTS, RESPONSES, WELCOME

THIRTY-SEVEN

QUERY LETTERS

A query letter is really a sales letter without the hype.
—LISEL EISENHEIMER

A query is a brief, well-written letter that sparks an editor's interest in publishing your article or book and ideally results in a request to submit the manuscript. A combination request letter and sales letter, the query letter is also used to persuade a literary agent to represent you or to pique someone's interest in a business proposal.

Editors like the query letter because it allows them to decide quickly if the idea is suitable for them and if it's interesting enough to pursue. They also use a good query letter to help them sell the idea in turn to their colleagues at editorial meetings.

For unagented writers, the query letter is the only way to approach publishers who no longer accept unsolicited manuscripts. And it may be a good way to approach even those publishers who do. Once an editor responds to your query letter with an invitation to send your manuscript, you can mark the package "Requested Material" and your manuscript will not end up doing time in the slush pile. You'll also know in advance that they're looking for material like yours.

Write Query Letters for

- books
- business opportunities
- dramatic scripts
- filmscripts/screenplays
- journal and review articles

- literary agents
- magazine articles

How to Say It

- Address your query to the right person. Familiarize yourself with the periodical or publishing house so that you are certain your material is suitable for them. Obtain the name and title of the editor receiving queries for your type of book or article (from a market book, online source, friend, writing group). Call the publisher and verify that the person is still there, that the name is spelled the way you have it, and that the person's title is current. (Don't ask to speak to the editor, who will usually be annoyed by the call; an operator, receptionist, or editorial assistant can answer your questions.)
- Orient your reader quickly to the purpose of your letter ("Would you be interested in seeing a 10,000-word article on . . . ?").
- Establish a strong hook to keep the editor reading. Some query letters open with the first paragraph of the proposed article or book.
- Tell what type of book or article it is (reference, biography, children's), how long it is (in number of words), its intended audience, and its title. In a few sentences, describe the work so that the editor itches to read it; this paragraph must be your finest writing.
- Tell why your article or book is different from others on the same subject, why you're the best person to write it (mention relevant expertise or knowledge), and why you chose this particular publisher.
- List your past publications.
- Thank the person for their time and attention.
- Include a self-addressed stamped envelope (SASE). Always. Every time.

What Not to Say

- Don't discuss payment, royalties, rights, or other business issues in the query letter; it isn't appropriate at this stage of the process.
- Don't include personal information (age, marital status, hobbies, education) unless it is highly relevant to the proposed work. You do, of course, include your full name, address, telephone number, e-mail address, and fax number.
- Don't use gimmicks to attract an editor's attention. Editors know how to zero in on the heart of the work and are not swayed by colored typefaces, joke or riddle openings (unless, of course, it's a joke or riddle book), or glitzy approaches. They usually consider gimmicks the mark of an amateur.

Tips on Writing

■ Follow instructions on how to query. Publishers that accept e-mail queries will say so; if they mention a self-addressed stamped envelope (SASE) they prefer a written query. Most publishers offer writer's guidelines; get a copy (either from their website or by writing and enclosing an SASE) for any publisher you are interested in selling to.

■ In general, address your query to associate editors and assistant editors, who are more likely to read your letter than are executive editors or editors-in-chief.

■ Your letter is one page long—two at the most. "A query letter is like a fishing expedition; don't put too much bait on your hook or you'll lose your quarry. Be brief and be tantalizing!" (Jane von Mehren)

■ Convey your enthusiasm for the material.

■ A clever, memorable, or intriguing title (as long as it's appropriate to the material) is helpful to your cause. It doesn't have to be your final title; select a working title or choose one solely for querying.

■ Proofread your letter as many times as it takes to be certain there are no spelling, punctuation, grammar, or usage errors; they can be fatal.

■ Multiple submissions involve sending the same manuscript to several editors at the same time. There is little agreement among authors and editors about the advisability of submitting multiply. In general, you can query several editors at the same time about the same project. A decision about submitting multiply is then made only if several editors reply to your query letter by asking to see the manuscript.

■ For assistance on writing great query letters, see John Wood, *How to Write Attention-Grabbing Query & Cover Letters*, and Lisa Collier Cool, *How to Write Irresistible Query Letters*, both published by Writer's Digest Books. There are also sections on query letters in books such as Judith Appelbaum, *How to Get Happily Published*, 5th ed., HarperPerennial.

Special Situations

■ The query letter has traditionally been used for works of nonfiction, but it is also being requested today for works of fiction. In those cases, the query letter is actually a cover letter, and an outline or synopsis and sample chapters are attached. To query about a fiction project, follow the guidelines in this chapter except that plot, characters, conflict, and resolution are described in the paragraph outlining your story or novel.

■ Unpublished writers commonly fear that someone at the publishing house will steal their idea after reading their query letter. This is an exceedingly rare and undocumented occurrence. In any case, there are no new ideas. What is always new—and saleable—is the way the idea is clothed and presented. Even two people working on the same idea (there are supposedly only thirty-six dramatic situations) will produce significantly different works. Then, too, how will you get published if you don't send a query letter? This is the way it's done.

■ When selling a reader on a business venture or idea, attach copies of charts or reports showing past successes, your résumé, your credit and business references, and any other data that relate to your proposal. Your object is to persuade the person to meet with you and discuss the matter. This letter differs from the literary query letter; you might profitably check with the chapters on APPLICATIONS, REPORTS, RÉSUMÉS, SALES.

Format

■ Query letters are always typed, preferably on personal letterhead stationery. Don't try to fit more than usual on the page by using a smaller typeface or reducing margin space.

■ E-mail queries are being accepted by some editors (you can tell who they are because their e-mail addresses are listed in marketing reports). Check to see if there are any special e-mail requirements.

■ Query by fax only if you have been invited to do so or if the market information suggests it.

WORDS

appeal	feature	nonfiction	round-up
audience	fiction	outline	summary
consider	interested	overview	synopsis
contemporary	manuscript	publication	viewpoint
expertise	material	review	

PHRASES

about 2,500 words	previous works include
aimed at long-distance runners	professional background supports
first-person narrative	publication credits include
most recent publications include	sample chapters and outline
mystery series	trade journal appeal
personal experience with	

SENTENCES

As you do not currently accept unagented submissions, I'm writing to ask if you'd like to see a picture book manuscript.

Can the market stand one more book on weight control? If it's this one—written by a physician with thirty years' success in helping patients lose weight—it can!

Enclosed are three sample chapters and an outline.

Enclosed is a SASE for your response.

I can submit the article by e-mail, on disks, or as hard copy.

I could deliver a 5,000-word article by September 1.

I look forward to hearing from you.

It was a dark and stormy night—or was it?

Thank you for your time and consideration.

When *should* you "cry wolf"?

Would you be interested in seeing a 40,000-word mystery for children set in the 1920s in one of Upper Michigan's Finnish settlements?

PARAGRAPHS

If education is not a preparation for life but life itself (John Dewey), why does today's education so little resemble the real world? What would happen if it did? Would you be interested in considering for publication the 75,000-word story of a real-life experiment in education?

What happens to romance after a couple has a baby? What can you do before the baby arrives to "baby-proof" your relationship? What skills and strategies will actually deepen your love after the baby arrives? As a family counselor with a new baby herself, I have been collecting anecdotes, quotations, studies, and firsthand stories to help your readers answer these questions.

"The Invisible Dragons" is an original Japanese folktale in which two brothers who try to outdo each other are rescued from a predicament of their own making by a girl whose name is too big for her.

Francesca Lia Block once wrote, "Love is a dangerous angel." She added, "Especially nowadays." Would you be interested in seeing an 80,000-word manuscript on the physical, emotional, intellectual, and spiritual dangers of sex today, supported by my current research?

A man with amnesia tries to negotiate the tricky steps of the life he is told is his. A familiar plot? Not in this novel.

Thank you for sending the submission guidelines for *Stucco City*. Having studied the guidelines and having also been a subscriber to your magazine for more than five years, I believe the article I want to submit to you is as new as it is highly appropriate to your readership.

Do you still believe in the existence of high-yield, low-risk stocks? You may not be as naïve as you think.

We met at a writers' conference in Los Angeles last month and briefly discussed the point at which a writer might need an agent. I believe I have reached that point.

I've been a season ticket-holder for the past three years and have thoroughly enjoyed your theater company's vitality, intelligence, and creativity. I am also a playwright with a script that I think is particularly appropriate for your ensemble.

On November 27, 1910, Marie Marvingt set the first women's world records in aviation. Earlier that month she had obtained her pilot's license, the third woman in the world to do so. An outstanding athlete (in 1910 the French government awarded her a gold medal for being expert in *all* sports), she was also a nurse, inventor, traveler, and the most decorated woman in the world. I would be surprised if your readers had ever heard of her.

SAMPLE LETTERS

Dear Ms. Dakers,

As the curator and principal scientist at the Leys Marmot Living Museum, I am in a unique position to write about the little-known but fascinating marmot (some species of which are more familiarly known as woodchucks). Studying them has given me a sense of the uncharted boundaries between so-called human and animal behavior.

I think the readers of Animal Life would be interested in the daily routine of a yellow-bellied marmot family, from the moment they wake up in their single-family dwelling to the moment they signal whichever family member has been guarding the door that it's time to come in and go to bed.

I am thinking in terms of a 10,000-word article with several sidebars on the folklore of the marmot. I can supply high-quality color slides.

I'm enclosing a SASE for your reply and I look forward to hearing from you.

————

Dear Ms. Ryder,

I am a regular customer of Ryder Exercise Equipment Inc. I am also the owner of three juice bars in the metropolitan area.

It occurred to me that a small line of take-home health foods and juices might be welcomed by your customers.

Enclosed are some articles on the growing popularity of juice bars and a summary of my own stores' financial health.

At this point, I am interested simply in exploring the possibilities of such an arrangement.

Would you like to discuss this sometime? Perhaps we could meet at my Mulcaster Avenue store, which is not far from you. I'd especially like to see what you think of our Apple-a-Day juice.

Sincerely,

————

Dear Mr. Wyndham,

An alumnus of the University, Louis Soltyk, has recently been honored for his successful efforts in saving two neighbor children from a fire. In addition, last year his masonry company was named Small Business of the Year by the local business council. In his personal life, he and his wife, Anastasya Vasek, have four children, all adopted.

Would you be interested in a profile of Mr. Soltyk for the University alumni/alumnae magazine? I'd like to focus on his drive and energy—where do they come from? How does he see himself?

My articles and interviews have been published in both local, state, and national publications (see attached list).

If you are interested, we can discuss word length and deadline.

Enclosed is a SASE for your response.

————

Dear Ms. Selston,

It's a question we'd all like answered: Is there life after death?

In September of 2000 I was pronounced clinically dead. As you might suspect, the diagnosis was correct only up to a point.

My experience fed a fierce curiosity to know how "normal" such experiences are. And what they mean. And whether they might be proof of anything.

Since that time, I have interviewed 184 people who have also been to the "other side" and returned.

Not since Moody's *Life After Life* has there been such a diverse collection of anecdotal evidence that there is indeed more to life than life.

Would you be interested in seeing some or all of this 70,000-word manuscript? Enclosed is a SASE for your reply.

Thank you.

————

From: jhall@email.com
To: query@email.com
Date: 06/26/2010 01:41 PM MST
Subject: Query: Renting a villa in Sicily

Hello. For my third stay in Sicily this fall, I'm renting a villa. Would you be interested in a 1,200-word piece comparing the benefits of villa life with hotel life, using as examples three of my favorite Sicilian hotels (one on the north coast, one on the south coast, and one in Taormina)? Travel information layered into the article includes getting to Sicily; the best times to visit; auto rental peculiarities there; the three best areas in which to rent villas and the day trips that are possible from each; the sites that no visitor to Sicily should miss.

I've written eighteen books published by mainstream publishers as well as a number of magazine and other articles. I'll be in Sicily Oct. 13–Nov. 13 and could get the piece to you several weeks after that. Because Sicily is best traveled in spring or fall, the article might appear in the spring for fall travel.

Thanks for your time and attention.

———

Dear Randy Shepperton,

Would you be interested in seeing an 85,000-word novel, *The Boarding House*?

Wealthy, intelligent, and isolated, Marshall is a house divided against himself. Denying important and life-giving facets of his self from an early age, he surrounds himself with shadows formed by his projected unacceptable imaginings. In this literary exploration of the divided self, Marshall struggles to resolve the four basic human conflicts—between freedom and security, right and wrong, masculinity and femininity, and between love and hate in the parent-child relationship. In daring to love with maturity and without reserve he is finally able to deal with the boarders living in his house and to trade his mask for a real face.

I can send the complete manuscript or, if you prefer, sample chapters and a detailed synopsis.

I am also the author of a number of short stories, one of which won the Abinger Prize last year, and I was recently awarded a grant by our state arts board based on a sample from this novel.

Enclosed is a SASE for your reply.

———

Dear Ms. Christina Furgeon Jaeger,

My family and I have just spent two months on a small island with no human company but our own. The strange story of why we went there and what we did while we were there is one that I think would interest your readers.

Each one of us—48-year-old husband/father, 49-year-old wife/mother, and 17-, 15-, 12-, and 10-year-old children—had a highly individual reaction to the experience and left the island changed in small and large ways.

Would you like to see a 5,000-word article, "Islands Within Islands"?

I am an architect with articles published in both professional journals and consumer magazines.

Enclosed is a SASE for your response.

See also: COVER LETTERS, REPORTS, REQUESTS, SALES

THIRTY-EIGHT

REFERENCES AND RECOMMENDATIONS

The hardest thing is writing a recommendation for someone we know.
—KIN HUBBARD

A letter of reference vouches for a person's general character. It tells a third party that the person is a responsible, functioning member of society. A reference is a verification: "Yes, I've known this person for some time."

A letter of recommendation is more specific and focuses on the person's professional qualities. It's often written by someone who knows the applicant on the one hand and the prospective employer, college, club, or awards committee on the other hand. A recommendation is an endorsement: "Yes, this person would be an excellent candidate for your program."

Letters of recommendation and letters of reference are so closely related that guidelines for writing them are similar.

A letter of commendation, written to congratulate a person on an achievement, is a combination of appreciation and congratulations; see the relevant chapters.

Letters of Reference and Recommendation Include

- applying for club membership (see also ORGANIZATIONS)
- asking someone to write a letter on your behalf
- credit references (see CREDIT)
- recommendations: individuals/ideas/companies/projects/products/services/

programs/workshops/new procedures/managerial decisions/ plans of action/ public office
- references: former employees/students/friends/family members/customers/ neighbors/babysitters
- refusing to write (see also REFUSALS)
- requesting information from a previous employer or from a reference cited by an applicant
- thanking someone for writing (see also THANK YOU)

How to Say It

- Give the person's full name at the beginning of your reference or recommendation. Later refer to the person as Ms., Mr., or Dr. plus the last name for the first reference in each paragraph and "she" or "he" after that. Never use the first name alone.
- State your connection with the person (former employer, teacher, supervisor, adviser, associate, neighbor, mentor) and how long you've known them ("for five years").
- Focus on the person's character for a general letter of reference (trustworthiness, sense of responsibility, enthusiasm, tact). In a letter of recommendation, focus on job experience and skills (length of employment with you, special abilities and accomplishments, your sense of the person as a prospective employee). Support your statements with facts or examples.
- Close with a summary statement reaffirming your recommendation of or confidence in the person.
- Offer to provide further information, if appropriate. Include your name, address, and phone number if you are not using letterhead stationery.
- Give the reference or recommendation to the subject of the letter, leaving the envelope unsealed so the person can read it if they wish. If you've been asked to mail your letter directly to a personnel office, scholarship committee, or other inquiring agency, it is sealed. Occasionally you might be asked to sign your name over the sealed flap to insure confidentiality. Sealed letters are generally more persuasive than unsealed ones.

What Not to Say

- Don't use the trite "To whom it may concern" if you can help it. A memo format is appropriate: "To:/From:/Date:/Re:." Or, give your letter a suitable heading such as "Introducing Letitia Fillimore," "To: Prospective Employers," "Recommendation of Helena Landless," "Letter of Reference for William Einhorn."

- Don't be too lavish or use too many superlatives—it undermines your credibility. Focus on two or three qualities and give examples of them.
- Don't tell the prospective employer what to do: "I'd hire her in a minute if she were applying here," "If I were you, I'd snap this one up," or "I can't think of anyone more deserving of this scholarship." Most people resent being told their business. You supply the information; they make the decision.
- Avoid saying anything you can't prove. This is often not so much outright dishonesty as misplaced enthusiasm, but it can work to the subject's disadvantage.

Tips on Writing

■ Be brief. One page, at most two, is sufficient to convey the general picture without repeating yourself, using unnecessary and fulsome phrases, or boring the other person.

■ Be specific. Don't tell; show the reader. Instead of saying someone is honest, explain that the person had access to the cash register, and even when experiencing personal financial hardship, turned in accurate receipts. Instead of saying someone is compassionate, tell how they missed a dinner party to help a troubled coworker.

■ When applying for a position, don't send letters of recommendation with your application letter or cover letter and résumé. Wait until they are requested.

Special Situations

■ When you want to list someone as a reference, call or write first and ask their permission.

■ When asking someone to write a letter of reference or recommendation for you, give the person enough information to be able to emphasize what will be most helpful to you ("I am applying for a position as a claims examiner"). Help the person tailor what they know of you with what you tell them of the company's needs and requirements. Enclose either a SASE for a return to you or a stamped envelope addressed to the person who is to receive the reference. Express your appreciation. Allow two to three weeks for the person to write the letter.

■ After thanking someone for writing you a recommendation or reference, share any news of your job search, membership application, or college admission efforts—or at least promise to let the person know what happens. Even if you don't get the position or choose not to take it, you will want to express your gratitude to the person for writing on your behalf.

■ When you believe that writing a positive letter of reference or recommendation for a former employee is unjustified or, in some cases, irresponsible, you may decline to provide one. Most employee records are accessible to employees, who may be inspired to legal action if they do not care for what you have written. According to some surveys, many employers are so wary of lawsuits that they don't give any information on former employees without their written consent and indemnification. Some companies will never under any circumstances provide references; defending a defamation suit can cost hundreds of thousands of dollars, even if the company wins. Many companies and personnel departments have a policy of either giving information only over the phone (thus, putting nothing in writing) or sending a form letter that acknowledges that the person worked there and verifies the dates of employment. Such a form might add: "It is against our policy to discuss the performance of former employees."

■ When recommending a service or product, relate your own experiences with it, but refrain from giving a blanket endorsement. Provide a few disclaimers: "This is only my opinion, of course"; "You may want to see what others think"; "It may not work for everyone, but we liked it."

■ When formally recommending a course of action, a policy change, or a decision, include: a subject line or first sentence stating what the letter is about; a summary of your recommendations; factual support for your recommendations; your offer to accept further negotiation, to engage in further research, or to submit additional information. If your recommendation is critical or negative, word it carefully. Point out the benefits along with the disadvantages, stating that you think the latter outweigh the former.

Format

■ Letters of reference and recommendation are typed on letterhead paper.

■ Thank-you notes sent to people who have written letters of reference or recommendation are typed or handwritten on plain personal stationery or foldovers.

■ In-house recommendations dealing with matters of policy are typed on memo paper.

WORDS

admirable	effective	integrity	resourceful
approve	efficient	intelligent	respect
capable	endorse	invaluable	responsible
commendable	energetic	inventive	self-motivated
competent	ethical	loyal	sensible
congenial	excellent	meticulous	successful
conscientious	experienced	outstanding	suitable
considerate	first-rate	personable	tactful
cooperative	hardworking	praiseworthy	thoughtful
creative	honest	productive	trustworthy
dependable	imaginative	professional	valuable
diligent	indispensable	recommend	
discreet	ingenious	reliable	
dynamic	initiative	remarkable	

PHRASES

able to energize a group of people

acquits herself/himself well

asset to any organization

attentive to detail

broad experience/range of skills

can attest to

creative problem-solver

dependable/eager/hard worker

did much to improve/increase/ better/upgrade

discharged his/her duties satisfactorily

distinguished herself/himself by

do not hesitate to recommend

energetic and enthusiastic worker

every confidence in

first-rate employee

for the past five years

gives me real satisfaction to

great respect for

happy to write on behalf

has three years' experience

have been impressed with

held in high regard here

held positions of responsibility

highly developed technical skills

I heartily/wholeheartedly/highly recommend

in response to your request for information about

many fine contributions

matchless record

nothing but praise for

one in a thousand

outstanding leadership abilities

rare find

recommend with complete confidence

responsible for all aspects of security

satisfactory in every way

set great store by

skilled in all phases of light
clerical duties

sterling qualities

take-charge person

take genuine pleasure in
recommending

takes pride in his/her work

vouch for

well thought of

SENTENCES

Although company policy prohibits my writing you the recommendation you requested, I certainly wish you every success with your career.

Ann Shankland has highly developed sales and marketing skills and has also proven herself invaluable in the recruiting, training, and supervising of an effective sales team.

Elizabeth Endorfield is one of our most knowledgeable people when it comes to custodial chemicals, equipment, and techniques.

Hiram G. Travers was in my employ for ten years.

I am proud to recommend Ellen Huntly to you—I always found her work, character, and office manner most satisfactory.

In response to your inquiry about Chester Nimmo, it is only fair to say that he seemed to need constant supervision and our association with him was not an altogether happy one.

In response to your inquiry about Michael Condron, we were obliged to let him go because of our own financial difficulties—he was a superior scaler and riveter.

I've known Richard Musgrove as a neighbor and employee for six years.

I would prefer not to comment on Jean Emerson's employment with us.

Mary Treadwell worked as an X-ray technician at Porter General Hospital from 2001 to 2008.

Mr. Tamson's record with our company was excellent.

Thank you for the wonderful and apparently persuasive recommendation you wrote for me—I've been accepted at the Maxwell School of Political Science!

Working with you has meant a great deal to me and I'm wondering if I may give your name as a reference when I apply for my first "real" job.

In order to fully evaluate your suitability for the sales position you applied for, we need to speak to at least four former employers or supervisors. Please provide us with names, addresses, and daytime phone numbers of people we may contact. You will hear from us as soon as we have made a decision.

The position turned out to be different from what I'd expected and I ended up declining it. I'm grateful to you for the positive recommendation you wrote (one of the reasons they wanted to hire me, I know!), and I'd like to use it again sometime. I'll let you know what happens.

It is a pleasure to confirm Kenneth Eliot's employment with Meynell Associates from 1992 through 2002. Mr. Eliot carried out his responsibilities with diligence and punctuality, and was a definite employee asset. We have no reservations about recommending him highly.

Lucas Cleeve comes to this job with a long history of community involvement. He has been a strong advocate for neighborhoods during his two terms on the city council. He has served as chair of the Rules and Policy committee and of the Energy, Environment, and Utilities committee; financial specialist with Sybil county; legislative aide; member of the Human Development Commission, the Board of Health, the Board of Water Commissioners, the Housing Redevelopment Authority, the Financing and Bonding Commission, and the Task Force on Neighborhood and Community Action. How can we afford *not* to return such an experienced, committed advocate to the city council?

Emily Wardle has asked that I write a letter of recommendation based on our professional association over the past several years. I've found Ms. Wardle to be intelligent and trustworthy as well as energetic in carrying out her duties. She is an asset to any organization. I would recommend her without reservation.

You asked what I thought of the Vanever-Hartletop contract. After looking into the matter, my best recommendation would be to return the contract unsigned with a request for renegotiation of the default clause.

In response to your request for information about Tasker Lithography, I must say that we've had nothing but exceptionally fine dealings with them for the past eight years. Deadlines were met, and the quality of their work has been superb. The few times we asked for changes, they were carried out quickly and cheerfully. It's possible that others have had different experiences with Tasker. I can only say that we are pleased with their work.

Nancy Lammeter-Cass is being considered for a position as pastry chef in our catering service, and has given your name as a reference. Will you please complete the attached form as soon as possible? Enclosed is a self-addressed stamped envelope for your reply. Thank you.

SAMPLE LETTERS

Dear Ms. Tartan,

You once offered to write me a letter of reference if ever I needed one. I would like to take you up on your kind offer now.

I am applying for a part-time teaching position in the Glendinning-Melville School District and have been asked to supply several letters of reference. In the hopes that you have the time and are still willing to write a letter, I'm enclosing an instruction sheet from the school district outlining what they need in a letter of reference as well as a stamped envelope addressed to the district personnel offices.

If for any reason you cannot do this, I will understand. Know that I am, in any case, grateful for past kindnesses.

Sincerely,

————

TO: Office of Admissions
FROM: Dr. Charles Kennedy
RE: Steve Monk
DATE: November 15, 2010

I have known Steve Monk for four years, first as a student in my earth sciences and biology classes and later as his adviser for an independent study in biology. I am currently helping him with an extracurricular research project.

Mr. Monk is one of the brightest, most research-oriented students I have encountered in eighteen years of teaching. His SAT and achievement test scores only begin to tell the story. He has a wonderful understanding of the principles of scientific inquiry, a passion for exactitude, and a bottomless curiosity.

I will be happy to provide any further information.

————

Dear Ms. Burnell,

You requested employment information about Dan Burke.

Mr. Burke was employed with us from 2001 through 2008 as a structural engineer. His work was satisfactory, and I believe he left us to pursue a more challenging job opportunity.

If we can be of additional assistance, please call.

Sincerely,

————

See also: APPRECIATION, EMPLOYMENT, INTRODUCTIONS, ORGANIZATIONS, REQUESTS, RÉSUMÉS, THANK YOU

THIRTY-NINE

REFUSALS

Most people hate to say no—but not nearly as much as other people hate to hear it.
—DIANNE BOOHER

When we have no interest in an activity and also have an ironclad excuse (being out of the country or out of money, for example), letters of refusal, regret, and rejection are easy to write. In all other cases, they are a challenge.

To write letters of refusal (also known as regrets and rejections), be certain that you want to say no; ambivalence will weaken your letter. A good reason for saying no is simply "I don't want to." When you have a specific reason for saying no, you can give it. However, the fact that someone wants you to do something confers no obligation on you to defend your decision. People who become angry with you for saying no, who try to manipulate you, or who make you feel guilty are confusing requests with demands.

Write a Refusal When Saying No to

- adjustment/claims requests
- applications: employment/franchise
- gifts
- invitations: personal/business
- proposals: contracts/bids/books
- requests: contributions/credit/introductions/time/volunteering/promotions/raises/loans of money or possessions/appointments/meetings/interviews
- sales: presentations/offers/invitations
- wedding invitations (see WEDDINGS)

How to Say It

- Thank the person for the offer, request, invitation (which you describe or mention specifically).
- Make a courteous remark, agreeing with the person that the cause is worthy, the proposal well thought-out, the résumé impressive, or the invitation appealing.
- Say no, expressing your regret at having to do so.
- If you wish, explain your position.
- Suggest alternate courses of action or other resources, if appropriate.
- Close with a pleasant wish to be of more help next time, to see the person again, or for success with their project, job search, or request.

What Not to Say

- Don't leave any doubt in the other person's mind about your response; your no is firm.
- Don't lie. It's too easy to be tripped up, and you'll be more comfortable with yourself and with the other person if you ground your refusal in some version of the truth.
- Don't offer lengthy, involved excuses and apologies; they are not persuasive, even when true. "Several excuses are always less convincing than one." (Aldous Huxley)
- Don't make personal remarks (about their appearance, personality, behavior, language skills) when turning down a person's request, job application, or proposal. Even if you think it would help the person in the future, leave this kind of comment to someone else in their life.
- Don't reply sarcastically to outrageous or inappropriate requests. It does you no good and angers the other person.

Tips on Writing

■ Respond promptly. "The prompter the refusal, the less the disappointment." (Publilius Syrus) In addition, most people asking for something or inviting you to an event need to know soon. By giving your refusal early, you allow them time to find another solution or invitee.

■ Be tactful. Avoid basing your refusal on the other person's résumé, program, invitation. Phrase it instead in terms of some inability or requirement on your part ("need someone who is bonded"; "another meeting that day"; "will be out of town"; or simply "will be unable to help").

■ Give your excuse before your refusal. The reader is thus prepared and the disappointment at your no doesn't keep them from "hearing" your reasons. Instead of saying, "I will not be able to attend your graduation because I'm going to be in California that week," say, "I am going to be in California the week of June 2, which means I won't, unfortunately, be able to attend your graduation."

■ In some cases you can use the word "policy," which conveys that your decision is nonnegotiable ("The family has a policy that leaves donations to the Board's discretion"). "Policy" shows you've put some thought into structuring your limits—and it's difficult to argue against.

■ You can play the "personal" card: "I'm dealing with several difficult issues right now and I don't feel I can handle anything else. But thanks for asking." No civilized person will dispute your assessment of what you can handle.

■ Lessen the disappointment: offer to help at a later date; suggest someone who might be able to provide the same assistance; agree with them on some point; apologize for your inability to approve the request; indicate some benefit to them from your refusal; thank them for their interest/request/concern.

■ The inimitable Miss Manners (Judith Martin) wouldn't want you to completely lessen the disappointment, however. She points out that you can't reject someone without them feeling rejected; if they don't feel rejected they don't go away. A painless rejection isn't one, so don't give false hope. She advises writing refusals that are bland, routine, and unoriginal.

■ Occasionally, the way you turn down an applicant, proposal, bid, or other business matter can lead to legal problems. If you have concerns, consult with a lawyer before writing your letter.

Special Situations

■ When unable to attend, always respond with regret to an invitation marked "RSVP," "Please reply," or "Regrets only." This is mandatory, obligatory, required, compulsory, imperative, and essential. If the invitation is issued in the name of more than one person, mention all of them in your refusal and mail it either to the person listed under the RSVP or to the first name given. To decline an invitation, use the same format as the invitation itself: If it is handwritten, handwrite your reply. If business letterhead stationery is used, reply on your own business letterhead. When the invitation is worded informally, your reply is also informal. When the invitation is formal, your reply uses the same words, layout, and style as the invitation.

■ White House invitations include the phone number of the Social Office where you telephone your regrets or ask how to respond to the invitation. General guidelines are: reply within a day of receiving the invitation; write the reply yourself (don't have a secretary do it); handwrite it on plain or engraved personal stationery; use the same format and person (first person or third person) as the invitation. There are only four generally accepted excuses for not accepting a White House invitation: a death in the family, a family wedding, prior travel plans, illness. Your reply says, "We regret that owing to the illness/recent death of . . ."

■ When turning down an applicant for a position, include: your thanks for the person's application; a simple statement saying that you are unable to offer the person the position; if necessary or helpful, an explanation of the decision; positive comments on the person's credentials, abilities, interview, résumé; if applicable, an invitation to reapply at some later time; your good wishes for success in the person's search for a suitable position. Some companies don't notify a job-seeker whose application is unsuccessful. However, it is courteous as well as good public relations to write a brief, tactful letter. When replying to an unsolicited application, express your appreciation for thinking of your company, state that there are no positions open, offer to keep the résumé on file, and invite a later contact, if that is an option.

■ When you refuse a job offer, do so with thanks and complimentary remarks about the company, your interviewer, the human resources department. Express your regret. If appropriate, tell why you made the choice you did, but phrase it in terms of your needs and not the company's deficiencies. Close on a positive note that leaves the door open for the future.

■ When denying a requested promotion or raise or application for an in-house position (1) show appreciation for the employee's contributions, listing specific talents and strengths; (2) explain honestly and concretely why the request was denied; (3) offer suggestions on how the promotion or raise or other position might be obtained or, if your no depended on external factors (too many managers, budget shortfalls), what changes might affect a future request. The goal is to leave the employee feeling valued, motivated, and encouraged.

■ Refuse an adjustment or claims request in a way that maximizes the chances of keeping the customer. Be tactful and considerate. Offer an alternative or compromise solution when possible. Tell the customer that you understand their position, that their complaint has been given every consideration, and that you wish you could say yes. Then give a credible explanation of your no. Use facts or copies of documents to show that an adjustment is not warranted. Most customers are satisfied with a brief, clearly written refusal. A few will write back and argue, point by point. When that happens, write a firm no with no further explanations.

■ Many companies and government agencies have codified procedures for handling bids. When you have a choice, notify bidders of your requirements as soon as possible. In rejecting bids, be courteous and supportive, and, when possible, explain briefly why the bid was rejected (especially if it concerned failure to follow directives or to stay within certain guidelines) or why the winning bid was accepted. Information like this is useful to your contractors. Close with an expression of appreciation and a reference to the possibility of doing business with them at a later date. You do not need to name the winning bidder.

■ When refusing a request for credit or a loan, be tactful; the person is still a customer, a potential customer, or a friend. Thank the person for applying or asking. Express appreciation of the interest in your company or faith in your friendship. In the case of an application for a commercial loan or commercial credit, tell how you arrived at your decision (the application, employer's recommendation, background check, credit bureau file). Suggest ways of improving an applicant's credit standing, alternative sources of credit, or reapplying to you after a certain period of time or after resolving certain financial problems. In the case of a personal loan, omit the advice and simply state that you're unable to help at this time.

■ Most manuscript rejections are made with form postcards or letters. Few are as witty as Samuel Johnson's: "Your manuscript is both good and original; but the part that is good is not original, and the part that is original is not good." When you write a personal letter, emphasize that the rejection is based on the needs and interests of your publishing house and that the situation at another publisher might be different. Assure the person that you've carefully considered the work, offer thanks for thinking of you, and send your good wishes for success in future endeavors.

■ Most fundraising appeals are mass-produced and you will not reply if you are uninterested. However, when you receive a personal letter with first-class postage, written over the signature of someone known to you, you might want to respond. Compliment the person on the work the organization is doing, give a plausible excuse for not contributing, and offer good wishes. You don't have to give any more detail than you choose; a vague statement that you are currently overcommitted elsewhere is fine. If you are refusing because you disagree with the organization's goals or policies, say so.

■ When terminating a business relationship, friendship, or dating relationship, aim for a no-fault "divorce": don't blame the other person or bring up past grievances. Help the other person save face by taking responsibility for the separation yourself. Be as honest as is consistent with tact and kindness. Above all, be brief and unequivocal; overexplaining or "keeping your options open" can be fatal if you sincerely want to end the relationship. Conclude with an encouraging, complimentary remark.

■ Sometimes people are extremely persistent about wanting your company, your time, your money. When refusing their requests, your note is firm, simple, and unequivocal (the moment you waffle, they are back in the door).

Give no explanations for your refusal ("I am sorry but I will not be able to" is sufficient). The moment you tell why you're refusing ("I'm very busy just now"), there will be an immediate response ("It will only take a minute"). When you offer another reason, there will be another rebuttal. Engaging you in wearying debate is part of the strategy; you wouldn't be the first person to say yes just to avoid being harangued. "I'm sorry, but no," repeated as many times as it takes, is the most effective response.

■ Sometimes you must refuse a gift. Express your gratitude for the person's thoughtfulness and for the choice of gift. Explain why you must return it ("Employees are prohibited from accepting gifts from suppliers" or "I hope you will understand, but I would feel uncomfortable accepting such an expensive gift from a client"). Word your refusal so that it does not imply the person was guilty of poor judgment in offering the gift.

Format

■ Business letters of refusal are typed on letterhead stationery.
■ Personal letters of refusal are most often handwritten.
■ Form letters are used for routine refusals.
■ You may e-mail your rejection of queries, suggestions, or requests that were made by e-mail.

WORDS

awkward	impractical	refuse	unavailable
contraindicated	obstacle	regretfully	unfavorable
decline	opposition	reject	unfeasible
difficult	overextended	reluctantly	unfortunately
dilemma	overstocked	respond	unlikely
doubtful	policy	sorry	
impossible	problem	unable	

PHRASES

after much discussion/careful evaluation	beyond the scope of the present study
although I am sympathetic to your problem/plight/situation	company policy prohibits us from
	current conditions do not warrant
although the idea is appealing	difficult decision
appreciate your asking me/us, but	disinclined at this time
because of prior commitments	doesn't qualify/warrant
	don't have enough information

due to present budget problems

hope this will be of some help even though

I appreciate your asking me, but

if it were possible

I know how understanding you are, so I'm sure

I'm sorry to tell you

I must say no to

I regret that I cannot accept

it is, unfortunately, out of the question that

it's a wonderful program, but

it's currently impossible

I wish I could say yes, but

I would like to help, but

must decline/demur/pass up/ withdraw from/say no to

normally I would be delighted, but

not a choice I can make right now

not an option at the moment

not currently seeking

no, thank you

not interested at this time

previous commitments

puts me in something of a dilemma

regret to inform you

remain unconvinced of the value of

runs counter to

sincerely regret

sorry about this, but

unable to help/comply/grant/send/ contribute/offer/provide

we appreciate your interest, but

we find that we cannot

we have concluded with regret

we have now had a chance to review

your idea has merit, but

SENTENCES

Although we appreciate your interest in Dempsey Toys, we do not feel that your product is one we could successfully market.

Although your entry did not win, we wish you good luck and many future successes.

At this time there does not appear to be a position with us that is suited to your admittedly fine qualifications.

Fundraising is not one of my talents—is there anything else I could do for the committee?

I appreciate your offer but I want to try a few things before I go outside the firm for a solution.

I don't have the energy just now to do the project justice.

I don't think this will work for us.

If you reread your contract, specifically clause C1, you will see that we have no legal obligations in this regard.

I have taken on more projects than I can comfortably handle.

I hope this will help you understand why we are unable to furnish the additional funding you are requesting.

I know we'll be missing a wonderful time.

I'm completely overwhelmed just now, and can't take on anything new.

I'm sorry not to be able to give you the reference you requested in your letter of November 3.

I sympathize with your request and wish I could help.

It's possible we would be interested sometime after the first of the year.

I've made it a policy never to make personal loans.

I will be out of town that evening—I regret that I'm unable to accept your kind invitation.

I wish I could be more helpful, but it's not possible now.

I wish I didn't have to refuse you, Jerry, but I'm not in a position to make you the loan.

May I take a raincheck?

Our present schedule is, unfortunately, inflexible.

Regarding your request to use my name in your fundraising literature, I must say no.

Thank you, but we have had a regular purchasing arrangement with Burnside Office Supplies for many years.

The Board has, unfortunately, turned down your request.

The position at Locksley International for which you applied has been filled.

Unfortunately, this is not a priority for Pettifer Grains at this time.

We appreciate your asking us, and hope that we will have the opportunity of saying yes some other time.

We are unable to approve your loan application at this time.

We have decided to accept another proposal.

We have reviewed your credit application and regret to inform you that we are unable to offer you a bank card at this time.

We regret that your work was not selected for inclusion in the symposium.

We regret to inform you that Spenlow Paint & Tile is no longer considering applications for its sales positions.

We regret to say that a careful examination of your résumé does not indicate a particular match for our present needs.

Your request comes at a particularly difficult time for me—I'm over-scheduled for the next two months.

PARAGRAPHS

Thanks for sending "Love in the Place Dauphine." Although this particular story isn't quite right for us, I'd like to see anything else you've done. I apologize for the long delay in getting back to you.

Thank you for your résumé. We considered your application carefully but have decided to offer the position to someone else. We will keep your application on file, however, and will contact you if we have a similar opening later. Please accept our best wishes as you seek a challenging and rewarding position.

I am sorry to report that we are unable to extend credit to you at the present time. Our decision is based primarily on your lack of a credit record and on the brevity of your employment history. Please contact us again in six months, when we would be happy to discuss your request again.

Dr. Gerda Torp regrets that because of a previous engagement she is unable to accept the kind invitation of Mr. and Mrs. Esdras B. Longer for Sunday, the third of June, at 8:00 p.m.

Thank you for your invitation to join Glowry Health Services as a pharmacy technician. The beautiful new facilities, the friendly staff members, and the good interview I had with you were all very persuasive. However, I have also been offered a position forty-five minutes closer to home. To have more time with my family, I plan to accept it. I thank you for your time, attention, and good humor. I hope our paths cross again someday.

Because we are financially committed to several charities similar to yours, we are unable to send you anything. However, please accept our best wishes for successful continuation and funding of your work—we certainly appreciate and admire what you're doing.

I've checked our production schedule and see no way of moving up your deliveries by two weeks. We are dependent on materials shipped to us by suppliers in other states who are unable to alter their timetables.

For a number of reasons, I am uneasy about writing you a letter of introduction to Sir Harrison Peters. I have discussed it with my superior, who would prefer that you find some other avenue of contact. I hope you understand.

We've just received your kind letter inviting us to Howards End. You can imagine how we'd enjoy seeing you again. However, Julia is graduating from college that weekend, so we have to say no this time. Thanks so much for thinking of us.

Dear J. T. Bullard,

We thank you for your interest in Marquand Advertising Inc. and for the time you spent interviewing with us.

We have carefully considered your qualifications and work history. While we are impressed with your accomplishments, we preferred that the candidate for this position have more experience in space sales than you have had, and we have offered the position to someone with over ten years' experience in that area.

We liked your energy and credentials, and we wish you continued success in your professional life.

Dear Ms. Partlit,

Your request for a transfer to the Manufacturing Operations Department has been carefully considered. We are sympathetic to your reasons for asking for the transfer and we hope to find a way of accommodating you in the future.

For the moment, however, you are irreplaceable where you are. In addition, the MO Department is in the process of downsizing so there is little likelihood that they would take on anyone else at this point.

I wish the answer could have been yes . . .

Dear Ms. Murchison,

We were sorry to hear about the problem with your Wimsey Electronic Digital Computerized Hairdryer.

Although your appliance is still under warranty, we are unable to repair it for you free of charge. The terms of the warranty appear to have been violated, which renders the warranty null and void. The machine was plugged into a European 220-volt outlet when it was intended for use only with 110-volt outlets or for 220-volt outlets with a converter. (This is explained in the owner's manual, and a small tag is affixed near the plug warning to use only 110-volt current.)

If you wish us to repair the machine at an approximate cost to you of $120, please let us know. Otherwise, we will return it to you.

We wish we could be more helpful, but the terms of the warranty are carefully spelled out. We cannot make exceptions, no matter how sympathetic we might feel.

Sincerely,

Dear Dean Arabin:

I regret that I am unable to represent Barchester College at the inauguration of Dr. Eleanor Bold as new president of Century College on September 16. I wasn't able to reschedule a previous commitment for that day.

My wife is a graduate of Century, so I would have particularly enjoyed being part of the ceremony. Thank you for thinking of me. I was honored to be asked to represent the College and would be glad to be of service some other time.

I hope you are able to make other arrangements.

Sincerely,

TO: Friends of the Library Committee

Thank you for your kind letter asking me to direct the annual fundraiser. I am flattered that you thought of me.

Because of several other time-consuming commitments, I am unable to accept your invitation. I would have enjoyed working with you and contributing in some way to our fine library system, but I feel sure that you will find the right person for this important project.

With best wishes, I am

Sincerely yours,

Dear Tony Cryspyn:

Thank you for submitting your work to us. As editors of the *Windsor Castle Review,* we have given your material careful consideration; every manuscript submitted to this office is read by one or more of us.

We regret that "The Ninth Son" is not suited to the current needs of the magazine, but we wish to thank you for having given us the opportunity of reading it. Unfortunately, the volume of submissions and the press of other editorial responsibilities do not permit us to make individual comments or suggestions.

Sincerely,

Dear Margaret Ivory,

We have appreciated having you as a patient these last two years. At this time, however, we feel that your best interests are not served by continuing treatment in this office. We would like to recommend that you make an appointment with Dr. Royde-Smith, Dr. Owen, or a dentist of your choice. We will be happy to send along your dental records, including X-rays.

Let us know how we can facilitate this change in dental care providers.

Dear Chris and David,

Thank you for sending us the information on your real estate trust investment opportunity.

Although it looks appealing, this is not something we are prepared to get into at the moment. I sent the prospectus on to my brother in Denver. It's possible he would be interested.

I'm sure you will find all the capital you need, and I wish you every success.

Best wishes,

Dear Mrs. Lanier,

We at Parker Investment Mortgage Inc. understand and appreciate how difficult this past year must have been for you.

However, given your history of missed payments (June 2010, September 2010, November 2010, and February, March, and April 2011), the fact that your account is now three months past due, and our inability to arrange a meeting with you to discuss solutions, we are unable to grant you any additional time.

Unless we receive your unpaid balance by May 15, you will receive a foreclosure notice.

Sincerely,

———

See also: APPOINTMENTS, CREDIT, DISAGREEMENT, RESPONSES, SENSITIVE

FORTY

REPORTS AND PROPOSALS

It may be said of me by Harper & Brothers, that although I reject their proposals, I welcome their advances.
—EDNA ST. VINCENT MILLAY

Standard proposals and reports aren't letters, but shorter ones are sometimes written as letters or memos. They use plainer language, do not have heads, subheads, and clauses, and are less formal and less complicated.

Proposals can be solicited (someone asks you for an estimate, bid, plan of action) or unsolicited (you want to sell your plan or service or program to someone who has not expressed a need for it). In either case, your proposal is a sales tool to persuade the other party that you are the best firm for the job (for a solicited proposal) or that it needs the service you are offering (for an unsolicited proposal).

Report and Proposal Letters Include

- acceptance of proposal/bid
- acknowledgment of receipt (see ACKNOWLEDGMENTS)
- bids and estimates
- book and article proposals (see QUERIES)
- compliance reports to government agencies
- credit reports (see CREDIT)
- investigative reports
- management, staff, policy, or recommendation reports
- progress/status reports
- proposals: products/grants/projects/programs/sales/services
- recommendations/suggestions

- rejection of proposal/bid/report (see REFUSALS)
- reports: annual/monthly/progress/management/staff/technical
- responses to inquiries/requests
- sales reports: weekly/monthly/annual

How to Say It

- Begin with a reference line that identifies the subject of the proposal or report.
- State why you are sending the report or proposal ("as requested," "for your information," "Charles O'Malley asked me to send you a copy," "in response to your request for a quotation").
- Describe the report in one or two sentences.
- The main body of the report or proposal—explaining the idea in detail, giving costs, specifications, deadlines, and examples of application—is organized into clear, logical units of information.
- Summarize the report in one or two sentences.
- Credit those who worked on the report or proposal.
- Offer to provide additional information and give the name and telephone number of the contact person.
- Tell what the next step is or what your expectations are ("call me," "sign the enclosed contract," "please respond with a written evaluation of the proposal").
- Thank the person for their time and consideration.

What Not to Say

- Don't include other topics or business. The report or proposal is a focused document.
- Don't use jargon unless you're sure it's familiar to your readers.

Tips on Writing

■ Before preparing a report or proposal, know the answers to these questions: Who will read the document? What is its purpose? What material will it cover? How will the material be presented?

■ The main body of a letter proposal or report can be as short as a paragraph or long enough to be divided into one or more of the traditional report elements: title page; summary, synopsis, or abstract; a foreword, preface, introduction, history or background; acknowledgments; table of contents; a presentation of data, options, conclusions, and recommendations; appendix, bibliography, endnotes, references, and notice of any attached supporting documents.

■ Before mailing the proposal or report, ask someone knowledgeable about the issues (in some cases a lawyer) to read it for clarity and precision. Double-check a proposal to be certain that every item in the original request has been responded to.

■ If timing is important to your report or proposal, send it return receipt requested so you can verify the date it was received.

Special Situations

■ When writing grant proposals, three guidelines will boost your chances of success: (1) follow directions scrupulously—no allowances are made for deviations from stated formats; (2) present your material faultlessly—neatly typed on high-quality paper, error-free, well spaced; (3) the content must be your finest writing and slanted specifically to that funding organization—the identical material can seldom be proposed to two different groups. Artist resource groups offer help to grant applicants, and sometimes people in your field will critique your material.

■ Many progress reports have a codified format, but others may be written in narrative letter form. Include: what has been done during the reporting period; what is currently being done; what outstanding projects are waiting for attention; good news and bad news during the reporting period; other comments that give readers an appreciation of the progress of the student, employee, department, or company.

■ If it appears that your proposal will be acceptable to the other party, turn the proposal letter into a contract letter or binding agreement by adding at the bottom, "Read and approved on [date] by [signature and title]." If the proposal is part of a larger contract, add "pursuant to the Master Contract dated March 2, 2010, between Raikes Engineering and Phillips Contractors" (see also CONTRACTS).

Format

■ Report or proposal letters are typewritten on letterhead or memo stationery.

■ When time is an issue, reports and proposals can be faxed or e-mailed, but send hard copies too.

■ Forms with blanks to be filled in are convenient for credit reports, school progress reports, routine production reports, and other reports that depend on numbers or short descriptions.

WORDS

abstract	display	judge	recommendation
advise	draft	layout	representation
agenda	establish	method	research
analysis	estimate	monograph	results
applications	evaluate	notification	review
appraise	exhibit	offer	statement
approach	explanation	opinion	strategy
assess	exploration	outcome	study
calculate	exposition	outline	subject
compute	findings	performance	suggest
conclude	forecast	policy	summary
conditions	gauge	preface	system
consider	guesstimate	preliminary	technical
critique	inquiry	presentation	terms
decision	inspect	procedure	text
design	instruction	program	undertaking
diagram	introduce	project	venture
disclose	investigation	projections	
discussion	issue	prospectus	

PHRASES

a considerable/significant/
   important advantage

address the problem of

along these lines

as you can see from the data

ballpark figure

close/exhaustive inquiry

copy of the proceedings

detailed statement

educated guess

estimated value

give our position on

gives me to understand

in-depth account of/look at

institute inquiries

make inquiry/known/public

map out

matter at hand/in dispute/under
   discussion/at issue

planning stages

plan of action

position paper

rough computation/calculation/
   draft/guess

subject of inquiry

summarizes the progress of

supplies/offers/provides some
   distinct advantages

take into consideration

take measures/steps

under consideration/discussion

Data on in-line skating injuries in the United States during the past two years are charted below.

East Side Neighborhood Service Inc. has developed a proposal to make our streets safer and cleaner.

I propose that we set up a subcommittee to study flex hours for all salaried employees.

Our annual report on homelessness in the six-county metro area reveals both good news and bad news.

Re: Acquisition of the Cypress Spa Products Corp.

Sperrit-Midmore Landscape Supply Center has had one of its most successful quarters ever—see below for details.

Subject: Proposed staffing changes in conference catering.

The following report was prepared by Robert Famish and Narcissa Topehall.

PARAGRAPHS

Your book proposal has been read with great interest. We will want to have several other people read and evaluate it before submitting it for discussion at our weekly acquisition meeting. I will let you know as soon as we have made a decision.

This report is a summary of your benefits and any optional coverage you have chosen as of January 1. Your benefits booklet provides further details. If you have any questions, please see your supervisor or the Benefit Information Coordinator. Although this report has been prepared for you as accurately as possible, the Company reserves the right to correct any errors.

A citizen task force composed of interested persons was formed last May and met almost the entire year to make recommendations to the Planning Commission, which, in turn, made its report to the City Council. Their report is summarized here.

Since our letter of September 3, in which we compared electroplating and sputtering for production of thin alloy films for recording, we have done some additional research on this subject. We have found that as long as the proper microstructure is achieved, both electroplating and sputtering are effective. It appears too early to exclude either of the processes. It may be helpful, however, to do a rough cost analysis either as more data from research in these two areas become available or by making a number of assumptions.

I've checked into the matter of buying versus renting an air compressor, and it seems far more cost-effective in the long run and convenient for us in the short run to buy a small portable air compressor rather than to rent one as needed. A study of our use of an air compressor suggests that although we need one only "infrequently," the rental charges and lost production time in not having one immediately available outweigh the cost of a new one. I suggest buying.

SAMPLE LETTERS

To: Members of the Humphrey Hills Orienteering Club
From: Elisa Minden
Date: Sept. 30
Subject: Report on the Mini-Goat Event

If we do say so ourselves, the Mini-Goat was a success. We had twice the number of entrants we had last year (52 compared to 25). Because of that, the modest $3 per person entry fee was enough to keep us in the black on this event. Mini-Goat T-shirts were donated by Orford Sports. We heard from many entrants that the event was a bargain: an afternoon of fun (although non-orienteering friends and family persist in questioning that what we do is "fun"!) AND a free T-shirt for only $3. It was the first orienteering event for many of the entrants. We think the allure of this sport is spreading by word of mouth, and we expect the local Club to keep growing, much as the U.S. Orienteering Federation has.

———

27 January 2010
Oliver Alden and Rose Darnley
100 Santayana Court
Great Falls, CT 06001

Dear Ms. Darnley and Mr. Alden,

I am a Visiting Professor at Oxford, and it has been my privilege to have your son, George, in class for the January term. Because this class has never been taught before, and because it turned out to be very special, I'd like to share a few details with you.

We studied the social, legal, and behavioral problems related to methamphetamine abuse and addiction and we examined sentencing and corrections systems with regard to methamphetamine offenders. The class has conducted field research to gather qualitative data using the interview method. We completed site research with law enforcement officers, with parolees and staff at a halfway house, and with prisoners and staff at a nearby prison.

I feel compelled to write this letter to the parents of my students because the class was such a joy; you must be very pleased with George. The students did a great deal of self-organizing, in terms of choice of books and articles to read and managing their group research and class presentations. Respectful, careful, and dedicated researchers, they asked insightful questions, and took every minute of the class seriously. Wherever we went, I was complimented on the students' conduct and professionalism.

Thank you for the opportunity of having George in class.

Best regards,

————

TO: Residents in the Larkin Road neighborhood
FROM: Larkin Road Task Force
DATE: April 12, 2010
SUBJECT: Report on changes to neighborhood streets

A citizen task force composed of interested persons was formed last May and met almost the entire year to make recommendations to the Planning Commission which, in turn, made its report to the City Council.

Residents living near the south end of Larkin Road wanted the road connected to the freeway immediately to ease traffic problems during rush hour. Our representatives asked that the problem of where to funnel the traffic at the north end be resolved before such a connection is considered.

There were, however, several areas of complete agreement, among them resolutions to have a direct westbound connnection to relieve some of the traffic on neighborhood streets and to reduce the Larkin Road speed limit to 35 mph as soon as possible. An Environmental Impact Statement was also suggested by the task force.

Unfortunately, the Planning Commission reversed the two major points of neighborhood agreement and did not recommend them to the City Council. The City Council said that the direct westbound connection was a future possibility that they could not now consider. It did, however, vote in favor of the Environmental Impact Statement and supported the enforcement of the current 45 mph speed limit.

————

Dear Etta,

Re: Proposed Budget for Design of Streets DRS—821.01

We have estimated the design cost to produce final plans for the relocation of Concannon Street from the bypass to the railroad tracks, and for Concannon Bypass from Blake Avenue to Nicholas. The design of Concannon Street is for a length of approximately 2,000 feet and consists of five traffic lanes, curb and gutter, and a raised median over 25 percent of its length. The Concannon Bypass design covers approximately 2,500 feet and includes curb and gutter along the outside lanes and median, pavement widening, intersection improvements, acceleration and deceleration lanes, and signals at three locations. The cost works out to $255,000, and we therefore propose that a budget for this amount be approved.

Please call me if you have any questions concerning our estimate. Thanks.

Sincerely,

————

To: Marketing Department
From: Stephen Rollo
Date: March 4, 2010
Re: Report on recent drop in sales

This memo report will serve as a summary of the attached 12-page in-depth report on what appear to be the mechanisms and underlying causes of the recent nationwide drop in sales at our restaurant equipment and supply outlets.

Based on these ideas, I'm planning experimental modifications to our outlets in Colorado Springs and Denver. If you have opinions on these ideas (especially if you disagree), I'd appreciate hearing from you.

The driving forces for sales to restaurants are of course need, immediate availability, accessibility, and price. We have isolated price as the critical factor in the recent downturn. Although our prices are, in fact, competitive with other suppliers, our prices do not *appear* to be competitive.

The report details the three potential ways of dealing with the perception that we are more expensive than our competitors. Please reflect, both individually and in groups, on our choices.

I will let you know the results of the planned changes in Del Mar and San Diego. In the meantime, I would appreciate getting as much feedback as possible (and as quickly as possible) on the attached report.

Proposal
Marryat Insulation Systems Inc.
54 Easthupp Boulevard
Frederick, IA 50501

Proposed work:

- Install fiberglass under boards in 900 sq. ft. attic area of two-story house.
- Remove and replace necessary boards.
- Install wind tunnels.
- Install 2 R-61 roof vents.
- Install fiberglass in sidewalls, approx. 2000 sq. ft.
- Drill siding and redwood plug, chisel and putty, owner to sand and paint.
- Remove and replace siding, drill above second floor windows only.
- Install 4 8" × 16" soffit vents, 2 front, 2 rear.

We propose hereby to furnish material and labor—complete in accordance with above specifications—for the sum of cash on completion, $5,307.

All material is guaranteed to be as specified. All work to be completed according to standard practices. Any alteration or deviation from the above specifications involving extra costs will be executed only upon written orders, and will become an extra charge over and above the estimate. All agreements are contingent upon strikes, accidents, or delays beyond our control. Owner to carry fire, tornado, and other necessary insurance. Our work is fully covered by Worker's Compensation Insurance.

Note: This proposal may be withdrawn by us if not accepted within 10 days.

Date: May 3, 2011
Authorized signature: F. Marryat

Acceptance of proposal: The above prices, specifications, and conditions are satisfactory and are hereby accepted. You are authorized to do the work as specified. Payment will be made upon completion.

Date of acceptance: May 6, 2011
Signature: Jack Easy

––––––––

See also: ACCEPTANCES, ACKNOWLEDGMENTS, COVER LETTERS, CREDIT, INSTRUCTIONS, MEMOS, REFERENCES, REFUSALS, RESPONSES, SALES

FORTY-ONE

REQUESTS AND INQUIRIES

*Know how to ask. There is nothing more difficult
for some people, nor, for others, easier.*
—BALTASAR GRACIÁN

Letters of request (when you want to ask for something) and letters of inquiry (when you want to know something) are critical in maintaining the flow of ideas and resources among individuals and organizations. Because they are often the first contact between businesses and potential customers, between those seeking something and the employers, publishers, and vendors they are seeking it from, these letters must be good ambassadors.

Most commonplace requests (to change a life insurance beneficiary, to claim insurance benefits, to apply for a VA loan, to purchase a home, for federal employment) are initiated by a phone call and completed with the appropriate forms. Only in the case of problems are letters required.

Write Letters of Request/Inquiry When You Want

- adjustments (see COMPLAINTS)
- advice (see ADVICE)
- appointments/meetings/interviews (see APPLICATIONS, APPOINTMENTS, EMPLOYMENT, RÉSUMÉS)
- assistance: business/personal
- bids and estimates
- contributions/donations (see FUNDRAISING)

- credit information (see CREDIT)
- documents or copies of business/personal records
- donation (see FUNDRAISING)
- extension of deadline
- favors: business/personal
- forgiveness (see APOLOGIES)
- goods/services: prices/samples/information/brochures/product literature
- information/explanations/instructions
- introductions (see INTRODUCTIONS)
- loan (see CREDIT)
- payment (see COLLECTION, CREDIT)
- permission to reprint/use copyrighted material
- raise in salary (see EMPLOYMENT)
- reservation (see TRAVEL)
- speakers for your conference/banquet/workshop
- to borrow money (see CREDIT)
- to check on an unacknowledged gift (see FOLLOW-UP)
- to interview for a job (see APPLICATIONS, COVER LETTERS)
- to learn if a company has job openings
- to query an editor about a book or article idea (see QUERIES)
- zoning changes

How to Say It

- State clearly and briefly what you're requesting, beginning with a courtesy phrase like "Please send me . . ." or "May I please have . . ."
- Give details to help the person send you exactly what you want (reference numbers, dates, descriptions, titles).
- If appropriate, and if it will help the person furnish you more precisely with what you need, briefly explain the use you intend to make of the material. (When writing the county pathologist for information on procedures in a murder case, it helps the person to know that you are a mystery writer looking for background rather than a prosecutor building a case or a physician in search of medical details.)
- State the specific action or response you want from your reader.
- Explain why your reader might want to respond to your request. "The best way to get on in the world is to make people believe it's to their advantage to help you." (La Bruyère)
- If appropriate, offer to cover costs of photocopying, postage, or fees.
- Specify the date by which you need a response.
- If your letter is a long one, restate your request at the end.

- Express your thanks or appreciation for the other person's time and attention and close with a confident statement that the other person will respond positively.
- Enclose a self-addressed stamped envelope (SASE), if appropriate. Otherwise, tell where to send the information or where to telephone, fax, or e-mail the response.

What Not to Say

- Don't simply request "information." Some companies have hundreds of brochures dealing with their products and services. A vague request for "information" may or may not net you what you need. If you don't know what other information might be available or useful, add, "I would appreciate any other information you think might be helpful."
- Don't be apologetic (unless your request is time-consuming or difficult to supply). Avoid phrases like "I hope this is not too much trouble" and "I'm sorry to inconvenience you." Indicate in passing your respect for the other person's time, talents, and resources ("I know how busy you are") but don't dwell on the negative. Everyone has requests, and the more matter-of-fact and courteous you are, the better your chances of getting a positive reply.
- Avoid a high-handed approach that implies you are entitled to the information, service, or favor. You are making a request, not a demand.

Tips on Writing

■ Be brief, avoiding unnecessary explanations or asking the same question in two different ways. Reread your letter to see if your questions are easy to answer. Most people sitting at information-supplying desks have too much mail and too little time.

■ Use a subject line to quickly orient your reader: "Subject: cellular phone service"; "Subject: horse transporting"; "Re: piano tuning rates"; "Subject: airbag safety information"; "Re: mountaineering and ice climbing expeditions in North America"; "Subject: recipes using cranberries." For simple, business-like requests, no salutation is necessary; the subject line can stand alone.

■ When you have several requests, number and place each one on a separate line (from most to least important) so that the recipient can tick off each item as it is responded to.

■ Be precise about the information you want: mailing instructions for the return of a hard drive, how to petition a county court for a legal name change, availability and rates for the high season, absentee figures for the period January 1 to June 30. The more information you give, the more helpful is the information you receive.

■ Several letter-writing authorities advise not to end a letter of request with "thank you" or "thanking you in advance" (because these expressions seem to signal an end to the exchange), but both have become common and acceptable in current usage. Some people like the brisk wrap-up sound of it and use it automatically. You can also end with "I appreciate your time and attention" or "I look forward to hearing from you."

■ Make it easy for someone to respond to you: enclose a survey or questionnaire; provide a postage-paid postcard printed with a message and fill-in blanks; leave space under each question on your letter so the person can jot down replies and return it in the accompanying SASE. When the other person is doing you a favor, and one of you must bear the cost of postage, materials, or other assistance, it is, of course, you who should offer to pay. Include a SASE when asking someone to make an effort on your behalf. When requesting information of companies who hope to make a sale to you, this is unnecessary.

Special Situations

■ When writing to ask if an unacknowledged gift was received, describe the item, tell when you sent it, and offer a face-saving excuse for the person ("I know you are especially busy just now"). You might say you're inquiring because you insured the package and if it did not arrive, you want to follow up on it, or that you are wondering if you should put a "stop" order on the check. You're not required to give a reason for your inquiry, but doing so is tactful.

■ When requesting reservations for facilities for conferences, meetings, sales presentations, and other business activities, begin your inquiries with a telephone call to determine rates, date availability, and description of facilities. When writing to confirm your arrangements, include: time, date, number of expected attendees, required equipment and supplies, refreshment arrangements, billing information, name of contact person in your organization (if not you), and any other agreed-upon items.

■ When requesting a pay raise in writing (as opposed to an interview), begin by identifying your position in the company and the amount of raise you want. List your reasons for thinking a raise is appropriate: longer hours, more responsibility, work successes, noteworthy results, new skills. Whenever possible, use figures ("increase of 10 percent"). Emphasize the work you've done since your last pay raise. It is not productive to point to other people in the department who do less than you and are better compensated. Repeat your strongest argument and close with good wishes and an expression of appreciation.

■ To request a copy of your or a relative's military personnel records, go online to www.archives.gov/veterans/evetrecs/ where you can fill out a request form. If you prefer, write: National Personnel Records Center, 9700 Page Avenue, St. Louis, MO 63132. Give your service or social security number, state what you need ("discharge papers"), and, if appropriate, why you need them or no longer have your copy of them. Include your mailing address and daytime phone number.

■ Your letter requesting a zoning change will become part of the public record, so it must be factual, accurate, unemotional, and businesslike. State your reasons for requesting the change, modification, or variance. Include as much information as you can showing that, first, a zoning change will not harm the environs and, second, that it has potential benefits. Attach statements from neighbors, petitions, assessments, and other documents that bear on the issue.

■ When requesting your physician to release your medical records to another physician, hospital, or insurance company, write: "Dear Dr. [name], I hereby authorize you to release my medical file to [name of recipient]. I will appreciate this being done as soon as possible. Thank you."

■ When requesting permission to reprint copyrighted material, make it easy to say yes. Include two copies of either a form or your letter so that the person can sign and date them and return one to you. Include a self-addressed stamped envelope. State precisely what you want to use (title of book or article, page numbers, line or paragraph numbers, and a photocopy of the excerpted material). Tell how you plan to use the material (the name of your book or article, approximate publication date, publisher, price, expected number of copies to be printed, whether you want U.S. or world rights, and anything else that describes the anticipated audience and distribution). Include the credit line you will be using, and ask for their approval of it. Express your appreciation for considering the permissions request and, if you wish, your admiration for the person's work.

■ When asking someone to speak at your meeting or conference, give the following information: your organization's name; date, time, and place of the event, with directions or a map; desired length and subject of the talk; the reason or focus for the event; a description of the group's interests and backgrounds to give the speaker some sense of the audience; an estimate of the size of the audience; your expectations of when the speaker would arrive and depart; whether you are paying a fee and the speaker's travel expenses and lodgings; what equipment (microphone, overhead projector) is available; the name and phone number of a contact person (if this is not you).

■ When requesting estimates, bids, proposals, or price quotes, be specific: quantities, deadlines (for bid and for completion of work); special requirements; types, model numbers, colors; a list of everything you expect to be included in the total. To ensure that no important consideration is omitted, use the eventual contract that will be offered as a model for your letter.

■ To compare different services (office maintenance, lawn care, driving schools, carpet cleaning) send the same letter requesting information to all such services in your area.

Format

■ Business requests that go outside the company are typed, usually on letterhead stationery. Memo paper is used for routine in-house requests.

■ Personal requests may be typed or handwritten on business or personal stationery. The more personal the request (advice, favors), the more suitable it is to handwrite the note on a foldover or personal stationery.

■ Postcards are useful for one-line requests.

■ If you make the same type of request repeatedly, use a form letter or memo paper with blank space to fill in the title of the article or sample you're requesting.

■ E-mail is often used to make requests of companies with websites and can be used for some casual or routine requests.

WORDS

appeal	grant	products	refer
assistance	grateful	prompt	require
brochures	immediately	query	rush
expedite	information	question	seek
favor	inquiry	questionnaire	solicit
furnish	instructions	quickly	urgent
generous	problem	reconsider	

PHRASES

additional information/time	direct me to the appropriate agency
answer the following questions	
anticipate a favorable response	have the goodness to
apply/ask for	hope you are able to
appreciate any information/your cooperation/your help	I'd appreciate having/receiving/ obtaining
as soon as possible	if you can find time in your busy schedule to
by return mail	
count on/upon	if you think it might be possible

I'm writing to ask you

institute inquiries

interested in receiving information/
learning more about

it would be most helpful

I would appreciate your
assessment of

I would be grateful/most
grateful if/for

look forward to hearing from you

offer some assistance

of great help to us

on account of/behalf of

please call me to discuss

please let me have your estimate by

please provide us with/send details
about

please reply by

reply by return mail

respectfully request

take into consideration

thank you for your efforts in/to

trouble you to/for

we would appreciate your taking
a few minutes to

would you be willing to/good
enough to

your considered opinion

SENTENCES

Can you tell me which government agency might be able to give me background information on Minamata disease in Japan?

Do you remember that you once offered to lend me Grandma's pearl ring for a special occasion?

Enclosed is a self-addressed stamped envelope/an International Reply Coupon for your reply.

How can a private citizen be named to the task force on the Resolution Trust Corporation?

I am preparing a report for which I need annualized total returns for one, three, and five years through December 31—can you provide these by March 15?

I'd like to know how one goes about getting on your talk show.

I have a favor to ask you, but I take "no" very well!

I'm wondering if you have the time to give us a little guidance.

Is it true that it's possible to have stars named for people and, if so, how does one go about it?

I would be interested in seeing some of the material that went into the preparation of your most recent occupational titles handbook.

May I use your name as a reference when applying for a cashier position with Mawson's Country Inn?

Please forward this letter to the appropriate person.

Please send me any literature you have on antioxidant vitamins.

This is a formal request to you to make some other arrangements for your cats; your lease clearly states that animals are not allowed in the building.

We are contacting several industrial window cleaning firms to invite estimates.

We do not understand footnote (b) of Exhibit H—could you please explain it?

Will you please send me a copy of your current foam and sponge rubber products catalog along with information on bulk order discounts?

Will you please send me a list of those trash haulers in Willard County that contract by volume rather than by flat fee?

Your order forms, prices, and ordering instructions are oriented toward institutions—can you tell me how an individual can obtain your materials?

PARAGRAPHS

My Maundrell watch, which is still under warranty, has stopped running for no apparent reason. I'm told there is nothing wrong with the battery. Please tell me where to bring or send it for repair under the warranty.

Please send a copy of your guide to the best American colleges. Enclosed is my check for $21.95.

We are interested in replacing the decorative stone brick on our home and would like you to give us an estimate on your lightweight "cultured stone." Please call either of us at work during the day or at home during the evening (see enclosed business cards) to set up an appointment. Thank you.

Several bowling teams in the tri-county area are establishing a league that will sponsor a series of competitions. We will be needing trophies, plaques, and ribbons. We are also interested in seeing your line of name tags, medals, incentives, T-shirts, caps, and jackets. Please send your catalog and price lists. Thank you.

The Somers County Extension office is revising its brochure on spot removal. We understand that you have been doing some interesting research in this area. May we have copies of any relevant papers? We will of course credit you in the brochure. Also, if you know of any other especially good resources on this topic, we would appreciate that information.

I am interested in learning more about Metro University. Would you please send me: (1) a catalog, (2) any brochures you might have, (3) financial aid information, (4) application forms for the 2010–11 school year, and (5) information on setting up an interview with the Admissions Office and a tour around the campus.

The Pallant County Arts Board is attempting to determine whether it is meeting the needs of county artists, writers, playwrights, and musicians. Would you be so kind as to take a few minutes to fill out the enclosed questionnaire and return it to us in the self-addressed, stamped envelope? Please do not fold the questionnaire as results will be tabulated by computer.

I was unable to attend your talk on "Texture Performance of Metals" but would greatly appreciate reprints or preprints of anything you have written in this area. Thanks.

I'm wondering if you could give me about five minutes of your time on the phone some time next week. I am writing a research paper on global economics, and think that you may have answers to some of my questions. I found when I interviewed other people that it takes from three to five minutes—no more. If you are unable to do this, I will understand. Enclosed is a self-addressed postcard—please indicate on it a time when I could call you.

I understand that the basement meeting room of the Oakdale Community Church is available for use by various small groups. Would it be possible for our study group to meet there one evening a month? Our own church does not have any such facilities, and we have found it difficult to move around to a different home each month. We could meet on nearly any Tuesday, Wednesday, or Thursday evening that is convenient for you.

We have just moved to the area and are interested in changing from our out-of-state insurance agent to someone local. Please send complete information for the following types of insurance: auto, home, whole life. We prefer that you do not follow up with a call or visit; as soon as we have studied the material, we will call you if we have questions or if we would like to schedule a meeting. Thank you.

I respectfully request to be excused from jury duty beginning Nov. 2. I am a veterinarian in a two-person practice. My partner will be in India (copies of airline tickets are attached) the entire month of November. The clinic would effectively be without a veterinarian, and I do not see how we could arrange for adequate care of our many patients during that time.

I will be calling on barbers in your area the week of June 4–June 11 to show a line of completely new Swedish barbering tools. Made of tempered steel, guaranteed for twenty years, and sold with a service contract at no extra cost, these implements have already won three first-place Mentions of Merit from the American Academy of Barbers. I would like to stop by The Hair Bear sometime during that week. Enclosed is a self-addressed, stamped postcard—please indicate a time that would be convenient for you. To thank you for your time, I will be bringing you a gift.

SAMPLE LETTERS

Dear Werfel Credit Advisers Inc.,

I believe I need a credit counselor to help with my current financial goals: to reestablish a good credit rating, to set up a workable debt repayment plan, to analyze and prioritize my present spending patterns, to learn how to budget, and, in general, to get my finances under control.

Would you please send me complete information on your services, including fees? I would also like the names of several people with whom you have worked who would be willing to recommend you. What I absolutely do not need at this time is more delay and confusion in my money life.

Thank you.

――――――

TO: Orme Woolen Products
FROM: Shamrock Gifts
DATE: January 4, 2011

As we plan our fall inventory, we are again in the market to buy woolens. We are principally interested in the traditional Aran sweater (men's and women's cardigans and pullovers), and would like to request a sample.

Please also send information on any other knitwear that your company produces and a current price list.

If you plan to have a representative at the Chicago Trade Fair at the end of July, please advise us of your stand number so that we can contact you at that time. (Note our new address and telephone number.)

Thank you in advance for your attention.

――――――

Dear Mr. Eldrige:

Would you be willing to speak to the Challis University English Department about your recent book, *Grammar and the Grammarian*, sometime this next spring? Several department members have heard you speak; all of us have read your book. We meet the third Wednesday of every month and hope that one of those Wednesdays will fit into your schedule.

If you think this is possible, please call me to discuss the honorarium.

Hoping for a favorable reply, I am

Sincerely yours,

――――――

Dear Mr. Imhof,

Would it be possible for me to move my desk?

A number of factors about my desk's present location make concentration difficult at times. The shipping clerk traffic just outside the door adjacent to my desk is unrelenting and distracting, the lighting over my desk is poor, and I have a direct view of an office in which the person spends some time every day tending to matters of personal hygiene.

The spot to the left of the lightboard would be perfect for my desk. I'd need an extension cord to reach an outlet for my computer and desk light, but that should be no problem. If Mr. Wahnschaffe could spare ten minutes to help me move my desk and computer, I'd be all set.

I would really appreciate being able to move. Thank you!

———————

Dear Axel,

I plan to be on Sanburan Island in the near future, and am wondering if you could schedule a tour for me of the Tropical Belt Coal Company. Coal is one of my hobbies.

Enclosed is a self-addressed envelope and an International Reply Coupon for your response.

Thanks so much for your time and attention.

Sincerely,

———————

Dear Mr. Babington:

I would like your permission to reprint the following material from your book, *Diplomacy Today:*

page iv: paragraph 2: "Since 1701 . . . and nothing was said."
page 294: final sentence: "If it appears that . . . only Henry VIII knows the truth."

This material would be used in my book, *The New Diplomacy*, to be published by Baines-Gandish in 2012. The book will retail for $16.95 and is expected to have a somewhat limited market. I will send you a complimentary copy, and you would of course be given credit as follows:

Diplomacy Today (New York: Goddard Publishing, 2007), pp. iv, 294. Reprinted with permission from Spencer Babington.

I'm enclosing two copies of this letter. If you agree to grant me permission, please write "permission granted," sign and date one of the copies, and return it to me in the enclosed self-addressed stamped envelope.

I would appreciate being able to use those two excerpts. Your book was an eye-opener when it appeared, and it has remained a standard for me of fine writing, clear thinking, and inspired research.

Sincerely,

———————

TO: Emmerick Demolition and Salvage

In September 2009 you submitted a bid to Brooker Real Estate to remove two structures, one at 1898 Stratfield and one at 1921 Cabell. Since that bid, two additional properties have been purchased by Brooker Real Estate that will require demolition this summer.

I invite you to submit a rebid to include the two additional sites plus tank removal at another site (please see attachment for description and addresses of sites).

Contact me if you will be submitting a bid as I would like to schedule a meeting to discuss this project further and to answer your questions.

———————

Dear Morris,

I'm thinking of leaving Langdon Glass Works (I'll tell you why next time I see you) and am currently on the lookout for a good sales management position.

You seem to know everyone in the industry (and everybody knows you)—would you mind letting me know if you hear of any openings?

I appreciate being able to ask you this. Let's get together soon.

Sincerely,

———————

TO: LeRoy Investment Services

Please send me information on investment opportunities for the small, independent investor. I would specifically like to know:

1. Requirements, interest rates, and other information on certificates of deposit, treasury bills, municipal bonds, mutual funds, and other investment programs.
2. The commission your company charges for handling such investments.
3. The performance records on your investment programs over the past two years.
4. The names of several people who have used your services recently.

———————

TO: Zoning Commission
FROM: Barbara Topham
DATE: March 10, 2010
RE: Zoning File 9117, Children's Playschool

I am writing to urge you to approve the Special Condition Use Permit sought by Children's Playschool. As we live directly across the street, we would be one of those most affected, and I believe it is important for you to know that the change would not appear to adversely affect the neighborhood.

———————

Dear Archie,

At the last meeting of the Open Door organizing committee, we discussed the need for new members. Your name came up several times as someone who has spent a good deal of time, money, and energy at the Food Shelf. We all felt you could add creativity, excitement, and inspiration to our efforts.

Would you consider a one-year commitment to the committee? This would involve one general monthly meeting, one weekly subcommittee meeting, some telephone work, and your regular weekly volunteer hours. I think you are currently spending about ten hours a week at the center. If you need to cut down on those hours to devote time to the committee, that would be fine.

Although this is something you'll need to think about, we are hoping to have your answer within the next two weeks so that we can publish the new roster in our year-end appeals. We are all hoping that you'll say yes but will understand if you cannot. In any case, we are grateful for the time and talent you have already given the center.

With best wishes,

————

TO: Metropolitan Council

I understand that you are funding a special multifamily recycling program for those who live in apartments or condominiums with twenty or more units.

I am writing on behalf of our neighborhood association, as we have a number of such buildings, and residents are interested in such a program. Please send information. We would also be interested in having someone from the Council speak at one of our meetings to explain the program.

Sincerely,

————

See also: APPOINTMENTS, COLLECTION, CREDIT, EMPLOYMENT, FUNDRAISING, INTRODUCTIONS, INVITATIONS, ORDERS, RESPONSES, SALES, THANK YOU, TRAVEL

FORTY-TWO

RESPONSES

I was gratified to be able to answer promptly. I said I didn't know.
—MARK TWAIN

Prompt and thoughtful responses to incoming mail may be as important to your business as your carefully drafted sales letters. They are equally rewarding in your personal life. "A prompt response is a sign of vigorous and authentic concern; nothing could be more flattering or touching to the recipient." (Jennifer Williams)

When responding with a straightforward yes or no, see ACCEPTANCES or REFUSALS.

Write Responses to

- announcements
- apologies
- complaints (see ADJUSTMENTS, APOLOGIES)
- congratulations
- expressions of sympathy
- gifts and kindnesses (see also THANK YOU)
- inquiries
- invitations (see also ACCEPTANCES, REFUSALS)
- letters addressed to someone temporarily absent
- requests: information/instructions/samples/introductions/contributions/payments/letters of reference

How to Say It

- In the first sentence, state what you are responding to (a letter, invitation, memo) so the other person knows immediately why you're writing. In some cases, use a reference line ("Re: Order #2K881").
- Briefly give all requested information.
- When you cannot respond completely to a request, include names, addresses, and phone numbers where more information can be obtained.
- If immediate action is not possible, tell what is being done and by what date results can be expected.
- If appropriate, offer further assistance.
- Let the other person know you appreciate them and are pleased to be responding.
- Close with good wishes, an expression of confidence in your product or service, or a remark about future contacts.

What Not to Say

- Don't give more information than your reader requested. In most cases, this is unnecessary and unhelpful.
- Don't misspell the other person's name. It is immediately noticed and weakens the effect of your response.
- Don't allow an irritated tone to creep in, even when you consider the letter you're responding to offensive, uninformed, or inane.

Tips on Writing

■ Respond promptly. "It should be the aim of every business office to answer all its mail the same day it is received." (Alexander L. Sheff and Edna Ingalls) That advice, written in 1942, may be an impossibility today, but it is still a good goal.

■ When responding to a number of questions or to a complicated letter, organize your letter elements by using numbers, bullets, or asterisks and leave plenty of white space.

■ If your response is brief and straightforward, you can sometimes note it on the bottom of the letter you've just received, refold the letter, address an envelope, and send it right back. A great time-saver, this works only when you don't need a record of the exchange.

Special Situations

■ Customer inquiries provide an unparalleled opportunity to promote your goods and services as well as your company. Handle them with the utmost respect, speed, efficiency, and good cheer—inquiries are generally forerunners of sales. Answer questions as completely as possible and enclose supplementary lists, articles, reports, brochures, flyers, or catalogs. Make it easy for the customer to follow up (place an order, find a local distributor, call a toll-free number).

■ When responding to a job offer, express pleasure in your future association with the company; say something complimentary about the job interview and interviewer; restate, when appropriate, the conditions of employment; renew your confidence that you and the company are a good match; thank the person. Sometimes your response is a qualified one; you want the position but cannot accept some condition of employment (hours, salary, vacation time). Explain that they are your first choice except for that issue; can anything be done about it?

■ Response to an invitation marked "RSVP" or "Please reply" is mandatory, obligatory, required, compulsory, imperative, and essential. If you do not plan to attend, the same is true for "Regrets only." If your invitation includes no RSVP, no "Regrets only," and no reply card, you need not respond. This type of invitation is used for large affairs—political gatherings, fundraising events, business cocktail parties, conventions. Guidelines for responding to an invitation: Reply within several days of receiving it. State clearly that you will or will not be able to attend. Mirror the invitation, using the same format, and almost all the same words. If you have cards with your name or personalized stationery, you can simply write under your name "accepts with pleasure the kind invitation of . . ." and repeat the kind of event, time, date, and place.

■ Invitations (wedding, bar mitzvah, bat mitzvah) and announcements (engagement, graduation, birth, adoption) require a response (letter or congratulatory card with handwritten note), but if you don't attend the event or celebration you aren't expected to send a gift.

■ Expressions of condolence require a response, which can take a number of forms, from handwritten formal notes of thanks (see THANK YOU) to printed newspaper announcements of appreciation (see ANNOUNCEMENTS). In the case of a public figure, printed acknowledgments can be sent to large numbers of people who were not personally known to the family (see ACKNOWLEDGMENTS). Responses may be brief, may be sent up to six weeks following the funeral, and may be written by someone on behalf of the person closest to the deceased.

■ Responding to fundraising appeals does not often involve a letter, or even a comment from you; most organizations simply want your check, which you tuck into the provided envelope. If you write a letter, mention the sum you're donating, ask for a receipt (for tax purposes) if you wish, and attach a completed matching gift form if your employer participates in this program. If you are not familiar with the sponsoring organization, you can obtain information about them at www.bbb.org/charity, which is sponsored by the Council of Better Business Bureaus.

■ Respond to an apology if only to acknowledge that you received it. What you do after that is your choice. "The person who can meet an apology more than halfway and forgive with a graciousness that makes the aggressor feel almost glad that the trouble occurred, but very certain that it shall never occur again, is the one who will make beautiful and lifelong friendships." (Julia W. Wolfe)

■ In responding to flattering and enthusiastic congratulatory messages, say "thank you" first of all. Then be gracious. "A compliment is a gift, not to be thrown away carelessly unless you want to hurt the giver." (Eleanor Hamilton) Reflect the compliment back to the giver ("how nice of you to write," "your letter touched me," "how thoughtful of you").

■ When asked what you or someone close to you would like for a graduation, anniversary, birthday, or holiday gift, mention a broad gift category ("books," for example, but not "money") that will provide a range of prices for the giver.

Format

■ Choosing a format for a letter or note of response is simple: do as you were done unto. If the original letter was typed, type yours; if it was handwritten, handwrite yours. If the invitation was formal, your response should be written in the third-person formal manner. If it was informal, first-person style on personal stationery, you respond similarly.

■ If you use formal notes engraved or printed with your name, respond to invitations by penning in "accepts with pleasure" or "declines with regret" under your name. Add the date so that your recipient knows which invitation you're responding to.

■ Forms are useful in responding to routine inquiries. Requests for information, materials, or samples can be handled with a printed card saying, "This comes to you at your request" or "Thank you for your inquiry. Enclosed are informational materials." Or, design a brief, general form letter that thanks the person for the inquiry and indicates what information is being forwarded. Include a checklist of publications so you can indicate those that you are enclosing or mailing under separate cover. You can also leave blanks: "Thank you for your inquiry about _____." Or design a form with every conceivable response and then check off the appropriate one ("Your order has been sent." "We are temporarily out of stock." "Please reorder in _____ days." "This is a prepaid item, and your payment has not yet been received." "Please indicate a second color choice.").

■ Reply to an e-mail message with an e-mail. When letter writers give an e-mail address in their letters, you may respond that way if your response is brief or routine.

WORDS

acknowledge	enclosed	inform	respond
appreciate	feedback	notify	return
confirm	grateful	regarding	send

PHRASES

according to your letter

appreciate your business

appreciate your calling our
   attention to

as mentioned in your letter

delighted to receive

enclosed you will find

for further information

happy to hear from you

I'm sending you

in response to your letter of

meant a great deal to me

pleased to be able to send you

thank you for your letter telling
   us about

to let you know

under separate cover

want to reply to your letter

we appreciate your interest in

we have carefully/thoughtfully
   considered your letter

your sympathetic/delightful/
   helpful/comforting/encouraging
   letter/note

SENTENCES

As requested, we are submitting a budget figure for construction surveillance for the water and sewer line project.

Here is the information you requested about the tank closure.

I have received your apology, and hope you will not give the matter another thought.

I hope this information is useful to you in resolving any remaining title issues.

In response to your request for sealed bids, a bid from Dale Heating and Plumbing is enclosed.

Letters like yours have been a great comfort to us all.

Mary Postgate has asked me to respond to your letter about the settlement agreement dated January 30.

Thank you for sharing with me the lovely memories you have of Father.

Thank you for taking the time to write, and please excuse my delay in responding to your letter.

Thank you so much for your kind words/for your letter.

This is to let you know that the report you requested will be mailed as soon as it is completed (Dec. 3).

We are pleased to send you the enclosed information about Weycock United Sugar Company.

We thank you for your inquiry, and are pleased to enclose a sample snack bar.

You have asked me to estimate the fees that would be required for our services.

PARAGRAPHS

Your grant proposal has been read with great interest. We will want to have several other people read and evaluate it before submitting it for discussion at our weekly meeting. I will let you know as soon as we have made a decision.

Thank you for your inquiry about Gabbadeo Wines. Enclosed are several brochures describing our vineyards and products and a list of vendors in your area.

In response to your fax of June 3, I'm sending the three original contracts along with two copies of each, four pro forma invoices with two copies of each, and a bill of lading. Please let us know at once if everything is in order.

We received your impressive résumé today and look forward to meeting with you. Because of the large number of responses we received to our advertisement, however, it may be two or three weeks before you hear from us.

Thank you for your generous and sincere apology. I am entirely willing to put the incident behind me, and I look forward to continuing our old association.

In response to your letter of September 16, we have made a number of inquiries and are pleased to tell you that most of the staff here is agreeable to helping you with your research project. Please telephone the department secretary Arthur Eden to let him know what day or days you would like to spend with us.

Dear Mr. Ruggles,

Thank you for your inquiry about Red Gap. We are enclosing some Chamber of Commerce brochures, a map of the area, and a list of events and activities through the end of the year.

If we can be of any further assistance, please let us know. We hope that you enjoy your stay in Red Gap.

Sincerely,

_____

Dear Ms. Stedman:

Thank you for your interest in our Quick Mail program. Due to an overwhelming demand, requests for our brochure and explanatory CD have far outpaced our supplies. However, a new shipment has been ordered, and we'll send you your materials as soon as we receive them.

Once you receive our kit, you'll learn all about the money-saving ideas that our program has to offer—reducing your mail float time, accelerating your cash flow, escalating your postage discounts, and still other techniques.

We look forward to hearing from you after you have had a chance to examine the materials.

Sincerely,

_____

Dear Mr. Einhorn:

In response to your inquiry of December 3, I am sorry to tell you that Mr. Belton was with us for only a short time and our records do not indicate a forwarding address. I believe he used to also work for Lorraine Linens. You might try them.

_____

Dear Barbara and Garnet,

Your love and support these past few weeks have been a great comfort to all of us. I am especially grateful for the way you took over with the children when I couldn't. And, Garnet, thank you for being a pallbearer. I know Edward would have wanted you there. I hope you have not exhausted your reserves of friendship, because I feel I am going to need your kindness and understanding for a while yet.

With love and gratitude,

_____

Dear Louisa William,

I was delighted to receive and read your letter of August 3, 2010. Thank you for your kind remarks about the Alconleigh Suites and the excellent team that operates the hotel.

Louisa Kroesig, Sales and Catering Manager, is honored to receive this recognition for her staff. In addition, Christian Talbot, General Manager, on behalf of the entire hotel team, is pleased with your compliments about our meeting and exceeding the expectations of the Jassy/Radlett wedding group.

Thank you for allowing us to be your hotel of choice—both for hotel accommodations and for your wedding reception—and for providing us with the privilege of introducing our brand of hospitality to your guests from across the United States.

We look forward to being of service in the future and feel privileged to have earned your continued business.

Thanks again for sharing your satisfaction with us.

————

See also: ACCEPTANCES, ACKNOWLEDGMENTS, ADJUSTMENTS, APOLOGIES, COVER LETTERS, FAMILY, FOLLOW-UP, GOODWILL, REFUSALS, SENSITIVE, THANK YOU

FORTY-THREE

RÉSUMÉS

We judge ourselves by what we feel capable of doing,
while others judge us by what we have already done.
—Henry Wadsworth Longfellow

A résumé gives prospective employers a written summary of your qualifications and work history. It convinces the reader that you're a good candidate for the position and that you should be invited for an interview.

Although it lacks most of the features of a sales letter (few employers are dazzled by extravagant claims and catchy language), the résumé is a letter in which you are both the seller and the product.

When applying for a job, you might use one or two of the following: *résumé*, a businesslike summary of your work history, education, and career goals; *cover letter*, a brief letter written to accompany a résumé; *letter of application*, a combination cover letter and brief, informal résumé. See COVER LETTERS and APPLICATIONS for assistance with the second two.

Send a Résumé When

- applying for a franchise
- applying for a job or internship
- applying for membership in certain organizations
- applying to universities/degree programs
- inquiring about openings at a company
- responding to an employment ad

How to Say It

- Place your name, address, daytime telephone number, e-mail address, fax number, and website address at the top right or at the top center of your résumé (the top left position may get stapled or punched).
- State the position or kind of job you're seeking.
- Detail your work experience and job skills. There are two basic approaches, with the second being more common today.

   1. The traditional reverse chronological employment format starts by listing your most recent position and going back through time. This is the easiest format to use, but it has its weaknesses if there are gaps in your job history, if you're new to the job market, or if your previous jobs don't seem to relate well to the one you are seeking. The emphasis in this listing is on concrete information: dates of employment, name and full address of employer, job title, job duties, reason for leaving, if appropriate.

   2. The nonchronological résumé (also called a skills-oriented or functional résumé) stresses your qualifications and abilities. You group job experiences according to a specific skill. For example, under "Leadership Skills" you write, "Supervised night shift at Hooper & Co. for two years." Under "Interpersonal Skills" write, "As the mayor's troubleshooter, I was often called upon to intervene in disputes, negotiate contracts, and otherwise deal with constituents, politicians, and city personnel under difficult circumstances." "Organizational Skills" might include: "I was hired at Arnold-Browne to reorganize the accounting department, which was barely functioning at the time due to staff turnover, low morale, lack of department guidelines, and poor use of office space. At the end of two years, I was commended by the company president for 'unparalleled organizing skills.'"

   You can also combine the two approaches; under each job listed in reverse chronological order, group skills used in that position. Or, slant your résumé directly toward the job under consideration by listing the general qualifications and specific qualifications you have for it.
- Give the essential facts of your education: name of school, city and state where it is located, years you attended, the diploma or certificate you earned, the course of studies you pursued, special training, significant honors or memberships.
- List publications, if appropriate.

What Not to Say

- Don't include a photograph or personal information (age or birth year, weight, height, marital or financial status, children, ethnicity, disability, religious or political affiliation) unless it is pertinent to the situation you are seeking. For example, to apply for a position as a weight control group leader, a mention of your weight history is probably indicated. It is often illegal for prospective employers to ask questions about age, sex, race, and religion.

- Don't tell what you expect the company to do for you. ("This position is a wonderful opportunity to learn about the marketing side of the automotive industry.") Emphasize instead what you can contribute to the company.

- Don't present your accomplishments so that they say, "Here is what I've done." Instead, phrase them to say, "Here is what I can do for you." For example, "I have the experience and ability to help you increase production efficiency. While I was supervisor at Fortis & Co., department overruns decreased 32 percent."

- Don't tell every single thing you've done. Filler material detracts from a strong résumé. People who throw in all the extras on the theory that it "can't hurt" may be wrong. Don't include information on childhood, early schooling, hobbies, or interests (unless they relate directly to the position). Omit work you've done in the past that you don't want to do again, unless this would leave unexplained holes in your résumé.

- Don't embellish, exaggerate, tell half-truths, or, of course, lie. Many companies have résumé fact-checkers and if you're found out, you will be dismissed, will suffer embarrassment and humiliation, and may be liable for civil charges. Trying to make yourself sound better than you are is often a tip-off that you may not be well qualified for that particular position—or happy in it.

- Don't be too modest either by playing down your accomplishments. Have someone who knows you evaluate your final draft.

- Don't use "etc." It is uninformative and irritating and conveys excessive casualness.

- Don't use weak adjectives and adverbs. Remove every "very" you find and such lukewarm words as "good," "wonderful," "exciting." Use instead strong, perhaps even unusual, nouns and verbs. See lists of adjectives, nouns, and verbs in this chapter.

- Don't use jargon, long, involved phrases, a bookish vocabulary you don't normally use, or acronyms (unless the acronym is so familiar in your field that it would be insulting to spell it out).

- Don't mention salary in a résumé; this is better discussed in an interview (and then try to get your interviewer to mention a figure before you do).

Tips on Writing

■ Before writing a résumé, assemble two kinds of information: facts about yourself and facts about your prospective employer and the position. Call the company to ask questions. Research the company at the library. Speak to people who work there or who know the company. When you tell a prospective employer what you can do for their company, the implication is that you've studied the company enough to know where you might fit in; this is appealing. Although you cannot change the facts of your employment history, you can emphasize certain skills and qualifications if you know that this is what the employer wants. The employer may want creativity, for example, and none of your previous jobs emphasized it. Check other areas of your life to see where you have shown creativity—art classes, hobby photography, teaching pottery. When prospective employers see a résumé that has obviously been written especially for them, they give it more than the sixty seconds that most résumés get. By presenting as clear a picture of yourself as you can in terms of the employer's needs, you make it easy for them to determine quickly whether there is a match. Linda Stern (*Newsweek*, 2008) recommends putting "at least 15 hours a week into it if you have a job; 35 or more if you don't. Call everyone you know who might be connected to your target and request informational interviews. Ask about job leads, and call back every six weeks to check in. . . . Expect to take six months or more to find a good job." That may or may not apply to your situation, but finding a good job is hard work.

■ Your résumé may be skimmed by a human resources assistant, scanned into a computer, or screened by a recruiter. It must appeal to all three: short paragraphs and white space and good headings to catch the eye of the assistant; plenty of appropriate keywords (see below) for the computer; a logical and persuasive organization of material for the recruiter.

■ Large companies use optical character readers (OCRs) to scan incoming résumés. Software identifies keywords and stores the résumés in a large database. When a new employee is needed, the database is searched by keywords to identify applicants who have the needed skills. Some career counselors recommend a special keyword section with a listing of terms that might get your résumé pulled. Others point out that the computer will find the terms whether they are in one paragraph or spread out through the résumé. What is critical is that your résumé contain the words most likely to identify you for the position you want. Tips for scanned résumés: put only your name on the first line as that's what the software is expecting; use jargon, acronyms, and other words commonly used in your field, along with their logical synonyms; identify abilities specifically, for example, name the computer software you're familiar with (don't simply list "word-processing skills"); use variations of words ("administrator," "administered") so that the program will pick up either; be specific ("advertising manager" instead of "manager" so that no matter which is searched for, it'll be caught); use only one date for your education (the date you received your degree) or the program will assume you simply spent time there; use both "R.N." and "Registered Nurse" in case only one has been requested; check the advertisement you're responding to and be certain the words used in it appear on your résumé.

■ Your résumé is only as long as it needs to be. Most authorities recommend no more than one or two pages. In *The Smart Job Search*, Mark L. Makos says, "Unless it is not important to you to get a job, a one-page résumé is your only choice." However, for many academic and professional positions, you may need more than two pages—as many as twelve perhaps, if you have a long list of publications, patents, cases, conference presentations, or other itemizations. Whether one page or twelve, your résumé must be tightly written and readable: use simple, short sentences, keep paragraphs short, and leave plenty of white space and ample margins. "Think of a résumé as a sixty-second television commercial: that's probably all the time the reader is going to spend on it." (Lassor A. Blumenthal)

■ Sample headings and divisions (you will generally have no more than five or six) that might be useful to you in constructing your résumé include:

Activities

Additional Accomplishments

Additional Experience

Awards, Honors, Offices

Background Summary

Career Highlights

Career Objective

Career Summary

Communication Skills

Copywriting Experience

Editorial Experience

Education

Employment Objective

Executive Profile

Experience

Extracurricular Activities

Highlighted Qualifications

Interpersonal Skills

Job Objective

Key Qualifications

Leadership Skills

Management Profile

Managerial Experience

Memberships

Negotiating Skills

New Product Development Skills

Office Management Skills

Office Skills

Organizational and Managerial
Skills

Overview of Qualifications	Résumé
Professional Achievements	Skills
Professional Affiliations	Skills Summary
Professional Background	Special Skills
Professional Experience	Summary of Qualifications
Professional History	Summary of Work History
Professional Profile	Supervisory Skills
Professional Qualifications	Systems Skills
Promotional Skills	Technical Experience
Related Experience	Training
Relevant Accomplishments	Volunteer Work
Relevant Experience	Work Experience
Retail Sales Experience	

■ Concentrate on your strengths. For each characteristic that you think your employer might want (leadership ability, responsibility, problem solving, initiative), assemble examples from your work history.

■ There are three ways to refer to yourself in a résumé: (1) in the first person ("I managed the Midway Pro Bowl for three years, and saw it double in profits during that time"); (2) in the third person ("She has worked in a number of areas of radio broadcasting, including . . ." or "Dr. Patikar organized a new patient outcare service"); (3) without a pronoun ("Developed a new method of twinning steel"). Each style has advantages and disadvantages. The first can be wearying with all its "I"s (omit as many as possible), the second can appear remote and pretentious, and the third may seem abrupt. Use the style you feel most comfortable with, regardless of what you perceive as its benefits or disadvantages. In any case, do not refer to yourself as "the writer" ("The writer has six years' experience . . .").

■ Use strong, active verbs. Instead of the weaker "I did this" or "I was responsible for that," write "I managed," "I developed," "I directed." See the list of active verbs in this chapter.

■ Make all listings parallel in form: "I directed . . . I supervised . . . I increased . . ." Not: "I directed . . . I was a supervisor . . . I have increased."

■ You will use two tenses in a résumé: the present tense for categories like career goal ("Desire position with . . .") and skills ("I am fluent in French, Italian, Spanish, and German"); the past tense for categories like work experience ("Headed all major advertising campaigns . . .") and professional accomplishments ("I won a six-state cabinetmaking competition").

■ Use numbers to report successful outcomes of your work. Even if you were only partly responsible for increasing sales, decreasing expenditures, or coming in under budget for the first time in ten years, mention the figures. State how many people you supervised, how many copies of your books were sold, how many projects you oversaw, how much time or money you saved the company, the size of the budget you were responsible for, the percentage reduction in absenteeism in your department, the percentage increase in productivity at your station. Figures are persuasive.

■ Resilience is an important qualification in a world where information and technology develop at high speeds. Emphasize your flexibility and ability to learn new tasks and adapt to new situations by making your past jobs sound different from each other. For example, if you've held several positions as an executive assistant, list under one position that you reorganized the filing system, under another that you trained employees in the use of the new telephone system, under yet another that you managed the office for three months while your supervisor was taking a leave of absence.

■ Use only years, not months, when dating your work history.

■ You need not mention the reason for leaving a position; if the employer wants to know, this will be brought up in the interview. Readily accepted reasons include: moving, returning to school, seeking a better position, unforeseen changes in your former job.

■ The old résumé standby, "References available upon request," isn't necessary since it is taken for granted that later in the process references will be requested by them and supplied by you. Include the line only if you need to fill white space at the end of your résumé. Always ask people in advance if you can use them as references.

■ Don't use the same boilerplate résumé for each job you apply for. Each résumé should be tailored to the particular company and typed or printed freshly (no photocopies).

■ After you proofread your final draft, have at least two other people read it for you. The error that two of you miss will jump out at your prospective employer.

■ Don't staple, glue, or seal your résumé into a binder or folder (unless requested to). The pages should be loose and paperclipped together; they are easier to handle. Mail your résumé and cover letter in a 9" × 12" envelope so they arrive unfolded and crisp-looking.

■ In some situations include work samples, publications, or other supplementary materials.

■ Check your library or bookstore for books devoted solely to résumé writing. Two suggestions: David F. Noble, *Gallery of Best Résumés: A Collection of Quality Résumés by Professional Résumé Writers*; Wendy S. Enelow has written a number of excellent books on résumés for particular audiences (for example, engineers, ex-military, teachers).

Special Situations

■ If you prefer that your present employer doesn't know you're job-hunting, refer inquiries to your home phone or address and ask that references from your present employer wait until you and the prospective employer feel sure of the match.

■ When given an application form to fill out for a job, you may attach a résumé to it.

■ First-time job seekers encounter the classic frustration: They won't hire me because I don't have experience, and I don't have experience because they won't hire me. It is, however, possible to structure an appealing résumé without a significant work history. Summer jobs show dependability, initiative, responsibility. Extracurricular activities illustrate leadership potential, the ability to complete projects, and special interests. Awards, honors, GPA, elected offices, and scholarships indicate accomplishments and show that you have been singled out from your peers. Volunteer work, athletics, and organization memberships help define you and give you a profile. This type of résumé benefits from a skills orientation; you state that you are responsible, dependable, hardworking, a quick learner, or loyal and give illustrative examples.

■ When asked to furnish a brief biographical sketch (or bio) for program notes, a newspaper article, or a company newsletter, your résumé will help you write it. A bio is written in narrative fashion, is far briefer and less specific than a résumé, and aims to capture the essence rather than the details of who you are professionally.

■ When applying for a franchise, follow FTC guidelines. You may want a lawyer to help with some of the correspondence.

Format

■ All résumés are typed, printed, or machine-produced on good bond paper (white or off-white), on one side only, in sharp black elite or pica type (no script or fancy font). They look professional, conservative, and straightforward. In a few fields, you might obtain a job using a highly creative résumé with graphics, colored inks, and an offbeat design. For this approach, however, you must understand your market—to the point perhaps of knowing someone at the company who obtained a job that way. This type of résumé receives admiring looks, but is often passed over for the more "stable"-looking résumé.

■ When your résumé will be scanned: use only white paper; don't use graphic elements, small type, or unusual fonts (Times Roman or Arial are good choices); don't use italics, underlining, or boldface; use asterisks instead of bullets as they are read as periods. OCRs like reading boring, homogeneous résumés; use only this style for them.

■ Fax your résumé only if you have been asked to do so or someone needs it at once. Faxed résumés don't look as good as those on résumé paper.

■ Résumés may be e-mailed in certain situations: the classified ad gives an e-mail address and asks that résumés be sent there; you find the job opening on the company website and they encourage sending your résumé by e-mail. Check with them first about any special e-mail requirements.

WORDS (ACTIVE VERBS)

accelerated	appointed	calculated	communicated
accentuated	appraised	captured	compared
accepted	approached	carried out	compiled
accommodated	appropriated	carved	completed
accomplished	approved	catalogued	composed
accounted for	arbitrated	categorized	computed
achieved	arranged	caused	conceived
acquired	articulated	celebrated	conducted
acted	assembled	centralized	confirmed
adapted	assessed	chaired	connected
added	assigned	challenged	conserved
addressed	assisted	championed	considered
adjusted	attained	charged	consolidated
administered	attended	charted	constructed
adopted	augmented	checked	consulted
advanced	authored	chose	contacted
advised	authorized	clarified	continued
advocated	awarded	classified	contracted
aided	balanced	cleared	contributed
allayed	began	closed	controlled
alleviated	bettered	coached	converted
allocated	bid	collaborated	cooperated
altered	blended	collated	coordinated
amassed	boosted	collected	corrected
amended	bought	combined	corresponded
analyzed	brought	commanded	counseled
anticipated	budgeted	commissioned	crafted
applied	built	committed	created

cultivated	elaborated	financed	incorporated
cut	eliminated	finished	increased
dealt	emphasized	fixed	indexed
decided	enabled	focused	influenced
decreased	enacted	followed	informed
defined	encouraged	forecast	infused
defrayed	enforced	forged	initiated
delegated	engineered	formed	innovated
delivered	enhanced	formulated	inserviced
demonstrated	enlarged	forwarded	inspected
deployed	enlisted	fostered	inspired
designated	enriched	fought	installed
designed	enrolled	found	instilled
detailed	ensured	founded	instituted
detected	entered	framed	instructed
determined	enticed	fulfilled	integrated
developed	equipped	functioned as	interacted
devised	established	funded	interpreted
diagnosed	estimated	furnished	intervened
directed	evaluated	furthered	interviewed
disbursed	examined	gained	introduced
discovered	exceeded	gathered	invented
dispatched	exchanged	generated	inventoried
dispensed	executed	governed	invested
displayed	exercised	grew	investigated
disseminated	exhibited	grouped	invited
dissolved	expanded	guided	involved
distributed	expedited	handled	isolated
diversified	experienced	headed	issued
divided	experimented	heightened	itemized
documented	exported	held	joined
doubled	extended	helped	judge
downsized	extracted	hired	justified
drafted	fabricated	hosted	launched
drew up	facilitated	hurried	learned
drove	factored	identified	lectured
earned	familiarized	illustrated	led
economized	fashioned	implemented	lessened
edited	fielded	imported	leveraged
educated	filed	improved	licensed
effected	finalized	improvised	liquidated

litigated	notified	processed	reduced costs
located	obtained	procured	reengineered
logged	offered	produced	referred
lowered	officiated	profiled	regained
maintained	opened	programmed	registered
managed	operated	progressed	regulated
mandated	optimized	projected	rehabilitated
maneuvered	orchestrated	promoted	reimbursed
manufactured	ordered	proofread	reinforced
mapped	organized	proposed	rejuvenated
marked	originated	protected	related
marketed	outdistanced	proved	remained
mastered	outlined	provided	remedied
masterminded	outsourced	publicized	remodeled
maximized	overcame	published	rendered
measured	overhauled	purchased	renegotiated
mediated	oversaw	quadrupled	renewed
mended	paced	qualified	reorganized
mentored	packaged	quantified	repaired
merged	packed	quoted	replaced
met	parlayed	raised	replicated
met deadlines	participated	ran	reported
minimized	partnered	ranked	repositioned
mobilized	perfected	rated	represented
modeled	performed	reached	reproduced
moderated	persuaded	read	researched
modernized	piloted	realigned	reshaped
modified	pinpointed	realized	resolved
molded	pioneered	rearranged	responded
monitored	placed	rebuilt	restored
motivated	planned	received	restructured
mounted	positioned	recognized	retained
moved	predicted	recommended	retooled
multiplied	prepared	reconciled	retrieved
named	prescribed	reconstructed	returned
narrated	presented	recorded	revamped
narrowed	preserved	recovered	reversed
navigated	presided	recruited	reviewed
negotiated	prevented	rectified	revised
netted	printed	redesigned	revitalized
nominated	prioritized	redirected	revived

revolutionized	sold	supported	trimmed
rotated	solicited	surpassed	tripled
routed	solidified	surveyed	troubleshot
safeguarded	solved	synchronized	turned around
salvaged	sorted	synthesized	tutored
satisfied	sourced	systematized	typed
saved	spearheaded	tabulated	uncovered
scanned	specified	tackled	underlined
scheduled	speeded	tallied	undertook
screened	spent	tapped	underwrote
searched	spoke	targeted	unified
secured	sponsored	taught	united
selected	stabilized	tended	unraveled
sent	standardized	terminated	updated
sequenced	started	tested	upgraded
served	steered	topped	upheld
serviced	stimulated	totaled	urged
set strategy	streamlined	traced	used
set up	strengthened	tracked	validated
settled	structured	trained	verified
shaped	studied	transacted	viewed
shepherded	submitted	transcribed	volunteered
shipped	succeeded	transferred	widened
shortened	suggested	transformed	withstood
showed	summarized	transitioned	won
signed	supervised	translated	worked
simplified	supplied	traveled	wrote

WORDS (NOUNS)

ability	experience	opportunity
background	goals	references
credentials	initiative	skills
education	objectives	

WORDS (ADJECTIVES)

adaptable	creative	dynamic	enthusiastic
ambitious	decisive	eager	flexible
assertive	dedicated	effective	friendly
capable	dependable	efficient	honest
competent	determined	energetic	imaginative
conscientious	discreet	enterprising	independent

HOW TO SAY IT

industrious	open-minded	professional	tactful
innovative	optimistic	progressive	tenacious
intelligent	persuasive	qualified	trustworthy
intuitive	persistent	reliable	versatile
loyal	pioneering	resourceful	well-organized
mature	practical	responsible	
methodical	problem-solver	self-confident	
motivated	productive	steady	

PHRASES

able to present facts clearly and succinctly

analytical and critical thinking skills

believe I could contribute/have a strong aptitude for

considered an enthusiastic worker

experience that qualifies me for

extensive experience with

good candidate/match for the job

good sense of/working knowledge of

in response to your advertisement

in this capacity

interested in pursuing a career with

may I have fifteen minutes of your time to discuss

my five years as

qualities that would be useful in

responsible for

serious interest in

sound understanding of

specialized in

supervisory abilities

take pride in my work

technical skills

well suited for

willing to travel

would enjoy attending/working/belonging

SENTENCES

I achieved a 19 percent capture rate on grants proposals submitted to local funders.

I am able to travel.

I am a skilled operator of the bridgeport mill and radial drill.

I have experience with light clerical duties.

I have three years' experience in product development.

I met every deadline while working at Brooker Associates, some of them under fairly difficult circumstances.

In my last position I performed complex CNC turning operations on diversified parts with minimum supervision, and also had Mazatrol experience.

In my two years at Arrow Appliance, I helped increase productivity by approximately 25 percent and decrease absenteeism by almost 20 percent.

I successfully reduced stock levels while maintaining shipping and order schedules, resulting in lower overhead costs.

I was responsible for all aspects of store management, including sales, personnel, inventory, profit and loss control, and overseeing the annual budget.

My work skills include data entry, alphabetical and numerical filing, photocopying, typing skills, good organizational skills, an affinity for detail, and previous experience in a legal office.

Previous employers have found me responsible and innovative.

PARAGRAPHS

Part of my duties as music director and liturgist involved instrument acquisition and maintenance, including revoicing seven ranks of the organ, constructing small percussion instruments, enlarging the handbell set from sixteen to thirty-seven, and acquiring a new studio piano for the choir. I also obtained estimates and made plans for a major overhaul of the forty-rank 1926 Casavant organ.

Because my previous jobs have all involved public contact, I am comfortable dealing with people on many levels. As an academic adviser in the MBA program at McKeown College, I provided academic guidance and course selection assistance to adult graduate students and program applicants, recruited students, and promoted the program in talks and seminars.

I am highly skilled in the use and interpretation of specifications drawings and measuring instruments, generally knowledgeable about mechanical and electrical principles, and have experience in the construction, maintenance, and machine repair industries.

My responsibilities at Edwards International included invoicing, logging deposits, resolving billing problems related to data entry, managing four other accounts receivable employees, and filing a monthly report on the department.

I have analyzed malfunctioning machines and systems (electrical, hydraulic, pneumatic), recommended corrective action, and, upon approval, made repairs or modifications. I also have a working understanding of recovery equipment, instrumentation, systems, and facilities, know how to use complicated measuring and sampling equipment, and can repair machines and equipment, working from written or oral directions and specifications.

JAMES PAWKIE
1822 Galt Road
Woodland, AL 36280
205-555-1234
pawkie@gmail.com

OBJECTIVE

An entry-level position offering future management opportunity and present learning challenges.

EDUCATION

Bachelor of Business Administration, Alabama University, 2008

Private security office license, Alabama Department of Public Safety, 2006

Certificate: Certified Security Officer, 2007

WORK EXPERIENCE

P. Picklan International, 2008–present. Duties include monitoring inventory of supplies, accounting, purchasing, stocking, clerking, scheduling, supervising five coworkers, and training fifteen new employees.

W.S. Caption Security Inc., 2007–2008. Duties included enforcing safety and pilferage rules, processing invoices, and data entry.

Alexander Clues Manufacturing, 2004–2007. Duties included assisting manager with inventory control operations, ticketing and distributing orders, receiving and shipping freight, evaluating daily reports, working with computer system, answering customer inquiries concerning inventories.

ACTIVITIES

Scoutmaster, 2006–present

Member, Rotary International

Commissioned Second Lieutenant, U.S. Army, 2004

Dean's List all four years of college

————

STELLA SUMMERSLEY SATCHELL
1913 Wells Avenue Chicago, IL 60657 312-555-1234

Professional Objective   To apply educational background, acquired experience, and creativity to a challenging position in photography.

Education   BA 2000 with photography major, University of Iowa

Knowledge & Skills	Black and white film development and printing. Color printing and filtration.
	Medium format and 35mm cameras.
	Black and white photofinishing and archival processing, including: archival washing and toning, spotting, trimming, and mounting.
	Alternative photographic processing, including: toning (selenium, sepia, copper, and iron), hand coloring, paper negatives, collage, Polaroid transfers, Liquid Light, solarization, and cross-processing.
Experience	Freelance artist/photographer/graphic designer May 2002 to present Create photographs for promotional, commercial, and educational purposes. Design, create, and layout advertisements, brochures, presentation materials, logos, and newsletters with Quark Xpress, Pagemaker, and Adobe Illustrator. Computer illustration. T-shirt design. Clients include: Ebbsworth Forms Inc., The Hutton Companies, Costanza Printing Co., Cochrane-Doyle Inc., and various individuals.
	Assistant to the Sound and Visual Collections Curator Bunker County Historical Society 1995 Accessioned new photography collections. Learned basic correct handling and storing of photographic archives. Helped coordinate informational mailing and check-in procedure for Society-sponsored statewide photodocumentary conference.
	Teaching assistant Glendower College Art Department 1995 Assisted in teaching a college-level beginning photography course. Demonstrated photographic techniques to students. Prepared and checked darkroom chemistry. Critiqued and evaluated students' progress and work.
Major Accomplishment	Fulfilled lifelong ambition to circumnavigate the globe. Traveled extensively through Western and Eastern Europe, the former Soviet Union, China, and South Asia (1990 to 1992).

JOAN PENROSE

Present Address	*Permanent Address*
14 Grace Lane	#4 Route 9N
Chance, UT 84623	Fairfield, UT 84620
801-555-2241	801-555-2789
penrose@email.com	penrose@email.com

OBJECTIVE

An entry-level management position in transportation and logistics with the opportunity to contribute to the efficient operation of a firm and to earn advancement through on-the-job performance.

EDUCATION

Bachelor of Business Administration, May 2009, from Merriam University, with a major in Transportation and Logistics and a minor in Psychology. Major GPA: 4.0; cumulative GPA: 3.4.

Coursework: Logistics Law, International Transportation and Logistics, Strategic Logistics Management, Transportation and Public Policy, Transportation Carrier Management, Transportation Economics; Accounting I and II, Business Communications, Business Law, Community and Regional Planning, Computer Science, Economics, Operations Management.

Financed 100% of college expenses through work, work-study programs, and grants.

EXPERIENCE

Merriam University Computer Lab, 2006–2009; supervised three other students; oversaw hardware repairs and updating of software library; assisted users with various software (15 hours/week, September to May only).

Swinney's Book Store, summers, 2005–2007: assembled and packed book, magazine, and giftware shipments; trained twelve employees (20 hours/week).

Creston Food Stores Inc.: Deli Manager and Clerk, summers, 2005–2007; controlled all facets of delicatessen, including catering large and small events; worked at five different stores (20 hours/week).

Lorimer Industries, Salt Lake City, June and July 2008, Transportation/ Distribution Intern: facilitated the relationship between Transportation and Customer Support Inventory Planning and Purchasing; assisted in the routing and controlling of inbound raw materials; gained experience in outbound logistics management, including warehousing and distribution.

Blaydon Logistics Case Study, August 2008: one of seven students selected to participate in logistics project at Blaydon Corporate Headquarters, San Diego;

evaluated performance measures used in the areas of transportation, customs, and export administration; presented initial findings and suggested alternative measures.

STRENGTHS

Communication: communicate well when speaking and writing; able to act as liaison between different personality types; comfortable and effective communicating with both superiors and staff.

Leadership: able to motivate a project team; background in psychology provides wide range of interpersonal skills to encourage and instruct others.

Responsibility: accustomed to being in positions of responsibility; self-motivated and willing to set goals and work to achieve them; never assume "the other person" is responsible.

Organization: use time and resources effectively; consider efficiency, planning, and accountability very important.

Computer expertise: experienced in Lilypad 1-2-3, Savvy Pagemaker, WordAlmostPerfect 9.0, ELEMENTAL programming, Venus-Calc spreadsheets, Cambridge Graphics, MacroTough Advance, and Bytewise.

Other: willing to relocate anywhere; have traveled to Europe (three times) and to the Orient (once) and thus have a global awareness of business and politics; quick learner and trained in analytical problem-solving skills; solid work ethic that finds satisfaction and pleasure in achieving work goals; daily reader of *Wall Street Journal, The Journal of Commerce, Christian Science Monitor*, and *The Utah Times*.

ACTIVITIES

Treasurer, Transportation/Logistics Club
Member, University Finance Club
Campus Chest (student-operated community service organization), business
    manager, 2008, public relations, 2009
Member, Professional Women in Transportation, Utah Chapter
Coordinator of the Business Council Peer Advisory to Transportation and
    Logistic Undergraduate Students

AWARDS

Creston's Employee-to-Employee Courtesy Award
Dean's List, eight semesters
Golden Key National Honor Society
National Collegiate Business Merit Award

———

FROM: Pip Thompson
TO: Raindance Film Festival
DATE: 4-9-2009
RE: bio for film festival program

Pip Thompson graduated magna cum laude from Yale University with a BA in Anthropology and Theater Studies. Two years in the film industry as script supervisor, production coordinator, and short-film director were followed by graduate school; she will receive her MFA in film (directing) from Columbia University in 2009.

Although Thompson admits her areas of specialization may seem unrelated to each other and a strange base on which to build a film career, she feels that anthropology, literally "the study of people," uncovers truths about human behavior while both theater and film convey those truths viscerally. Her viewfinder might not look like a microscope and her notebook contains storyboards, not observations on Inuit rituals, but she strives to direct films that give viewers insight into different cultures as a means of better understanding their own ways and the broader human experience.

A native of Minnesota, Thompson brought her interest in anthropology home with "The Windigo." Set in the preserved wilderness of northern Minnesota, the story derives its title and subject from a local Ojibwe Indian myth and dramatizes the misunderstandings that can arise between cultures. Gerard strives to emulate native ways, but he embodies a recent trend that appropriates Indian legends and beliefs without truly understanding them. Sandy, on the other hand, learns the hard way that he is biased in favor of laboratory wisdom. "The Windigo" examines ancient myths through the eyes of contemporary culture in order to shed light on the past and the present.

———

Regina Alving
1939 Norway Street
Cleveland, OH 44101
216-555-1234

OBJECTIVE

To obtain a position as an administrative assistant commensurate with my experience, capabilities, and need to be challenged

EDUCATION

2-year degree from Engstrand Technical College in office administration, 2009

WORK EXPERIENCE

Manders Realty, assistant to the president, 2006–present

Oswald Engineering Consultants Inc., administrative assistant, 2003–2006

Ibsen Manufacturing International, assistant to the vice president, 1999–2003

SKILLS

All general office duties

Typing 65 wpm

Extensive experience with Microsoft Word, Excel, Oracle Data Base, PowerPoint, Peachtree Accounting

Good oral and written communication skills

Fluent in written and spoken Spanish

Personal characteristics include being highly organized, able to take a multitask approach to the workday, self-motivated, tactful, discreet

———

See also: APPLICATIONS, APPOINTMENTS, COVER LETTERS, EM-PLOYMENT, FOLLOW-UP, REFERENCES, THANK YOU

FORTY-FOUR

SALES LETTERS

*The advertisement is one of the most interesting and difficult
of modern literary forms.*
—ALDOUS HUXLEY

Almost every letter sent by a company, business, or organization is a sales letter. Even nonbusiness letters like sympathy notes, congratulations, thank-you letters, or apologies carry a second-level message that asks the recipient to think well of the firm. Courtesy, clarity, correctness, and persuasiveness are found in letters sent by successful companies.

Sales letters aren't appropriate for all products and services, but they can get the reader to make the call or visit the store where the real selling can be done. Because they're effective and economical (compared to print and video advertising, for example), they're an integral part of most firms' marketing strategies.

Sales letters have become so sophisticated that many businesses no longer generate their own. The buzzword is "integration"—using full-service agencies to handle every aspect of advertising, including sales letters.

Kinds of Sales Letters

- announcements: changes/new products
- asking for meeting/appointment (see APPOINTMENTS)
- congratulations: purchase/new account/payment
- direct mail advertising
- follow-up: inquiries/sales letters/sales
- form letters

- goodwill (see GOODWILL)
- introducing new products/services
- invitation: open house/sale/membership/new account
- questionnaires/surveys
- responding to inquiries
- special promotions/sales/gifts/free services
- thank you: sale/new account/revived account
- trial offers: products/programs/services/subscriptions

How to Say It

- Get the reader's attention with your opening sentence, question, anecdote, or statistic.
- Create an interest in what you're selling with a strong central sales message.
- Arouse the reader's desire for your product by using specific, vivid words as well as active power verbs. One word that never gets old is "new."
- Point out how your service or product differs from similar ones, emphasizing quality and dependability.
- Convince the reader that responding to your offer is a smart move, and offer "proof" (samples, testimonials, statistics).
- Tell how to obtain your product or service.
- Give a reason for acting immediately: limited supply, expiring sale offer, future price increase, early-response discount.
- State clearly what immediate action you want them to take: "Telephone now for an appointment"; "Order one for every family member"; "Call today to arrange a demonstration"; "Return the postage-paid reply card now"; "Send for your free copy of the planning guide."
- Make it convenient to respond: order blanks with postage-paid reply envelopes, prepaid form postcards asking for a sales rep to call or for additional information, a toll-free number to call for local distributors or to place orders, order now-pay later procedures, listing of store hours and locations. (Business reply mail, with the seller paying the postage, has a 10 to 20 percent higher response rate than courtesy reply, where the buyer pays the postage.)
- Finally, echo your letter opening in some way. If you began by quoting a celebrity, finish by saying something like, "And that's why So-and-So won't drive anything but a . . ."
- Add a P.S. to repeat your main point, to emphasize an important feature, or to offer a new and strong sales point such as a money-back guarantee, a time limit for the offer, an additional bonus for buying now: "P.S. To offer

you these sale prices, we must receive your order by June 30"; "P.S. Don't forget—your fee includes a gift!"; "P.S. If you are not completely satisfied, return your Roebel Pager and we will cheerfully issue you a full refund." Lin Yutan wrote, "A letter is a soliloquy, but a letter with a postscript is a conversation."

What Not to Say

- Don't make too many points in one letter. Concentrate on your strongest one or two sales points, add one in the postscript if you like, and save the others for follow-up letters.
- Don't, in general, use numerous exclamation marks or exaggerated adjectives such as astonishing, revolutionary, incredible, sensational, extraordinary, spectacular. Describe instead concrete features, benefits, details, and product claims.
- Don't ask questions relating to the sale ("Can you afford to throw this letter away?" "Can anyone today get along without one?"). It's poor psychology to enlist readers in a dialogue in which they might not answer your question "correctly." Questions derail your reader from the one-way train of thought that leads to a sale and bring to full consciousness the idea of refusal.
- Don't say, "We never hold a sale! Our everyday prices are so low we don't need to." Human nature likes a sale. Even customers who regularly use your products or services and think they're reasonably priced are attracted by a bargain. By offering occasional discounts, sales, clearances, and special purchase promotions, you'll create a sense of excitement and willingness to buy in both old and new customers.
- Avoid jargon unless you're sure that your target audience is familiar with it.
- Don't threaten ("You'll be sorry if you don't order now"). It is off-putting and it tempts people to call your bluff. However, telling customers that their names will be removed from the mailing list if they don't order soon is sometimes effective because people fear missing out on something.
- Don't preach, scold, correct, or write down to customers ("you probably don't know this, but . . ."). Ask others to read your letter to be sure no patronizing tone has crept in.
- Avoid the first-name, pseudo-friend approach. Business columnist Louis Rukeyser received an impressive reader response after a column on form sales letters. According to him, "The artificially intimate stuff appears particularly irritating."
- Don't make assumptions: that your reader knows what you are talking

about, is familiar with an industry term, can picture your product, agrees with your premises. Dale Carnegie wrote, "I deal with the obvious. I present, reiterate and glorify the obvious—because the obvious is what people need to be told."

Tips on Writing

■ Whether you're selling a product, service, idea, space, credit, or goodwill, the sales letter requires more work before you write than it does to actually write it. You need to know everything about your product or service. You need to know your reader, assembling as much data as possible. "Knowing something about your customer is just as important as knowing everything about your product." (Harvey Mackay) Pinpoint and develop a strong central selling point. Consider other factors (timing, design, length, developing a coupon or sample). Only after adequate preparation is a successful letter written.

■ Everyone agrees on the best way to begin a sales letter: with a bang! There's no agreement, however, on the type of "bang." Possibilities include: a surprising fact or statistic; a touching or dramatic anecdote; a personal story; significant savings; the offer of a gift, coupon, or booklet; a thought-provoking question or quotation; a joke or riddle; a celebrity endorsement, quote, or tie-in; a who-what-when-where-why paragraph; your strongest selling factor; a reference to something you have in common or to a previous contact or purchase; telling readers in a convincing way that they are special; asking or offering a favor; perhaps even a negative or unexpected statement.

■ It's hard to distinguish between the clever gimmick, hook, or attention-getter and the too-cute-for-its-own-good approach. When taking a risk with a novel overture, ask others to evaluate your letter. If it's clever, the rewards are great. If you stray on the side of coy or insensitive, the results can be fatal.

■ State the cost of your product or service. Customers ignore sales messages without prices, assuming they can't afford the item. Cost determines most purchases, and if the customer has to call to find out what it is, the extra trouble is often not worth it when a competitor's cost is available in its sales message.

■ Although both are necessary, emotional appeals tend to outpull intellectual appeals. Tie your message to some basic human emotion: love ("your child will have hours of fun!"); the need for love ("heads will turn when you wear this"); prestige ("your home will be a standout with . . ."); ambition ("learn new management techniques overnight"); security ("smoke-alarm with built-in battery tester"). Show how your service or product will bring the customer better health, popularity, pride of ownership or accomplishment, success, more money, improved appearance, more comfort and leisure, social and business advancement, loyalty.

■ From start to finish, the focus of a sales letter is on the prospective customer. Use the words "you" and "your" frequently, and describe the product in terms of benefits to the customers: how it relates to their needs, problems, and interests; how it can improve their lives, save them money, and make them feel more confident. The customer has only one question: "What will this do for me?" Persuade potential buyers that they need your product not so much because it's a great product, but because it is great for *them*.

■ Choose a consistent "voice" that complements your product or service and maintain it throughout your letter: friendly, neighbor-to-neighbor; serious and intellectual; humorous, lively, and fast-moving; brisk and businesslike; urgent and hard-hitting; sophisticated; soothing and reassuring; mysterious; technical or informational; emotional.

■ Use colorful descriptive words, strong verbs, appealing images. Sometimes sales letter writers are so intent on either educating the prospective customer or building up a case with statistics, background information, and reports that they forget how boring and how un-client-centered such a message is.

■ Use repetition to emphasize a main point, clarify complicated material, and lend an attractive rhythm to your letter.

■ Sales messages can mimic other familiar letters: letters of congratulations, thank-you letters, announcements, invitations, letters of welcome, holiday greetings.

■ Create and foster credibility by means of testimonials, case histories, research studies, statistics, company reputation, product usage test results, comparison with similar products, free samples or trial periods, guaranties/warranties, celebrity endorsements, photographs of actual use, user polls. Whenever possible, guarantee the buyer's satisfaction in some way.

■ How long should a sales letter be? The key is that each word does its job, each word sells. A poorly written letter is in no way redeemed by being short, and some well-written long letters have enjoyed a high response rate. In general, however, shorter letters are better letters. Concentrate on what absolutely needs to be said—whether that takes one page, two, four, or ten. What needs to be kept short in any case are your paragraphs.

■ To increase the desirability of responding, offer discounts, bargain prices, special offers, delayed no-interest payments, gifts, in-store certificates, enclosures, coupons, brochures, samples, or trial period.

■ Attention-getting devices make your message more memorable: a message on the envelope that inspires the person to open it (studies show that mailers have about fifteen seconds to get customers to open the envelope or they lose them); handwriting part of the message (the P.S., for example); underlining certain words to look as though you personally emphasized the important points; yellow highlighting of key phrases; colored inks and papers; graphics; questionnaire or survey format; boxed information; italics, capital letters, quotation marks, unusual typefaces; design elements such as heads, subheads, white space, short paragraphs, indented material, and bulleted lists. Attention-getting devices are not always appropriate; to sell bank cards, life insurance, healthcare services, or other sedate products and services, you want a more traditional format.

Special Situations

■ When responding to customer inquiries, the cover letter is a sales letter of the most potentially effective type because you've been given a focused opportunity to sell your product or service. Although the enclosure should sell itself (or the product it describes), the cover letter offers a strong sales message and additional incentives.

■ A series of letters is often effective. When a segment of the market is susceptible to your product (because of previous purchases, for example), contact them several times—but with a different focus each time: a new premium, an additional benefit of your product or service, time growing short with the offer expiring soon, two-for-one price, discount. Or, target customers buying one of your products with a sales letter promoting another product or service that, out of long habit, they don't "see" anymore. For example, customers who regularly use a hair salon may forget that they can also buy an extensive line of hair-care products, use tanning booths, or schedule manicures.

■ With a versatile product or service (or a number of different products in your line), you can reach different target audiences with letters tailored to their needs. A greenhouse manufacturer might write different sales letters to farmers, suburban homeowners, businesses, apartment dwellers, and even college students (the desktop miniature greenhouse).

■ Sales letters aimed at former customers emphasize your appreciation for past business, your desire to serve them again, products or services introduced since your last contact with them, your confidence that you can satisfy their needs. You could ask if there is a reason that they no longer bring their business to you. This may provide you with useful information. Or it may remind the customer that there is no particular reason.

■ E-mail sales messages have exploded, with the greatest number of them classified as spam—that is, messages people do not want to receive, will not read, and defend themselves against by means of filtering software. E-mail is being used successfully, however, to sell products and services by individuals and companies who respect their customers: (1) they e-mail only those people who have first contacted them via the sellers' websites; (2) they always offer, and honor, requests by recipients to unsubscribe; (3) they are careful not to flood e-boxes with their messages; (4) they make their e-mails worth reading by offering special sales, discounts, or useful information.

Format

■ Most sales letters are computer-generated—either standard form letters or letters in which names, addresses, and salutations are personalized using a mass mail merge feature. The latter gives form letters a more personal look (unless you are also inserting the person's name here and there throughout the letter, which actually gives the opposite impression).

■ For highly select audiences, use good quality stationery, first-class postage, a real person's signature, and an individually typed address.

WORDS

absolute	demonstrated	high-quality	pledge
acquaint	dependable	immediate	portable
adaptable	details	indulge	powerful
advanced	discovery	inexpensive	practical
advantages	durable	informative	precision
affordable	economical	ingenious	premium
all-new	effective	innovative	productive
attractive	exceptional	instant	professional
authentic	exciting	invaluable	profitable
benefits	exclusive	investment	proven
brand-new	expert	lasting	quality
breakthrough	exquisite	low-cost	rapid-action
choice	extensive	low-priced	reasonable
classic	facts	luxurious	rebate
clever	features	moneymaking	refund
comfortable	flair	natural	reliable
compact	flexible	new	results
confident	genuine	nostalgic	revolutionary
contemporary	guaranteed	offer	reward
convenient	half-price	opportunity	safe
dazzling	handy	optional	satisfaction
delightful	helpful	personalization	secure

solution	successful	unconditional	versatile
sophisticated	super	up-to-date	warranted
spectacular	thrifty	urgent	waterproof
state-of-the-art	tremendous	useful	wholesale
stunning	trial	user-friendly	
substantial	unbreakable	valuable	

PHRASES

add a new dimension to

advanced design

all for one low price

all-in-one convenience

as an added bonus

at a discount/a fraction of the cost/
  great savings/no expense to you

avoid worry/embarrassment/
  discomfort/risk

be more efficient

be the first to

both practical and beautiful/
  decorative

budget-pleasing prices

built-in features

business advancement

buy with confidence

can pay for itself in

carefree upkeep

choose from over 20 styles/cards/
  models/varieties

come in and try

compact design

complimentary copy

contemporary/gracious design

customer support

cutting edge

direct-to-you low prices

direct your attention to

discover for yourself

dramatic difference

easier and more enjoyable/
  comfortable

easier to use than ever before

easy/carefree maintenance

easy-to-follow instructions

elegant styling

engineered for dependability

exciting details/offer

exclusive features

experience the pleasure of

express your personality

fast, safe, easy-to-use

finely crafted

fit-any-budget price

fully automated/warranted

get full details

gives you your choice of

greater safety/convenience/
  pleasure/popularity

great gift idea

have the satisfaction of knowing

if not completely satisfied

if you accept this invitation/respond
     right away/send
     payment now

impressive collection

improved appearance

increased enjoyment

incredibly low introductory rate/
     price of

indulge yourself

influence others

intelligent way to

in these fast-moving times

invite you to

join millions of others who

just pennies each

key to your peace of mind

lasting beauty

lets you enjoy more of your favorite

look forward to sending you

low, low prices

loyal customers like you

make it easy for yourself

makes any day special

many advantages of

money's worth

more advanced features

more money/comfort/leisure

more than fifty years of service

most versatile, powerful, and
     exciting study aid available

no matter which set you choose

no more mess/lost sales/errors/fuss/
     worry

no-risk examination

no strings attached

now for the first time

of particular importance to
     you

one easy operation

one of the largest and most
     respected

one reason among many to order

one size fits all

order today

our top-seller

outstanding features

over 50,000 satisfied customers

perfect gift for yourself or a loved
     one

pleased to be able to offer you

preferred customer/rates

previously sold for

price you'll appreciate

pride of accomplishment

privileges include

professional quality

prompt, courteous service

proven reliability/technology

provides the finest home hair care
     at the least cost

ready to spoil you with its powerful
     features

reasonably priced

reduced price

revolutionary approach

reward yourself with

risk nothing

rugged and dependable

save money/time

satisfaction guaranteed

security in your later years

see for yourself

simple steps

so unusual and striking that

special benefits/introductory offer/
value

state of the art

step in the right direction

stop those costly losses with

supply is limited

surprise your special someone with

take advantage of this opportunity

take a giant step forward toward

take a moment right now to look
over this

takes the gamble out of choosing

time is growing short

timeless elegance

time-tested

top of the line

treat yourself to

unconditional money-back
guarantee

under no obligation to

under our simple plan

unequaled savings and
convenience

unique limited edition creations

unique opportunity

urge you to

use it anywhere, anytime

we're making this generous offer
because

what better way to

whole family can enjoy

with no obligation on your part

with our compliments

won't cost you a thing to

won't find better quality anywhere

world of enjoyment waiting for you

you can be proud of

you don't risk a penny

you'll be amazed to discover

you might expect these to cost as
much as

your money back

you will appreciate the outstanding
quality of these

SENTENCES

At this low price, every home should have one.

Be the first in your community to have one!

But act now—we expect a sizable response and we want to be certain that your
order can be filled.

Call today to arrange a demonstration.

Discover savings of up to 50 percent.

Discover the elegance of a genuine leather briefcase with discreet gold initials.

Don't miss out!

Do your holiday shopping the easy way.

Enjoy it for a 15-day home trial.

Every item is offered at a discount.

If you are not completely satisfied, simply return it for a full credit.

In order to make this offer, we must have your check by September 1.

It's a first!

It's a no-strings offer.

Join us today.

Just bring this letter with you when you come in to sign up.

Just what makes the Blount Filing System so great?

May I make an appointment with you next week to explain/show/demonstrate our latest line of products?

Now there's a new magazine just for you.

Order one for every family member.

Please don't delay your decision—we expect a heavy demand for the Ellesmere filet knife.

P.S. To lock in these great rates, we must receive your deposit by October 15.

Returning the postage-paid reply card does not obligate you in any way.

Send for your free copy of the Bemerton planning guide.

Send today for free, no-obligation information on rates and available discounts, special services, and easy claims filing.

Take a look at the enclosed brochure for a sneak preview.

Telephone Sarah Lash, your personal representative, for an appointment.

The Art Deco look fits almost any decorating scheme.

There is absolutely no risk on your part.

There's no cost or obligation, of course.

These low prices are effective only until June 1.

This is just one more reason why our products have won such overwhelming acceptance.

Use the order form and postpaid reply envelope enclosed to receive your first Holiday Bell absolutely free.

We cannot extend this unusual offer beyond May 25, 2011.

We invite you to complete the enclosed reservation request form and return it now to confirm your choice of dates.

We're making this unprecedented offer to a select group of business executives.

We take all the risks.

We've missed you!

You can choose from over 150 different programs.

You can now acquire a two-line telephone for far less than you ever thought possible.

You'll appreciate these fine features.

You'll like our convenient evening and weekend hours; you'll love our brand-new equipment and experienced teachers!

You'll see that Rockminster China isn't like other china.

You may not have ever used a hibachi, which is why we are making you this no-risk trial offer.

You must see the complete series for yourself to appreciate how it can enrich your life.

PARAGRAPHS

Are you still paying premiums for the same homeowner's policy you signed up for ten years ago? Things have changed. You may want to compare what's available today with what you bought ten years ago.

The enclosed Special Introductory Invitation can be guaranteed for a limited time only. We urge you to reply within the next 10 days.

Congratulations on your election to membership in the Society for Historic Preservation! If you accept this membership offer—and I certainly hope you will—you will become part of a unique and influential group. As a member you will enjoy such important benefits as voting privileges on matters of national importance, a subscription to the monthly magazine *Preservation*, and many more. Please mail the enclosed Confirmation of Election by May 31.

If for any reason, at any time, you are not satisfied with your Haverley Air Cleaner, you can return it to us for a complete and prompt refund. No questions asked.

P.S. The cookbook of your choice and the lucite book stand are both yours free—without obligation. All you need to do is send in the enclosed form.

Send no money now. You will be billed at the time of shipment for any items ordered, plus shipping and sales tax (if applicable). You do not have to pay until you are totally convinced of the high quality and outstanding appeal of our lithographs and prints. If you are not delighted in every way, return your purchases within ten days, and you'll owe nothing!

There's one sure way to convince you that Bryerley Bath Beads are the last word in luxurious skin-softeners. We're enclosing sample packets of two of our most popular Bryerley scents, Gardenia and Lily of the Valley.

P.S. This is your last chance to buy the kits at these low prices. Rising material costs require a moderate price increase effective next month.

You want to give that special child in your life the finest reading—her or his very own books—but you don't have the time to look at thousands of children's books to find the best. That's where we come in.

Is a housecleaning service for you? We think so because you want the best for yourself and your family . . . and that takes time. Time you don't always have after working all week and meeting important family needs after hours. We can offer you thorough, reasonably priced, once-a-week housecleaning that will make a big difference in your life. Think about what you could do with the hours you now spend on housework. Think about walking into a clean house at night. And then think about giving us a call to schedule an estimate interview.

SAMPLE LETTERS

Dear MasterGold Cardmember,

A revolutionary new service is now available to valued MasterGold cardmembers—and you're among the first invited to enroll.

CreditReport service is a valuable new credit tool that allows you to guard your privileged credit status. Membership in CreditReport entitles you to:

- Unlimited access to copies of your CreditReport record.
- Automatic notification when anyone receives a copy of your CreditReport files.
- One convenient document that organizes all your personal finances.
- Convenient application for loans or financing at participating credit grantors.
- Credit card protection: At no extra charge we'll register all your credit, charge, and ATM cards in case of loss or theft.

Best of all, your membership includes an unconditional money-back guarantee, so you can enjoy all the privileges of membership without risk.

This is a valuable service for MasterGold cardmembers. I urge you to look over the enclosed materials and consider this special offer now.

Sincerely,

————

Dear Executive:

According to several management studies, the single most important characteristic of an effective executive is the ability to manage time.

Are you meeting your deadlines? Can you list your current projects in order of importance? Do you know where you're headed over the next week, month, year? Can you find things when you need them? Do you assign work in the most time-effective ways?

If you answered no to any of these questions, you're sure to benefit from our popular, effective Time Management Workshop.

In just two days you learn how to set priorities, how to use special tools to help you organize your time, and how to develop interpersonal skills to help you deal with unnecessary interruptions, inefficient staff, and group projects.

In fact, we don't want to be one of those interruptions, so we'll make this short. We simply suggest that you save time by making time for the next Time Management Workshop in your area. You can do this in under a minute by checking off a convenient date and signing the enclosed postage-paid reply card or by calling 800-555-1707 to register.

This is one workshop that won't be a waste of time!

Sincerely,

————

Dear Marietta Lyddon,

You were a member of the Atlas Fitness Club from March 15, 2002, to November 18, 2008, and according to our records you worked out regularly.

Whatever your reasons for not being with us the past several years, you may want to know about some changes that have taken place since you were last here:

New this year: Olympic-size pool with extended hours, 5:30 a.m. to midnight. A lifeguard is on duty at all times.

New this year: Membership packages designed to fit your use patterns. You may now choose between an all-use pass or a pass that specifies morning hours, early morning hours, after-five hours, evening hours, late evening hours.

New this year: Peripheral services that our members—most of whom are busy working people like yourself—have requested: a personal check-cashing service; yogurt, soup, and mineral water machines in the lobby; a telephone for the use of members making local calls; all-new padlocks for the lockers.

New last year: We have 50 percent more equipment in the weight lifting room, and three new Nautilus units.

If you liked us before, you'll love us now. I think it's worth a look, and I'm so convinced of this that I'm offering you a two-week membership for FREE.

Just bring this letter with you when you come to give us another look!

Sincerely yours,

———

See also: ANNOUNCEMENTS, APPRECIATION, CONGRATULATIONS, COVER LETTERS, CREDIT, FOLLOW-UP, GOODWILL, HOLIDAYS, INVITATIONS, ORDERS, REQUESTS, THANK YOU

FORTY-FIVE

SENSITIVE LETTERS

*When it comes to bombshells, there are few that can be more effective
than that small, flat, frail thing, a letter.*
—MARGARET DELAND

In some difficult situations, writing a letter is more effective than a face-to-face encounter. "Most people think better on their seat than on their feet." (Dianna Booher) When writing a letter, you have time to reflect on what has happened, to inform yourself of related or supporting facts, to choose your words so that they convey exactly what you want to convey, and to rewrite the letter as many times as you need to until it accurately presents your position.

Letters Require Sensitive Handling When You Must

- ask someone to return an engagement ring
- borrow money from a friend or family member
- break off a relationship
- claim credit for your work
- clear yourself of an unjust accusation
- deliver bad news
- inquire about a gift or check that hasn't been acknowledged
- offer unsolicited and probably unwelcome advice
- remind someone of an unpaid personal loan
- report a child's unpleasant behavior
- report sexual harassment

- reprimand an employee (see also EMPLOYMENT)
- respond to someone with a terminal illness (see "GET WELL")
- tell the other person they're wrong
- turn someone down for a job whom you know well
- uninvite guests

How to Say It

- Write promptly. Nothing will make a difficult letter more difficult to write than putting it off.
- Begin with a courteous expression about something, however small, that you can agree upon or that you have in common.
- Admit (if it's true) that you're uncomfortable with the situation.
- State the issue clearly and directly. Dressing up your message in big words, roundabout phrases, and conciliatory sentences only antagonizes the other person. If you have trouble writing this part of the letter, say your message aloud as though speaking to a friend. Boil down your "conversation" to a sentence or two that expresses the heart of the matter.
- Provide facts and details of the issue.
- Convey your understanding of the other person's position.
- Admit your role in the situation, if you have one. When you take responsibility for your contribution, others are more likely to own up to theirs.
- Examine your position for areas of negotiation. Can you trade one point for another? Can you accept anything less than what you originally wanted?
- State what you are asking or what solution you want.
- Close with a wish to put the matter behind you, with an expression of confidence that the situation will be resolved, with a statement that a satisfactory solution will benefit both of you, or with a sentence conveying your goodwill.

What Not to Say

- Don't tell people what to do (this sentence doesn't count). Words like "must," "ought," and "should" raise most people's hackles. Replace them with "might like to," "could consider," or other more open-ended phrases.
- Don't write unpleasantries. They live forever and you will not forget—or be allowed to forget—them.
- Don't use words that trigger negative reactions in the reader. Although almost any words, when strung together in the right order, could annoy a person, some are immediately inflammatory: "obviously" and "clearly" (of course it isn't obvious or clear, or the other person would have known

it—are you saying they're stupid?); "you appear to think," "according to you," "you claim," and "if you are to be believed" (these belittle the other person's word); "you must agree" or "at least you will admit" (not so—these phrases make the person want to not agree and not admit).

- Don't use words like "problem," "argument," "battle," "disagreement," or those labeling a situation negative or adversarial.
- Don't exaggerate or dramatize: "You egregiously underestimated"; "In all my years as a coach I've never seen anything as reprehensible"; "I will never be able to forget what you did"; "You have contributed absolutely nothing to the department." When the words "never" and "always" appear, you are probably exaggerating or dramatizing. "Magnifying a matter is not the way to mend it." (Ivy Compton-Burnett)
- Don't be too "sensitive" when writing a letter about a sensitive issue: "I hesitated a long time before writing this . . ."; "I hate to write because I know how upset you get"; "Now don't be mad, but . . ."; "Promise me you won't take this the wrong way . . ." State calmly and neutrally what the issues are; leave the emotions (theirs and yours) out of it.
- Concentrate on facts instead of feelings. "I don't feel this is fair" does not carry as much weight as, "The guidelines for the competition stated that . . ."
- Don't assume you have all the facts. Check your assumptions. Particularly when several people are involved, an issue can become muddled.
- Don't make a decision sound negotiable if it is not. It is kinder to be clear that the answer is no, the news is bad, the response is negative.
- Don't deal with other matters in a letter about a touchy situation; save them for later. Sometimes people try to hide the difficult part of the letter in a jumble of news, offhand remarks, or other distractions. It doesn't work.
- Don't try to teach people a lesson, lecture them, or label their behavior if you want to achieve a specific goal (the return of a tool, repayment of a debt, stopping a behavior, undoing a wrong). If you want to vent and don't care if you ever see the person again, it doesn't matter what you say.
- Don't put people on the defensive by attacking them or disparaging their personality, character, intelligence, or looks. People who have been made to feel stupid and little are not apt to give you what you want. Focus on the behavior, the facts, the central issue. Getting personal indicates a weak position and "anger is not an argument." (Daniel Webster)
- Don't threaten (lawsuit, loss of your friendship, some action). It won't solve the problem and it weakens your side of the issue. "Never give anyone an ultimatum unless you are prepared to lose." (Abigail Van Buren)

Tips on Writing

■ Think twice before offering unsolicited advice or "help." "It's awfully important to know what is and what is not your business." (Gertrude Stein)

■ Before writing the letter, finish this sentence: "I want them to . . ." Do you want a rebate, an exchange, repairs? Do you want an apology, a corrected statement, a credit? Do you want something redone? Do you want to convince the person that facts, statistics, opinions are wrong? Be clear about your goal.

■ Link some good news to the bad news. This shouldn't be artificial or inappropriate good news, but any upbeat items help put the unpleasant part of the letter in a more hopeful context.

■ When possible, help the other person save face. Set up the situation so that the person can do what you want and at the same time feel generous, gracious, powerful, and willing.

■ We usually prefer active voice to passive voice. However, the passive voice is more tactful in a touchy situation. Instead of writing, "You did this," write, "This was done."

■ You can say you are angry, disappointed, upset, distressed, appalled, or anything else you might feel. In fact, the more carefully you choose the words that describe your position, the clearer the communication will be. What is unacceptable is abusing the other person verbally. The difference often lies between "I" statements and "you" statements: "I am upset about the dent in my car door" is appropriate; "You are an idiot and they should take away your license" is not—unless, of course, you don't care if the person pays for the dent or if you ever see them again. Strive for a letter that is factual, dispassionate, considerate, and evenhanded. When you write a letter in the midst of your anger, don't mail it; reread and rewrite your letter several times over a period of days.

■ When writing a letter about a sensitive subject, ask someone you trust to read your letter before you send it.

Special Situations

■ A profoundly bitter, prejudiced, hostile, accusatory, or hate-mongering letter requires careful handling. If you think the writer could be dangerous, consult with police or an attorney. In any case, you need never respond to an abusive letter. At the mild end of the spectrum, when the person simply seems to be letting off steam (and you think a response is called for), reply with "I am sorry to hear you feel that way."

■ When writing to borrow money from a friend or relative, remain business-like about how much you need, why you need it, and when you will repay it. Offer to sign an agreement. Reassure the person that you will understand if they have to refuse you.

■ Sexual harassment consists of unwelcome, unsolicited, nonreciprocated sexual advances, requests for sexual favors, sexually motivated physical contact, or communication of a sexual nature, usually by someone who has power over another person. It includes comments, jokes, looks, innuendoes, and physical contact, and emphasizes a person's sex role over any function as a worker. It is against the law. If you are on the receiving end of such behavior, a good first step is a letter notifying the person that you consider the conduct sexual harassment. It used to be that saying anything about another's offensive behavior not only got you nowhere, but got you in trouble. This is no longer quite as true. Depending on your situation, a quiet warning note might be all that's needed. If you are the offender and have been called on it, (1) educate yourself about the issues until you feel sure you know where the boundaries are; (2) write a brief note of apology, thanking the person for letting you know and stating that you will comply with the request; (3) never repeat the behavior. Few reasonable people will bring a charge of sexual harassment against a one-time offender who didn't realize the original harm done and who is now apologetic and reformed.

■ In the case of a serious disagreement, begin by referring to the previous correspondence or to the event responsible for the present letter. Outline the two opposing views or actions. Give clear (perhaps numbered) reasons for your stand, using statistics, quotations from an employee handbook, supportive anecdotal material, and names of witnesses or others who agree with you (with their permission). If appropriate, suggest an intermediate stage of negotiation: a reply to specific questions in your letter; further research; a meeting between the two of you or with third parties present; visits to a lawyer, accountant, or other appropriate adviser. If the disagreement has reached the stage where you can effectively do this, finish by stating clearly the outcome you desire. End with your best wishes for a solution acceptable to both of you and a reference to good future relations.

■ When requesting a favor that makes you uncomfortable, admit it. You will make the request more easily if you can accept no for an answer, and if you make this clear to the other person.

■ When reprimanding an employee, begin with a positive or complimentary remark. Describe the employee behavior and tell why it is unacceptable. Mention how it came to your attention. Suggest how the employee can improve or change. Outline any previous history of the same behavior (documenting this with dated reprimands). State the consequences of continuing the behavior. Tell exactly what you expect the employee to do (apologize, take a class, speak to you, not repeat the behavior). Say that this letter will be placed in their file. Close with an expression of confidence that the situation will be successfully dealt with. You may want the employee to sign and date the letter to verify having read it. A reprimand is brief, respectful, encouraging, and positive (instead of writing, "Don't send out any letters with misspellings," write, "Please use your spellcheck function followed by a dictionary check of any questionable words").

■ Assumptions are dangerous. Don't assume that when you send invitations, everyone will be able to make it up your front steps. Don't assume that a divorce is either good or bad. Don't assume that a death is a "blessing" or a "release" or "God's will." Don't assume that having children is a universal human undertaking; some people's tragedy is that they are unable to have the children they long for, while other people have good reasons for not having them. In short, be sensitive to other people's realities. When dealing with a sensitive situation, reread your letter with an eye for unthinking assumptions about the other person and their feelings.

Format

■ Sensitive business matters are typed on letterhead stationery to convey formality and a certain neutrality. This will have a "cool" tone. When a business matter has personal aspects, handwrite it. This letter will have a "warm" tone.

■ A sensitive personal matter is dealt with in a letter written by hand or typed on personal stationery.

■ E-mail and fax are inappropriate for sensitive issues.

WORDS

ambiguous	distressing	negotiate	troublesome
annoyance	disturbing	object	troubling
arrange	embarrassment	oppose	unfavorable
bothersome	extent	predicament	unfortunate
burdensome	hardship	problem	unhappy
circumstances	impede	protest	unpromising
complex	inconvenient	puzzling	unsuccessful
difficult	inopportune	refusal	untimely
dilemma	intervene	regrettable	unwilling
discuss	involved	reluctant	upsetting
disinclined	mediate	thorny	worrying

agree to disagree	look forward to
apologize for my part	pleased to be able to discuss
appreciate your willingness to	rough going
come to terms	state of affairs
deal with	ticklish situation
difficult to understand	with your help
find a middle ground	work for a happy ending
give and take	work out a solution
happy to sit down and discuss	would like to hear your side
in the future	

SENTENCES

Do you have time to discuss this over a cup of coffee?

I feel sure you will make the best decision for all involved.

I hope you will understand that while I am in the early stages of recovery I simply can't be around some of my old friends—wish me well and I will call you when I can.

I understand you have some thoughts about my work, behavior, and looks, and I would like to discuss these with you directly instead of hearing them secondhand.

The language and tone of your last letter is unacceptable to us. Please forward our file to someone else in your organization who can handle this matter.

You don't have to understand where I'm coming from or agree with me or even like what I'm saying, but would you—as my good, dear friend—do me the great favor of not using crude language around me?

PARAGRAPHS

I'm sorry to have to write again about the $500 you owe me. I helped you with the clear understanding that the money would be repaid within two months. I've given you at least a month's grace, but I must insist on receiving the money before the end of the week.

I was surprised to learn last week from Miles MacPhadraick that you and he had been discussing your new alarm system. I suspect I misunderstood him because it sounded like the system I've been working on. You might be interested in seeing my record of invention (enclosed). I'd be happy to show you what I'm doing if you stop by the lab sometime.

Alert! Alert! Jay, I need my kayak. Now! Every time I've called I was sure we understood each other. Maybe a note will do the trick. Just keep saying to yourself: Kayak. Back. To Jack.

I'd like to set the record straight: it was not I who called you an ugly name. I don't know who it was. The person who ascribed it to me was mistaken. In any case, that's not my style—and I think you know that.

As you know, the Financial Commission has been very pleased with your work. Unfortunately, there is not quite enough of it. Your coffee breaks and lunch hours have been growing increasingly lengthy over the past few months. I realize it's tempting to slip out to run an errand or two or to go to the gym for a workout, but the company has a zero tolerance policy for short workdays. Please let us have a full measure of your fine work.

As you can imagine, I wish I had any other response to give you. I would have enjoyed working with you. The decision has been made, however, to hire someone with more experience in livestock production.

Christy and Ben tell me that Jimmy and Letty have been teasing them unmercifully about having two mothers instead of a mother and father. Some of the remarks sound oddly adult—not the sort of thing that preschoolers would come up with on their own. I know you have not been particularly happy to have us in the neighborhood, but we're sad to see the children involved this way. We'd like to invite the two of you and Jimmy and Letty for a couscous dinner one night next week. Perhaps we can find enough common ground to allow us to live in a neighborly way.

About your visit this weekend—Biddy is upset at the thought of having L'il Dickens in the house again. She isn't frightened of all dogs but L'il Dickens feels unpredictable to her. At any rate, we've made reservations for you at the Gargery Motel nearby. They welcome pets. Let us know if this is all right with you.

You're my brother and I love you, but please don't come to the house again when you've been drinking. It disturbs the children, and because they look up to you it sets an unfortunate example. You'll be welcome any other time. When you've been drinking, I will not be able to invite you in.

SAMPLE LETTERS

Dear Mrs. Burdock,

You may not have noticed the wine stains on my linen tablecloth when you returned it. Because they had set, the stains needed special treatment by the dry cleaners.

Knowing you, I thought you would want to take responsibility for the dry cleaning bill, which I'm enclosing.

(This will also make me much more likely to lend it the next time!)

Sincerely,
H. Rimini

———

Dear Rev. Dawkbell,

I am able to write this letter only because I am sure that you are well convinced of my deep admiration for you. Leyminster Grammar School has become everything a good school ought to be—and you know that I credit you with the fine progress made these last few years.

I am not sure that you are aware that the students have taken to joking among themselves about how noticeable your aftershave lotion is. My own experience is that a person becomes so used to it himself that he rarely notices its effects on others.

We needn't ever mention this again, but I thought you wouldn't mind this little note.

Truly yours,
J. S. Fletcher

———

Dear Brett,

I was pleased to get your note saying that your divorce is final—pleased because I know this is the way things had to be.

Did you ever see these lines by Elizabeth Cady Stanton? "Such is the nature of the marriage relation that a breach once made cannot be healed, and it is the height of folly to waste one's life in vain efforts to make a binary compound of two diverse elements. What would we think of the chemist who should sit twenty years trying to mix oil and water, and insist upon it that his happiness depended upon the result of the experiment?"

Congratulations on making it through this painful and often inhuman process. Surviving the past two years the way you have shows a strength of character that I know will stand you in good stead as you establish a new, fuller, and happier life.

I am always ready, dear friend, for a cup of tea, a chat, or a visit to the art gallery of your choice.

Love and a hug,
Frances

———

Dear Ms. Lucas,

I think you know I was unhappy with the author's override of almost all my editing suggestions on the golf book. You and I agree that in general the author should have the last word. However, in this case, the final manuscript contains many universally recognized grammar errors, inappropriate capitalizations, spelling inconsistencies, and such a "creative" approach to outlining that even a fourth-grader would notice.

Would you please see that I am not listed anywhere in the book as its editor? I don't mind if the author prefers his version, and I received a check for the hours I spent on the manuscript, so I have no complaints about the work itself. But I wouldn't like anyone to think that book was an example of my editing skills.

Thank you!

————

Dear Friends,

Your stay with us at the lake last week was delightful. It made me determined not to let so much time go by before our next visit. I especially enjoyed getting to know James and Camilla—they were toddlers the last time I saw them!

I am assuming (I hope correctly, for the sake of our friendship) that you would want to know this. After you left, I discovered that several of our bottles of liquor were missing, and others had been seriously depleted. I was also missing a half bottle of antianxiety pills and my prescription allergy medication. I have tried to think of all other possibilities (theft, other visitors, misplaced items) but find none that make sense.

I thought you needed to be alerted to the possibility of a problem, but now that I've done so, I will not mention this again.

I send all our love and remain

Your loving friend,

————

Dear Mr. Torpenhow,

I have received your letter demanding the return of your dog and your mention of taking legal action.

It would be helpful to review the situation. I found the dog on July 18 in a ditch off Highway 48, nearly dead of malnutrition and heat prostration. It also had a broken leg. It wore no collar or other identification.

Thus far, I have only your unsupported word that she is your dog.

My veterinarian and her associate have confirmed that the leg was broken approximately six months ago but was not set and apparently received no treatment whatsoever. Since the leg was broken, the dog was bred and gave birth to a litter. They tell me this neglect of the broken leg and continued use of the animal for breeding purposes in spite of it is animal abuse.

I am enclosing photocopies of my veterinary bills. So far they amount to $845.

I would need to be certain that the dog is in fact yours. I would need to be repaid for the veterinary bills, as well as for dog food and vitamins. I would need to be certain the SPCA considers you a fit owner for the dog.

I am sending copies of this letter to my lawyer, my veterinarian, the local Humane Society, and the national Society for Prevention of Abuse to Animals.

Sincerely,

Dear Sandra,

We feel so lucky to have you as our Babysitter in Chief—the children are crazy about you. We're looking forward to seeing you again this weekend.

One thing: Our last phone bill had a number of long-distance charges that we didn't recognize. Upon checking the dates and after speaking with several of the recipients of the calls, we realized they were yours.

I'm enclosing a copy of the bill with those calls circled. I noticed that all the calls were made after 10:30 p.m., when the children would have been asleep. This agrees with my sense of you—that you would not be talking on the phone when the children were awake. Because of this good sense of responsibility, I felt you would want to reimburse us for the calls.

And, now, that's the end of that, OK?

Dear Mrs. Tilford,

We all enjoyed Mary's stay with us last weekend. Because it was so pleasant, I'm sorry to be writing with this problem.

When I was a child, my father brought me back a small carved giraffe from Africa. As he died soon afterward, I have always treasured this memento. I missed it Sunday evening and spent several days looking for it. Karen told me that Mary now carries it around in her schoolbag and freely admits to "finding" it here. In her six-year-old way, Karen demanded it back, but Mary was evidently not ready to let it go. I trust that you will find some good way of convincing Mary to return it.

Thank you for taking care of this.

Sincerely,

My dear Annie-Laurie,

I've lost the rhinestone necklace you lent me for the dinner-dance last week. I am devastated. I've looked everywhere for it. I've called the hotel, the taxi company, everyone who was at the dance. Nothing. I'm not giving up (I'm putting an ad in the paper this week), but the situation is looking hopeless and I need to let you know what is going on.

I will of course replace it, but since it was your mother's, there's no way to make up for its sentimental value. I'll call you tomorrow to see what's the best way of going about this. My deepest apologies for an unforgivable loss.

My dear Bryn,

I've been doing a lot of thinking lately. I know you noticed because you've asked me several times what's wrong. What's wrong is that I've realized I don't have the kind of feelings for you that I want to have if we are to spend the rest of our lives together.

I think the world of you—and you know that's true—but I'm convinced my love for you is not a marrying kind of love. It's a friendship kind of love.

I waited to write this letter until I was very, very sure of my thoughts and feelings. You've done nothing wrong and there is nothing you can do to spark something that isn't there. I don't want to leave you with any doubts or hopes about what I'm saying.

I'm probably the last person who can be of support to you, but if there's anything I can do to make this easier, let me know. In the meantime, know that you are and will always be one of the dearest people in my life.

———

TO: Gus Parkington
FROM: Alice Sanderson
DATE: Nov. 13, 2010
RE: Request

I need to tell you that repeatedly touching my arm or putting your arm around my shoulder is inappropriate in a business setting (it would actually also be inappropriate outside the business setting because I don't welcome such gestures from people I don't know well). In the office, this is considered sexual harassment. I would appreciate keeping our exchanges on a professional level. Knowing how intelligent and quick-on-the-uptake you are, I feel sure we need never discuss this again.

———

Dear Lizzie and Jim,

We are still talking about your beautiful wedding! I meant to ask you if the singer was a friend of yours—his voice was stunning.

I'm wondering if you received my wedding gift. As it was rather fragile, I hesitate to pay my Cecil-Roberts charge balance until I am sure that (a) you did indeed receive it and (b) it arrived in one piece. I have visions of it having arrived damaged and you not knowing quite what to do about it.

Give my love to your mother when you see her, will you, Lizzie?

Fondly,
Bert

———

Dear Hamilton,

We are fortunate that in such a large, high-pressure office we all get along so well. You are one of the ones who keep the social temperature at such a comfortable setting. I don't know anyone in the office who is better liked than you.

You can perhaps help with this. The collection of contributions toward gifts for employees' personal-life events is becoming a little troubling. Certainly, the communal sending of a gift is justified now and then. In the past month, however, there have been collections for two baby shower gifts, one wedding shower gift, two wedding gifts, one funeral remembrance, four birthday gifts, and three graduation gifts.

It's not only the collected-from who are growing uncomfortable (and poor), but the collected-for feel uneasy receiving gifts from people who don't know them outside the office, who wouldn't even recognize their graduating children, their marrying daughters and sons, or their deceased relatives.

This is essentially a kind gesture (and one that people think well of you for), but the practice seems to have become too wide-ranging and feels inappropriate in today's office setting.

Thank you for understanding.

———

See also: ADJUSTMENTS, BELATED, COMPLAINTS, DISAGREE-MENT, REFUSALS, SYMPATHY

FORTY-SIX

LETTERS OF SYMPATHY

A good letter of condolence is like a handclasp, warm and friendly.
—LILLIAN EICHLER WATSON

Letters of condolence and sympathy are some of the most difficult to write. People who are shocked and saddened and who feel inadequate and tongue-tied are writing to people who are grief-stricken and vulnerable and who feel life is hardly worth living.

However painful they are to write, letters of sympathy are imperative if you have a personal or business relationship with the deceased's family or friends. It will not be easy for them to overlook your ignoring something as all-important as the death of a loved one.

Condolences are offered only in the event of a death; sympathy may be expressed for a death, but it is also extended to those who have suffered from a fire, flood, storm, or natural disaster; burglary, theft, or violent crime; a lost job, bankruptcy, personal reverses, or other misfortunes.

Send Letters of Sympathy in Cases of

- absence of a superior who would normally respond
- anniversary of a death (see also ANNIVERSARIES)
- death of a family member of friend/neighbor/relative/customer/client/employee/colleague
- death of an employee (write to next of kin)
- death of a pet
- divorce
- hospitalization due to serious illness or accident (see also "GET WELL")

- miscarriage or stillbirth
- misfortune: loss of job/bankruptcy/burglary/violent crime
- natural disaster: flood/hurricane/drought/storms
- terminal illness (see also "GET WELL")

How to Say It

- Simply and directly express your sorrow about the other person's loss or trouble.
- Mention by name the person who died or the unfortunate event.
- Tell how you heard the news, if appropriate.
- Express your feelings of grief, dismay, loss.
- Offer sympathy, thoughts, prayers, good wishes.
- In the case of a death, mention what you liked or loved about the deceased; relate some happy memory, anecdote, favorite expression, or advice they gave you; mention the virtues, achievements, or successes for which they'll be remembered; tell about something they said or did that touched you. Especially welcome is recalling a complimentary or loving remark made by the deceased about the bereaved person. The more specific you are, the more memorable and comforting your letter will be.
- Close with a general expression of concern or affection or an encouraging reference to the future: "You are in my thoughts and prayers"; "My thoughts are with all of you in this time of sorrow"; "In the days ahead, may you find some small comfort in your many happy memories."

What Not to Say

- Don't say too little (sending only a commercial card with your signature) and don't say too much (offering clichés, advice, or inappropriate comments).
- Don't use overly dramatic language ("the worst tragedy I ever heard of," "the dreadful, horrible, appalling news"). If you were shocked or appalled at the news, say so—but avoid being excessively sentimental, sensational, or morbid. A simple "I'm sorry" is effective and comforting.
- Don't discuss the philosophy of death and disaster or offer religious commentary unless you are certain that sympathy grounded in a shared philosophic or religious orientation is appropriate with this person. Avoid pious clichés, simplistic explanations of the tragedy, or unwarranted readings of God's activities, intents, or involvement.
- Don't give advice or encourage big changes (leaving town, moving into an apartment, selling the spouse's model ship collection). It's usually many months before survivors can make well-thought-out decisions.

- Don't make generic offers of help like "Let me know if I can help," or "Feel free to call on us." This requires a response from people who already have much to deal with; most people will not take you up on such vague invitations. Instead, just do something: bring food, have the dress or suit the person is wearing to the funeral dry-cleaned, put up out-of-town relatives, watch children for several hours, address acknowledgments, take over work duties for a few days, cut grass or shovel snow or water the garden, help clean the house. If you're not close to the bereaved, an offer of help will be seen for the empty gesture it is. If you are close, you will either know what is helpful or you know whom to ask (friend, neighbor) about what needs doing.
- Don't focus on your feelings: "I've been just devastated—I can't seem to keep my mind on anything"; "I start crying every time I think of him"; "Why didn't you call me?" In the chapter entitled, "P.S. Don't tell *me* how bad you feel!" of her bestselling book, *Widow*, Lynn Caine says most of the condolence letters she received were more about the writer's awkwardness, discomfort, and inadequacies than about her sorrow or their shared loss. She says many letters were "full of expressions of how uneasy the writers felt, how miserable the writers were—as if they expected *me* to comfort *them*." There is a fine line between expressing your sorrow and dramatizing your own reactions.
- Don't offer false cheeriness or optimistic platitudes. In a *Reader's Digest* article, "An Etiquette for Grief," Crystal Gromer says, "In the context of grief, clichés are simply bad manners. . . . 'At least he didn't suffer,' people say. 'At least he's not a vegetable.' Any time you hear 'at least' come out of your mouth, stop. Creating an imaginary worse scenario doesn't make the real and current one better. It trivializes it." C. C. Colton once said, "Most of our misfortunes are more supportable than the comments of our friends upon them." Avoid the following comments:

Chin up.	Keep busy, you'll forget.
Be brave.	I know just how you feel.
Don't cry.	God never makes a mistake.
You'll get over it.	Be happy for what you had.
It's better this way.	He's in a better place now.
She is better off now.	It's a blessing in disguise.
Time heals all wounds.	At least she isn't suffering.
He was too young to die.	You must get on with your life.
Life is for the living.	He was old and had a good life.

Every cloud has a silver lining.

I heard you're not taking it well.

She is out of her misery at least.

Be thankful you have another child.

At least you had him for eighteen years.

Don't worry, it was probably for the best.

I feel almost worse than you do about this.

God had a purpose in sending you this burden.

You're young yet; you can always marry again.

It's just as well you never got to know the baby.

You're not the first person this has happened to.

I have a friend who's going through the same thing.

God only sends burdens to those who can handle them.

Life must go on—you'll feel better before you know it.

Tips on Writing

■ When your condolences are belated, send them anyway. A person can overlook tardiness, but it's almost impossible to overlook being ignored at a time like this.

■ In most cases, be brief. A lengthy letter may be overwhelming in a time of grief. On the other hand, if your letter is lengthy because you are recounting wonderful memories of the deceased person, it will be comforting and welcome. A letter that is lengthy because it includes other news or because it dwells on your own feelings is not appropriate.

■ Be tactful, but don't fear being honest—using the word *death* or *suicide,* for example. Circumlocutions like *passed on, passed away, departed, left this life, gone to their reward, gone to a better life, the deceased,* and *the dear departed* are no longer seen very often.

■ Accept that nothing you write will take away the person's grief, grief that is a necessary part of the healing process. Too many people agonize about finding the words that will make everything right again. There simply aren't any.

■ Observe the fine line between sympathy and pity. Sympathy respects the person's ability to survive the unfortunate event; pity suspects it has beaten them.

■ Let the person know you don't expect a response to your note or letter. After writing thank-you notes for flowers, condolences, memorials, honorary pallbearers, and special assistance, there is often little energy left to acknowledge sympathy letters.

■ If you're writing to one member of the family, mention the others in your closing.

■ To ensure that you don't write anything awkward, pitying, or tactless, reread your letter as though you were the one receiving it.

Special Situations

■ Miscarriages and stillbirths are devastating. Sympathize as you would for the death of any child. Avoid such unfortunately common remarks as: "You already have two lovely children—be grateful for what you have"; "This may have been for the best—there might have been something wrong with the baby, and this was nature's way of taking care of it"; "You're young yet—you can try again." And the worst of all: "Don't feel so bad. After all, it isn't as though you lost a child." The person *has* lost a child.

■ In the case of a suicide, offer sympathy as you would to any bereaved family. Because many survivors experience feelings of guilt, rejection, confusion, and social stigma, they need to know that you're thinking of them. Although it is generally appropriate to say you were "shocked to hear about" someone's death, avoid the phrase in this case. Don't ask questions, speculate about how the death could have been prevented, or dwell on the fact of the suicide; what matters is that the person is gone and the family is grieving. Instead, talk about how the person touched your life, share a happy memory, or express sympathy for the bereaved's pain.

■ Those who live with AIDS are first of all your friends, neighbors, and relatives, and only second someone with a usually fatal illness. Write as you would to anyone with a serious illness. Don't assume the person's time is short. Some AIDS patients have good years ahead of them in spite of recurrent crises. It's more important to be supportive and to send a card than to say exactly the right thing. Focus on how special the person is to you rather than on their illness, their prognosis, the sadness of it all. Ask if they'd like company; because of the perceived nature of AIDS, some people are unwilling to visit and your friend may appreciate seeing you all the more.

■ Responding to news of a divorce or separation is difficult, unless you're well acquainted with the person you're addressing. Neither expressions of sympathy nor congratulations are entirely appropriate in most cases. However, whether the person is "better off" or not, such life changes are never without their sad aspects and mourned losses, and a message of sympathy and support is often welcome.

■ Don't hesitate to write to people experiencing a misfortune considered embarrassing (a family member convicted of a crime, for example); if friends and family are hurting, your warm message of support will be welcome.

■ When business associates, customers, clients, or employees lose someone close to them, write as you would for friends or relatives, although your note will be shorter and more formal. Avoid personal remarks; it is enough to say you are thinking about them at this time. Extend sympathy on behalf of the company and convey condolences to other members of the person's family. When writing to the family of an employee who has died, you can offer assistance in gathering personal effects, discuss the pension plan, or make a referral to someone in the company who can help with questions.

■ Those who are grieving the death of a companion animal will appreciate a note of sympathy. This loss can be devastating; whether one can identify with the feelings or not, expressing sympathy is a loving, respectful gesture.

■ When someone has lost a close family member, remember the person with a special note on the anniversary of the person's death and (in the case of a spouse) on the couple's wedding anniversary date. Don't worry about bringing up sad memories. The person will hardly think of anything else on that day, and will be grateful for the supportive note that says somebody remembers. Those who plan class reunions might send cards or flowers to parents of deceased classmates to assure them that their children are remembered.

■ A letter to someone terminally or very seriously ill is more of a sympathy letter than a "get well" letter, but be careful not to anticipate someone's death. Avoid mention of imminent death unless the person has introduced the subject and shows a desire to talk about it. Instead, say how sorry you are to hear that the person is ill and that you are thinking of them. Instead of a "Get Well" card, choose one of the "Thinking of You" or no-message cards.

■ When sending flowers to a funeral home, address the accompanying small card's envelope to "The family of Emily Webb Gibbs." Insert a plain white card from the florist or your own visiting or business card with a brief message ("Please accept my sincerest sympathy" or "My thoughts and prayers are with you and the children"). If you make a donation to a charity in the deceased person's name, give the name and address of a family member as well as your own. The charity will send a notice of the contribution to the family and acknowledge to you that the donation was received.

Format

■ The personal letter of sympathy is always handwritten, unless a disability prohibits it. Use plain personal stationery or foldovers (no bright colors or fussy design).

■ Commercial greeting cards are acceptable as long as you add a personal line or two (or more).

■ Sympathy letters can be typed when writing a customer, client, employee, or colleague whom you don't know well but with whom you have business dealings. Use business-personal rather than full-size letterhead stationery.

WORDS

affection	distressed	mourn	sorry
bereavement	faith	ordeal	suffering
bitter	grief	overcome	sympathy
blow	hardship	regret	touched
comfort	healing	remember	tragic
commiserate	heartache	saddened	trouble
compassion	heartbroken	severe	trying
concerned	heartsick	shaken	unfortunate
consolation	heavyhearted	share	unhappy
devastating	hope	shocked	unwelcome
difficult	misfortune	sorrow	upset

PHRASES

although I never met	I remember so well
at a loss for words	I was saddened to learn/so sorry to hear that
beautiful/blessed/cherished memories	in your time of great sorrow
deepest sympathy	legacy of wisdom, humor, and love of family
deeply saddened	long be remembered for
during this difficult time	made a difference in many lives
extremely/terribly/so sorry to hear of	many friends share your grief
family sorrow	no words to express my great/ overwhelming/sincere/deep sorrow
feel fortunate to have known	offer most sincere/heartfelt/deepest sympathy
feel the loss of	one of a kind
grand person	profound sorrow
greatly saddened	rich memories
greatly/sadly/sorely missed	sad change in your circumstances
grieved to hear/learn of your loss	sad event/news/bereavement
grieve/mourn with you	
heart goes out to	

send my condolences/our deepest sympathy

sharing in your grief/sorrow during this difficult time

shocked and profoundly grieved/saddened

sick at heart

sincere condolences

so special to me

sorry to learn/hear about

stunned by the news

terrible blow

touched to the quick

tragic news

trying time

upsetting news

warmest sympathy

wish to extend our condolences/sympathy

with sincere feeling/personal sorrow/love and sympathy/sorrow and concern

SENTENCES

All of us are the poorer for Patrick's death.

Dora was a wonderful person, talented and loving, and I know that you and your family have suffered a great loss.

How sad I was to hear of Hsuang Tsang's sudden death.

I am thinking of you in this time of sorrow.

I can still see the love in his face when he watched you tell a story.

I feel privileged to have counted Fanny as a friend.

I hope you don't mind, but Marion Halcombe told us about your recent bad luck and I wanted to tell you how sorry we were to hear it.

I know how hard it is to lose a beloved father—I hope the memories of the happy times you shared will be some solace.

I know Phillip had many admiring friends, and I am proud to have been one of them.

I remember the way your mother made all your friends feel so welcome with her questions, her fudge, and her big smiles.

It seems impossible to speak of any consolation in the face of such a bitter loss.

It was with great sadness/sense of loss/profound sorrow that I learned of Ramona's death.

I was so sorry to hear that Mr. Golovin's long and courageous battle with cancer has ended.

I wish I weren't so far away.

I write this with a heavy heart.

Like so many others who were drawn to Yancy by his charm, courage, and warmth, I am deeply grieved and bewildered by his unexpected death.

Please extend our condolences to the members of your family.

Professor Bhaer will always remain alive in the memories of those who loved, respected, and treasured him.

The loss of your warm and charming home saddened us all.

The members of the Crestwell Women's Club send you their deepest sympathy.

The world has lost someone very special.

We always enjoyed Dr. Stanton's company and respected him so much as a competent, caring physician and surgeon.

We were grieved to hear that your baby was stillborn.

We were stunned to hear that you lost your job, but are hopeful that someone with your experience and qualifications will find something suitable—maybe even better.

We who knew and loved Varena have some idea of how great your loss truly is.

You and the family are much in our thoughts these days.

Your grief is shared by many.

PARAGRAPHS

How sad I was to hear of Eugenia's sudden death. I will miss seeing her gentle, smiling face every Sunday across the church. She was the first person I always thought of when anyone said the word "volunteer." What the parish will do without her, I can't imagine. And your own loss is, of course, immeasurably greater.

I was so sorry to hear about your wife's death. She was one of those truly gracious individuals who make life so much more pleasant for everyone around her. You will miss her very much, I know.

We felt so bad when we heard about the burglary. Something similar happened to us, and it affected me much more deeply and took longer to get over than I would ever have expected. I hope you are not too undone. May we lend you anything? Help put things back in order? Type up an inventory of what's missing? I'll stop by to see what you need.

This will acknowledge your letter of the 16th. Unfortunately, Mr. Newman is vacationing in a wilderness area this week, but I know he will be most distressed to learn of your brother's death when he returns. Please accept my sympathy on your loss—Mr. de Bellegarde visited here only once, but he left behind the memory of a charming, generous man.

Helen's death is a sad loss for you and for many others at Zizzbaum & Son. We too will sorely miss her, both from a personal and from a professional standpoint. As you know, we could not have been more pleased with her work for us over the past five years. She made many good friends here, and we all send you our heartfelt sympathy.

It's been a year today since Hebble died, and I wanted to tell you that we think of him often and with great affection. You must still miss him very much. I hope you are keeping busy and managing to find small happinesses in everyday things. We will be passing through Cool Clary in March, and hope to see you then.

The staff and student body join me in extending our sympathy to you on the death of your father. I have heard the stories you tell about this delightful and determined man, and I am sure this is a great loss for you. A special donation has been made to the scholarship fund. Next year, one of the scholarships will carry his name.

There is no good time for a tragedy, of course, but I know that you were in the midst of completing plans for the national conference. Would it help if I tied up the loose ends for you? You are so organized I'm sure I'll have no trouble following your notes. Just say the word if this is something I could do for you. And, again, please accept my most sincere sympathies on your sister's death.

SAMPLE LETTERS

Dear Mrs. Miller,

Saturday is the first anniversary of Daisy's death, and I couldn't let the day go by without writing to see how you are getting along and to tell you that all of Daisy's friends here in Switzerland miss her as much as ever. Her beauty, innocence, and enthusiasm will always live in our hearts.

With warmest regards and renewed sympathy, I am

Sincerely yours,

———

Dear Rollo,

I felt so bad when Mother called to say Mary died this morning. I know how happy the two of you have been these past years, despite health problems for both of you. I never saw a couple who traveled as much and were as involved in so many organizations as you two. Your love and respect for each other was obvious to all who knew you. I know that life will be very lonely for you without this splendid companion.

My memories of Mary go back forty years to the doughnuts and apple cider she made for us in your big farm kitchen after a hayride.

I will visit the next time I'm back in Iowa. Until then, dear Rollo, you will be in my thoughts. I am also thinking of your "boys" (all grown up now, and I still call them boys) and their families. This is a very sad time for all of you.

Affectionately,

Dear Adam,

Please accept my sincerest sympathy on the death of your mother. Although I never had the pleasure of meeting her, I know how much she meant to you. I also know she left behind a great many friends in the accounting department from her years of excellent work there.

My thoughts are with you and your father on this sad occasion.

Sincerely,

Dear Mr. Latch,

I was so sorry to hear of Mrs. Latch's death. Although I haven't seen you since I left Barfield, I have often thought with great affection and pleasure of those wonderful days we spent together at the races. Please accept my sympathy on your sad loss.

Yours truly,

Dear Mary and Jessie,

We were all so sorry to hear about your father's death. He was a fine man, and all of Cranford is in mourning for him. I remember seeing him take the two of you for a walk each evening after dinner when you were just little girls. I hope your memories of him will be some comfort to you.

Please accept our sympathy and good wishes.

Sincerely,

Dear Lydia,

I was shocked to hear of Noel's death; you must be devastated. You and Noel were always closer than any married couple I know. I can only hope that your years of happiness and your many good memories will enable you to live with this sad loss.

Affectionately yours,

Dear Dr. and Mrs. Primrose,

Please accept my sympathy on the fire that leveled your home. I understand you and your family are staying temporarily with the Thornhills. As soon as you begin rebuilding, please let me know—I would like to help.

My husband joins me in hoping that you and the children will soon be back in your own home.

With best wishes,

————

Dear Jody,

We were all sorry to hear the sad news. Flag was much more than a pet, I know, and you must be wondering if you'll ever feel happy again. I'm enclosing a picture that I took of you and Flag about a month ago. I hope it doesn't make you sad, but brings back good memories instead.

Love,

————

Dear Eden,

Harriet tells me that your divorce from Alayne is now final. Please accept my sympathies for the difficult experience this must have been. I also send my best wishes for a bright and happy future. I'll call you next week to see if you have time to get together.

Your friend,

————

Dear Ms. Abinger:

I was sorry to hear of the recent flooding you've had at the Corner Stores. It is one of those horror stories that haunt the dreams of self-employed businesspeople everywhere. I wish you all good luck in getting things back to normal as quickly as possible.

I wanted to assure you that although I will temporarily order my supplies elsewhere, I will be bringing my business back to you as soon as you are ready. I appreciate our long association and am looking forward to doing business with you again.

Sincerely,

————

Dear Leora and Martin,

Please accept our most heartfelt condolences on your miscarriage. I know how much you were both looking forward to welcoming this child into your lives.

Will you let us know the moment you feel up to a quiet visit? We would like to stop by with a couple of our warmest hugs.

With love and sympathy,

————

Dear Kitty and Chris,

We were stunned to hear the tragic news about Oliver. Everyone who knows you must be appalled and heartbroken at the loss of your bright, charming, lovable son. There are no words to adequately express our sympathy for the devastation and profound loss you must be feeling. Please know we are thinking of you and praying for you every minute.

In talking with Chris's mother, we learned that you are without a car because of the accident. We're leaving one of the demo cars for your use as long as you need it. Please let us do this; there is no need to call or to discuss it.

We'll be seeing you in the next couple of days. Until then, we send all our love and deepest sympathy.

Sincerely,

———

See also: ACKNOWLEDGMENTS, ANNOUNCEMENTS, BELATED, "GET WELL," RESPONSES, THANK YOU

FORTY-SEVEN

THANK-YOU LETTERS

His courtesy was somewhat extravagant. He would write and thank people who wrote to thank him for wedding presents and when he encountered anyone as punctilious as himself the correspondence ended only with death.
—EVELYN WAUGH

Thank-you letters enhance business and personal relationships and handsomely reward those who make a practice of sending them. Despite this, people find them difficult to write, which is perhaps why so many arrive late or not at all.

When you're unsure if a thank you is necessary, err on the side of "necessary." Even when you have graciously thanked someone in person, a written thank you is often expected or required or, at the least, appreciated.

For wedding gift thank yous, see WEDDINGS.

Write Thank-You Letters for

- appreciation/congratulations/recognition
- contributions: fundraising drives/memorials/charities
- employee suggestions/outstanding efforts/jobs well done
- expressions of sympathy
- favors/kindness/assistance/special help/advice
- gifts: business/personal
- hospitality: business/personal
- job interviews
- money: gifts/bonuses/loans
- orders: new/unusual
- patronage: new account/first purchase/good customer

- referrals: customers/clients/patients
- requested information/materials/documents
- sales prospects
- wedding and wedding shower gifts (see WEDDINGS)

How to Say It

- Describe in some detail what you are grateful for (not just "the lovely gift" or "the nice present").
- Express your gratitude in an enthusiastic, appreciative way.
- Elaborate on your appreciation. Tell how useful or appropriate it is, how you plan to use it, where you have placed it, or how it enhances your life, home, office, wardrobe. Be specific about what pleased you.
- Close with one or two sentences unrelated to the object of your gratitude (expressing affection, promising to see the person soon, sending greetings to family members, saying something nice about the donor).

What Not to Say

- Don't dilute your thanks by including news, information, questions, and comments; save them for another time.
- When you receive duplicate gifts, don't mention this to the givers.
- Don't ask where the gift was purchased so you can exchange it.
- Some etiquette authorities say not to mention the amount of a money gift. They suggest instead speaking of the giver's kindness, generosity, or, perhaps, extravagance. However, if both you and the gift-giver are comfortable with a mention of the amount, this is an acceptable choice.
- A few letter-writing experts dislike the "Thanks again" that concludes so many thank-you letters and notes. However, it is a popular and benign way of reminding the reader of the purpose of the letter. If you like it, use it.
- "Never express more than you feel" is a good guideline, especially in thank-you letters, where we try to make up in verbiage what we lack in enthusiasm. A simple "thank you" is effective.

Tips on Writing

■ Write soon. It's easier to find the words when you feel grateful than it is after your enthusiasm has cooled. It's also more courteous. Most givers don't need your thanks as much as they need to know if the gift arrived (especially if it was sent from a store) and if it pleased you. Some people think a thank-you note should be written within three days of receiving a gift. Certainly two weeks would be a maximum. For a stay in someone's home, write within one to three days, but certainly within a week; for dinners and other hospitality, within a day or two. When responding to expressions of sympathy, you have up to six weeks because of the special hardships involved. For "get well" gifts, wait until you are well enough to write comfortably (a friend can acknowledge gifts for you in the meantime).

■ A picture is still worth a thousand words. Enclose with your thanks a photo of the gift being used: the clock hanging on the wall, the glasses being filled with wine, your dog posing in the new plaid coat. A couple who received a gift certificate for dual massages sent photos of themselves—tired and irritable before their massages, relaxed and happy afterward.

■ You are not obliged to write a thank you (although of course it is always in excellent taste and will be greatly appreciated if you do) for: a party at which you were not the guest of honor; a casual dinner, lunch, or cocktail party; birthday, anniversary, congratulations, and "get well" cards and greetings; favors and hospitality extended by people with whom you are close (a sibling, a neighbor) and with whom you have reciprocal arrangements. In these cases, thank the person by telephone or the next time you see them.

■ Overnight hospitality always warrants a thank-you note—and usually a gift, which you bring with you or send afterward (popular items are specialty foods, houseplants, flowers, something for the house, toys for the children). When you write a family, address the parents, but mention the children by name (and if you say something complimentary about them, you will have more than justified your invitation). If you write to only the one who invited you or the one who was primarily responsible for your comfort, extend your thanks to the other household members.

Special Situations

■ A late "thank you" is harder to defend than any other delayed message, but it is better to write late than not at all. In his delightful manners book for children, *How Rude!* Alex J. Packer tells them, "Thank-you notes get exponentially more difficult to write with each day that passes. By the second day, they are *four* times harder to write. By the third day, they are *nine* times harder, and if you wait twelve days, they are *144* times harder to write!" Don't spend more than a phrase or a sentence apologizing for the delay: "My thanks are no less sincere for being so unforgivably late." "I am sorry not to have told you sooner how much we enjoyed the petit fours."

■ Yes, you send a thank-you note for a thank-you gift, if for no other reason than to let the person know it arrived.

■ When someone donates money to a charity in your honor or in memory of a deceased relative, the charity will acknowledge the contribution to the donor, usually with a printed card or form letter, but you also write a thank-you note.

■ Although the guest or guests of honor at an anniversary party, birthday party, or shower always thank each friend warmly for gifts as they are opened, thank-you notes are still required. The party or shower host should receive a special thank you as well as a small gift.

■ An essential job-seeking technique as well as a gesture of courtesy is to thank the person who interviews you. Write a note immediately after the interview and before a decision has been made. State what you liked about the interview, the company, the position. Emphasize briefly and specifically your suitability for the job. Address concerns about your qualifications that came up during the interview. Mention any issue that you didn't have the opportunity to discuss. If you felt you misspoke or left the wrong impression, this is where you can correct your interview—but be brief and subtle. You don't want to remind the interviewer of a weak point.

■ Although business entertaining is often taken for granted, a thank you is appreciated and builds good relations. Notes to a colleague, client, employee, or supplier inspire loyalty, enthusiasm, and increased productivity. When you receive a gift from a business contact, write a thank you, even though you suspect hundreds of gifts were sent. When you are unable to accept a business gift, avoid any implied accusation of poor taste on the giver's part when you write your thank-you-but-I-must-refuse letter; explain simply that your firm doesn't allow you to accept gifts.

■ In the business world, frequent, well-written thank-you notes can foster professional success in unimaginable ways. Beginning with the "thank you" for your first job interview and ending with the "thank you" for your retirement party, your career can benefit enormously from simple notes of gratitude written along the way. Harvey Mackay, outstanding business executive, bestselling author, and popular speaker, says, "Anyone too busy to say thank you will get fewer and fewer chances to say it."

■ When gifts arrive early for an event, write thank-you notes after the special day.

■ When you receive a gift from more than one person, write personalized thank-you notes to each one. You don't need to do this when you receive a gift from a family (even when all five of them sign the card) or when you receive a gift from a group such as your bridge club, teachers at your school, your coworkers. You can write one letter to the group but circulate or post it so that everyone who contributed sees it.

■ After a death in the family, thank-you notes are written to people who sent flowers or donations, and to those who helped with hot meals, hosted dinners, put up out-of-town relatives, lent chairs, or were otherwise supportive. You also respond to those who sent notes of condolence (exception: those who sent printed cards with only a signature and no personal message). You may use the printed cards supplied by the funeral home if you add a personal note. When the person closest to the deceased is unable to manage the correspondence, a family member or friend writes thank-you notes on their behalf. The notes need not be long and, traditionally, you have up to six weeks after the funeral to send them. To keep track of who sent flowers, a family member or funeral home official should collect the attached cards and write a description of the flowers on them.

■ Send thank-you notes to sales prospects for the time they spend with you on the phone or in the office. Your notes—which take only minutes to write—will secure for you their goodwill and their increased willingness to speak with you next time. (You also may surprise yourself by liking this part of your work—after the first few notes anyway.)

■ For a few special gifts, you may want to write two thank-you notes, the first when you receive the gift (a check or a fondue set, for example) and the second when you use it ("we used your gift to enroll in a ballroom dancing class, something we've wanted to do for years" or "we invited the cousins over for fondue and told them that they could thank you too!").

Format

■ Thank-you messages are almost always handwritten on foldovers, note cards, or personal stationery. Typewritten thanks are acceptable when they are part of a long, personal letter to family or friends.

■ Use formal printed or engraved stationery to write thank-you notes for important events (weddings, for example).

■ Business thank yous are typed on letterhead stationery, personal-business stationery, or good bond paper. When you want a warmer tone, handwrite your note.

■ Commercial foldovers with "Thanks" or "Thank you" are convenient and acceptable; a handwritten note goes on the inside page. Contemporary thank-you cards with sentimental or humorous messages are also appropriate as long as a handwritten message is added.

■ When you need to thank many people, it is appropriate (and, in some areas, expected) to insert a thank-you notice in the local newspaper. The nurses, doctors, hospital staff, friends, and family who helped someone through a long and demanding illness are often thanked. The funeral of a public figure may inspire hundreds of notes of condolence, which are best acknowledged in a newspaper announcement. Recently elected public officials thank those who worked and voted for them. The wording is simple and warm: "We wish to thank all the generous and loving friends and family who sent cards and gifts on the occasion of our twenty-fifth wedding anniversary."

■ Can you e-mail your thanks? In most cases, no. Certainly e-mail is suitable for quick thanks between longtime friends for the loan of a book, a small favor, a light lunch. It can also be used as a down payment on a "real" thank-you note, written primarily to say that the gift arrived and that a letter will follow. The point of a thank-you note is that it is personal. E-mail has many virtues, but graciousness and formality are not among them.

■ Miss Manners (Judith Martin of the *Washington Post*) warns against faxing a thank you to someone who has just bought your product. She points out that the recipient must pay for such a thank you (fax paper, the time the letter occupies the machine, machine depreciation).

WORDS

appreciate	favorite	lovely	sensational	thrilled
bountiful	flattered	luxurious	sophisticated	timeless
captivated	generosity	memorable	special	timely
charming	gracious	needed	spectacular	touched
cherished	grateful	one-of-a-kind	striking	treasure
classic	hospitable	overjoyed	stunned	treat
delighted	impressed	overwhelmed	sumptuous	unique
elegant	indebted	perfect	superb	useful
enchanted	invaluable	pleased	surprised	valuable
enjoyed	keepsake	priceless	tasteful	well-made
excited	kindness	remarkable	terrific	wonderful
fascinated	largehearted	satisfying	thoughtful	

PHRASES

absolutely perfect choice for me	consider me deeply in your debt for
appreciate your confidence/interest/ kind words/referral	convey my personal thanks to everyone who
a rare treat	deeply appreciate
cannot tell you how delighted I was	derived great pleasure from
charming of you	did us good/our hearts good

enjoyable and informative tour

enjoyed it/ourselves enormously

excellent/splendid suggestion

felt right at home

from the bottom of my heart

generous gift

great gift for us

heartfelt/hearty thanks

how kind/dear/thoughtful/sweet of you to

how much it meant to us

I am indebted/very much obliged to you for

I have seldom seen such

I'll long remember

important addition to

I plan to use it for/to

I really treasure

it was a great pleasure

it was hospitable/kind of you to

I will never forget

made us feel so welcome

many thanks

meant a great deal to me

more people have remarked on the

more than kind

most sincerely grateful to you for

most thoughtful and generous

much obliged

one of the most memorable days of my trip

one of your usual inspired ideas

perfect gift/present

please accept my gratitude/our sincere appreciation

pleased as Punch

profoundly touched by

quite out of the ordinary

really appreciate your help

seventh heaven

so characteristically thoughtful

thoroughly enjoyed myself

tickled our fancy

truly a marvel

truly grateful

very special occasion

we want you to know how much we value

we were especially pleased because

we were simply thrilled/delighted/ stunned with

what a joy it was to receive

will be used every day/often

with your usual inimitable flair/style

wonderful addition to

you made me feel so special by

you may be sure that I appreciate

you must be a mind reader

your generous gift

your gift meant a lot to me at this time because

your thoughtful/kind expression of sympathy

All of us were touched by your thoughtfulness.

As soon as we decide what to do with your wonderful gift [money] we will let you know.

How dear of you—we are delighted!

How did you know we needed one?

I appreciate your advice more than I can say.

I can't remember when I've had a better/more pleasant/more relaxing/more enjoyable time.

I can't thank you enough for chauffeuring me around while my knee was in the immobilizer.

I'll cherish your gift always.

I love it!

I'm grateful for your help, and hope that I can reciprocate some day.

In the past several weeks, you have kindly referred Harvey Birch, Frances Wharton, and Judith Hunter to the Cooper Architectural Group—we are grateful!

I owe you one!

I plan to use your gift to buy a wok—we've always wanted one.

I treasure the paperweight—it will always remind me of you.

It was kind of you to let me know about the job opening—I'll keep you posted.

I very much appreciate your concern.

Madeleine will be writing you herself, but I wanted to thank you for knowing just what would please a nine-year-old.

More people have remarked on our new Mondrian glassware.

On behalf of the family of Violet Effingham Chiltern, I thank you for your kind expression of sympathy.

Special thanks to the doctors and the nurses at Trewsbury County Hospital.

Thanks a million.

Thanks for recommending Bates Craters and Freighters—they've been as good as you said they were.

Thanks for the great advice on patio brick—I'm pleased with what we finally bought.

Thanks for thinking of me.

Thanks for your order and for the interest in Leeds Sporting Goods that prompted it.

Thank you for including me in this memorable/special event.

Thank you for opening a charge account with us recently.

Thank you for shopping regularly at Farrell Power & Light.

Thank you for your courtesy and patience in allowing me to pay off the balance of my Irving Products Inc. account in small installments.

Thank you for your generous donation to the Dunstone Foundation in memory of James Calpon Amswell; he would have been pleased and I appreciate your comforting gesture very much.

Thank you for your kind hospitality last night; I have never felt less a stranger in a strange city.

Thank you so much for agreeing to speak to our study club.

The letter of reference you so kindly wrote for me must have been terrific—Goodman & Co. called yesterday with a job offer!

This is just a note to thank you for rushing the steel shelving to us in time for our event.

Visions of Paradise is a stunning book, and we are all enjoying it immensely.

We all thank you for the tickets to the science museum.

We are thrilled with the handsome brass bookends you sent!

We will never forget the autumn glories of the North Shore—thank you so much for inviting us to share your cabin with you last weekend.

You can see what a place of honor we've given your gift the next time you stop by.

You couldn't have found anything I'd enjoy more.

You shouldn't have, but since you did, may I say that your choice was absolutely inspired!

PARAGRAPHS

We are still talking about the wonderful weekend we spent with you—thank you, thank you! You are the busiest people we know, yet you welcomed us into your home as if nothing in the world were more important. We particularly enjoyed the comedy at the Wharton Theater—sharing a laugh with dear friends is surely one of life's greatest pleasures.

The extravagantly flowering azalea plant absolutely transformed my hospital room and has given me a great deal of pleasure these past few weeks. I'm looking forward to thanking you in person once I get back on my feet.

Thank you for agreeing to write a letter of recommendation for me, especially since I know how busy you are this time of year. I'm enclosing a stamped envelope addressed to the personnel officer at Strickland Construction. I will, of course, let you know at once if I get the job. In the meantime, thanks again for your kindness.

I want to thank you for all the time you put into coaching the Crossley-area baseball team this summer. It was a joy to watch you and your enthusiastic players model sporting behavior and team spirit to some of the younger teams. The assistance of our volunteer coaches is crucial to the survival of this program, and the Board of Directors joins me in sending you our admiration and thanks.

Your dad said you picked out my tie all by yourself. Thank you! Aunt Belinda just took a picture of me wearing the tie and eating a piece of birthday cake. When we get the pictures developed I'll send you one so you can see how nice I look in my new tie.

On behalf of the directors, staff, and employees of Mallinger Electronics, I want to thank you for your splendid arrangements for the Awards Banquet Night. Decorations, food, program, and hospitality were all first-rate. Please convey our admiration and thanks to your committee chairs. If you can possibly face the thought, we'd like you to chair next year's celebration. The evening was an outstanding success in every way, primarily due to your organizational abilities, creativity, and interpersonal skills.

Thank you so much for the graduation check. As you know, I'm saving everything I earn for college, so when I received your card and gift, I knew right away what I was going to do with it! I've been needing and wanting a decent watch for a long time, and I can hardly wait to choose one. Every time I look at my new watch, I'll think of you with affection and gratitude.

It is my understanding that you wrote a letter supporting my nomination by the Department of Materials Science and Engineering as a Distinguished Professor. I am happy to inform you that I was indeed honored with this title on June 3, 2009. I am deeply appreciative of your kind support in this regard. Many thanks.

The kindness and generosity you showed to all of us at the time of Edgar's death are much appreciated. What a good idea to send a plant; we've put the chrysanthemums in Edgar's perennial garden. Thanks too for the hot meals, the touching letter that I know you put your whole self into, and for your constant support. We're blessed to count you as a friend.

What a wonderful engagement gift! We haven't even begun to think of planning our wedding as we've heard it's so much work and so complicated. With this marvelous book on wedding planning, I think we can quit worrying.

I would like to thank one of your sales staff for being helpful, tactful, and speedy—all at the same time! I foolishly tried to buy a wedding gift on my lunch hour, and I am a poor shopper at the best of times. Within minutes, this young man helped me select the absolutely perfect gift at the price I wanted to pay. It was all done so smoothly that I was out of the store before I knew it—and before I thought to ask his name. The initials on my sales slip are R.J. Can you identify him and pass on my thanks?

Thanks for the Mozartkugeln! One of my favorite annual rituals is watching the Wimbledon tennis finals in bed (they start at 7:00 a.m.). The women's final was great, and that's when I ate the Mozartkugeln—they were deliciously decadent. When I lived in Salzburg, a shop near my apartment made them daily. They cost about a quarter each then, and every day after class I made my little journey there to get one.

Thank you for the assistance, information, and encouragement you offered us when Hannah was applying to the U.S. Air Force Academy. We're convinced that her acceptance was due in no small measure to your support and advocacy.

Thank you for your most welcome letter of September 28. I am impressed with your generosity in sending complimentary subscriptions of the magazine to our doctors and nurses presently working in Tanzania. They will make good use of them—they estimate that each copy of the magazine is held by over fifty pairs of hands!

I enjoyed this morning's discussion of the research position you want to fill. I was pleased to know that my advanced degree is definitely an asset. I've been "overqualified" for several jobs, and was beginning to wonder if my extra years of study were of any value in the job market. Thanks so much for your time and for the congenial interview.

SAMPLE LETTERS

Dear Major Hugo Cypress,

Thank you so much for agreeing to speak to our study club. We are looking forward to hearing your presentation.

Our district includes ninety-seven veterans, although usually only twenty-five to thirty attend the study club meetings.

The best way to reach the St. George Hotel is to take the Arlen exit off I-35 north. Continue one mile west to 100 Arlen Avenue.

Again, thank you.

Best regards,

————

Dear Elsie and Joe,

You made our day with your funny anniversary card and warm message. In one way or another, you've been a part of many of our "big" days, so it was good to have you with us again, in a manner of speaking, on our twenty-fifth wedding anniversary.

We both send our thanks and love for your faithful friendship (with the promise of a letter to follow).

Fondly,

————

Dear Mr. Hollingford,

Thank you for remembering my five-year anniversary with the company. I didn't think anyone would notice except me! I've enjoyed working here and plan to stay as long as you'll have me. Thank you, too, for the gift certificate to Sweeney Inn. I have another anniversary coming up (three years of marriage), and I know where we'll celebrate it.

Sincerely,

————

Dear Aune Esther Koskenmaki Lilley,

Thank you so much for sending us a copy of your book, *Father Said, "Eat, Don't Giggle!"* You are quite right in thinking that our collection of folklore materials can benefit from your contribution, especially since Finnish folklore is of particular interest to our Folk Arts Division.

Again, thank you for your book.

Sincerely,

————

Dear Agnes and Walter,

Thank you for the lovely silver piggy bank you gave Anabel. It's a classic, and I know she will treasure it all her life. In the meantime, it has a place of honor on her dresser, and we've gotten into the habit of putting our change into it at the end of the day.

Can you come by to see your new little grandniece sometime next week? We're all feeling rested by now and would love to see you. Give me a call.

With much love,

————

Dear Millicent,

The dinner party was elegant and memorable, and we were delighted to be included. I don't know anyone who has as much flair and style as you do when it comes to entertaining!

Fondly,

Dear Vincent Crummles:

Thank you for your contribution of $200 to the Alumni Annual Giving Campaign. As stipulated on the donor card returned to this office, your gift will be designated for the Annual Giving Fund to be used where most needed.

We also appreciate your use of the Langdon Co. matching gifts program and look forward to receiving their one-for-one matching gift. This matching gift will also be directed to the Annual Giving Fund.

Thank you again for your generosity, which will make it possible for many young women and young men to have the advantage of a quality education.

Very truly yours,

See also: ACCEPTANCES, ACKNOWLEDGMENTS, APPRECIATION, BELATED, RESPONSES

FORTY-EIGHT

LETTERS RELATED TO TRAVEL

A trip is what you take when you can't take any more of what you've been taking.
—ADELINE AINSWORTH

Today most travel arrangements (airline, car, hotel reservations; requests for tourist, passport, health information; cancellations) are made by phone, e-mail, or on the Internet. Occasionally, however, a letter or faxed letter is the best choice to outline complicated arrangements, confirm reservations, address special problems, or register a complaint.

Every letter that a travel business writes to customers—even a one-sentence response to a query for information—is a sales or goodwill letter and is courteous, positive, and presentable.

Write Travel Letters to

- airlines
- bus companies
- campground/RV facilities
- convention and visitors bureaus
- cruise companies
- customers of a travel business
- employers for travel reimbursement
- entertainment/amusement complexes
- friends and relatives

- hotels/motels/B&Bs
- national parks
- railroad companies
- resorts/spas/dude ranches
- tourist information centers
- travel agents

How to Say It

- Begin with your question or item of business.
- Include specifics: dates; number of nights, people, rooms, type of accommodation, extras, verification of information about accessibility, pool, cable TV, entertaining facilities; type of car, number of days, pickup and drop-off points; record, confirmation, or other locator number; credit card number; your address and telephone number; names of guests or passengers.
- Mention enclosed deposit or coupons.
- Repeat terms or information you were given over the telephone.
- Ask for a confirmation number.
- Close with a courtesy.

What Not to Say

- Don't volunteer unnecessary personal information.
- Don't put your credit card number in a letter unless you know the company well.
- Don't assume anything. Ask for information when you are not sure about details.

Tips on Writing

- Aside from standard courtesies ("thank you for your assistance/attention"), you are brief when writing about travel arrangements.
- Put each unit of information on its own line:

  compact car
  standard transmission
  airconditioning
  3 days, May 11–14
  pickup: New York—JFK
  drop-off: Boston—Logan

- When requesting confirmation or a response from a non-U.S. hotel, resort, or travel bureau, especially one on the low-budget end, enclose an International Reply Coupon (available at post offices) to assure a response. If you don't have an IRC, suggest they e-mail or fax their response.
- Take copies of reservations and confirmation letters with you as you travel, along with notes on arrangements made by telephone.
- To inspire you to write travel letters home, read Rudyard Kipling's *Letters of Travel*, Pierre Teilhard de Chardin's *Letters from a Traveller*, John Steinbeck's *A Russian Journal*, Michael Crichton's *Travels*. From Phillip Brooks' 1893 *Letters of Travel* and Gertrude Bell's 1894 *Persian Pictures* to Freya Stark's 1929 *Baghdad Sketches* to Joanne Sandstrom's 1983 *There and Back Again* and Erma Bombeck's 1991 *When You Look Like Your Passport Photo, It's Time to Go Home*, you'll find letters to inspire and entertain.

Special Situations

- When making requests for hotel or motel reservations, include such information as the number of persons in your group, how many rooms you need and whether you want single or double beds, your times of arrival and departure, and any extras you'll need (crib, poolside room, connecting rooms, additional bed, nonsmoking room). Ask for confirmation of your reservation, and indicate how the rooms are to be billed—to you, to a credit card, to your company account—and if you are entitled to a discount of any kind.
- When canceling a travel arrangement, repeat the information in your original letter. (Canceling has become more than courtesy; if you forget to cancel a reservation, your credit card may be charged for the first night.)
- One can hardly say "travel" without thinking "postcards." If you choose the cards carefully, you will already have something to write ("Our hotel is right by this canal" or "We toured this castle yesterday" or "We went to the top of this mountain in a funicular"). A postcard shows recipients something colorful, interesting, or unknown to them. Your message focuses on your pleasure being there (nobody wants to hear that you've had trouble). Tell what you've liked best, a food you've eaten for the first time, an interesting fact or bit of history, the impact your trip is having on you.
- To obtain a passport, writing a letter isn't your best bet. Instead, go online at www.travel.state.gov/passport for information and downloadable forms or call the National Passport Information Center (NPIC) at 877-487-2778. In any case, for your first passport, you need to appear in person at one of the 9,000 passport facilities in the United States.

Format

■ Except for postcards and letters to family and friends, all travel correspondence should be typed to avoid errors.

■ Fax and e-mail are often used for travel arrangements.

WORDS

accommodation	deposit	nonrefundable	schedule
arrangement	directions	register	sightseeing
availability	discount	reimburse	tour
booked	excursion	rental	visa
cancel	fare	reservation	voyage
charter	lodging	roundtrip	

PHRASES

activities for children	hold for late arrival
advance purchase requirements	map of the area
areas of interest	nearby horseback riding
bed and breakfast (B&B)	sightseeing/tour package
discount for those over 55	sports facilities
eighteen-hole golf course	travel insurance
especially interested in	youth hostel
flexible schedule	

SENTENCES

Attached is a completed form about the luggage lost November 8 on flight #78 as well as photos and descriptions of the missing luggage.

Enclosed are the reimbursable hotel, meal, and car rental receipts from my trip to Miami February 10–14.

Is your resort fully accessible to someone who uses a wheelchair?

I would like to dispute the $150 charge for changing the return date on my ticket.

Please send a brochure and rates for the Kokua Family Resort.

Sweeting-Nunnely Telecommunications is considering holding its annual shareholders' meeting in your area and would appreciate your sending us information on your convention center, hotels, area attractions, and any other material that would be helpful in making our decision.

This will confirm the cancellation of our reservation at the Doddington Dude Ranch.

We will be spending the month of July in Sundering-on-Sea and would appreciate receiving a map of the area, train schedules, a calendar of local events, and anything else that would help acquaint us with your area.

PARAGRAPHS

We spent the night camped at a remote campground in Badlands National Park. The stars were stunning, and there were buffalo everywhere—we had to drive through a herd to get to our campsite. Right now we're in Wall Drug eating breakfast. I wish you were here with us.

I am interested in flying from Denver to Hong Kong sometime after June 7 and returning to Denver from Hong Kong approximately three weeks later. I will need two roundtrip tickets Denver–Hong Kong, and I am hoping you can find the most inexpensive seats available. I understand that if I purchase tickets by March 1, there will be a discount. My plans are fairly flexible as to departure and return dates if that helps obtain lower-priced tickets. Please call me as soon as you have some information.

I would like to reserve a single, nonsmoking room on one of the lower floors for July 7–17. I will be arriving late on the evening of the 7th so please hold the room for my arrival.

You asked about transportation between the airport and the hotel. We operate a free shuttle service that leaves the airport every half-hour between the hours of 7:00 a.m. and midnight from the Ground Transportation area. Look for the Crossley Hotels logo on the bus.

Your room will be billed on the group account for the convention so you do not have a confirmation number. However, at check-in give your name and say you are with Gammon, Quirk & Co.

As discussed in our telephone conversation this morning, we will arrive at the Lowborough Hotel at approximately 3:00 p.m., Thursday, August 31. Thank you for your willingness to reserve a parking space with orange traffic pylons for our 24' rental moving truck. I wouldn't like to depend on chance to find a parking place for a truck that size, especially in Boston!

I very much enjoyed my stay at the O'Reilly McMurrough International Hotel. However, I thought you'd like to know that when I tried to use the telephone, the "2" dialed 911. So did the "9." So did every other button. It was most disconcerting and a worrying nuisance for the emergency personnel on the other end of the calls. The iron also needs to be replaced; the plate is stained and it slightly damaged my dress.

Please accept this coupon good for one free night at the O'Reilly McMurrough International Hotel to apologize for the malfunctioning telephone and iron. We value your business and appreciate the courtesy of your letter.

We are planning to vacation in Seattle next June. Will you please send us information on hotels, a map of the area, descriptions of attractions, a list of events scheduled for that month, and a report of average June temperatures and rainfall?

SAMPLE LETTERS

TO: P. Bottome
FROM: Amelie von Rohn
DATE: April 3, 2012
RE: Travel arrangements

Phyllis,

Johan Roth, Freya Breitner, and I will represent the Department at the XVI International Meteorological Conference in Tokyo. Convention dates are October 14–18. We'd like to arrive in time to get a good night's sleep, and it would help if the flight home would also allow us to get a night's sleep before returning to work. But do what you can.

Can you arrange for the three of us:

   roundtrip airline tickets
   hotel reservations (see attached Convention brochure)
   a rental car to be picked up and dropped off at the airport
   the current allowable travel cash times 3 (in yen)

Thanks!
Amelie

_____

Dear Mr. Dallas,

Vivian Grey Hotels International is pleased to learn that you are considering the Burnsley area for your August family reunion. We look forward to an opportunity to extend our warm hospitality to your group for this special event. Although we are not currently holding space for your group, we have accommodations available at this time that meet your needs. Please call or fax your reservations to us as soon as possible.

_____

Signor Gian-Luca Boselli,

I would like to make reservations for October 31 (1 night). We will need 2 rooms for 4 people (each room must have 2 beds).

May we please have rooms with a view of the Temple of the Concord? The last time we had rooms #6 and #15, and they were perfect.

Below is my credit card number to hold the rooms.

I am looking forward to enjoying your lovely hotel once again.

————

Re: Rental agreement #AI9946X, dated May 18, 2012

Before returning this car to the rental car return area at the Cairo Airport on June 3, I stopped at a gas station one block away and filled the tank to the brim. My bill indicates that I am being charged for 17 liters of gasoline in addition to the penalty charge for returning a car without a full tank of gas. Please look into this, and refund the inappropriate charges. Thank you.

————

Dear Family,

I have to tell you where you want to spend your next vacation: Colorado! Even those of you who live there, and you know who you are, can enjoy a vacation in your home state.

The most amazing thing to us out there was (1) no bugs and (2) no humidity. I am not making that up. The first night I mistakenly left my tennis shoes outside the tent. It took me about an hour the next morning to get over the fact that they weren't wet. It seemed unlikely to me that shoes could spend a night outdoors and still be completely dry. This dryness and no bug thing went on for days and days and days—beyond our understanding.

The only frightening wildlife we saw was Kevin's hair in the morning. If you study our photos carefully, you will notice that there is no humidity and no bugs!

With love,
Mary

————

Dear Mrs. Hawkins,

I would like to reserve a single room at the Admiral Benbow Inn for July 7–17. I will be arriving late on the evening of July 7 so please hold the room for my arrival. Enclosed is a check for the first night.

Thank you.

Sincerely,

————

To: Granby Airlines
FAX: 212-555-1000
FROM: Julia Hazelrigg
DATE: Sept. 4, 2010
RECORD LOCATOR: #4GMEN5
NUMBER OF PAGES: 2

In reference to today's telephone conversation, please cancel both reservations under record locator number #4GMEN5.

My traveling companion was hospitalized suddenly yesterday for an indefinite period (attached is a note from the physician's office).

I understand that according to your policy for international flights, you offer a complete refund of all tickets in a party when one of the party must cancel due to illness.

I appreciate your compassion and prompt help at this difficult time.

———

Dear Knox Motor Inn,

I would like to reserve a no-smoking room in your hotel for two nights, June 19 and 20.

My husband and I have two sets of twins (ages six months and two-and-a-half years) so we will need four cribs and an extra set of sheets per crib. The room should also have two double beds since I spend much of the night nursing the infants and my husband spends much of the night comforting the toddlers.

We have lots of nighttime crying in our life just now so if you could please give us a room in a secluded wing of your hotel I'm sure your other patrons would appreciate it very much.

Please send confirmation of our reservation to our address as shown below.

Thank you!

———

See also: ACKNOWLEDGMENTS, ADJUSTMENTS, COMPLAINTS, FAXES, MEMOS, REQUESTS

FORTY-NINE

WEDDING CORRESPONDENCE

*I joined a singles group in my neighborhood. The other day the president called
me up and said, "Welcome to the group. I want to find out what kind of activities
you like to plan." I said, "Well, weddings."*
—LYNN HARRIS

All correspondence relating to weddings or commitment ceremonies, including engagements, is in this chapter. However, supporting advice may also be found in the
chapters on ACCEPTANCES, ACKNOWLEDGMENTS, ANNOUNCEMENTS,
BELATED, CONGRATULATIONS, INVITATIONS, REFUSALS, REQUESTS,
RESPONSES, THANK YOU.

The only hard-and-fast rules for weddings and wedding correspondence today
are those requiring courtesy, appropriateness, and common sense. The guidelines
given below blend tradition and contemporary custom to provide you with a frame-
work onto which you can sculpt your own individual tastes and circumstances.

Wedding Correspondence Includes

- acknowledging gifts
- announcements: printed/engraved/newspaper
- cancellation
- confirmation of arrangements
- congratulations on wedding
- families of wedding couple exchanging letters
- informing ex-spouse of remarriage

- invitations: showers/parties/dinners/wedding
- postponement
- responses: invitations/announcements
- save-the-date notices
- selecting ceremony participants: attendants/presider/organist/musicians/reception helpers
- showers: invitations/thank yous
- thanking people for gifts/favors/greetings/assistance

How to Say It

- Engagement announcements can be made in one of four ways. (1) Handwrite individual letters to family and friends that include: name of the person you are to marry; wedding date (if known); if you choose, tell briefly how you met and how long you've known the person; some expression of your happiness; a personal comment (the other person is the first to know, you can't wait for them to meet your intended). (2) Insert an announcement in the newspaper that includes: your full names; hometowns; parents' names and hometowns; education backgrounds and places of employment; date of wedding or general plans ("a spring wedding is planned"). Some newspapers have requirements and deadlines for engagement announcements, and some will run either an engagement or a wedding announcement, but not both, so check beforehand. (3) Send formal printed or engraved engagement announcements: "Maria and Ernest Rockage announce the engagement of their daughter Phyllis to Stephen Newmark. An August wedding is planned." (4) Invite family and friends to a dinner party or other event at which the engagement is announced.
- Broken engagements need no announcement if no formal announcement was made. If you've written family and friends of the engagement, write the same type of personal note saying simply that you and the other person have broken your engagement; there's no need to explain why.
- When writing to ask friends or relatives to serve as attendants, state what you are asking and who pays for what. Offer them a graceful way of refusing so that they don't feel pressured. Express your appreciation for their friendship.
- Although many arrangements for weddings and commitment ceremonies are made by telephone, you often write letters of confirmation to the temple, church, or location where the ceremony is to be held; to the person who will officiate; to the sexton, organist, cantor, soloist, musicians; to your attendants, ushers, and others; to the photographer and videographer, to the florist, jeweler, bakery; to hotels to make honeymoon arrangements; to the

caterer or club for the reception; to order gifts for attendants, the aisle carpet, candles, ribbons, decorations. These different letters have three requirements in common: give all possible details; ask everything you need to know at the outset; keep copies of your correspondence.

- When hosting a wedding shower send handwritten invitations or commercial shower invitations that include: name of the honoree or honorees (bride-to-be, groom-to-be, the couple); type of shower (kitchen, tool, bath, garden, recipe, household); time, date, and place; RSVP or Regrets only; name, address, and telephone number of the host. Each guest is thanked for their gift at the shower, but thank-you notes are still sent to each person (even those who "went in together" on a gift) soon after the shower. The shower host receives a small gift as well as an especially warm thank you.

- Wedding invitations are engraved, printed, or handwritten. Many papers, typeface styles, inks, and designs are available at printers, stationery stores, and large department stores. The more formal the wedding, the more formal the invitations. Formal wedding invitations have two envelopes: the outer one is sealed for mailing, carries your return address, and is hand-addressed; the inner envelope, which contains the invitation (faceup as you open the envelope), is unsealed (the flap has no glue) and carries the names of the invitees on the front. There may also be a sheet of tissue paper to protect the engraving, and enclosures such as at-home cards, reception cards, pew cards for a large wedding, maps indicating location of ceremony and reception, and admission cards if the ceremony or reception is held in a public place. Reply cards are inserted in envelopes addressed to you (printed or engraved) and stamped, and then placed in the inner envelope. Concern about our wasteful use of paper prompts some people to omit the inner envelope or to use recycled paper for their invitations. Reply envelopes are at least $5" \times 3\frac{1}{2}"$ to comply with postal regulations. If you aren't using reply cards, include an address or telephone number below the RSVP so that guests know where to respond. For a small, casual wedding, handwrite invitations in black ink (perhaps a friend will offer calligraphy skills) on good-quality white or off-white notepaper or foldovers. Write in the first-person, in the same way that you would extend any informal invitation. Printed or engraved invitations are rarely sent for a small wedding. Your invitation includes: names of bride and groom; date, time, place; mention of hospitality to follow, if any; expression of pleasure at having guests celebrate with you. The invitation, whether formal or informal, may be issued by the couple, by both their parents, by the woman's parents, by the man's parents, or by a relative or family friend—in short, by whoever is hosting the event or whoever is most appropriate. A deceased parent is not named in the invitation as though it were being issued by her or him, but the person can be included if the invitation is sent by the bride and groom ("Jean Lucas, daughter of Martha Lucas and the late George Lucas, and Bruce Wetheral, son of Mr. and Mrs. John Henry Wetheral, request the honour of your presence . . .").

- Addressing invitations is an art in itself. On the outer envelope, list full names and addresses, with no abbreviations, if possible. On the inner envelope, repeat last names only ("Mr. and Mrs. Hollingrake"). Don't include young children's names on the outer envelope but list their first names under the parents' names on the inner envelope. (Never add "and family.") Older children (between thirteen and eighteen) receive their own invitations. Address one invitation using both full names to an unmarried couple living together. Your return address goes in the upper left-hand corner, unless you use embossed or engraved envelopes, in which case it is on the back flap. (Note that the U.S. Postal Service discourages placing return addresses on the back flap.) Use a good-quality fountain pen, felt tip, or narrow-tipped calligraphy pen to address the envelopes.
- Wedding cancellation announcements are similar in style and format to the invitations. If formal wedding invitations were sent, formal cancellation announcements are sent; they shouldn't be as lavish as the invitations, but should be of approximately the same quality. The message is simple: "Marjorie Corder and Theodore Honey announce that their marriage on the twenty-first of April, two thousand and eight, will not take place."
- Printed, engraved, or handwritten announcements, modeled on the wedding invitation, are sent to those who weren't invited to the ceremony or reception. The same type of stationery is used, and the wording is similar. If formal invitations were sent, the announcements will also be formal; if the wedding was small and informal and invitations were handwritten, the announcements will also be handwritten. They are mailed as near the wedding date as possible (address them in advance), and may include at-home cards. The announcement is made by the bride's family ("Mr. and Mrs. Raymond Gray announce the marriage of their daughter Polly to . . ."); by the couple themselves ("Camilla Christy and Matthew Haslam announce their marriage on Saturday, the fifth of June . . ."); or by both sets of parents ("Evelyn and Peter Gresham and Bridget and Henry Derricks announce the marriage of their daughter and son, Audrey Gresham and George Derricks, on Friday, the third of April, two thousand and eight, Emmanuel Lutheran Church, Golding, Nebraska").
- Reply to all wedding invitations. Use the formal reply card or, if there isn't one, use the same wording and degree of formality as the invitation to ei-

ther "accept with pleasure" or "decline with regret." It is not improper to reply informally to a formal invitation. What is absolutely imperative is that you respond. (You need not respond if you are invited to the wedding ceremony only.) When accepting an invitation to a wedding reception, accept only for those people named on the invitation. If your children are not listed, they are not invited. It is highly improper to bring them to the reception. In the same way, if your envelope doesn't have "and guest" written on it, do not bring someone with you.

- Etiquette on thank-you notes for wedding gifts is inflexible: a handwritten thank you is sent for every gift, even if you thanked the individual in person or if you work with the person every day. Both newlyweds are responsible for thank-you notes; whoever writes mentions the other person ("Mae and I appreciate . . ."; "Hugh joins me in . . ."). Tradition allowed a month after the wedding to mail thank-you notes and contemporary authorities allow up to three months. However, the advice here is to send them immediately after the honeymoon. "The path of later leads to the house of never" (Donald E. Walker) and for many couples the three months turn into six, which turn into a year, which turns into embarrassment and denial and, finally, a guilty forgetfulness. Because everybody is busy today—even the people who found time to send you a gift—there's no excuse for not making a priority of sending wedding thank-you notes.

- Each thank-you note includes: a mention of the gift ("the silver bread tray," not "your lovely gift"); an expression of pleasure; a mention of how you'll use it, why you like it, how much you needed it; a sentence or two unrelated to the gift ("so good to see you at the wedding" or "hope you will come see our new home"). Don't mention dollar amounts of money gifts in your thank you, but tell how you plan to spend the money. Write separate and different thank yous to friends who sent joint gifts, unless the gift is from a large group, such as coworkers. If you use commercial thank-you foldovers or note cards, choose the plainest type. When a wedding gift is not to your taste, focus on the kindness of the giver rather than on the gift. For additional guidelines on writing thank-you notes, see THANKS.

- When you can't write immediate or at least timely thank-you notes (because of a large number of gifts, extended honeymoon, illness), send a handwritten or printed or engraved acknowledgment card for each gift. This lets the person know the gift arrived safely and assures them that you'll write a personal note as soon as you can. Acknowledgment cards in no way replace thank-you notes and are followed by them as soon as possible.

What Not to Say

- In formal wedding invitations and announcements, don't abbreviate anything except "Mr.," "Mrs.," "Ms.," "Jr.," and sometimes military rank. ("Doctor" is written out unless the name following it is too long.) In the case of initials in names, either supply the name for which an initial stands or omit the initial altogether. Write out "Second" and "Third" after a name or use Roman numerals ("Caspar Goodwood II"). There is no comma between the name and the numeral. The names of states are spelled out ("Alabama," not Ala. or AL) as are dates ("November third") and the time ("half past eight o'clock," "half past five o'clock"). All numbers under 100 are spelled out. No punctuation is used except for commas after the days of the week ("Saturday, the sixteenth of June") or periods after "Mr.," "Mrs.," "Jr." No words are capitalized except for people's names, place names, and days of the week or months. The year is not included on wedding invitations, but is usually included on announcements.
- When writing thank-you notes for wedding gifts, don't ask where a gift was purchased so that you can exchange it, and don't mention duplication of gifts.

Tips on Writing

- Traditionally "the honour of your presence" indicates a religious ceremony and "the pleasure of your company" is used for civil weddings or for wedding receptions.
- Watch for nonparallel forms when referring to the wedding couple in invitations, announcements, and other wedding correspondence—for example, "the marriage of Adela Polperro to Mr. Lucian Gildersleeve." Use honorifics for both (Ms. and Mr., for example) or for neither (neither is preferred). The phrase "man and wife" is "husband and wife" or "man and woman."
- Timing: ask friends to be your attendants as soon as you have a date; order printed or engraved invitations at least three months before the wedding; begin to address invitations two months or more before the wedding (the envelopes can be picked up earlier than the invitations); mail all invitations at the same time—between three and six weeks before the wedding.
- If you use reply cards, invitees will know how to respond. If you don't, insert an address or telephone number below the RSVP so they know where to send their responses.
- In her 1941 book, Mary Owens Crowther tells readers mailing wedding invitations: "Do not use two one-cent stamps in place of a two-cent stamp. Somehow one-cent stamps are not dignified." Although her advice is dated,

considering the appearance of your postage stamps is not; most invitations and announcements use attractive or meaningful commemorative stamps.

■ When you receive an engagement or wedding announcement, there is no obligation to send a gift, but it is customary to write your congratulations to the engaged or newly married couple. You may properly offer either one your "congratulations" or "best wishes." (These expressions used to be sex-linked; one was limited to use for the woman, one for the man.)

■ If you are late with your wedding congratulations, write anyway. Most people will understand and will be pleased that you remembered at all. Apologize only briefly for the delay.

■ Jot a brief description of the wedding gift on the back of the signed card that accompanies it. This has proved useful to more than a few newly married couples trying to determine which of the mystery gifts came from whom.

Special Situations

■ In today's over-scheduled world, many couples send "save the date" letters or even e-mails to notify family and friends of a wedding that may be a year or more in the future. Invitations are sent later in the normal way, six weeks before the wedding. While six weeks' notice was ample in the days when families and friends lived in the same small town and knew each other's news, today it is inadequate for making flight reservations, scheduling vacations around the date, or keeping the work calendar free for that day.

■ For a wedding announcement published in the newspaper, include as much of the following as allowed: bride's and groom's full names; date, time, and place of wedding; name of officiator or presider; names of members of the wedding party (and relation to the wedding couple); names, hometowns, and occupations or accomplishments of the couple's parents (and occasionally grandparents); information on the couple's education and careers; description of the flowers, music, and wedding party's clothes; where the reception was held; the couple's address after marriage. (If the woman keeps her birth name or if the couple adopts a hyphenated name, this is a good way to let people know: "Marian Belthem and Augustus F. G. Richmond will be living at 1871 Meredith.") Avoid nicknames and abbreviations. Call your newspaper in advance for guidelines on submitting wedding announcements. Some newspapers publish information about weddings only if there is news value. Others charge a fee for announcements. Some will publish either an engagement notice or a wedding announcement, but not both. And others will not print an announcement if it is "old news"—arriving more than several weeks after the wedding. Some want the information about three weeks before the wedding so that it can be run the day after the wedding. Wedding announcements can also be sent to employee newsletters, alumnae/alumni magazines, or other affiliation publications.

■ When the bride, the groom, or both are members of the military, it's customary to use their rank on invitations and announcements unless they are noncommissioned officers or enlisted personnel, in which case it may be omitted.

■ Prospective in-laws appreciate a gracious note of welcome by members of the family.

■ When you invite some people to the wedding and others to both wedding and reception, your wedding invitation mentions the ceremony only. Enclose a card (about 3"×4", and of the same style stationery as the invitation) with an invitation to the reception. It is a shortened form of the wedding invitation: "Nora Hopper and George Trimmins request the pleasure of your company at their wedding reception [or: a reception following their wedding], on Saturday, the twelfth of June, Walter Village Inn, 55 North Walter Street. RSVP." If all guests are invited to both the wedding and reception, you add, after the place of the wedding on your invitation, "Reception immediately following" or "and afterward at . . ." or "followed by a reception at . . ."

■ When prospective wedding guests indicate in their acceptance that they are bringing a friend or their children, whom you have not invited, write that you are pleased they can come to the wedding but that the reception is limited to those invited because of space or is for adults only. When you invite friends who may not know anyone at the reception, you can either call them for the name of a companion (so you can send a personal invitation) or add "and Guest" to their invitation.

■ To inform friends and relatives of your address after marriage, enclose an at-home card in your wedding invitation or announcement. It is usually the same style as your other wedding stationery, about 2¾"×4": "Linda Condon and Arnaud Hallet will be at home after the sixth of June at 1918 Hergesheimer Road, Waunakee, Wisconsin 53597."

■ To let family and friends know that the woman plans to keep her birth name or that the couple is adopting a hyphenated or an altogether new surname, insert a small printed or engraved card (matching the wedding stationery) in the wedding invitation or announcement: "After their marriage, Clarissa Graham and Charles Belton will use the surname Belton-Graham," or "Clarissa Graham wishes to announce that following her marriage she will retain her birth name."

Format

■ Engagement or wedding announcement notices sent to newspapers are typed and double-spaced. If a photograph accompanies it, identify it on the back in case it gets separated from the announcement. (Use a return-address label or taped-on piece of paper; don't write directly on the back of the photo.)

■ Wedding invitations and announcements are engraved, printed, or hand-written. A bewildering variety of papers, type styles, inks, and designs are available at printers, stationery stores, and large department stores. Ecru remains the most popular color for invitations and social stationery. Your choice depends on the type of wedding—the more formal the wedding, the more formal the invitations and announcements. You can order matching name cards, thank-you notes, informals, notepaper, or other stationery at the same time.

■ Envelopes (for example, for reply cards and thank-you notes) must be at least 3½" × 5" to comply with postal regulations. And if your invitations are oversized or weigh more than an ounce (which happens with high-quality paper and two envelopes) they will need extra postage.

■ When responding to an invitation that contained no reply card, use formal notepaper or foldovers. If you have a card with your name on it, write underneath your name "accepts with pleasure" or "declines with regret" and then repeat the information about the event and the date.

WORDS

acknowledge	ceremony	marriage	ritual
announce	congratulations	matrimony	union
bless	happiness	nuptials	vows
celebrate	joy	pleasure	wishes

PHRASES

acknowledges with thanks the receipt of	rehearsal dinner
groom's dinner	request the honour of your presence
happy to announce/to invite you to	request the pleasure of your company
help us celebrate our wedding	share in the joy
invite you to celebrate with us	united in wedlock
joined in holy matrimony	wedding party
our fondest congratulations	we would be honored to
	wish to acknowledge the receipt of
	witness our marriage

SENTENCES

Aurelia and I were greatly touched by the beautiful family tea service you gave us for our wedding—we feel we're now connected to all the family that's gone before and all that is yet to come.

Best wishes on your wedding day!

Jane Vallens and Andrew Satchel gratefully acknowledge the receipt of your beautiful wedding gift and look forward to writing you a personal note of thanks at an early date.

Jesse joins me in thanking you for the oil painting you did especially for us—it is our first piece of original art!

Mary Llewellyn and Martin Hallam request the pleasure of your company at the marriage of their daughter Mary Frances.

Our very best wishes to you both for many years of happiness, health, and prosperity.

Please join us in celebrating the marriage of our daughter Sally to William Carter.

Thank you for your generous check, which will go a long way toward helping us buy the piano we have our eye on!

The ceremony will take place at 1:30 p.m., and a reception at the house will follow.

We're sorry, but we are limited in the number of guests we can have at the reception—we hope you'll still be able to come and that we can meet your cousin some other time.

We were delighted to hear of your engagement—Anita is an intelligent, beautiful, and kind young woman, and the two of you are beautifully matched!

We wish you every happiness as you celebrate the love you have for each other.

PARAGRAPHS

Mr. and Mrs. Solomon Darke accept with pleasure Mr. and Mrs. Charles Heath's invitation to the marriage of their daughter Margaret to Rupert Johnson on Saturday, the twelfth of June.

Congratulations and best wishes to both of you on this, your wedding day. May you take with you into the years ahead some beautiful memories of those who love you and of your shining love for each other.

We would like to make an appointment with you to discuss the music for our wedding, which is scheduled for June 16 at 1:00 p.m. We have some ideas (and will bring some music with us), but we would appreciate some suggestions from you.

Julia and I will be married at our apartment on Saturday, June eighteenth at 5:30 p.m. It would mean a great deal to us if you would join us for the ceremony and for dinner afterwards.

You could not have chosen a more exquisite gift than the Waterford clock. I was deeply moved by your love and generosity. Unfortunately, Kit and I have canceled the wedding and we are returning all gifts. As you can imagine, I will never forget your thoughtfulness and I will always think of you whenever I see Waterford crystal.

Christina Hossett and Albert Edward Preemby were married June 18, 2010, at Wells First Christian Church. The Reverend Wilfred Devizes performed the ceremony. Parents are Mr. and Mrs. H. G. Hossett of Wells and Mr. and Mrs. A. E. Preemby Sr. of Waynesville. Christina and Albert want to thank all the guests who celebrated with them. Both are employed at Stephens Insurance.

Bernice and I are absolutely delighted with the electric blanket. You must have been poor students yourselves once, living on the third floor of an old brownstone, hoping that perhaps today the heat might make it all the way upstairs. It's a beautiful, thoughtful, practical gift, and we're grateful.

SAMPLE LETTERS

Mr. and Mrs. David Herries
announce that the marriage of
their daughter Dorothy
to Arthur Bellairs
on Saturday, the tenth of May
will not take place.

———————

Mr. Edmund Roundelay
regrets that owing to
the recent death of
Evelyn Ferguson Roundelay
the invitations to the marriage
of their daughter Crystal
to Maxwell Dunston
must be recalled

———————

The honour of your presence
is requested at the marriage of
Sybil Anstey Herbert
to
Harry Jardine
on Saturday, the tenth of October
at one o'clock
Lehmann Methodist Church
and afterward at
The New Lehmann Inn

RSVP
Sybil Anstey Herbert
20 Ianthe Court
Lehmann, OH 45042

———

Dear Lucy and Fred,

Christopher and I are so pleased you will be able to attend our wedding celebration. I'm afraid there's been a misunderstanding, however. You know how much we enjoy Freddy, Elsa, and Charles, but we are not planning on having any children at the reception. I hope you can find a babysitter so you can still come. Thanks for understanding.

Love,

———

Miss Laetitia Prism
regrets that she is unable to accept
the kind invitation of
Mr. and Mrs. Oscar Fairfax
to the marriage of their daughter
Gwendolyn Fairfax
Saturday, the sixth of June
two thousand eight
at half past seven o'clock

———

Dear Marjorie,

Will and I have finally made the great decision—we're going to be married next August 19! And the really important question is: will you be my attendant? I can't imagine having anyone but you. However, if you can't get away—and what with your job, Richard's new business, and the children's activities, I know it will take some doing—I will certainly understand.

Enclosed is a sketch of the dress you'd wear. I want to pay for it, so don't worry about that. And of course you'll stay at the house, but unfortunately my budget won't run to your airfare. Will that be a problem?

I'll call next week after you've had time to think about this. In the meantime, Will sends his love along with mine.

———

Mr. and Mrs. Orville Jones
accept with pleasure
the kind invitation of
Belinda Jorricks
and
Charles Stobbs
to their marriage on
Friday, the tenth of May
two thousand and eight
at 7:00 p.m.
St. James A.M.E. Zion Church
Reception following
Surtees Country Club
1838 Plains Highway

———

Christina Allaby and Theobald Pontifex
announce with great pleasure
their marriage on
Saturday, the twenty-third of June
two thousand and nine
Butler, Maine

———

Dear Grace and Harold,

Our dear Stella and Stanley Kowalski are being married on Saturday, September 4, at 3:00 p.m. in an informal ceremony at our house.

We'd love to have you celebrate with us, and stay after the ceremony for a small reception. Let me know if you can join us.

Fondly,

———

Mimi Wynant and Christian Jorgensen
announce that their marriage
has been postponed from
Saturday, the third of June
until

Saturday, the sixth of August
at two o'clock
St. Anselm's Church
Webster City
Reception to follow
Webster City Country Club

———

See also: ACCEPTANCES, ACKNOWLEDGMENTS, ANNOUNCE-MENTS, BELATED, CONGRATULATIONS, INVITATIONS, REFUS-ALS, REQUESTS, RESPONSES, THANK YOU

FIFTY

LETTERS OF WELCOME

Come in the evening, or come in the morning,
Come when you're looked for, or come without warning.
Kisses and welcomes you'll find here before you,
And the oftener you come here the more I'll adore you.
—THOMAS OSBORNE DAVIS

Because they're optional, letters of welcome are read with surprise, pleasure, and gratitude. They are a powerful sales tool for businesses, and a charming approach to smoothing and cementing interpersonal relations among neighbors, coworkers, and people with whom we have frequent dealings. For the naturally hospitable among us, they are a way of life and a joy to write.

Write Letters of Welcome to

- new business contacts/customers/clients
- new businesses in the neighborhood
- new coworkers/employees
- new members of club/organization/temple/church
- new neighbors
- new students/teachers
- potential customers/clients
- prospective in-laws

How to Say It

- State how happy you are to have the person join your company, store, division, club, family, group, neighborhood.
- Offer to help the person become acquainted with their new surroundings, duties, colleagues, neighbors.
- Tell something positive about the neighborhood, company, or organization the person is joining. If a special event is coming up, mention it to give the person something to look forward to.
- Suggest a possible future meeting, a store visit, an invitation to call you, or at least say that you're looking forward to meeting sometime soon. Assure the person you'll be glad to answer questions (include your telephone number).

What Not to Say

- Don't refer to negative aspects of the person's new situation, for example, the mountains of unfinished work left by a predecessor or the roof problems that troubled the previous owner.
- Don't say "Good luck!" It implies that good luck will be needed.
- Avoid a strong selling message when welcoming customers.

Tips on Writing

■ Send your welcome promptly; it is most appreciated when the new kid on the block still feels insecure.

■ Find common ground between you or your organization and the person you're welcoming ("I understand you're a gardener—you'll be interested to know that many of us are!").

■ The welcome letter is a fitting place to let the newcomer subtly know about any unwritten rules you might have. ("Although there's never time to chat during office hours, I'd like to get to know you better over lunch someday" or "We look forward to seeing you once you're settled in—but do give us a call first.")

Special Situations

■ When welcoming new employees, include detailed terms of employment to avoid later misunderstandings: hours, duties, salary, title, starting date, supervisor. If the newcomer receives packets of information—building regulations, benefits, contact numbers—include a letter of welcome as the first sheet in the packet. A brief handwritten note from a superior, sent separately, is a powerful way to inspire loyalty and enthusiasm.

■ In late August, some elementary school teachers send postcards to welcome incoming students and to help them feel positive about returning to school. Mention a project that the class will enjoy or say, "I think we're going to have a great year." As this requires money for stamps and stationery, access to class lists, time, and energy, the parents of a child who isn't looking forward to the new school year might offer to help the teacher with welcome notes.

■ When welcoming a new business or new family to your market area, establish name-recognition and product-association in their minds. Offer a free service or product to introduce the potential customer to your goods and services and to encourage a visit to your office or store. Enclose a coupon for a small gift or a discount. A relatively inexpensive but useful gift to newcomers is information, for example, a card with phone numbers of area services, hospitals, day-care centers, schools, or hotlines. In a welcome letter, the sales message is more effective when it is unobtrusive and undemanding. A personal letter of welcome to potential customers over the manager's or president's signature will be more cost-effective than mass-produced flyers stuck between a door.

■ After a customer or client visits your place of business, follow up with a letter of welcome. If you have not done so earlier, you might now offer some sort of discount or coupon to encourage the customer to return a second time—the possible beginnings of a habit.

■ To invite prospective customers to an open house or to visit your new store or offices at their convenience, see INVITATIONS.

Format

■ Letters to new neighbors, prospective in-laws, and new students or teachers are handwritten on foldovers or personal stationery.

■ Welcome letters that carry a sales message and letters to new employees, colleagues, and organization members are typed on letterhead or business-personal stationery.

■ Postcards are often used to welcome new customers with a special offer or discount.

WORDS

community	greetings	meet	reception
congregation	hope	neighborhood	together
delighted	hospitality	organization	visit
excited	introduce	pleased	
future	invite	questions	

PHRASES

bid a cordial welcome

delighted to make your acquaintance

eager to serve you

expect long and fruitful years of association

extend a welcome

family circle

good place to pitch your tent

help you get established

look forward to meeting/seeing you

look us up

make yourself at home

open arms/door/house

pleasure to welcome you

so happy you can join

take great pleasure in

to help you get acquainted

warm reception waiting

welcome aboard/back

welcome mat

SENTENCES

I look forward to a mutually satisfying business relationship.

I'm pleased to welcome you to the Board of Directors of the Margaret Peel Museum.

It is with the greatest pleasure that I welcome you to Paragon Photo Processing.

Let us know how we can help you feel quickly at home.

The door is always open to you.

The Packles & Son Theatrical Agency is pleased to welcome you to our select family of talented clients.

To introduce you to the faculty, there will be a welcome reception Thursday, September 8.

We believe you will enjoy meeting this challenge with us.

We hope you'll enjoy this area and the great neighbors as much as we have.

Welcome to the team!

We welcome you to Daphnis Wool and Textiles and look forward to a long, productive, and satisfying collaboration.

You've made a wonderful choice (in my opinion)!

PARAGRAPHS

Welcome to the Guest & Company family of shoppers! It is always a pleasure to greet a new customer. Customer satisfaction has had the highest priority at Guest & Company since 1860. Although the value, variety, and dependability of our products probably inspired your first order, it is only great service that will keep you coming back. If you are not satisfied with your purchase for any reason, just return it for a refund, exchange, or credit—no questions asked! Thank you for shopping with us, and we hope you are pleased with your first order.

It is my great pleasure to welcome you to the Rivermouth Centipedes. The enclosed preapproved membership card entitles you to all benefits and privileges of club membership.

We officially welcome Ottila Gottescheim as Director of Education on Friday, August 7 at 6:30 p.m. Please join us for services and an Oneg Shabbat in her honor.

Welcome to *SportsStory*, the best sports fiction published today! You will receive your first issue shortly. Don't forget to vote for your favorite story every month on our Internet site.

Nothing pleases us more than to be able to say "welcome back" when an inactive account is revived. We appreciate your return to our list of active accounts and look forward to serving you again.

Welcome to Plattsville! All of us here at The Tarkington Gift and Card Shop hope that you soon feel at home in your new surroundings and that you find much to enjoy and appreciate in Plattsville. To help acquaint you with your new town, we have put together a packet of information in conjunction with the chamber of commerce that we hope you will find helpful. Also enclosed is a coupon for 25 percent off your first purchase with us.

Welcome to Clyde Episcopal Church. I hope you felt "at home" with us at your first service last Sunday. On February 16 at 7:00 p.m. we are having a welcome party for new parishioners in the church hall. Newcomers have found it helpful to meet some of their neighbors and to hear about the programs we offer. We hope that the whole family will be able to come.

Thank you for your first purchase at Eyvind Hardware, and welcome to our store! We are more than "just a hardware store." You can ask any of us for advice and information on a wide range of topics—whether it's the most appropriate floor finish for your home, the differences between grades of sandpaper and steel wool, how to use our rental products, or the advantages and disadvantages of various grout cleaners. Bring us all your home maintenance questions. To show our appreciation for your business, we are enclosing a coupon good for a free pair of gardening gloves. Visit us again soon!

Dear Rose Lorimer:

Welcome back! We're pleased that you are renewing your membership in the Medieval History Round Table. We know you'll continue to be satisfied with the many benefits that are yours to enjoy in the next year.

You are entitled to tuition discounts at the University, admission discounts at all conferences, workshops, and special lectures, and a subscription to the monthly newsletter. A less tangible benefit is the opportunity to meet people with interests and pursuits like your own.

Your membership dollars help support our programming, and your participation helps make the Round Table more responsive to the people it serves.

Sincerely,

————

Dear Ms. Spenser-Smith:

It is with the greatest pleasure that we welcome you to the E. H. Young Literary Society. Enclosed please find: a list of members, a copy of our bylaws, a schedule of this year's meetings, minutes from the last meeting, and an annotated bibliography of the books we'll be reading this year.

Your mentor—to make your introduction into the Society as pleasant as possible—will be Ms. Hannah Mole. If you have any questions, please feel free to direct them to her or to me.

I am looking forward to visiting with you after the next meeting.

Sincerely yours,

————

Dear Mr. Jellyband:

The Dover Business Association welcomes you to one of the busiest and most successful retail areas on the south coast. Those of us who own or manage businesses here have been working together for the past eleven years to bring new business in and to promote the area. Enclosed is a description of the group's purpose and activities.

As the new owner of The Fisherman's Rest, you are cordially invited to join the Association. The next meeting will be held June 15 at The Crown and Feather. We hope you will enjoy doing business in Dover as much as we have.

Feel free to contact any of the listed members for information or assistance.

Sincerely,

————

Dear Dr. and Mrs. Townshend-Mahony,

Welcome to Buddlecombe! We're having a neighborhood barbecue/potluck dinner on August 3 at our place, and we would love to have you come. Most of the neighbors will be there, and we think you'll enjoy meeting them. If you'd like to bring something, a cold salad would be perfect.

Yours truly,

Dear Mr. Harness,

I am pleased to tell you that your six-month review shows that your work is more than satisfactory, your sales record is exceptional, and your relationships with managers, co-workers, and customers are all very cordial and productive. As of today, you are being upgraded from temporary to permanent employee status. Welcome to Trengartha Tin Plate Works.

With best wishes,

Dear Godfrey,

Nancy just told us the good news, and we are both happy that she has chosen to spend the rest of her life with you, and you with her. We were not entirely surprised, as we've been hearing about you quite a bit lately! You already feel like part of the family, and we're looking forward to seeing you both at the end of the month. Welcome to the family!

Dear Mr. and Mrs. Webb,

Welcome to Groves Corners. We sincerely hope you'll enjoy living in this friendly community. We at Thornton Furniture offer you a special welcome and invite you to come in and say hello to our friendly, courteous salespeople who are eager to serve you. To make your shopping even more convenient and enjoyable, we are pleased to extend credit privileges to you. Just fill out an application form the next time you are in the store.

We are always happy to answer questions, help you find what you need, or place special orders. Don't hesitate to ask. We pride ourselves on satisfying our customers!

Yours truly,

See also: EMPLOYMENT, GOODWILL, NEIGHBORS, SALES

MECHANICS

It was very pleasant to me to get a letter from you the other day. Perhaps I should have found it pleasanter if I had been able to decipher it. I don't think that I mastered anything beyond the date (which I knew) and the signature (which I guessed at). There's a singular and a perpetual charm in a letter of yours; it never grows old, it never loses its novelty.
—Thomas Bailey Aldrich

Appendix I covers the concrete aspects of letter writing, for example, types of stationery, letter formats, envelope addresses, and postal regulations. For assistance with the content of your message (tone, style, language, grammar), see APPENDIX II.

STATIONERY

Business stationery

Traditionally, business stationery size is 8½"×11"—for the practical reason that odd-sized stationery is difficult to file. White, off-white, cream, light gray, or other neutral shades are acceptable colors.

Twenty-pound rag bond paper is a popular choice for business stationery; for higher quality, go to a thirty-pound paper. Textures and finishes—flat, matte, smooth, woven, linen-look, watermarked—are a matter of personal taste; all are acceptable. Many businesses use recyclable paper, which is good for public relations as well as for the environment.

All business organizations and many individuals use a letterhead on their stationery, which includes the name of the firm (or the individual); address including ZIP code (ideally ZIP+4); area code and telephone number; e-mail address; optionally, fax number, website address, telex number. The letterhead can also include a logo, an employee's name and title, a list of board of directors or other governing bodies (if lengthy, this list is arranged along the left edge of the page). A good letterhead is readable, informative, attractive, and not too insistent. Printers can show you many formats, inks, styles of type, papers, and engraving and printing methods. The most formal and conservative choice is black ink on white or off-white high-quality paper.

Second sheets are of the same quality as the letterhead paper. They are either plain or are printed or engraved with the company's name. The print is smaller than on letterhead and the address isn't included.

Envelopes match your stationery in color, weight, general style, and typeface. Your return address always goes in the upper left corner of the front of the envelope. "The return address. Don't let your letters leave home without it." (Steve Sikora) The United States Postal Service (USPS) discourages return addresses on the back flap because sorting machines can't flip envelopes over to check for a return address.

Personal-business stationery

The size referred to as personal-business or executive stationery is 7" or 7½" × 10". Choose white, off-white, neutral, or pale shades of good-quality bond paper. The letterhead includes: the company name and address with the person's name, or name and title, set underneath or off to one side. An e-mail address is often included.

Although its use is declining, personal-business stationery is convenient for brief notes; when writing to someone as individual-to-individual rather than as company representative to employee or customer; when the information is casual; or for matters that cross over into the social or personal arena (congratulating a colleague on an award, for example).

Memos

Memos include anything from 8½" × 11" stationery to small pads of printed memo sheets. In white, off-white, neutral, or pastel colors, memo stationery matches the firm's regular business stationery but has only the company name at the top. Memos sent outside the company are printed with the company name, address, telephone and fax numbers. Some memo paper is labeled "Internal Correspondence" and at the top has "TO: FROM: DATE: SUBJECT:" with a space after each.

Personal stationery

You may need 8½" × 11" paper for some personal uses (complaints, household business matters), but personal stationery is generally 7–8" × 10½" or 5½" × 6½"–7½" and has matching envelopes.

Formal stationery (for handwritten invitations, condolences, thank yous) is white, off-white, cream, eggshell, straw, beige, gray, or other neutral color with a self border, contrasting border, or no border. For informal use, almost anything is acceptable, with the exception perhaps of stationery that's perfumed, decorated with tiny objects, ruled, oddly shaped, or otherwise says too loudly, "Look at me!" On the other hand, nobody appears to have ever returned a letter because the stationery had too much personality.

If you use a letterhead, monograms, or other printing on your personal stationery, your second sheets have no printing but are the same color and quality as your first sheets.

One-page notecards and foldovers (at least $3\frac{1}{2}$" × 5" when folded) are of a heavier weight paper than stationery and are popular for thank-you notes, handwritten invitations, replies to invitations, condolences, and other formal and informal messages. They usually come with matching envelopes and may be engraved or printed. If your name, address, initials, or other printing appear on the front panel, write on the inside—beginning at the top of the two panels for a long letter or using the bottom panel for a short note. Otherwise, begin your note on the front panel. The Postal Service discourages printing or engraving your return address on the envelope's flap. Letter-Sorting Machines (LSMs) cannot flip a letter to check the other side when it fails to find the return address on the front.

ENVELOPES

Business

The Postal Service says that for the best service you should use the optical-character-reader (OCR) format for your envelopes, a machine-readable style for rapid sorting. Type or machine-print all address information in capital letters, using black ink on white paper and sharp, clear print with no overlapping or touching letters. Problem fonts include extended fonts, italic fonts, condensed fonts, bold fonts, and stylized scriptlike fonts. Do not underline address information as that will interfere with character recognition. Scanners can read a combination of uppercase and lowercase characters but prefer all uppercase. Addresses appear flush left style, that is, the first letter of each line in the address should be directly under the first letter of the line above. Include as much address information as possible: apartment, floor, suite number, ZIP code or ZIP+4. Omit all punctuation (except the hyphen in the ZIP+4). Use abbreviations preferred by the Postal Service (see list at the end of this Appendix). Leave at least one space between words and two spaces between word groups. Two spaces are preferred between city and state, and two spaces between state and ZIP code (with no punctuation). Leave the bar code area free of any writing. Allow at least $\frac{1}{2}$" on either side of the address and $\frac{5}{8}$" from bottom of address to bottom of envelope. Every address must have a minimum of three lines and a maximum of five lines. If you have an attention line ("ATTN: Tom Bowling"), it goes on the second line (under the company name). If the address contains both a post office box and a street address, it will be delivered to whichever appears directly above the city and state. Hand-stamp or type mailing directions ("Priority," "Media Mail") under the area where the postage will go.

Personal

For all formal and many informal personal letters, handwrite your return address (upper left corner) as well as the addressee's (lower right). For less formal personal correspondence the envelope may be typed (single-spaced). Although formal personal stationery is sometimes engraved or printed with the person's name and address on the back flap, the Postal Service prefers the return address on the front. For the other person's address, use either block style (each line's left edge lines up with the others) or indented style (each successive line is indented one or two spaces). Formal correspondence traditionally does not use abbreviations for "Street," "Avenue," "Parkway," "Road," or state names. However, the Postal Service requests that, for optimum sorting and delivery, the address be printed all in capital letters, with no punctuation except the hyphen in the ZIP + 4, using approved two-letter state abbreviations. The European "7" is not recommended because of the possibility of its being confused by the scanner with f, h, p, or t. USPS guidelines differ from traditional addressing of personal correspondence. When Judith Martin ("Miss Manners") was asked if we must forgo etiquette rules on envelopes, she recommended following the USPS rules to ensure delivery, but suggested that the double envelope system (used for wedding invitations) can permit the writer to send a personal letter that is both prettily addressed and properly delivered.

ZIP codes

All letters need correct ZIP codes to be delivered. When you know it, use the ZIP + 4 number; it indicates local routes and can speed your letter significantly. Use your ZIP + 4 on outgoing correspondence so that people use it when writing to you. Find ZIP codes online at www.usps.com/zip4 or by calling 800-ASK-USPS or by purchasing a ZIP code directory. For in-town mail, check your local phone book, which often lists ZIP codes by street names.

The Postal Service prefers that there not be less than one full character space and not more than five full character spaces between city, state, and ZIP code; it prefers two spaces between city and state, and two spaces between state and ZIP code.

Note that there should be no information on the envelope below the ZIP code line. This area is reserved for bar coding.

Folding and inserting

When inserting a sheet of 8½" × 11" paper into a #10 envelope, fold it in horizontal thirds, and insert it with the back of the top third facing the flap so that the recipient pulls out the letter, flips up that third, and is ready to begin reading. When using window envelopes, letters need to be folded so that the name and address appear in the window.

When inserting a full-size sheet into an envelope smaller than a number ten, fold it in half horizontally and then again in thirds and insert it so that the open end is on the left and the top fold faces the flap. The recipient pulls it out, rotates it a quarter turn to the right, opens it, and is ready to read.

Personal stationery is folded once with the writing inside and inserted into its matching envelope, open edges down. The recipient removes the letter and flips up the top half to read.

When folding any size sheet of paper, the top and bottom edges are not perfectly even with each other (although the sides are). It is easier to unfold a sheet of paper if one end extends just slightly beyond the other.

No matter what stationery you're using, the salutation (which will be inside the folds) faces the flap of the envelope.

Enclosures

Flat enclosures (checks, folded flyers, business cards) are placed inside the folds of the letter. To safeguard against your reader overlooking them, add an enclosure line to your letter ("Enc.: subscription blank"). For larger enclosures, use an appropriately sized manila envelope (many businesses have their own imprinted larger envelopes). When there is no urgency about bulky or heavy enclosures, send them third class and advise your correspondent by first-class mail of the package being sent separately.

WRITING, TYPING, PRINTING

Handwritten

Black or blue ink is preferred to other colors, and pencil is never used. Certain notes are almost always written by hand: thank-you notes, messages of sympathy, replies to invitations, invitations that are not engraved or printed. Write by hand to convey personal feeling or informality or, in the case of an interoffice memo, when you have a one- or two-line message.

Typewritten or computer-generated

Business correspondence is being word processed in almost all companies.

Engraved or printed

Acknowledgments, announcements, invitations, and response cards are commonly engraved or printed (engraving is more expensive). Printers can explain the differences between the types of engraving and printing; show you dozens of samples; and offer you a wide variety of papers, formats, type styles, and inks as well as advice on how to word your message.

ELEMENTS OF A LETTER

Personal letters

DATE: The date is placed near the top of the right side of the page. When the person is unfamiliar with your address and you aren't using stationery with your address on it, start with your address in the upper right corner (usually two lines) followed by the date. The left edges of these three lines line up underneath each other.

SALUTATION: Begin the salutation a few spaces down and flush left. It is followed by a comma ("Dear Jean,"). You don't usually put the person's address above it, as you would with a business letter.

BODY OF THE LETTER: Indent the first paragraph—five spaces if you are typing the letter, about ¾" if you are handwriting it. Indent all other paragraphs the same way.

CLOSING: The complimentary close ("Love," "Sincerely,") is set about one line below your last sentence and to the right, its left edge on a line with the left edge of your date. Sign your name on the line below the complimentary close.

If your letter is more than one page long, generally write only on one side of your stationery.

Memos

HEADINGS: At the top of the memo are the headings, the to/from/date/subject lines, which replace the letter's salutation. The most common ways of arranging the headings on the page are:

TO:	Paul Rayley	TO: Rowena Ravenstock
FROM:	Minta Doyle	FROM: Max Tryte
DATE:	April 23, 2010	DATE: November 1, 2010
RE:	Lighthouse repairs	SUBJECT: Gouache supplies

———

TO: Martin Fenner	DATE: July 14, 2009
FROM: Owen Kettle	SUBJECT: Series on tuberculosis

MESSAGE OR BODY OF THE MEMO: There are no rigid rules for spacing in a memo, but two or three blank lines are commonly left between the headings and the text, which is single-spaced. Each paragraph begins flush left and is separated from other paragraphs by a single line of space.

NOTATION LINES: Notations such as "Enc.:" or "cc:" are placed flush left at the bottom, as in a letter.

No signature is necessary on a memo, but people often sign or initial it at the bottom or next to their name in the "From:" line. Some memos are arranged in two parts so that the recipient can respond on and return the second half.

Business letters

RETURN ADDRESS: If you aren't using letterhead stationery, use the two lines immediately preceding the date line for your street address, city, state, and ZIP code. Unless the letter is extremely formal, abbreviations ("Rd.," "Apt.," "NY") are acceptable.

DATE: For dates use this format: "October 12, 2010." The month is not abbreviated, the day is not spelled out, and endings for numbers ("16th," "2nd") are not used. You may see "12 October 2010," particularly for international or government business. If you are typing in your return address, the date line goes directly beneath it. Otherwise, it is placed two to six lines below the printed address. When using the shortened date form ("10/12/2010") in a memo, remember that this is used primarily in the United States; in other countries the first number is the day, the second the month.

CONFIDENTIAL OR PERSONAL NOTATION: Indicate "Confidential" or "Personal" halfway between the date line and the inside address, flush left.

INSIDE ADDRESS: The number of spaces between the date line and the inside address depends on the length of your letter. Balance the elements of the letter so that there's not too much white space above the inside address or below the last printed line. The inside address is always flush left and single spaced. If one line is long, put half of it on the next line, indenting two or three spaces. The person's name goes on the first line. A brief title follows the name, preceded by a comma. Otherwise the title goes on the second line or, if you need the space, can be omitted. When writing to two or more people, list them one to a line in alphabetical order. The company's name is on the next line, and the department or division is on the following line (unless space is a problem, in which case omit it). Information such as suite, room, floor, or apartment usually has its own line, unless it and the street address are short enough to fit on one line. It used to be standard practice to spell out all words of the inside address, but the use of two-letter state abbreviations has spread from the envelopes (where the Postal Service wants to see them) to the inside address, and if the letter is not formal, other abbreviations ("Ave.") may appear as well. Spell out compass directions that precede a street name but abbreviate those that follow it ("14 North Cedar," "14 Cedar N.W.").

ATTENTION LINE: When you don't know the name of the individual to whom you are writing or you want to direct the letter to a particular person's attention, the attention line ("ATTN: Customer Service Representative") is placed below the inside address, leaving one line of space between them. You can also include an attention line as part of the inside address on either the first or second line (after the company name).

SUBJECT LINE: To indicate the subject of your letter, type "Subject:" or "Re:" (for "regarding") between the salutation and the body of your letter or between the inside address and the salutation. A brief phrase follows it ("Subject: block and brick work" or "Re: vacation dates"). Many people replace the salutation with a subject line when writing an impersonal letter to an anonymous recipient (your credit card statement was incorrect, for example). The subject line is popular with people handling stacks of incoming letters, trying to quickly identify the purpose of each. It is not recommended when your letter deals with several subjects.

REFERENCE LINE: When referring to an order number or to a reference number used either by your correspondent or by your firm, handle it like a subject line and place it between the inside address and the salutation or between the salutation and the body of the letter (leaving one line of space on both sides in each case). It may also be placed between the date line and the inside address.

SALUTATION: Leave one line of space between the inside address (or the subject line) and the salutation. The salutation is followed by a colon (which is more formal) or a comma.

BODY OF THE LETTER: Leave one line of space between the salutation (or the subject line) and the body of the letter. In general, single space within paragraphs and leave a line of space between paragraphs. If your letter is brief, however, double-spacing (or even 1½ spacing) will make it look better on the page. Wide margins will also balance brief letters on the page just as narrow margins (but not less than 1¼) modify long letters. To indent paragraphs, start in five to ten spaces.

Do not justify the right margin.

If your letter runs to a second page, indicate the name of the recipient, the page number, and the date across the top of the page (about six lines below the paper's edge). When writing to two individuals, put both names on the left, one under the other, and on the right indicate the date with the page number under it. Then leave three to five lines before resuming the body of the text. There should be a minimum of three lines of type in addition to the signature block to justify a second page.

COMPLIMENTARY CLOSE: Leave one line between the body of the text and the complimentary close ("Yours truly").

SIGNATURE: Your handwritten signature goes between the complimentary close and your typed name and title.

NAME AND TITLE LINES: Four spaces (or more, if your signature is large) below the complimentary close, type your name with the first letter directly beneath the first letter of the complimentary close. If you use a title, it is typed on the line beneath your name, and also lined up with the left edge of your name and the complimentary close. Omit the title if it appears on the letterhead.

IDENTIFICATION LINE: Leave one line of space between the name or title line and the identification line. Type the letter-signer's initials in capital letters flush left, followed by a slash or colon and the typist's initials in lowercase letters ("DCK/jp," "IN:pjm"). Or, since it is obvious who has signed the letter, the typist's initials appear alone. The identification line is no longer much used.

ENCLOSURE LINE: Leave one line of space between the identification line or the name/title line and the enclosure line. Set flush left, this line begins with "Enc.:" and lists any enclosures in the order in which they are found in the envelope, one to a line. You may also use "Encl." or "Enclosures" followed by the number of items enclosed: "Enclosures (4)".

COPIES LINE: Leave one line of space between previous material and the copy line. After "cc:" (from the old "carbon copy") list those receiving copies of the letter in alphabetical order, one to a line, either by their full name, initials and last name, or title and last name only. The person's address may also be included. If you don't want the recipient of the letter to know that copies were sent, indicate "bcc:" (blind carbon copy) with the names of those receiving copies on the office copy of the letter.

POSTSCRIPT: A postscript, preceded by "P.S.," is typed flush left two spaces below the last typed line.

MAILING NOTATION: Instructions for mailing (Special Delivery, Overnight Express) used to be noted on copies of the letter, but not on the original. This is rarely used today.

LETTER FORMATS

There is no "best" way to arrange the elements of a letter on the page (unless your company has a house style). You do, however, need to be consistent (if you indent one paragraph, you indent them all) and the layout must be readable and appealing. The following four formats are the most common, but any arrangement is acceptable if it makes sense, is readable, and is spaced nicely on the page.

Full-block letter
The easiest format for the typist, full-block style means that every line begins at the left margin—no exceptions. If you have a second page, the name of the recipient, the page number, and the date are typed flush left, one under the other.

CHANNING FURNITURE RENTAL
1927 James Avenue
Huntly, WI 53597

March 15, 2010

Confidential

Yorke Furniture Rental
ATTN: Constance Yorke
1862 Wood Street
Huntly, WI 53597

Dear Constance Yorke:

Re: bad checks

We spoke at the Huntly Business Association meeting last month about exchanging lists of customers who have written at least three unbankable checks. Enclosed is my list.

Yours truly,

[signature]

Hamish Channing

President

Enc.: list

P.S. I don't feel too bad about passing these names along because I keep this same list posted by my cash register.

Block letter

The block letter is identical to the full-block with two exceptions: the date line is typed flush right and the signature block (complimentary close plus signature plus name line and title line) are also set flush right or at least to the right of center. Otherwise, everything is flush left and there are no indentations. This format, which has a more traditional look than the full-block format, is used in the majority of business letters.

CHANNING FURNITURE RENTAL
1927 James Avenue
Huntly, WI 53597

March 15, 2010

CONFIDENTIAL

Yorke Furniture Rental
ATTN: Constance Yorke

1862 Wood Street
Huntly, WI 53597

Dear Constance Yorke:

Re: bad checks

We spoke at the Huntly Business Association meeting last month about exchanging lists of customers who have written at least three unbankable checks. Enclosed is my list.

> Yours truly,
>
> [signature]
>
> Hamish Channing
> President

Enc.: list

P.S. I don't feel too bad about passing these along because I keep this same list posted by my cash register.

Modified-block

Also known as the semi-block, this format is identical to the block format with one exception: it has indentations. All paragraphs are indented five to ten spaces. The subject line may also be indented. As in the block style, the date line and the signature block are all set flush right or at least to the right of center. This format, which appears a little warmer than the block formats, is probably the second most popular business letter format.

CHANNING FURNITURE RENTAL
1927 James Avenue
Huntly, WI 53597

> March 15, 2010

CONFIDENTIAL

Yorke Furniture Rental
ATTN: Constance Yorke
1862 Wood Street
Huntly, WI 53597

Dear Constance Yorke:

Re: bad checks

We spoke at the Huntly Business Association meeting last month about exchanging lists of customers who have written at least three unbankable checks.

Enclosed is my list. I'll look forward to receiving yours when you have time to send it along.

Yours truly,

[signature]

Hamish Channing
President

Enc.: list

P.S. I don't feel too bad about passing these along because I keep this same list posted by my cash register.

Simplified

With its streamlined contemporary look, the simplified format is easily identified by its lack of salutation and complimentary close. Like the full-block style, all lines begin at the left margin. But it has a subject line (typed in capital letters) instead of a salutation. The letter-writer's name and title are typed in all capital letters.

CHANNING FURNITURE RENTAL

1927 James Avenue

Huntly, WI 53597

March 15, 2010

CONFIDENTIAL

Yorke Furniture Rental
1862 Wood Street
Huntly, WI 53597

RE: BAD CHECKS

As decided at the Huntly Business Association meeting last month, I am forwarding to other stores a list of my customers who have given me at least three unbankable checks.

Enclosed is my list. I'll look forward to receiving yours.

[signature]

HAMISH CHANNING
PRESIDENT

Enc.: list

UNITED STATES POSTAL SERVICE GUIDELINES

The United States Postal Service (USPS) provides a number of useful handbooks, manuals, and publications that can be downloaded free online (www.usps.com/publications).

Other services include online or by-mail sale of postage stamps, automated telephone information on postal services, ZIP code listings, and instructive videos.

Suggestions from the Postal Service on improving your mail handling include:

- Make sure your mail is readable by the optical character readers (OCRs) used in automated sorting: use envelopes of standard size and shape (first-class mail must be rectangular—a square envelope, for example, will be assessed a surcharge); use only white, ivory, or pastels; avoid unusual features like odd papers or bright graphics; type the address IN CAPITAL LETTERS with no punctuation (except for the hyphen in ZIP+4 codes), with one or two spaces between words, and with nothing but the address in the lower right part of the envelope.
- Don't use paperclips; they often jam the Letter-Sorting Machines (LSMs).
- Put your return address on envelopes; many people fail to do this.
- Use the two-letter state abbreviations and ZIP+4.
- Through stamps.com (an approved, licensed USPS vendor) you can print your own postage. With their free digital scale and assistance, you can have a virtual post office at your home or office. For information, call 888-307-8267.
- Or, set up your own postal center, investing in a small postage scale, relying on USPS online information for postage rates, and buying stamps of various denominations to keep in small nine- or fifteen-drawer organizers.
- Bar code your mail. Using ZIP+4 and bar codes gives you the largest postal discount available, and the bar coding equipment eventually pays for itself.
- Keep current with new publications, programs, rates, and services; the USPS constantly updates old services and introduces new ones.

ENVELOPE ABBREVIATIONS

Alabama	AL	Federated States of	
Alaska	AK	Micronesia	FM
American Samoa	AS	Florida	FL
Arizona	AZ	Georgia	GA
Arkansas	AR	Guam	GU
California	CA	Hawaii	HI
Colorado	CO	Idaho	ID
Connecticut	CT	Illinois	IL
Delaware	DE	Indiana	IN
District of Columbia	DC	Iowa	IA

Kansas	KS	Northern Mariana Islands	MP
Kentucky	KY	Ohio	OH
Louisiana	LA	Oklahoma	OK
Maine	ME	Oregon	OR
Marshall Islands	MH	Palau	PW
Maryland	MD	Pennsylvania	PA
Massachusetts	MA	Puerto Rico	PR
Michigan	MI	Rhode Island	RI
Minnesota	MN	South Carolina	SC
Mississippi	MS	South Dakota	SD
Missouri	MO	Tennessee	TN
Montana	MT	Texas	TX
Nebraska	NE	Utah	UT
Nevada	NV	Vermont	VT
New Hampshire	NH	Virginia	VA
New Jersey	NJ	Virgin Islands	VI
New Mexico	NM	Washington	WA
New York	NY	West Virginia	WV
North Carolina	NC	Wisconsin	WI
North Dakota	ND	Wyoming	WY

Apartment	APT
Attention	ATTN
Building	BLDG
Center	CTR
Company	CO
Corporation	CORP
Department	DEPT
Division	DIV
Floor	FLR
Government	GOVT
Headquarters	HDQTRS
Hospital	HOSP
Institute	INST
National	NATL
Parkway	PKWY

Post Office Box	PO BOX
Room	RM
Rural Route	RR
Suite	STE

CONTENT

*I once read a survey that said the moment in the daily routine
that people look forward to most is opening the mail.*
—NANCY BERLINER

Appendix I tells *how* to put a letter on the page (and what kind of a page to put it on). Appendix II tells *what* to put on the page, discussing principles of good letter writing and effective form letters; grammar and usage; respectful, unbiased language; names and titles; salutations, complimentary closes, and signatures; frequently misspelled words; superfluous words and phrases.

GENERAL GUIDELINES ON LETTER CONTENT

These guidelines apply primarily to business letters. For example, brevity is highly prized in a business letter, but it may not be appreciated by a dear friend. You aren't obliged to state your main idea (if indeed you have one) in the first sentence of a letter to a family member, whereas the business reader wants to know immediately what your letter is about. However, these suggestions will improve all your letter writing.

- Before beginning to write, identify the purpose of your letter (to get a refund, to set up a meeting, to issue an invitation). Gather necessary information. Think about your reader—the more you know about the recipient of your letter, the more precisely you can tailor your message.
- State the main idea in the first or second sentence.
- Be brief. George Burns's advice on a good sermon applies equally well to letters: "a good beginning and a good ending . . . as close together as possible." Give brief explanations, instructions, reasons.

- Be specific. Nothing gives writing more power than details—not unnecessary details, but details that replace vague words and phrases. Readers want to know how much, what color, what date, what time, how big, how little. Reread your letter and question every adjective—is it pulling its weight? Could it be more specific?
- Be pleasant, courteous, positive, and encouraging. For being so inexpensive, upbeat attitudes are startlingly effective.
- Be factual and avoid emotion in business letters. (It is fine—even desirable—in personal letters.) Your readers do not really care about your feelings; they want facts, they want to know outcomes, they want results, they want reasons. Don't exaggerate, or your message will lose credibility with your reader. It's better to mildly understate your case and let the reader take credit for seeing how wonderful it really is.
- Use (but don't overuse) the word "you" throughout your letter, and particularly in the opening sentences. The most important letter-writing rule is "Keep your reader in mind." Phrase your message in terms of your reader's interests, needs, and expectations. The "you" involves the reader in the letter. The exception to the use of "you" is the letter of complaint or disagreement, in which "you"-statements are perceived as (and often are) accusing and hostile. Phrase your message in terms of "I" statements.
- Use the active instead of the passive voice ("I received your letter last week," not "Your letter was received last week"). Use strong, direct, action-filled verbs ("is/are," "do," and "make" are not some of them). Use a thesaurus to find dynamic (but not unusual, unfamiliar, or unpronounceable) substitutes for your most overused words.
- Use a lively, conversational tone. Reading your letters out loud for several weeks will help you spot awkwardnesses.
- Choose a tone for your letter and stick to it. A letter might be formal or informal, cool or warm, serious or lighthearted, brisk or relaxed, simple or complex, elegant or down home. But it is, above all, consistent.
- Avoid overused words like "very" and "basically." Basically, neither of them means very much, and they become annoying to the reader.
- Avoid slang, jargon, clichés, buzzwords, legalese, elitist language, and stilted usage like "I shall." Choose the familiar word over the unfamiliar.
- When writing abroad, keep sentences and syntax simple. Avoid slang, jargon, figures of speech, references to facets of American culture, the passive voice, and complex verb constructions. Keep to the present and simple past tenses. Instead of "If we had only known . . . ," say "We did not know . . ." If using numerals for the date, use day/month/year instead of month/day/year. If you know them, use social titles from the reader's own language ("Madame," "Signore," "Herr," "Señora"). Use the address exactly as given;

it is most deliverable in that form. Letters from other countries often have ritualized closing sentences that express the writer's respect and good wishes; take your cue from your correspondent's letter and reply in kind.

- Make it easy for your correspondent to reply: enclose a postage-paid reply envelope or a self-addressed stamped envelope.

FORM LETTERS

Form letters have done away with the numbing and time-consuming chore of typing the same letter thousands of times. They are invaluable in direct sales marketing and in the processing of routine business letters (confirmations, acknowledgments, cover letters, rejections).

Joseph Heller poked fun at form letters in *Catch-22*: "Dear Mrs, Mr, Miss, or Mr and Mrs Daneeka: Words cannot express the deep personal grief I experienced when your husband, son, father or brother was killed, wounded or reported missing in action."

To avoid this aspect of form letters, direct your message to the individual reading it. Inserting the person's name at intervals isn't the way to do this; too many spelling errors can creep in, and people do not in any case mistake this cheery and obviously phony friendship for real intimacy.

Personalize your letter by using "you" and using mailing lists of specific market targets. Then, if you are writing to members of a list who are all gardeners or who have all contributed to a charity within the past six months, you know how to frame your letter. For important mailings, use high-quality paper, sign each letter individually (there are people who look first to see if the signature is "real" or not and then either read the letter or toss it), and mail the letter first-class.

GRAMMAR AND USAGE

Some common grammar and usage issues are outlined below. If you write more than the occasional letter, invest in a mini-library for your desk: dictionary, basic grammar, usage guide, style manual, thesaurus.

- Use **periods** at the end of sentences. Or sentence fragments. A period also follows an abbrev. Ellipsis points are used to replace missing words: three dots in the middle of the sentence, four at the end.
- **Commas** separate items or lists of things. It is correct either to use or not to use a comma before "and" in a series ("Milk, butter and eggs" or "Milk, butter, and eggs")—the only rule is to do it one way or the other consistently. If you don't know when to use a comma, read the sentence aloud dramatically. The place where you pause to group a thought phrase together may need a

comma. Commas are used before and after "etc.," years of a date ("On May 27, 1678, the sun rose . . ."), and academic degrees. Always place a comma before a name ("Are you eating, Jim?" not "Are you eating Jim?").

■ Don't use **question marks** after indirect questions or requests ("He asked what went wrong" or "Please sweep up here after yourself"). Omit the comma after the question mark in cases like "Do you like it?" she asked.

■ Except perhaps for sales letters, business correspondence doesn't need—and shouldn't have—**exclamation marks**. Be stingy with them in personal correspondence as well. J. L. Basford believed that "One who uses many periods is a philosopher; many interrogations, a student; many exclamations, a fanatic." Exclamations give your letters a certain manic look, like people laughing at their own jokes. At first, it will tear at your heart to remove them; by and by, you will be pleased to find that you can get along nicely without them.

■ **Quotation marks** are used for quoted words and for the titles of magazine articles and TV and radio shows. All punctuation goes inside the quotation marks ("What?" "Egads!" "I won't," he said). Common sense ought to indicate the rare exceptions. If the punctuation in no way belongs to the quotation, you can leave it outside, as in the following sentence: How many times have you heard a child say "But I'm not tired"?

■ **Parentheses** are used to enclose asides to your main train of thought. When the aside is an incomplete thought (incomplete sentence) it is placed in the middle of a regular sentence; the first word inside does not begin with a capital, nor is there any punctuation. (Sometimes, however, your thought is a complete thought, or complete sentence, in which case it is set inside parentheses and has its own initial capital letter and final punctuation.) When using parentheses within a sentence, all punctuation goes after the parentheses: Please order more ribbons, paper (30#), and file folders.

■ In general, **hyphens** are used to help word pairs or groups form one easy-to-read thought group. Traditional exceptions are words ending in -ly ("newly appointed") and adjective groups that follow a noun ("well-known telecaster" but "she was well known"). The trend is to one word rather than hyphenated words or two separate words ("headlight," not "head-light" or "head light"). A quick check with a dictionary will give you the correct form for most words.

■ Use **apostrophes** to replace missing letters ("isn't" = "is not") and to show possession ("Simon's"). The apostrophe most commonly shows up in the wrong place in "its" and "it's." If you can write "it is" in place of your word, it needs the apostrophe. If you have trouble with this pair, write only "it is" or "its" until you are comfortable with the difference. When more than one person is involved, show the plural possessive by placing the apostrophe after the "s" ("union members' votes" or "the parents' recommendations"). Omit the apostrophe when making plurals of number and letter combinations: PhDs, the 1990s, the 2000s, the '50s, three 100s, IBMs.

- **Colons** often precede a list or a long quotation ("We carry the following brand names: . . ." or "The hospital issued the following apology: . . ."). Do not use a colon when it unnecessarily breaks up a sentence (remove the colon in "Your kit contains: a lifetime supply of glue, four colors of paint, and a set of two brushes"). The colon is also used after a business or formal salutation ("Mr. President:").

- **Semicolons** tend to give a stuffy, old-fashioned look to a letter. However, they are still useful on occasion. When writing a long list that has internal punctuation, separate each element with a semicolon ("New members for January: Rachel and Darke Solomon of Velindre, their children Peter, Jasper, Ruby, and Amber; Constantine Stephanopoulos; Catherine, Lize, and Fritz Steinhart"). You may also separate two independent clauses of a sentence with a semicolon ("In prosperity our friends know us; in adversity we know our friends."—J. Churton Collins).

- The overuse of **dashes** indicates a rather slapdash (you see where it comes from?) style. If you are a regular dash-user, check to see if other punctuation might not do as well. Dashes tend to mate in captivity, so once the dash habit takes hold, they proliferate on the page, giving a letter a rather forward-leaning, breathless quality.

- A common grammar error involves **noun-verb agreement**. In complicated sentences in which the noun and verb become separated from each other, it's easy to make a mistake. When proofreading your letters, pick out long sentences, find your noun and verb, put them together, and see if they still make sense. Some nouns that look singular ("data") take a plural verb; some that look plural take a singular verb ("a series of books is scheduled for"; "the board of directors is investigating"). What do you do with "None of them has/have voted yet"? When in doubt, reword the sentence ("Nobody has voted yet"; "Not one of them has voted yet") or ask what the sense of the phrase is. If you are speaking of only one person, use "has"; if the sense of the phrase indicates many people, use "have." "A number of accountants are signing up for . . ." but "The number of accountants is decreasing."

- **Underline or italicize** titles of books and movies; other titles go in quotation marks.

- **Capitalize** proper names and places. To see the difference between a lowercase noun (dad) and an uppercase noun (Dad) decide whether it is a classification (a parent) or a name ("Hi, Dad"). If you say "my father is great," it's like saying "my piano is great." But if "Dad" acts as his name, it's capitalized ("Thanks, Leo"; "Thanks, Dad").

■ One of the best things you can do for your writing is to become aware of **parallel structures**—from little things like capitalizing or not capitalizing all the words in a list to making sure each word in the list is the same part of speech. In long sentences, writers often forget that they started one phrase with "to interview . . ." but later used "calling the candidate" and ended up with "and, finally, you could meet with . . ." A parallel form would have "to interview . . . to call . . . to meet with . . ."

■ Keep **paragraphs** short. Let each one develop a single idea. Start with your broadest idea and support it with detailed refinements. Or start with details and lead the reader to your final, topic sentence.

■ The easiest way to decide whether you need **"that"** or **"which"** is to see if you need commas. Commas and "which" tend to go together: "The file, which eventually turned up on Frank's desk, had been missing for a week." "The file that had been missing eventually turned up on Frank's desk." Do not set off a phrase beginning with "that" with commas, but do set off a "which" clause with commas.

■ "Howard and Paul had lunch together before he left." Which "he" left? Check pronouns ("who," "she," "they") to be sure the **antecedents** (the persons they refer to) are clear.

■ **Dangling modifiers** consist of words tacked onto a sentence, front or back (sometimes even in the middle), in such a way that the reader doesn't know what they modify. In *Watch Your Language*, Theodore M. Bernstein gives several examples, among them: "Although definitely extinct, Professor Daevey said it had not been too long ago that the moa was floundering around his deathtrap swamps." "As reconstructed by the police, Pfeffer at first denied any knowledge of the Byrd murder." The phrase has to refer to, or be about, the first noun that comes after it. They must be related.

■ **"Between"** is generally between two people, no more. (And the correct expression is always "between you and me," "between Flory and me.") **"Among"** is generally for three or more: "We should have the necessary know-how among the four of us."

■ Watch the placement of **"only"** and **"not only"**; they should go right next to the word they modify. Instead of "I am only buying one," write "I am buying only one."

■ **"Whom"** and **"whomever"** do not occur nearly as often as people suppose. Use them only when you can show they are the object of a verb. The most common misuse of "whomever" occurs in a situation like this: "Please mail this file to whoever is elected secretary." "Whoever" is correct; it is the subject of the clause. If you are troubled by this construction, see a good grammar book; until then, it is perhaps enough to be aware of the problem.

■ **"Should have"** is always correct. "Should of" is *never* correct.

TALKING ABOUT PEOPLE

Stereotypical language forgets that people are individuals. Exclusive language forgets to include certain people. When you invite customers to an open house and fail to say that the event is accessible, you exclude people with disabilities. When you begin your letter "Dear Sirs:" you forget that women might be reading it. When you refer to the "Judeo-Christian ethic" you exclude large numbers of highly ethical non-Jews and non-Christians. Words can exclude, stereotype, and discriminate against people on the basis of sex, age, ethnicity, disability, socioeconomic class, sexual orientation, and religion.

For information on using respectful people language, see *Talking About People* (Rosalie Maggio, The Oryx Press and *Unspinning the Spin* (Rosalie Maggio, Women's Media Center). The rationale is that it is good business; you can't sell anything or obtain any information or favors from someone whom you've just excluded or stereotyped. A few guidelines:

■ The "people first" rule says we are people first, and only secondarily people who have disabilities, people who are over sixty-five, people who are Baptists, people who are Finnish-Americans. In your letters, decide first if you need to mention classifications such as sex, age, race, religion, economic class, or disability; most often they're unnecessary. When in doubt, omit them. Don't identify the whole person by part of the person. Madeline is someone who has paraplegia. Referring to her as "a paraplegic" identifies the whole Madeline by one part of her. People aren't "confined to a wheelchair"; they use wheelchairs.

■ Check for parallel constructions: do you mention one person's marital status and not the other person's? One person's race, and not the other's? Identify some people as gay but not others as heterosexual? Is she Mrs. William Gostrey, but he is Ray Parker? Or he is Ray Parker and she is Sheila?

■ Instead of "man" or "mankind" use words that include everyone, for example, people, we, us, humanity, human beings, individuals, human society, nature, planet earth, the world. Don't use "he" when you mean "he or she." Instead of "A mail carrier has his work cut out for him today" use the plural: "Mail carriers have their work cut out for them today." You can also rewrite the sentence to use "you" or "we." Sometimes "he," "his," or "him" can be omitted or replaced with a noun. Avoid the awkward "his or her" or "she or he." The centuries-old use of singular "they" ("to each their own"), which is found throughout this book, is accepted or endorsed by most language authorities, including *Oxford English Dictionary; Chicago Manual of Style*, 15th ed.; *American Heritage Dictionary of the English Language*, 4th ed.; *American Heritage Book of English Usage*; the National Council of Teachers of English; *Random House Dictionary II*; *Webster's Third New International Dictionary*; Randolph Quirk et al., *A Grammar of Contemporary English*. With a few exceptions ("layperson," for example), words ending in *-person* are contrived-looking; good alternatives exist for almost all of them. Use *chair* instead of *chairperson*; *chair* is the older and tidier term. We use *head* ("the head of the department") and *headed* ("she headed the organization") without fearing a disembodied head; in the same way, no one mistakes the committee chair for what they're sitting on.

NAMES

There is only one rule about names: use whatever name your correspondent prefers. Guidelines include:

■ Spell your correspondent's name correctly. It is worth the few minutes and the long-distance charge to call to obtain the correct spelling and current title of the person to whom you're writing.

■ Although it is acceptable in some fields and in some parts of the country to call people by their first names, write "Dear Mr. Cokeson" rather than "Dear Bob" until you're sure the latter is welcome. Miss Manners says: "To prevent the unauthorized use of her first name, Miss Manners took the precaution of not having one." She says she is far from alone in cringing when strangers assume the privileges of intimacy by using her first name. When unsure about the degree of formality between you and a correspondent, choose the more formal approach.

■ When ordering business cards or personal calling cards, spell out your full name. Social titles (Mr., Ms., Mrs., Miss) used to precede the name, but they are largely omitted today. Medical specialists use "Dr." or "Doctor" on social cards ("Doctor Christopher Bembridge"), but use "M.D.," "D.O.," "D.D.S.," "O.D." on business cards ("Muriel Eden, D.D.S."). Either "Joseph Farr Jr." or "Joseph Farr II" is correct. When using "Esq." (short for Esquire) after a lawyer's name ("Marian Beltham, Esq."), omit all other titles (Mr., Ms., Mrs., Miss) before it.

■ For a woman, use the social title (also called courtesy title or honorific) she uses (see her last letter or call her home or office to check on the spelling of her name and to ask "Do you prefer Miss, Mrs., or Ms.?"). If there's no clue to her marital status (and remember that we've been addressing men for years without worrying about this), use her full name without a social title ("Dear Florence Churchill") or use "Ms." and her last name. The worst that can happen is that the letter you receive in return is signed by a "Mrs." or a "Dr." or some other title. Now you know. In business, women use their own first names. This used to indicate that a woman was single, divorced, or possibly widowed. Today it just means that that is her first name. Socially, some women use their husbands' names. Some may still sign a letter "Nelly Christie" but type underneath "Mrs. John Christie." Traditionally, married or widowed women used their husbands' names ("Mrs. Philip Halliday"), while divorced women used their own first name and either their family-of-origin name, their married name, or both. Single women were to use "Miss" or not, as they pleased. This marital coding system for women is no longer as reliable or as popular as it once was.

■ When addressing couples, use the form they use themselves: "Mr. and Mrs. Walter Evson"; "Adela and George Norrington"; "Dr. Guy and Mrs. Elizabeth Phillips"; "Katherine Halstead and Frank Luttrell"; "Dr. Linda and Mr. Arnaud Hallet." When addressing envelopes or typing the inside address, and each name is fairly long, put one to a line in alphabetic order.

■ When writing to more than one person, use each person's full name or use a social title plus last name for each. For single-sex groups, you may use "Mesdames" ("Mmes.") for women and "Messieurs" ("Messrs.") for men, although these terms have an old-fashioned ring to them. These titles are followed by the individuals' last names only. When addressing both women and men, use an inclusive salutation such as "Dear Friends," "Dear Cochairs," "Dear Committee Members," or "To: (list names, one to a line in alphabetic order)."

SALUTATIONS, COMPLIMENTARY CLOSES, AND SIGNATURES

Salutations

The salutation (also referred to as a greeting) is set flush left. The first letter of the first word is capitalized but other modifying words are not ("My very dear Joanna"). All titles and names are capitalized. Use abbreviations for Ms., Mr., Mrs., Dr., but spell out religious, military, and professional titles such as Father, Major, Professor, Sister, Colonel. The salutation generally ends in a comma for personal or informal letters, and in a colon or a comma for business letters.

When possible, obtain the name of the person who is best suited to receive your letter and verify the correct spelling of their name and their current title; call the company if necessary.

When you know the person's name, write: "Dear Neil A. McTodd" or "Dear Agnes Bailey" (full name with no social title) or "Dear Ms. Lee," "Dear Captain Crowe," "Dear Inspector Hopkins," "Dear Senator Burnside" (social title plus last name). The first convention is useful when you don't know the person's sex ("Audley

Egerton") or which social title (Ms., Mrs., Miss) the person uses. Professional or academic titles (Dr., Representative) are always used instead of social titles (Mr., Miss).

When writing a form letter or when you don't know your correspondent's name, you can still write "Dear . . ." with nouns like: Neighbor, Subscriber, Friend, Motorist, Reader, Colleague, Student, Customer, Gardener, Client, Employee, Potential Employee, Parishioner, Collector, Cardholder, Concerned Parent, Initiate-Elect, Handgun Control Supporter, Member, Homeowner, Supplier, Executive, Aquarist, Equestrian, Do-It-Yourselfer. Or try job titles: Dentist, Copywriter, Electrician, Metallurgist, Customer Service Manager. Or use the company's name: Poulengay Upholsterers, Elliot-Lewis Stationers, Handford Lawn Care. You can also use an impersonal salutation like Good morning! Hello! Greetings! The best solution may be to replace the salutation with a subject line. (The outdated "Dear Sir or Madam" and "To Whom It May Concern" are not recommended.)

Complimentary Closes

The complimentary close follows the body of your letter, with one line of space between them. It always begins with a capital letter and ends with a comma. Words in between are not capitalized.

The most everyday, acceptable, and all-purpose complimentary closes are: Sincerely (used perhaps three-fourths of the time), Yours truly, Sincerely yours, Very sincerely yours, Very sincerely, Very truly yours. You cannot go wrong with one of these. Miss Manners (Judith Martin) says that business letters should close with "Yours truly"; "Can Miss Manners be the only person still alive who knows that?"

For a highly formal letter involving White House, diplomatic, judicial, or ecclesiastical correspondence, use: Respectfully yours or Respectfully. An informal letter in the same instances uses: Very respectfully yours, Yours respectfully, or Sincerely yours. In formal letters to members of Congress, senators, high-ranking politicians and government figures, priests, rabbis, imams, mullahs, and ministers, use: Yours very truly. The informal form is: Sincerely yours.

For most formal letters—regular business and personal—choose from among: Sincerely, Sincerely yours, Yours sincerely, Very sincerely yours, Very sincerely, Truly yours, Yours truly, Very truly yours, Yours very truly, Very cordially yours.

Informal closes include: Love, With all my love, Lovingly, Lovingly yours, Fondly, Affectionately, Yours affectionately, Sincerely, Sincerely yours, Cordially, Cordially yours, Yours cordially, Faithfully, Faithfully yours, Yours faithfully, As ever, As always, Devotedly, Yours, Best regards, Kindest regards, Warmest regards, Cheers, Your friend, Be well, Until next time.

Complimentary closes somewhere between formal and informal include: With all kind regards, Warm regards, Best regards, Best, Best wishes, With best wishes, With all best wishes, Cordially, Sincerely, All the very best, With every good wish, Warm personal regards.

After studying the above lists, choose one or two complimentary closes that reflect your letter-writing style and use them for most of your correspondence. It's rarely worth the trouble to fit a special complimentary close to each letter.

Signatures

Although there used to be many rules governing signatures, it's fairly simple today: use the version of your name that you want the person to use for you. If there is any ambiguity (for example, the person knows you only under your pen name, birth name, married name, or business name), put the name that might be more easily recognized in parentheses under your signature. Signatures rarely include social titles, so omit the "Dr.," "Ms.," or "Mr." (They may be typed on the name line, however.) In personal letters, your signature stands alone. In business letters, it is followed by your name and title (on one or two lines, depending on length). The name and title lines are typed four lines below the complimentary close—more, if you have a particularly sweeping signature. If your name and title are given on the letterhead, omit them under your signature. When signing a letter for someone else, put your initials just below and to the right of the signature, often after a slash. When you write a letter on someone else's behalf, sign your own name above a name line that identifies you: "Son of Christina Light" or "Secretary to Cavaliere Giacosa."

If your salutation uses the person's first name, sign the letter with your first name (although in a business letter, your full name and title will be printed below your signature). Nonparallel salutations and signatures can be insulting and offputting. If you write "Dear Fred," and sign it "Dr. Francis Etherington," you have assumed a superior position; writing it the other way around presumes an intimacy that may not exist. Except in rare cases, the salutation and signature should be strictly parallel: "Dear Rosa, . . . Love, Judy"; "Dear Thomas Eustick, . . . Sincerely, Margaret Kraft."

FREQUENTLY MISSPELLED WORDS

Bill Nye once said, "The dictionary is a great book; it hasn't much plot, but the author's vocabulary is wonderful." It is also useful for verifying correct spelling. A handful of the most troublesome words:

abscess	acknowledge/acknowledgment/
absence	acknowledging
accommodate	acquaintance
accumulate	acquire

a lot
all right (never alright)
amateur
appall/appalled/appalling
apparatus
aquarium
arctic
barracks
barrage
beneficiary
benefited
canceled, cancellation
Caribbean
category
cemetery
conscious
concur/concurred/concurrence
consensus
consistency
correspondence/correspondent
definitely
desperate
discernible
elegant/elegance
eligible
embarrass/embarrassment
exhaustible
exhilarate
existence
fascinate
February
fluorescence
foreign
fulfill/fulfilled/fulfillment
genealogy
grievance
harass/harassment
height
hemorrhage
hitchhike/hitchhiker

hypocrisy
indispensable
in regard to (not in regards to)
inoculate
iridescent/iridescence
irresistible
jewel/jeweled/jeweler/jewelry
judgment
knowledge/knowledgeable
liaison
lieutenant
maintenance
miniature
mischievous
missile
misspell
niece
noticeable
occasion
occur/occurred/occurrence
omitted
parallel
paraphernalia
pastime
perennial
permissible
personnel
precede
prejudice
privilege
proceed
realtor
receive
reference
regardless (never irregardless)
reminisce
rhythm
sacrilegious
seize
separate

siege
sieve
subtle
supersede
threshold

toward
vacuum
vengeance
yield

FREQUENTLY MISUSED TERMS

Your spell check won't single out the words below because they are all spelled correctly. However, these look-alikes and sound-alikes are often confused with each other. When in doubt, consult a dictionary.

accept/except
adapt/adept/adopt
adverse/averse
advice/advise
affect/effect
all ready/already
all together/altogether
allusion/illusion
altar/alter
alternate/alternative
amend/emend
among/between
amount/number
anyone/any one
appraise/apprise
assure/ensure/insure
auger/augur
beside/besides
biannually/biennially
bloc/block
born/borne
brake/break
can/may
canvas/canvass
capital/capitol
carat/caret/karat
censer/censor/censure
cite/site/sight

clamber/clamor
colossal/colossus
compare/contrast
complacent/complaisant
complement/compliment
compose/comprise
confidant/confident
continuous/continual
council/counsel/consul/councilor/
    counselor
credible/creditable
deduce/deduct
definite/definitive
defuse/diffuse
demur/demure
deprecate/depreciate
disassemble/dissemble
disburse/disperse
disinterested/uninterested
disorganized/unorganized
each other/one another
elicit/illicit
emigrate/immigrate
eminent/imminent/immanent
energize/enervate
ensure/insure
exacerbate/exasperate
exercise/exorcise

farther/further
ferment/foment
flair/flare
flaunt/flout
flounder/founder
forbear/forebear
foreword/forward
formerly/formally
gage/gauge
gamut/gantlet/gauntlet
gibe/jibe
gorilla/guerrilla
gourmand/gourmet
hail/hale
hoard/horde
hurdle/hurtle
imply/infer
incredible/incredulous
ingenious/ingenuous
it's/its
later/latter
less/fewer
liable/libel
lie, lay, lain/lay, laid
liqueur/liquor
loath/loathe
main/mane
mantel/mantle
notable/notorious

palate/palette/pallet
peak/peek/pique
pedal/peddle
persecute/prosecute
personal/personnel
prescribe/proscribe
principal/principle
prophecy/prophesy
rack/wrack
ravage/ravish
reaction/response
rebuff/rebuke/rebut
rein/reign
retch/wretch
rise/raise
sit/set
stanch/staunch
stationary/stationery
than/then
that/which
their/there/they're
throe/throw
tortuous/torturous
trustee/trusty
vain/vane/vein
verses/versus
who's/whose
who/that
your/you're

WORD WEEDS

Thomas Jefferson said, "The most valuable of all talents is that of never using two words when one will do."

In general, delete qualifiers, intensifiers, and fillers. The worst offenders are: very, so, quite, rather. Others include: absolutely, always, apparently, as a rule, generally, in general, in many instances, in most cases, in my opinion, it is possible that, it seems/appears, kind of, more or less, mostly, normally, often, ordinarily, perhaps, seemingly, seems to indicate, sometimes, somewhat, there is a possibility that, there is some potential that, totally, type of, usually.

After doing this for a while, you'll be surprised at how clean and crisp your writing is; and you won't even miss these words.

The wordy, euphemistic, or outdated terms listed below to the left of the equal sign are weeds in our garden of words. Read through the list several times to develop a sense of constructions that you'd like to delete from your writing. Your letters will be easier to read and will have a more contemporary, confident voice. Note that occasionally a term on the left will be precisely what you need; in that case, use it.

above-mentioned = OMIT
absolutely essential/necessary = essential/necessary
accompanied by = with
accordingly = so
according to our records = we find, our records show, or OMIT
according to them = they say
acknowledge receipt of = thank you for
acquaint = tell/inform/let know
acquire = get, gain
activate = begin/start
active consideration = consideration
actual experience/truth = experience/truth
advance forward = advance
advance planning/preparation/warning = planning/warning/preparation
advise = tell/inform
afford an opportunity = allow/permit
aforementioned = OMIT
aggregate/aggregation = total
a great deal of = much
all and sundry = all
all of = all
almost similar = similar
along the lines of = like
already exists = exists
a majority of = most
am/is of the opinion = think/thinks
and etc. = etc.
and so on and so forth = and so on
an early date = soon
anent = about/concerning/regarding
anticipate = expect
a number of = about

a number of cases = some

any and all = any/all, but not both

applicable to = suitable for, relevant, appropriate, apply to

appreciate = realize

appreciate in value = appreciate

appreciate your informing me = please write/tell me

approximately = about

are in receipt of = have received

are of the opinion that = think that

around about [number] = about [number]

as a consequence = so

as a matter of fact = in fact, or OMIT

ascertain = learn/find out

as far as I am concerned = as for me

as I am sure you know = as you know, or OMIT

as per = according to

as per your request = as you requested

as regards = regarding/concerning/about

assemble together = assemble

assist/assistance = help

as the case may be = OMIT

as to = about

as you know = OMIT

at about = at

at all times = always

at an early/later date = soon/later

at a time when = when

at hand = OMIT

at present = now

attached please find/attached herewith/attached hereto = attached/I am
    attaching/I am enclosing

attach together = attach

at that/this point in time = then/now

at the conclusion of = after

at the earliest possible moment = immediately/very soon

at the moment = now/just now

at the present/at this writing = now

at this (point in) time = now/just now

at your earliest convenience = soon

awaiting your instructions = please let me know

baby puppies = puppies

balance of equilibrium = balance/equilibrium, not both

based on the fact that = because

basic fundamentals/essentials = fundamentals/essentials

be cognizant of = know that

be dependent on = depend on

beg to [state/differ/advise] = OMIT

be in possession of = possess

be that as it may = OMIT

be the recipient of = receive

beyond a shadow of a doubt = undoubtedly

big in size = big

blended together = blended

bona fide = genuine

both alike = alike

brief moment = moment

but even so = but/even so, not both

but in any case = but/in any case, not both

but however/nevertheless/nonetheless = one or the other, not both

but on the other hand = but/on the other hand, not both

by means of = by/with

call your attention to = please note

cancel out = cancel

cease = stop

circle around = circle

classify into groups = classify

clearly apparent/unambiguous = apparent/unambiguous

climb up = climb

close proximity = proximity/nearby/close by

coequal = equal

cognizant = aware

collaborate together = collaborate

come to the realization = realize

commence = begin/start

commendation = praise

communicate/communication = write, telephone/letter, telegram

commute back and forth = commute

completely fill/finish = fill/finish

completely accurate/compatible/finished/unanimous = accurate/compatible/
   finished/unanimous

complete monopoly = monopoly

concerning the matter of = about

conclude = close/end
conclusion = closing
conclusive proof = proof
connected together = connected
consensus of opinion = consensus
consequently = so
construct = make
cooperate together = cooperate
could care less = couldn't care less (if you use this at all)
course of time = time
crucial/critical = important
current news = news
customary channels = usual way/regular procedure
customary practice = practice
cylindrical in shape = cylindrical
deeds and actions = deeds or actions, not both
deem = consider, think
deem it advisable = suggest
definite decision = decision
demonstrate = show
depreciate in value = depreciate
deserving of = deserve
desire = want
despite the fact that = although
different [two different dresses/several different movies] = OMIT
direct confrontation = confrontation
discontinue = stop
disincentive = penalty
doctorate degree = doctorate
do not hesitate to = please
drop down = drop
due consideration = consideration
due to the fact that = because
duly = OMIT
during the course of = during
during the time that = while
effectuate = effect
either one of the two = either one/either of the two/either
eliminate = get rid of
empty space = space
enclosed herewith is/enclosed please find = enclosed is/I enclose

encounter = meet

endeavor = try

endeavor to ascertain = try to find out

endorse on the back = endorse

end product/result = product/result

engineer by profession = engineer

equivalent = equal

essentially = OMIT

etc. = avoid whenever possible

eventuate = result

exactly identical = identical

exactly the same = the same

exact replica = replica

exact same = exact or same, not both

exhibit/show/have a tendency to = tend to

exhibits the ability to = can [check with preceding]

existing condition = condition

expedite = hurry

extreme hazard = hazard

facilitate = ease/simplify/chair the meeting

fact of the matter = fact

false pretenses = pretenses

famous far and wide = famous

fearful of = fear

feedback = comments/advice/reactions/opinions/thoughts

feel free to call/write = please call/write

fellow colleague = colleague

few and far between = few

few in number = few

field of anthropology/politics = anthropology/politics

filled to capacity = filled

fill up = fill

final conclusion/outcome = conclusion/outcome

finalize = end/conclude/complete/settle

financial remuneration = remuneration, pay

find necessary = need

first and foremost = first or foremost, not both

first created = created

first of all = first

floral bouquet = bouquet

following behind = following

foot pedal = pedal
for all intents and purposes = OMIT
foreign imports = imports
formulate = form
for the period of a week/month/year = for a week/month/year
for the purpose of = for
for the reason that = because/since/as/for
forthwith = now, at once
frankly = OMIT
free gift = gift
fullest possible extent = fully
full satisfaction = satisfaction
fully complete = complete
furnish = give
future plan = plan
gather together = gather
get more for your money's worth = more for your money/
    get your money's worth
give an answer = answer
give encouragement to = encourage
give this matter your attention = OMIT
good benefit = benefit
grand total = total
grateful thanks = thanks
great majority = majority
had previously = had
have a belief in = believe
heir apparent = heir
hence = so
herein = in this
herinafter = from now on
herewith = enclosed/attached
homologous = alike
honestly = OMIT
hopefully = it is to be hoped, we hope
hopeful that = hope
if and when = if or when, not both
if it meets with your approval = if you approve
if at all possible = if possible
if you desire = if you wish/want
I have ascertained that = OMIT

immediately adjoining = adjoining

implement = carry out, do

I myself personally = I myself/I

in about a week's time = in a week

in accordance with = with/as/by/under

in addition to = besides, also

inadvertent oversight = oversight

in all honesty = OMIT

in a matter of seconds/minutes/hours/days = in seconds/minutes/
 hours/days

in a number of cases = sometimes

in a satisfactory manner = satisfactorily

inasmuch as = as/since/because

inaugurate = begin/start

in back of = behind

in close proximity = near

incombustible = fireproof

in compliance with your request = as you requested/as you asked

in connection with = in/on/to, or OMIT

increase by a factor of two = double

indicate = show

individual person = individual or person, not both

inform = tell

initial = first

initiate = begin/start

in lieu of = instead of

in many cases = often

in order that = so that

in order to = to

input = advice/opinions/thoughts/reactions

inquire = ask

in re = about

in receipt of = received

in reference to = about

in regard to = about/concerning

in relation to = toward/to/about

in respect of = about/concerning

inside of = inside

integral part = part

interface with = meet with

in the absence of = without

in the amount of = for
in the case of = of/in, or OMIT
in the course of = during
in the event of/that = if
in the final analysis = OMIT
in the form of = as
in the majority of instances = usually/often
in the matter of = about/in/of
in the meantime = meanwhile
in the nature of = like
in the near future = soon
in the neighborhood of = about
in the time of = during
in the vast majority of cases = in most cases
in this connection = OMIT
in this day and age = today, or OMIT
intravenous IV = IV
intrinsically = OMIT
in view of = because/since
in view of the fact that = as
invisible to the eye = invisible
invited guest = guest
irregardless = regardless/irrespective
I share your concern = like you, I believe
is indicative of = indicates
is of the opinion = thinks
is when/is where = is the day/is the place
it goes without saying = OMIT
it has been brought to our notice = we note/we have learned
it is clear/obvious that = clearly/obviously
it is interesting to note that = OMIT
it is my belief that = OMIT
it is my intention = I intend
it is often the case that = often
it would not be unreasonable to believe/think/assume =
    I believe/think/assume
I would hope = I hope
I would like to express my appreciation = I appreciate
Jewish synagogue = synagogue
joint collaboration = collaboration
join together = join

keep in mind the fact that = remember that

kindly = please

kind of/sort of = OMIT

kneel down = kneel

last but not least = finally, or OMIT

let me add that = OMIT

likewise = and, also

lift up = lift

literally = OMIT 99 percent of the time

literally and figuratively = OMIT 99 percent of the time

little baby = baby

lose out = lose

lot/lots/a whole lot = OMIT

major breakthrough = breakthrough

make a decision = decide

make a mention of = mention

make contact with = call/write/see

make inquiry regarding = inquire

mandatory requirements = requirements

may perhaps = may

meet with approval = approve

merge together = merge

meet together = meet

meet up with = meet

mental telepathy = telepathy

mesh together = mesh

modification = change

modus operandi = method

month of December = December

more importantly = more important

mutual agreement/cooperation = agreement/cooperation

my personal opinion = my opinion/I believe that

native habitat = habitat

natural instinct = instinct

necessary prerequisite = prerequisite

needless to say = OMIT

never before = never

new initiative/record/recruit = initiative/record/recruit

none at all = none

not in a position to = unable to

no trespassing allowed = no trespassing

not to mention = OMIT
notwithstanding the fact that = although/even though
obviate = do away with
obviously clear = clear or obvious, not both
official business = business
off of = off
of the opinion that = think/believe
old adage = adage
on a continuing basis = constantly/continually
on a daily/monthly/weekly basis = daily/monthly/weekly
on a few occasions = occasionally
on a regular basis = regularly
on a theoretical basis = theoretically
on behalf of = for
one and the same = the same
only other alternative = alternative
on the grounds that = because/since
on the order of = about
on the part of = for/among
opening gambit = gambit
open up/close up/fold up/settle up = open, close, fold, settle
original source = source
originally created = created
other alternative = alternative
overall = OMIT
overexaggerate = exaggerate
over with = over
owing to = because of
owing to unforeseen circumstances = unexpectedly
pare down = pare
particulars = details
past experience/history/memories = experience/history/memories
peace and quiet = peace or quiet, not both
per = a
per annum = a year
per diem = a day
perfectly clear = clear
perform an examination = examine
permeate throughout = permeate
permit me to say = OMIT
per se = as such

personal friend/opinion/belief = friend/opinion/belief

peruse = study

pervasive = widespread

pervasively = throughout

physically located = located

pick and choose = pick or choose, not both

pink in color = pink

pizza pie = pizza

place emphasis on = emphasize

positive identification = identification

postponed until later = postponed

preclude from happening = preclude

predicated on = based on

preparatory to = before

prepared to offer = able to offer

preplanned = planned

present a conclusion = conclude

present status = status

preventative/orientated = preventive/oriented

previous to = before

previous experience = experience

prioritize = list/rank/rate (in order of importance)

prior to = before

proceed ahead = proceed

prove conclusively = prove

pursuant to = according to

quantify = measure

quite a = OMIT

quite unique = unique

radically new = new or radical, not both

raison d'être = reason for

rarely ever/seldom ever = rarely/seldom

rate of speed = speed

reach an agreement = agree

rectangular in shape = rectangular

reduce to a minimum = minimize

red/yellow/blue in color = red/yellow/blue

refer back = refer

regardless of the fact that = although

reiterate again = reiterate

relating to = about

relative to = about/regarding/concerning
remuneration = pay
repeat again/twice = repeat
reside = live
respectively = OMIT
return back = return
revert back = revert
rise up = rise
root cause = cause
round in shape/round circles = round or circles, not both
same (as in "will send same") = it/them/the items, or OMIT
same identical = same or identical, not both
seldom ever = seldom
separate entities = entities
serious crisis/danger = crisis/danger
shuttle back and forth = shuttle
sine qua non = essential
sink down = sink
six in number = six
skipped over = skipped
slanted diagonally = slanted
small in size = small
so advise us = advise us
so as to be able to = to
so consequently/therefore = so consequently or therefore, but not both
square in shape = square
stacked together = stacked
state of Minnesota = Minnesota
streamlined in appearance = streamlined
still persists = persists
string together = string
subject matter = subject or matter, not both
subsequent to = after/following
substantiate = prove
successful achievement = achievement
sudden impulse/crisis = impulse/crisis
sufficient = enough
sum total = total
take and (e.g., "take and read this") = OMIT
take the liberty of/take this opportunity to = OMIT
technical jargon = jargon

terminate = end/complete/finish/conclude
the above = OMIT
the better part of = most of/nearly all of
the bulk of = most/nearly all of
the earliest possible moment = soon/immediately
the party = (replace with specific noun)
therein = in
the undersigned/this writer = I
this is to inform you = OMIT
this is to thank you = thank you
thusly = in this way/as follows
too numerous to mention = numerous
total destruction = destruction
to tell the truth = OMIT
transmit = send
true fact = fact
ubiquitous = widespread
undergraduate student = undergraduate
under separate cover = separately
unexpected emergency = emergency
unfortunate mishap = mishap
uniformly homogeneous = homogeneous
unintentional mistake = mistake
unless and until = unless or until, not both
until such time as = until
untimely death = death
up to this writing = until now
usual custom = custom
utilization/utilize = use
vacillating back and forth = vacillating
various different = various or different, not both
verbal discussion = discussion
very = OMIT
visible to the eye = visible
vitally essential = vital or essential, not both
wall mural = mural
we are writing to tell you = OMIT
we beg to advise = OMIT
when/after all is said and done = OMIT
wish to advise/state = OMIT
wish to apologize = we apologize

with all due regard = OMIT
with a view to = to
without further delay = now/immediately
with reference/regard/respect to = about/concerning/on/OMIT
with the exception of = except for
with the result that = so that
with this in mind, it is certainly clear that = therefore
words cannot describe = OMIT
worthy of merit = worthy or merits, but not both
would appreciate your informing/advising us = let us know
writer by profession = writer
written down = written
young boy/foal/lad = boy/foal/lad

FORMS OF ADDRESS

Using the correct form of a person's title and the correct form of addressing the person says you are interested in accuracy and respectful of the person's position. On the other hand, our democratic underpinnings and common sense indicate that a respectful letter addressed to the person by name and beginning "Dear . . ." would be equally effective and acceptable.

The list below will help you compose the inside address and the address on the envelope. At the end of each entry are appropriate salutations. If more than one is given, the first is always the formal salutation, the second the informal. Where addresses are known and permanent, they are given.

Government Officials

PRESIDENT OF THE UNITED STATES
The President
The White House
1600 Pennsylvania Avenue
Washington, DC 20500
Mr./Madam President: / Dear Mr./Madam President:
The President and Mrs. Dozier
Dear Mr. President and Mrs. Dozier:

VICE PRESIDENT OF THE UNITED STATES
The Vice President
The White House
1600 Pennsylvania Avenue
Washington, DC 20500
    or

The Vice President
Executive Office Building
Washington, DC 20501
The Vice President: / Dear Madam/Mr. Vice President: / Madam/Sir:

SPOUSE OF THE PRESIDENT OF THE UNITED STATES
Ms. Hannah Marryat/Mr. Louis Rony
The White House
1600 Pennsylvania Avenue
Washington, DC 20500
Dear Ms. Marryat/Mr. Rony:

FORMER PRESIDENT OF THE UNITED STATES
The Honorable Jasper Petulengro
Dear Mr. Petulengro: / Sir:

CABINET MEMBERS
The Honorable Mark Sabre or Mabel Sabre
The Secretary of Health, Education, and Welfare
(or The Postmaster General or The Attorney General)
Dear Mr./Madam Secretary:

GOVERNOR (STATE OR TERRITORY)
The Honorable Oswald Henshawe/Sarah Denburn
Governor of California
Sir:/Madam: / Dear Governor Denburn/Henshawe: / Dear Governor:

Note that instead of "The Honorable . . ." the correct form in Massachusetts is "His/Her Excellency, the Governor of Massachusetts." This form can be used for other governors too.

LIEUTENANT GOVERNOR/ACTING GOVERNOR
The Honorable Ada Herbert/Horace Beveridge
Lieutenant Governor/Acting Governor of Texas
Madam/Sir: / Dear Ms. Herbert/Mr. Beveridge:

UNITED STATES SENATOR
The Honorable Jack Worthing/Gwendolyn Fairfax
United States Senate
Washington, DC 20510
    or
The Honorable Jack Worthing/Gwendolyn Fairfax
United States Senator
(local address)
Madam/Sir: / Dear Senator Worthing/Fairfax:

UNITED STATES REPRESENTATIVE
The Honorable Marjorie Frant/Peter Standish
United States House of Representatives
Washington, DC 20515
   or
The Honorable Marjorie Frant/Peter Standish
Representative in Congress
   (local address)
Sir/Madam: / Dear Ms. Frant/Mr. Standish: / Dear Representative Frant/
   Standish:

SPEAKER OF THE HOUSE
The Honorable Philip Liu/Rebecca Linnet
Speaker of the House of Representatives
United States Capitol
Washington, DC 20515
Dear Mr./Madam Speaker:

SENATE/HOUSE COMMITTEE/SUBCOMMITTEE CHAIR
The Honorable Richard Gettner/Gelda Rosmarin
Chair, Committee/Subcommittee on Foreign Affairs
United States Senate/United States House of Representatives
Washington, DC 20515
Dear Senator/Representative Gettner/Rosmarin:

Members of Congress-elect and former members of Congress are also addressed as "The Honorable . . ." and "Dear Madam/Sir:" or "Dear Mr./Ms. . . ." Members of Congress holding special positions are addressed as "The Honorable . . . ," followed by their title ("Speaker of the House of Representatives"), with a salutation of "Sir:/Madam:" / "Dear Madam/Mr. Speaker:" or "Dear Ms./Mr. . . . :"

MAYOR
The Honorable Anna Fitzgerald/Nick Faunt
Mayor of Caldwell
City Hall
Dear Madam/Sir: / Dear Mayor Fitzgerald/Faunt: / Dear Mr./Ms. Mayor:

CHIEF JUSTICE OF THE UNITED STATES SUPREME COURT
The Chief Justice
The Supreme Court of the United States
   or

The Honorable Alvin Belknap/Constance Nevil
Dear Sir/Madam: / Dear Madam/Mr. Chief Justice: / Dear Madam Justice
    Nevil/Mr. Justice Belknap:

Heads of State

President of a Republic
His/Her Excellency Abdou Diouf/L. Sédar-Senghor
President of the Republic of Senegal
Excellency: / Dear Madam/Mr. President:

PRIME MINISTER

His/Her Excellency Lt. Colonel Ramahatra Victor/Gabrielle Ranavalona
Prime Minister of Madagascar
Excellency: / Dear Mr./Madam Prime Minister:

PRIME MINISTER OF GREAT BRITAIN/CANADA

The Right Honorable Julia Lancester/John James Ridley
Prime Minister of Great Britain/the Dominion of Canada
Sir:/Madam: / Dear Madam/Mr. Prime Minister: / Dear Mr. Ridley/Madam
    Lancester:

PREMIER

His/Her Excellency Major Pedro Pires/Luzia Sotavento
Premier of the Republic of Cape Verde
Excellency: / Dear Mr./Madam Premier:

When writing to officials of another country, check the country's exact
name (a desk almanac will help) and the correct spelling of the official's
name. Country leaders include queens, kings, rulers, co-regents, presidents,
prime ministers, premiers, governor-generals, chancellors, emirs, episcopal
co-princes, and sultans; verify the correct title. For example, in Mauritania,
you write to the Chief of State and Head of Government, The Islamic Republic of Mauritania. Letters are traditionally sent to reigning monarchs via
their private secretaries, thus you are not addressing a king or queen directly.

Diplomats

Ambassador to the United States
Her/His Excellency Elizabeth Tenbruggen/Kristian Koppig
The Ambassador of The Netherlands
    or His/Her Excellency the Ambassador from The Netherlands
Excellency: / Dear Mr./Madam Ambassador:

Use the full name of the country except for Great Britain; address British representatives as British Ambassador or British Minister. If an ambassador has a personal title, use it before the name ("Her Excellency Lady Catherine De Bourgh"). For an ambassador with a military title, substitute that title for "The Honorable" ("Colonel Jean Albert De Charleu").

U.S. AMBASSADOR
The Honorable Grace Carden/Harold Dakers
The United States Ambassador/Ambassador from the United States
The United States Embassy
Madam/Sir: / Dear Madam/Sir: / Dear Mr./Madam Ambassador: / Dear Ambassador Carden/Dakers:

U.S. CONSUL-GENERAL, CONSUL, VICE-CONSUL, CHARGÉ D'AFFAIRES
Mr. Christopher Pumphrey/Ms. Margaret Hart
Consul-General/Consul/Vice-Consul/Chargé d'Affaires of the United States of America
Madam:/Sir: / Dear Ms. Hart/Mr. Pumphrey: / Dear Madam/Sir:

FOREIGN CHARGÉ D'AFFAIRES
Mr. Horatio Hieronimo/Ms. H. G. Nuñez
Chargé d'Affaires of Spain
Sir/Madam: / Dear Mr. Hieronimo/Ms. Nuñez:

U.S. OR FOREIGN MINISTERS
The Honorable Nathan Rosenstein/Adèle Rossignol
United States Minister to Pakistan/Minister of France
Madam/Sir: Dear Sir/Madam: or Dear Mr./Madam Minister:

HIGH COMMISSIONER
The Honorable Waris Dane/Ethel Armitage
United States High Commissioner to Argentina
Madam/Sir: / Dear Mr. Dane/Ms. Armitage:

SECRETARY GENERAL OF THE UNITED NATIONS
Her/His Excellency Anne Menzies/Peter Levi
Secretary General of the United Nations
The Secretariat
United Nations
United Nations Plaza
New York, NY 10017
Excellency: / Dear Ms./Mr. Secretary General: / Dear Ms. Menzies/Mr. Levi:

UNDERSECRETARY OF THE UNITED NATIONS

The Honorable Rose Mei-Hua/Thomas Henry Fould
Undersecretary of the United Nations
Sir/Madam: / Dear Mr./Ms. Undersecretary / Dear Ms. Mei-Hua/Mr. Fould:

U.S. DELEGATE TO THE UNITED NATIONS

Mr. Hans Kleinhans/Ms. Isabella Woodhouse
Chief of/Delegate from the United States Mission to the United Nations
Dear Mr. Kleinhans/Ms. Woodhouse:

U.S. REPRESENTATIVE TO THE U.N. WITH RANK OF AMBASSADOR

The Honorable Arethusa Gaunt/Manuel Chaver
United States Representative to the United Nations
Sir/Madam: / Dear Mr./Madam Ambassador:

FOREIGN REPRESENTATIVE TO THE U.N. WITH RANK OF AMBASSADOR

His/Her Excellency Pietro Spina/Eline Vere
Representative of Italy to the United Nations
Excellency: / Dear Mr./Madam Ambassador:

Academics

COLLEGE/UNIVERSITY PRESIDENT

Dr. Clare Browell/George Heyling
President, Montague College of the Arts
Madam/Sir: / Dear Dr./President Browell/Heyling:

PROFESSOR/ASSOCIATE PROFESSOR/ASSISTANT PROFESSOR

Professor/Dr./Ms. or Mr. Wat Ollamoor/Joan Heseltine or Wat Ollamoor/
    Joan Heseltine, PhD
Department of English
Aspent University
Dear Professor/Dr./Ms. or Mr. Heseltine/Ollamoor: / Dear Madam/Sir:

"Dr.," meaning someone who has received a doctoral degree, and "PhD" do
not appear together; use one or the other. If the instructor does not have a doctoral degree, use a social title (Mr., Ms., Mrs., Miss) instead of "Dr." Do not
use "Professor."

DEAN/ASSISTANT DEAN

Dr. Frederick Mulliner/Jane Oliphant
Dean/Assistant Dean, School of Veterinary Medicine
University of Minnesota
Dear Madam/Sir: / Dear Dean/Dr. Mulliner/Oliphant:

CHANCELLOR

Dr. Jane Geoghegan/Edward Bronckhorst
Chancellor
Robinson University
Sir/Madam: / Dear Dr. Geoghegan/Bronckhorst:

CHAPLAIN

Chaplain/The Reverend Sarah Brockett/Martin Whitelaw, DD, PhD
Crowther United College
Dear Chaplain/Dr. Brockett/Whitelaw:

Members of the Clergy

For a member of the clergy, use the religious title first and put affiliations and degrees after the name ("The Reverend Malachi Brennan, SJ, PhD" or "Sister Mary Beatrice Fitzclare, CSJ, PhD") and use either "Dear Dr. Brennan/Fitzclare:" or "Dear Father Brennan/Sister Fitzclare:").

RABBI

Rabbi Miriam Ephraim/Benjamin Ezra or Rabbi Miriam Ephraim, DD/Benjamin Ezra, DD
Temple of Mount Zion
Madam/Sir: / Dear Rabbi/Dr. Ephraim/Ezra:

CANTOR

Cantor Simon Rosedale/Leah Dvoshe
Temple Ben Aaron
Sir/Madam: / Dear Cantor Rosedale/Dvoshe:

CANON

The Reverend/The Very Reverend Esmé Howe-Nevinson, DD
Canon of St. Elizabeth's
Reverend Sir: / Dear Canon Howe-Nevinson:

NUN/SISTER

Sister Donna Agnes Rebura, CND
Dear Sister Donna Agnes: / Dear Sister: / Dear Sister Rebura:

BROTHER

Brother Casimir Lypiatt, OSB
Dear Brother: / Dear Brother Casimir: / Dear Brother Lypiatt:

MINISTER, PRIEST, OR MEMBER OF THE CLERGY

The Reverend George B. Callender, PhD/Martha Rodd, PhD
or The Reverend Martha Rodd/George B. Callender

or The Reverend George B. Callender, DD
or The Reverend Dr. Martha Rodd
Reverend Sir/Madam: or Dear Reverend Madam/Sir: / Dear Dr./Father/Ms.
  or Mr./Reverend Callender/Rodd:

An Eastern Orthodox priest's title is "Reverend Father Kostes Palamas" and
  the salutation is "Dear Father Palamas:"

DEAN (CATHEDRAL/SEMINARY)
The Very Reverend Andrew Montfitchet, DD
Dean of St. Philip's Seminary
Very Reverend Sir: / Dear Dean Montfitchet:

MONSIGNOR
The Right Reverend Monsignor John Woodley
Reverend Monsignor: / Dear Monsignor Woodley: / Dear Monsignor:

ABBOT
The Right Reverend Gilbert Belling Torpenhow, OSB
Abbot of Heldar Abbey
Right Reverend Abbot: / Dear Father Abbot: or Dear Father
  Torpenhow:

FATHER/BROTHER SUPERIOR
The Very Reverend William Falder, M.M.
Director/Superior of The Mission Fathers/Brothers
Dear Father/Brother Superior: / Dear Father Falder/Brother William:

See the Official Catholic Directory if you are unsure whether the individual
is a priest or a brother or if he has other titles.

MOTHER/SISTER SUPERIOR
The Reverend Mother/Sister Superior Ellen Mary Montgomery, ACM Con-
  vent of St. Joseph
  or Mother Ellen Mary Montgomery
  Superior of St. Joseph's Convent
  or Mother Ellen Mary Montgomery, Superior
  Convent of St. Joseph
Reverend Mother/Sister: / Dear Reverend Sister/Mother: / Dear Mother/Sis-
  ter Superior: / Dear Mother Ellen Mary Montgomery: / Dear Mother Ellen
  Mary: / Dear Madam:

There are also titles such as Regional Superior, Provincial Superior, and
President, and salutations like "Dear Religious Leader" are used when writing to large or international orders. Someone within the order might write

simply "Dear Sister." For the correct title, check the Official Catholic Directory.

ANGLICAN BISHOP
The Right Reverend James Crowther
The Lord Bishop of Oxford
Right Reverend Sir: / Dear Bishop Crowther:

ANGLICAN ARCHBISHOP
The Most Reverend Reginald Kershaw
Archbishop of Salisbury
   or The Most Reverend Archbishop of Salisbury
   or The Lord Archbishop of Salisbury
Your Grace: / Dear Archbishop Kershaw: / Dear Archbishop:

EPISCOPAL BISHOP
The Right Reverend Dinah Morris
Bishop of New York
Right Reverend Bishop: / Dear Bishop:

The Presiding Bishop of the Protestant Episcopal Church in the United States has that title in place of "Bishop of New York." You can also replace "The Right Reverend" with "The Most Reverend" and address him as "Most Reverend Sir:"

PROTESTANT BISHOP
The Reverend George Cassilis
Bishop of Los Angeles
Dear Bishop:

METHODIST BISHOP
Bishop Richard Feverel of the Miami Area
   or The Reverend Richard Feverel
   Methodist Bishop of Miami
Reverend Sir: / Dear Bishop Feverel:

LDS BISHOP
Bishop Roger Dainton
The Church of Jesus Christ of Latter-day Saints
Dear Bishop Dainton: / Sir:

ROMAN CATHOLIC ARCHBISHOP/BISHOP
The Most Reverend Jean Latour
Archbishop/Bishop of Santa Fe
Your Excellency: / Dear Archbishop/Bishop Latour: / Most Reverend Sir:

EASTERN ORTHODOX ARCHBISHOP/BISHOP
His Eminence Archbishop George, Archbishop of Denver
Your Excellency:
His Grace Bishop George, Bishop of Denver
Reverend Father George:

EPISCOPAL ARCHDEACON
The Venerable Nicholas Broune
Archdeacon of San Francisco
Venerable Sir: / Dear Archdeacon:

CARDINAL
His Eminence James Cardinal Wickham
Archbishop of New York
Your Eminence: / Dear Cardinal Wickham:

ROMAN CATHOLIC POPE
His Holiness, Pope Benedict XVI
    or His Holiness, the Pope
Vatican City
00187 Rome, Italy
Your Holiness: / Most Holy Father:

> The complimentary close is always "Respectfully yours."

APOSTOLIC PRO-NUNCIO
His Excellency, The Most Reverend John Sylvester Clayton
Titular Archbishop of Greece
The Apostolic Pro-Nuncio
Your Excellency: / Dear Archbishop Clayton:

GREEK ORTHODOX PATRIARCH
His All Holiness Patriarch George
Your All Holiness:

RUSSIAN ORTHODOX PATRIARCH
His Holiness the Patriarch of Chicago
Your Holiness:

Military Personnel
When writing to officers and enlisted personnel use full rank (may be abbreviated), full name, comma, initials for the branch of service ("Captain Marguerite Evelyn Falconer, USA"). For retired personnel, add "(Ret.)" after the service affiliation. Abbreviations for the service branches are:

Air Force, USAF
Army, USA
Army Reserve, USAR
Coast Guard, USCG
Coast Guard Reserve, USCGR
Marine Corps, USMC
Marine Corps Reserve, USMCR
Naval Reserve, USNR
Navy, USN

Salutations include the rank and last name ("Dear Commander Marlow:") or rank only ("Dear Commander:"). You may write "Dear General:" when addressing a general, a lieutenant general, a major general, or a brigadier general. "Dear Admiral:" includes fleet, vice, rear, and ordinary admirals. The salutation for junior officers, petty officers, warrant officers, enlisted personnel, ensigns, and noncommissioned officers is "Dear Ms./Mr. Marcovitch."

For chaplains use: "Chaplain," full name, comma, rank, comma, initials of their branch of service ("Chaplain Michael Sabrov, Captain, USA"). In the Navy, the order is reversed: "Captain Michael Sabrov (Ch.C.), USN." The salutation is "Dear Chaplain."

INDEX

special situations for, 299–300
tips on, 299
what not to say in, 299
words for, 300
Military, 370, 476
Miss Manners' Guide for the Turn-of-the-Millennium (Martin), 305
Mother's Day, 198–99

Name, change of, 476
Names, parallel form of, 188
Nash, Ogden, 291
National Personnel Records Center, 370
Neighbor letters, 305
  about children, 307
  format for, 307
  how to say it, 306
  paragraphs for, 308–9
  phrases for, 307–8
  sample letters for, 309–12
  sentences for, 308
  special situations for, 306–7
  tips on, 306
  what not to say in, 306
  words for, 307
Noble, David F., 393

Obituary, 45–46
OCR. *See* Optical character readers
The 100 Most Difficult Business Letters You'll Ever Have to Write, Fax, or E-mail (Heller), 216
Optical character readers (OCR), 390–91
Orben, Robert, 184
Order letters, 313
  for cancellation, 315
  format for, 315
  how to say it, 314
  paragraphs for, 317
  phrases for, 316
  sample letters for, 318–20
  sentences for, 316–17
  special situations for, 315
  tips on, 314–15
  what not to say in, 314
  words for, 316

Packer, Alex J., 450
Paragraphs
  for acceptances, 5
  for acknowledgment and confirmation, 13–14
  for adjustment, 22–23
  for advice, 32–33
  for anniversaries and birthdays, 40
  for announcements, 48–50
  for apologies, 59–60
  for application letters, 67–68

  for appointments and interviews, 76–77
  for appreciation letters, 84–85
  for belated letters, 91
  for club/organization letters, 325
  for collection letters, 103
  for complaints, 115–16
  for congratulations, 127–28
  for contract letters, 134
  for cover letters, 144–45
  for credit letters, 153–54
  for disagreement letters, 160–61
  for e-mail, 179–80
  for employment letters, 190–92
  for family and friend letters, 202–3
  for faxes, 210–11
  for follow-up letters, 218–19
  for fundraising letters, 229–30
  for get well letters, 240
  for goodwill letters, 247
  for holiday letters, 255–56
  for instruction letters, 263
  for introduction letters, 271–72
  for invitations, 284–85
  for letters to editor, 168–69
  for love letters, 295
  for memos, 301
  for neighbor letters, 308–9
  for order letters, 317
  for query letters, 332–33
  for reference letters and recommendations, 342–43
  for refusal, 353
  for reports and proposal letters, 361–62
  for requests and inquiries, 373–75
  for responses, 384
  for résumés, 400
  for sales letters, 418–19
  for sensitive letters, 428–29
  for sympathy letters, 443–44
  for thank-you letters, 456–58
  for travel letters, 465–66
  for wedding correspondence, 478–79
  for welcome letters, 486–87
Passport, 463
Pay raise, 186, 369
Pen pal, 200–201
The Perfect Cover Letter (Beatty), 139
Persian Pictures (Bell), 463
Phillips, Ellen, 111
Phrases
  for acceptances, 4
  for acknowledgment, 12
  for adjustment, 21
  for advice, 30–31
  for anniversaries and birthdays, 39
  for announcements, 47
  for apologies, 57–58